Learning Truth

A concise guide to
the King James Bible

Greg Cetton

Learning Truth: Acts
A concise guide to the King James Bible

Greg Cetton

"Seek ye out of the book of the Lord, and read"
Isaiah 34:16a

Contents

What is the Bible?

Biblical definition: An actual book based on the text preserved by God that stands as absolute authority.
Non-biblical definition: The Bible is the word of God in the original writings, which no longer exist; extant (existing) manuscripts (hand-written copies) are the word of God insofar as they reflect the wording of the non-extant originals.

1. The Bible is an actual book

"Seek ye out of the book of the Lord, and read: no one of these shall fail, none shall want her mate: for my mouth it hath commanded, and his spirit it hath gathered them." (Isaiah 34:16)

The Bible is an actual book (whether physical or digital), not a set of lost manuscripts that never constituted a book.

"Then said I, Lo, I come (in the volume of the book it is written of me,) to do thy will, O God" (Heb 10:7). The author of Hebrews states that the promise of Jesus the Messiah can be found in an actual book (not merely some lost originals). He proves his point by quoting from a copy of Psalm 40:7, which was originally written some 1,000 years earlier. So the scripture available in the 1st century AD (when Hebrews was written) is the authoritative word of God, as was the scripture available in David's day (when Psalm 40 was written), even though one is a copy of the other. The Old Testament scripture available in the 1st century AD was faithfully copied by Hebrew scribes and eventually used as the basis of the King James Bible.

"And that from a child thou hast known the holy scriptures, which are able to make thee wise unto salvation through faith which is in Christ

Jesus" (2 Tim 3:15). Timothy apparently received biblical education from his mother Eunice and grandmother Lois (2 Tim 1:5) who would not have access to the original manuscripts, yet nevertheless had access to "the holy scriptures."

"All scripture is given by inspiration of God, and is profitable for doctrine, for reproof, for correction, for instruction in righteousness: That the man of God may be perfect, throughly furnished unto all good works" (2 Tim 3:16-17). Paul assures Timothy that everything that makes the Bible the word of God – attributes of inspiration, power, truth, and authority – are present in the scriptures that he possesses. The "problem" of not having access to the original manuscripts is an issue invented by those who wish to weaken the authority of the Bible and is not an issue in the eyes of anybody in the New Testament.

It is not about the original manuscripts; it is about the Book that "turned the world upside down"!

2. The Bible is based on the text preserved by God

The Old Testament

"For verily I say unto you, Till heaven and earth pass, one jot or one tittle shall in no wise pass from the law, till all be fulfilled." (Matt 5:18)

The Old Testament was written in Hebrew. The Levites were commanded by Moses to preserve the scripture (Deut 31:24-26) and to read the law to the people of Israel every seven years (Deut 31:9-12). They were to see that any future Israelite king had an authentic copy (Deut 17:18). The Levite priest Hilkiah found a book of the law of the Lord which had been lost or hidden during the reign of evil King Manasseh. Hilkiah presented it to the scribe Shaphan who read it to King Josiah (2 Kings 22:8-10).

Before the time of Christ "about 200 BC and perhaps a century earlier .. . there was deposited in the court of the Temple a standard copy of the Bible for the benefit of copyists."[1] This official copy would be used to create and validate other copies of scripture, such as the Isaiah scroll read publicly by Jesus in the synagogue of Nazareth (Luke 4:16-20).

After the destruction of the Jerusalem temple in AD 70, there was no longer a central repository of biblical text until Hebrew scribes combined their efforts in AD 600. "The Masoretic text that resulted from their work shows that every word and every letter was checked with care." A sophisticated system was used to ensure the accuracy of the text. "When the final codification of each section was complete, the Masoretes not only counted and noted down the total number of verses, words, and letters in the text but further indicated which verse, which word, and which letter marked the centre of the text. In this way any future emendation could be detected. The rigorous care given the Masoretic text in its preparation is credited for the remarkable consistency found in Old Testament Hebrew texts since that time ... experts have been astonished at the fidelity of the earliest printed version (late 15th century) to the earliest surviving [hand-written] codices (late 9th century). The Masoretic text is universally accepted as the authentic Hebrew Bible."[2]

"What advantage then hath the Jew? or what profit is there of circumcision? Much every way: chiefly, because that unto them were committed the oracles of God" (Rom 3:1-2). Jewish scribes faithfully preserved the Hebrew Masoretic text of the Old Testament from the time when Moses gave the law until the King James Bible was translated. Modern versions, however, do not rely exclusively on the Hebrew text preserved by God.

ESV - "The ESV is based on the Masoretic text of the Hebrew Bible ... [but] in exceptional, difficult cases, the Dead Sea Scrolls, the Septuagint, the Samaritan Pentateuch, the Syriac Peshitta, the Latin Vulgate, and other sources were consulted."

NASB - "In the present translation the latest edition of Rudolf Kittel's

---

[1] Crawford Howell Toy, Caspar Levias. "Masorah." *Jewish Encyclopedia*, 1906
[2] "Masoretic text." *Encyclopedia Britannica Online*, accessed 9 Dec 2019

BIBLIA HEBRAICA has been employed together with the most recent light from lexicography, cognate languages [ancient non-Hebrew texts], and the Dead Sea Scrolls."

NIV - "For the Old Testament the standard Hebrew text, the Masoretic Text as published in the latest edition of Biblia Hebraica, has been used throughout... Readings from [ancient non-Hebrew] versions, the Dead Sea Scrolls and the scribal traditions were occasionally followed where the Masoretic Text seemed doubtful."

NKJV - "For the New King James Version the text used was the ... Biblia Hebraica ... The Septuagint (Greek) Version of the Old Testament and the Latin Vulgate also were consulted. In addition to referring to a variety of ancient versions of the Hebrew Scriptures, the New King James Version draws on the resources of relevant manuscripts from the Dead Sea caves."

Examples of modern versions rejecting the Masoretic Hebrew text preserved by God:

"And he smote the men of Beth-shemesh, because they had looked into the ark of the Lord, even he smote of the people fifty thousand and three-score and ten men:" (1 Sam 6:19a)
Masoretic Text: 50,070
Challenge: 50,070 is a massive slaughter for such a small town.
Possible Solution: The total 50,070 may encompass divine judgment on Bethshemesh plus the cities of the Philistines that mishandled the ark.
Non-Solution: ESV and NIV ignore the Masoretic text and subtract 50,000 from the total; the one writes "he struck seventy men of them" and the other "putting seventy of them to death."

"Forty and two years old was Ahaziah when he began to reign" (2 Chron 22:2a)
Masoretic Text: 42 years old
Challenge: "Forty two years old" seems to contradict the statement "Two and twenty years old was Ahaziah when he began to reign" (2 Kings 8:26a).
Possible Solution: Consider that Ahaziah (the son of Athaliah of Israel and Jehoram of Judah, 2 Kings 8:25-26) may have become co-ruler of

Israel with King Ahab at age twenty-two and then king of Judah at age forty-two.

Non-Solution: ESV, NASB, and NIV all ignore the Masoretic text and change 42 years to 22 years in 2 Chronicles.

"Thou hast multiplied the nation, and <u>not</u> increased the joy: they joy before thee according to the joy in harvest, and as men rejoice when they divide the spoil." (Isa 9:3)

Masoretic Text: not increased the joy

Challenge: The phrase "<u>not</u> increased the joy" contrasts with "they joy before thee."

Possible Solution: An increased rebellious population "shall have no joy" (Isa 9:17). Furthermore, the context of Isa 9:2-4 read with its fulfillment in Matt 4:12-17 raises the possibility that the enlarged, yet joyless nation is the Gentile "oppressor" (Isa 9:4) contrasted against the joyous Hebrews.

Non-Solution: ESV, NASB, NIV, and NKJV all ignore the Masoretic text and remove the word "not."

The New Testament

1st Century AD
"Heaven and earth shall pass away: but my words shall not pass away." (Luke 21:33)

God gave the New Testament scripture
The New Testament was written in Greek in the first century AD. The Apostle Peter recognized God speaking His word through him (1 Peter 1:25) and even compared his words to those of the Old Testament prophets (2 Peter 3:2). Peter identified Paul's writings as scripture (2 Peter 3:15-16), and Paul identified Luke's gospel as scripture on the same level as the writings of Moses (compare 1 Tim 5:18 with Deut 25:4 and Luke 10:7). The Apostle Paul and the Apostle John each declared that his own words are from God (1 Thes 2:13 and Rev 1:1-3, 22:18-19).

Autographs mostly sent to specified locations
The original autographs (i.e., original writings) of the New Testament
were apparently sent to the eastern half of the Roman Empire. Simon
Peter wrote to a large geographical area of five Roman provinces in Asia
Minor, to believers "scattered throughout Pontus, Galatia, Cappadocia, Asia,
and Bithynia" (1 Peter 1:1b). The Apostle Paul wrote to an even larger geo-
graphical area, from Galatia in the east to Rome in the west. The book of
James was written by "James the Lord's brother" (Gal 1:19) apparently from
Jerusalem where he was the head of the church (Acts 12:17, 15:13, 21:18);
copies were sent "to the twelve tribes which are scattered abroad" (James
1:1b). At least 18 of the 27 books of the New Testament were sent to Asia
Minor (John, Galatians, Ephesians, Colossians, 1 & 2 Timothy, Philemon, 1
Peter, 1-3 John, Revelation) and the Aegean area (1 & 2 Corinthians, Phi-
lippians, 1 & 2 Thessalonians, Titus).

Believers knew the importance of faithfully copying scripture
Copies of Peter's epistle were made for at least five provinces (1 Peter
1:1), and he instructed his recipients to preserve his writings after his
death (2 Peter 1:15). Paul sent an epistle "unto the churches of Galatia"
(Gal 1:2), which would have included at least the congregations of Antioch in Pisidia, Iconium, Lystra, and Derbe (Acts 14:20-21). Although Paul
wrote to individual churches, he intended his letters to be read by churches beyond the original recipients (1 Thes 5:27, Col 4:16). He addressed 2
Corinthians "unto the church of God which is at Corinth, with all the saints
which are in all Achaia" (2 Cor 1:1b). Therefore Paul's writings would have
been promptly copied for distribution to multiple churches. Copies were
also needed for new congregations beyond these, as Paul implied writing
"unto the church of God which is at Corinth ... with all that in every place
call upon the name of Jesus Christ our Lord" (1 Cor 1:2). So from the very
beginning, copies of scripture were being made from pure sources, with
the vast majority accurately reflecting the original text.

2nd Century AD
**"For this cause also thank we God without ceasing, because, when ye
received the word of God which ye heard of us, ye received it not as the
word of men, but as it is in truth, the word of God, which effectually wor-**

keth also in you that believe." (1 Thes 2:13)

Canon of scripture informally recognized

Believers quickly recognized the divine origin of the books of the New Testament. In about AD 115, Polycarp wrote a letter to the Philippians in which he referred to "sacred writings" while quoting Ephesians 4:26 and calling it "scripture."[3] In his letter he cited or alluded to almost every New Testament author. Verses from all 27 books are found in the writings of Polycarp, Clement of Rome, Justin Martyr, Melito of Sardis, Athenagoras of Athens, Theophilus of Antioch, and Irenaeus.[4]

In the second-century AD, Justin Martyr wrote of the scripture being read in churches every week. "And on the day called Sunday, all who live in cities or in the country gather together to one place, and the memoirs of the apostles or the writings of the prophets are read, as long as time permits; then, when the reader has ceased, the president verbally instructs, and exhorts to the imitation of these good things."[5] Believers were therefore busy copying scripture for the many churches worldwide that would need a copy for their weekly reading.

Deliberate corruption introduced into some manuscripts

The Apostle Paul repeatedly warned of false teachers (Rom 16:17-18, 2 Cor 11:1-15, Gal 1:6-9, 2 Tim 4:3-4); some would even try to pervert the biblical text. Dionysius of Corinth wrote in about AD 170 of unscrupulous men altering his letters and apparently the scripture as well. "As the brethren desired me to write epistles, I wrote. And these epistles the apostles of the devil have filled with tares, cutting out some things and adding others. For them a woe is reserved. It is, therefore, not to be wondered at if some have attempted to adulterate the Lord's writings also, since they have formed designs even against writings which are of less account."[6]

Tertullian (AD 155 – 240) wrote against Marcion's (AD 85 – 160) corruption

---

[3] Polycarp, *Letter to the Philippians*, 12:1
[4] Wilbur Pickering, *The Identity of the New Testament Text IV* (2014), p.58-60
[5] Justin Martyr, *First Apology*, 67
[6] Dionysius, Bishop of Corinth, AD 170

of scripture. "Marcion is seen to have chosen Luke as the one to mutilate[7]. ... That gospel of Luke which we at this moment retain has stood firm since its earliest publication ... For if the apostolic gospels have come down to us in their integrity, while the gospel of Luke, in the form in which we have it, is in such agreement with the standard of those others that it is retained in the churches along with them, it is at once evident that Luke's also came down in integrity until Marcion's act of sacrilege. In fact it was only when Marcion laid hands upon it, that it became different from the apostolic gospels, and in opposition to them."[8]

Christians knew the importance of making *accurate* copies of scripture and the importance of rejecting corrupted texts (Rev 22:18-19). Tertullian rejected Marcion's falsification by comparing those writings to authoritative church copies of scripture. Likewise, Irenaeus (AD 130 – 200) wrote that the number 666 is found "in all the most approved and ancient copies" of Revelation 13:18 in contrast to erroneous copies which have the number 616.[9]

Byzantine readings present in the early papyri

There are no existing second-century manuscripts from Asia Minor or the Aegean region (i.e., no extant Byzantine manuscripts). Only those writings left in the dry sands of Egypt have survived. Most of these papyri (sheets made from the stem of the papyrus plant) are tiny fragments with a limited number of verses that Egyptian scribes copied in a rather careless manner. P66 is a prime example of the poor quality of manuscripts produced in Egypt. "This papyrus manuscript is perhaps the oldest (c. 200) ... [yet] it is one of the worst copies we have. It has an average of roughly two mistakes per verse – many being obvious mistakes, stupid mistakes, nonsensical mistakes."[10] A corrector modified some of the errors; it is evident that both the original copyist and subsequent corrector of P66 appear to have had access to both an Alexandrian and a Byzantine exem-

---

[7] Tertullian, *Against Marcion*, 4.2

[8] Ibid., 4.5. Tertullian also condemned those who pervert the scripture "by means of additions and diminutions ... by the contrivance of diverse interpretations ... by an adulteration of its meaning ... by a corruption of its text" (Tertullian, *Prescription Against the Heretics*, 17).

[9] Irenaeus, *Against Heresies*, 5.30.1

[10] Wilbur Pickering, *The Identity of the New Testament Text IV* (2014), p.64

plar manuscript from which to choose readings as they saw fit. "There are several occasions where P66 agrees with the Byzantine-Western alignment, then corrects to the Alexandrian-WH type of text... In addition to these there are several instances where P66 reads with the Alexandrian text-type ... but corrects to the Byzantine-Western combination."[11]

The studies below examine Egyptian papyri (pages made from the papyrus plant) from the 2nd and 3rd centuries ("whose evidence takes us back into the mid-2nd-century at least"[12]). Lists show the percentage of times the papyri agree with various codices (a codex is a book comprised of hand-written pages): the 4th-century manuscripts Codex Sinaiticus (Aleph) and Codex Vaticanus (B); the 5th-century manuscripts Codices A, C, D, and W; and the Greek *Textus Receptus* (the basis of the King James Bible, produced mainly from Byzantine manuscripts).[13]

1. Papyrus P45 (AD 200 – 300) in Mark 6-9 agrees with:[14]

Codex B	42%
Codex D	38%
Textus Receptus	40%

15

2. Papyrus P66 (AD 200 – 225) in John 1-14 agrees with:[15]

P75	51%
Codex Aleph	45%
Codex B	50%
Codex A	46%
Codex C	49%

---

[11] Harry Sturz, *The Byzantine Text-Type & New Testament Textual Criticism* (Nashville, TN: Thomas Nelson, 1984), p.74

[12] "In these third-century manuscripts, whose evidence takes us back into the mid-second century at least, we find no pristine purity, no unsullied ancestors of Vaticanus, but marred and fallen representatives of the original text." Wilbur Pickering, *The Identity of the New Testament Text IV* (2014), p.41, citing J.N. Birdsall, *The Bodmer Papyrus of the Gospel of John* (London, 1960), p.17

[13] Wilbur Pickering, *The Identity of the New Testament Text IV* (2014), p. 41, citing G. Zuntz, *The Text of the Epistles*, p.55

[14] Ibid., p.95, citing Eldon Epp, "The Twentieth Century Interlude in New Testament Textual Criticism," *Journal of Biblical Literature*, XCIII (1974), p.394-396

[15] Ibid., p.95, citing G.D. Fee, *Papyrus Bodmer II (P66): Its Textual Relationships and Scribal Characteristics* (Salt Lake City: U. of Utah Press, 1968), p.14

Codex D	39%
Codex W	45%
Textus Receptus	48%

3. A group of many papyri agrees with:[16]

Alexandrian (reflecting Aleph and B)	34%
Byzantine (basis of the *Textus Receptus*)	31%
Western (called "undisciplined and wild"[17])	35%

Textual critics promote the Alexandrian text while arguing that the Byzantine text is "an inferior form,"[18] which is a "later development in the history of transmission."[19] However, Professor Harry Sturz, who performed the above study (the group of many papyri), came to a different conclusion. "Numerous distinctively Byzantine readings now proved early would seem to reverse the burden of proof. Instead of assuming that characteristically Byzantine readings are late, it may be more logical and more in accord with the facts to assume they are early. The burden of proof now appears to rest on whoever claims that a Byzantine reading is late. Furthermore, making textual decisions on the basis of how three or four 'old' uncials [such as Aleph and B] read should he abandoned because they do not give a complete picture of the second century traditions."[20]

Critics object by circular reasoning. They presuppose that the Byzantine text is late.[21] When they find Byzantine readings in the papyri which also match readings in Alexandrian or Western texts, they attribute the readings only to the latter two texts because they believe the Byzantine text

---

[16] Harry Sturz, *The Byzantine Text-Type* (1984), p.228. Papyri from early 2nd through early 4th century (ibid., p. 140). "These 150 readings are early. They go back to the second century, for they are supported by papyri which range from the third to the second century in date" (ibid., p.62).

[17] Bruce Metzger and Bart Ehrman, *The Text of the New Testament*, 4th edition (New York, NY: Oxford University Press, 2005), p.276

[18] Ibid., p.67

[19] Ibid., p.279

[20] Harry Sturz, *The Byzantine Text-Type* (1984), p.65

[21] "Since the Syrian [Byzantine] text is only a modified eclectic combination of earlier texts independently attested, existing documents descended from it can attest nothing but itself." Brooke Westcott and Fenton Hort, *The New Testament in the Original Greek*, Vol 2, (Cambridge and London: Macmillan and Co., 1882), p.118

is late. Because few readings are attributed to the Byzantine text through this process, critics conclude that the Byzantine text is late.

In conclusion, "The papyri supply valid evidence that distinctively Byzantine readings were not created in the fourth century but were already in existence before the end of the second ..."[22] Although the Egyptian papyri can validate various readings found in later Byzantine manuscripts, the overall quality of their content is too low to be helpful in building the New Testament text. They show the futility of assuming that the oldest manuscripts are the best.

Byzantine readings present in ancient Christian writings
Ancient Christian writers ("church fathers") recite scriptures that match the Byzantine text.
First half the second century: the Didache, Diognetus, Justin Martyr
Second half the second century: the Gospel of Peter, Athenagoras, Hegesippus, Irenaeus[23]

Critics object by circular reasoning: they presuppose that the Byzantine text is late; when they find Byzantine readings in the ancient Christian writings, they ignore these quotes by arbitrarily declaring that later scribes altered the writings to make them more closely match the Byzantine text-type; because no passages are attributed to the Byzantine text through this process, critics conclude that the Byzantine text is late.

However, evidence shows that some ancient Christian writings that match the Byzantine text **also** match Egyptian papyri and therefore cannot be considered late. Two examples:

"And many of the brethren in the Lord, waxing confident by my bonds, are much more bold to <u>speak the word</u> without fear." (Phil 1:14)
Papyrus P46: "speak the word"
Alexandrian text (Aleph and B): "speak the word of God" ("of God" is *added*)
Byzantine Majority: "speak the word"

---

[22] Harry Sturz, *The Byzantine Text-Type* (1984), p.69
[23] Wilbur Pickering, *The Identity of the New Testament Text IV* (2014), p.40-41

Tertullian (3rd century) quoting Marcion (2nd century): "speak the word"[24]

"But rather seek ye the kingdom <u>of God</u>; and all these things shall be added unto you." (Luke 12:31)
P45: "kingdom of God"
Alexandrian text (Aleph and B): "kingdom" ("of God" is *omitted*)
Byzantine Majority: "kingdom of God"
Tertullian (3rd century) quoting Marcion (2nd century): "kingdom of God"[25]

3rd Century AD
"For we are not as many, which corrupt the word of God: but as of sinceri-ty, but as of God, in the sight of God speak we in Christ." (2 Cor 2:17)

The scripture was never lost!
Early in the third century, Tertullian told his readers where they could assuredly find accurate copies of scripture. "Run over the apostolic church-es, in which the very thrones of the apostles are still pre-eminent in their places, in which their own authentic writings are read, uttering the voice and representing the face of each of them severally. Achaia is very near you, (in which) you find Corinth. Since you are not far from Macedonia, you have Philippi; (and there too) you have the Thessalonians. Since you are able to cross to Asia, you get Ephesus. Since, moreover, you are close upon Italy, you have Rome, from which there comes even into our own hands the very authority (of apostles themselves)."[26] By "authentic writings" Tertullian apparently speaks of original autographs or authentic copies of Paul and perhaps other apostles (recall that at least 18 of the 27 books of the New Testament were sent to Asia Minor and the Aegean area). Tertul-lian makes it clear that **the text of the New Testament has not been lost** or made uncertain in any way; it has always been available in the Byzan-tine manuscripts.

---

[24] "When (the apostle) mentions the several motives of those who were preaching the gospel, how that some, waxing confident by his bonds, were more fearless in speaking the word, while others preached Christ even out of envy and strife, and again others out of good-will ..." (Tertullian, *Against Marcion*, 5:20)
[25] "And your own gospel likewise has it in this wise: Seek first the kingdom of God, and these things shall be added unto you" (Tertullian, *Against Marcion*, 3:25).
[26] Tertullian, *Prescription Against the Heretics*, 36

In contrast to the faithful copies of scripture circulating in Asia Minor and the Aegean area, Origen of Alexandria, in about AD 244, complained of the poor quality of manuscripts in Egypt. "Now it is clear that many differences in the copies have come about either from the lazy indifference of certain scribes, or the misguided daring of some, or from those neglectful of the correction of the things written, or even from those who, in their correction, either added or subtracted those things according to their own opinions."[27]

Byzantine readings present in ancient Christian writings

Ancient Christian writers ("church fathers") recite scriptures that match the Byzantine text.

First half the third century: Clement of Alexandria, Tertullian, Clementines, Hippolytus, Origen

Second half the third century: Gregory of Thaumaturgus, Novatian, Cyprian, Dionysius of Alexandria, Archelaus[28]

Corruption of scripture is now rejected

Efforts to deliberately alter scripture were sometimes successful in the first and second centuries. Some of these corruptions were preserved in the Egyptian papyri and copied into the Alexandrian and Western texts. However, believers in the 3rd century were on guard against those who would change the scripture. Origen tried to introduce false readings into the biblical text and failed to do so. "From the early third century onward the freedom to alter the text which had [been] obtained earlier can no longer be practiced. Tatian [AD 120 – 173][29] is the last author to make deliberate changes in the text of whom we have explicit information. Between Tatian and Origen Christian opinion had so changed that it was no longer possible to make changes in the text whether they were harmless or not."[30]

---

[27] Origen of Alexandria, *Commentary on the Gospel according to Matthew*, translation by Justin M. Gohl (revised 2019), 15.14

[28] Wilbur Pickering, *The Identity of the New Testament Text IV* (2014), p.41

[29] "Tatian." *Encyclopedia Britannica Online*, accessed 3 Feb 2020

[30] Harry Sturz, *The Byzantine Text-Type* (1984), p.69, citing Kilpatrick, "Atticism and the Text of the Greek New Testament," *Neutestamentliche Aufsatze* (Regensburg: Verlag Friedrich Pustet, 1963), p.129-30

4th and 5th Centuries AD

"I said, Days should speak, and multitude of years should teach wisdom. But there is a spirit in man: and the inspiration of the Almighty giveth them understanding. Great men are not always wise: neither do the aged understand judgment." (Job 32:7-9)

"Oldest and best" manuscripts?
The oldest surviving manuscripts with substantial portions of scripture are called "uncials" (or "majuscules") because they are written in all capital letters with no spaces between the words. Each manuscript is designated by a capital letter (e.g., Codex Vaticanus is "B").

4ᵗʰ century (only two exist):
Codex Vaticanus (B) – part of the Vatican library in Rome. Contains the New Testament except for the Pastoral Epistles, Philemon, Hebrews from 9:14 onward, and Revelation. Text-type is Alexandrian.[31]
Codex Sinaiticus (Aleph) – "discovered" by Tischendorf in 1844 at the St. Catherine monastery. The only uncial to contain the entire New Testament. Text-type is Alexandrian.[32]

Codices Aleph and B are usually called the "oldest and best" by textual critics and weigh heavily in modern translations. Yet they contain numerous errors[33] and also contradictions between each other. H.C. Hoskier thoroughly examined both manuscripts and documented "three thousand differences between Aleph and B in the four Gospels" alone.[34] According to textual critics, "for a group of witnesses to be considered a text type, they need to agree in approximately 70% of all places."[35] The Byzantine text demonstrates this sort of uniformity, whereas "Aleph and B do not

20|

---

[31] Bruce Metzger and Bart Ehrman, *The Text of the New Testament*, 4th edition (2005), p.67-68
[32] Ibid., p.62
[33] "T. C. Skeat of the British Museum has suggested that Codex Vaticanus was a 'reject' among the 50 copies [made for the Emperor Constantine], for it ... has many corrections by different scribes" (Bruce Metzger and Bart Ehrman, *The Text of the New Testament*, 4th edition (2005), p.68-69).
[34] H.C. Hoskier, *Codex B and its Allies* (London: Bernard Quaritch, 1914), II.1
[35] Bruce Metzger and Bart Ehrman, *The Text of the New Testament*, 4th edition (2005), p.234

qualify."[36] As a consequence, the Critical Greek Text (published as the United Bible Society and Nestle-Aland texts) assigns a cover letter to the Byzantine text-type (capital "M" for "majority") but does not assign an Alexandrian cover letter because there does not exist a uniform Alexandrian text, only individual manuscripts that sometimes vary from each other more often than they agree.

When a judge in court observes that two witnesses disagree much of the time, he will not find them credible. John Burgon called Aleph and B "two false Witnesses ... We suspect that these two Manuscripts are indebted for their preservation, *solely to their ascertained evil character*; which has occasioned that the one [Codex B] eventually found its way, four centuries ago, to a forgotten shelf in the Vatican library; while the other [Codex Aleph] ... got deposited in the waste-paper basket of the Convent at the foot of Mount Sinai.[37] Had B and Aleph been copies of average purity, they must long since have shared the inevitable fate of books which are freely *used* and highly prized; namely, they would have fallen into decadence and disappeared from sight."[38]

5th century:
Codex Alexandrinus (A) – Byzantine text in the gospels, Alexandrian in the rest of the New Testament.[39]
Codex Ephraemi Rescriptus (C) – the original text was overwritten but later restored and found to be "compounded from all major text types."[40]
Codex Bezae (D) – "Codex Bezae's special characteristic is the free addition (and occasional omission) of words, sentences, and even incidents." One example is "the Acts of the Apostles ... being nearly one-tenth longer than the text generally received." The text-type of the Gospels is Western.[41]

---

[36] Wilbur Pickering, *The Identity of the New Testament Text IV* (2014), p.24
[37] Tischendorf claimed to find pages of Codex Sinaiticus "at the foot of Mount Sinai, in the convent of St. Catherine ... [in] a large and wide basket full of old parchments ... destined for the fire." Constantine Von Tischendorf, *When were our Gospels Written* (New York: American Tract Society, 1866), p.28
[38] John Burgon, *The Revision Revised* (1883), p.319, emphasis his
[39] Bruce Metzger and Bart Ehrman, *The Text of the New Testament*, 4th edition (2005), p.67
[40] Ibid., p.70
[41] Ibid., p.70-73

Codex Washingtonianus (W) – varied readings including Alexandrian, Byzantine, Caesarean, and Western.[42]
Codex Guelferbytanus B (Q) – fragments of Luke and John, mainly Byzantine readings.[43]
Codex Freerianus (I) – fragments of Paul's epistles, Alexandrian readings.[44]
Codex Borgianus (T) – fragments of Luke and John, mainly Alexandrian readings.[45]

Byzantine readings present in ancient Christian writings

Ancient Christian writers ("church fathers") recite scriptures that match the Byzantine text.
Fourth century: Eusebius, Athanasius, Macarius Magnus, Hilary, Didymus, Basil, Titus of Bostra, Cyril of Jerusalem, Gregory of Nyssa, Apostolic Canons and Constitutions, Epiphanius, Ambrose[46]

Byzantine churches accurately copy scripture

While the Alexandrian text was being copied in Egypt, believers in the Byzantine region remained acutely aware that men would try to corrupt the text of scripture. They would compare questionable manuscripts with ones they knew to be authentic. In the year 324, Eusebius of Caesarea wrote of Asclepiodotus and Theodotus, who "fearlessly lay their hands upon the holy Scriptures, saying that they have corrected them," but actually did "mutilate the Scriptures," which they "perverted for their own objectives." Their guilt was readily apparent "for neither can they deny that they have been guilty of the daring act, when the copies were written with their own hand, nor did they receive such Scriptures from those by whom they were instructed in the elements of the faith; nor can they show copies from which they were transcribed."[47]

---

[42] Ibid., p.80
[43] http://textus-receptus.com/wiki/Codex_Guelferbytanus_B, accessed 02-02-2020
[44] Bruce Metzger and Bart Ehrman, *The Text of the New Testament*, 4th edition (2005), p.77
[45] Ibid., p.80
[46] Wilbur Pickering, *The Identity of the New Testament Text IV* (2014), p.41
[47] Eusebius Pamphilus, *Ecclesiastical History*, 5.28

A Tale of Two Cities

Antioch – Asia Minor and the Aegean area subsequently became part of the Byzantine Empire. This nation continued to speak Greek and was in a unique position to preserve the Greek manuscripts of the New Testament. This "Byzantine text" is also called "Syrian" or "Antiochian" because of its association with the work of faithful believers in Antioch, Syria. "The disciples were called Christians first in Antioch" (Acts 11:26b), which is the location of the first major combined Jewish and Gentile church (Acts 11:19-21) and the origin of Paul's three missionary journeys (Acts 13:1-3, 15:35-36, 18:22-23). From Antioch he brought the gospel to Asia Minor and the Aegean Area, which was called "the heartland of the Church."[48]

Alexandria – Whereas Antioch had a reputation for faithfully copying scripture, Alexandria, Egypt did not. "At the close of the 2nd century," the Egyptian church was "dominantly gnostic [they valued their exceptional 'knowledge' above scripture]. The copies existing in the gnostic communities could not be used because they were under suspicion of being corrupt."[49]

Four factors allowed believers in the Byzantine region to produce faithful copies of scripture: access to autographs, proficiency in the source language, the strength of the church, and attitude toward the text.[50]
-   The Byzantine region received at least 18 of the 27 New Testament original autographs; Egypt received none.
-   Greek remained the primary language of the Byzantine empire; Coptic predominated in Egypt from the 2nd century onward.[51]
-   Asian Minor and the Aegean region were "the heartland of the Church;" Egypt was dominated by the false teaching of Gnosticism.[52]
-   The "school of Antioch" believed in the literal interpretation of scripture (the text means what it says); the "school of Alexandria" believed in allegorical interpretation (the text means what a person

[48] Wilbur Pickering, *The Identity of the New Testament Text IV* (2014), p.65, citing K. and B. Aland, *The Text of the New Testament* (Grand Rapids: Eerdmans, 1981), p.53
[49] Ibid., p.65, citing K. Aland, "The Text of the Church?", *Trinity Journal*, 1987, 8NS:138
[50] Four factors identified by Wilbur Pickering, *The Identity of the New Testament Text IV* (2014), p.63-67
[51] "Coptic language." *Encyclopedia Britannica Online*, accessed 4 May 2020
[52] Wilbur Pickering, *The Identity of the New Testament Text IV* (2014), p.65

imagines it to mean).[53]

6th to 14th Century AD

"Oh that my words were now written! oh that they were printed in a book! That they were graven with an iron pen and lead in the rock for ever!" (Job 19:23-24)

Byzantine text flourishes

Scribes in the Byzantine region highly valued scripture and made thousands of accurate copies that survive as "minuscule" or "cursive" manuscripts written in lower-case letters. As an example, "the list of Greek manuscripts containing the Gospel of Mark is over 1,500;"[54] most surviving Greek manuscripts are minuscules, and over 90% of minuscules are of the Byzantine text-type.[55] Whereas Alexandrian manuscripts typically survived because they were set aside (being neither read in churches nor copied due to their inferior quality), most Byzantine manuscripts were worn out with use and discarded. Textual critics Lake and associates wrote, "There must have been in existence many thousands of manuscripts of the gospels in the great days of Byzantine prosperity, between the 4th and the 10th centuries. There are now extant but a pitiably small number... [It is] hard to resist the conclusion that the scribes usually destroyed their exemplars when they copied the sacred books."[56]

Textual critics argue that the **Alexandrian** text was the **primary** text of the New Testament. They theorize that scribes created the Byzantine text either through an abrupt or a gradual process. Some critics postulate that Lucian of Antioch around AD 350 constructed the Byzantine text[57] where-

---

[53] Harry Sturz, *The Byzantine Text-Type* (1984), p.115

[54] James Edward Snapp, Jr., "The Authenticity of Mark 16:9-20" (2007), p.4

[55] Edward Hills, *The King James Version Defended* (1983), p.147 quoting Kurt Aland, "The Significance of the Papyri for Progress in New Testament Research." *The Bible in Modern Scholarship* (Nashville: Abingdon Press, 1965), p.342-45

[56] Ibid., p.150, quoting Kirsopp Lake, Robert P. Blake and Silva New, "The Caesarean Text of the Gospel of Mark." *Harvard Theological Review*, vol. 21 No. 4, (1928), p.345-346

[57] "The Syrian [Byzantine] text must have been due to a revision which was in fact a recension, and which may with fair probability be assigned to the time when Lucianus taught at Antioch." Brooke Westcott and Fenton Hort, *The New Testament in the Original Greek*, Vol. 2,

as others argue that successive edits of scripture over time formed the text. However, there is no historical corroboration for either theory. Furthermore, readings from the early Egyptian papyri correlate with readings in Byzantine manuscripts.

The explanation that best fits the evidence is that the **Byzantine** text was the **primary** text of the New Testament, and the Alexandrian text was contrived. The thousands of Byzantine manuscripts exist because it was known from the earliest ages to be the true text-type going all the way back to the apostles.

15th to 18th Century AD

"The Lord gave the word: great was the company of those that published it." (Psalm 68:11)

The New Testament of the King James Bible was translated from the Greek *Textus Receptus* that was compiled mainly from Byzantine Greek manuscripts.

1453 Byzantine empire falls[58]
1455 Gutenberg prints the Bible in Latin[59]
1516 Erasmus prints his first edition Greek New Testament using five primary manuscripts and his extensive research of all major variant readings[60]

(Cambridge and London: Macmillan and Co., 1882), p.182
[58] "Byzantine Empire." *Encyclopedia Britannica Online*, accessed 2 Feb 2020
[59] "Johannes Gutenberg." *Encyclopedia Britannica Online*, accessed 2 Feb 2020. Only two years after the Byzantine Empire fell (whose scribes had been faithfully copying Greek manuscripts), the printing press was invented (which made hand-written manuscripts obsolete). Might this be the providential working of God?
[60] "Did Erasmus use other manuscripts beside these five in preparing his Textus Receptus? The indications are that he did... It is well known also that Erasmus looked for manuscripts everywhere during his travels and that he borrowed them from everyone he could. Hence although the Textus Receptus was based mainly on the manuscripts which Erasmus found at Basel, it also included readings taken from others to which he had access... Indeed almost all the important variant readings known to scholars today were already known to Erasmus more than 460 years ago and discussed in the notes (previously prepared) which he placed after the text in his editions of the Greek New Testament" (Edward

1517 Martin Luther posts the *95 Theses*, which spark the Protestant refor-mation[61]

1522 Martin Luther publishes the Bible in German (translated from Eras-mus' 1519 Greek text)[62]

1526 William Tyndale publishes the New Testament in English (translated from Erasmus' 1522 Greek text)[63]

1598 Beza publishes his 5th edition Greek New Testament (based on the text of Erasmus later modified by Stephanus)[64]

1611 King James Bible published (translated from Beza's 1598 Greek text, later called the *Textus Receptus*)[65]

1769 King James Bible Oxford edition published – the final in a series of minor edits to correct printing errors and update spelling and punctua-tion; this is the edition commonly available today[66]

19th to 21st Century AD

"Who is this that darkeneth counsel by words without knowledge?" (Job 38:2)

The *Textus Receptus* vs. Aleph and B

In the 19th century textual critics Westcott and Hort, who did not believe the Bible is the infallible word of God,[67] set out to attack what Hort called "that vile *Textus Receptus*."[68] They argued that the *Textus Receptus* (the basis of the King James Bible) is a recension (a deliberate corruption of

---

Hills, *The King James Version Defended* (1983), p.160).

[61] "Ninety-five Theses." *Encyclopedia Britannica Online*, accessed 2 Feb 2020

[62] http://textus-receptus.com/wiki/Luther_Bible, accessed 02-02-2020

[63] Floyd Nolan Jones, *Which Version is the Bible?*, 20th edition (Humboldt, TN: KingsWord Press, 2010), p.64

[64] Ibid., p.65

[65] Ibid.

[66] http://textus-receptus.com/wiki/King_James_Version, accessed 02-02-2020

[67] Westcott: "I reject the word infallibility of Holy Scripture overwhelmingly." (Arthur West-cott, *Life and Letters of Brooke Foss Westcott*, Vol. 1 (New York: Macmillan and Co., 1903), p.207). Hort: "If you make a decided conviction of the absolute infallibility of the New Testament practically a sine qua non for co-operation, I fear I could not join you." (Arthur Fenton Hort, *Life and Letters of Fenton John Anthony Hort*, Vol. 1 (New York: Macmillan and Co., 1896), p.420).

[68] Ibid., p.211

scripture) from the 4th century. In contrast, codices Aleph and B are the "neutral text," which is closest to the original autographs. They offered three main "proofs" of their theory:

1. Conflation – Westcott and Hort argued that the Byzantine text was created in the 4th century as a combination of Alexandrian and Western texts. As evidence they gave eight examples,[69] one of which is Luke 24:53. **"And were continually in the temple, praising and blessing God. Amen." (Luke 24:53)**
Alexandrian reading (Aleph and B): "blessing"
Western reading (D): "praising"
Byzantine reading: "praising and blessing"
Westcott and Hort argued that the Byzantine "praising and blessing" is a conflation of the Alexandrian and Western readings. **However**, this is hardly proof since there is no reason that "praising and blessing" cannot be the authentic reading which an Alexandrian copyist truncated as "blessing" and a Western scribe as "praising."

27

2. Ancient Christian writings – Westcott and Hort argued that in the texts of ancient Christian writers ("church fathers"), "we have no historical signs of the existence of readings, conflate or other, that are marked as distinctively Syrian" (Byzantine) in regular use before the time of Chrysostom.[70] **However**, Edward Miller wrote how "I made a toilsome examination for myself of the quotations occurring in the writings of the Fathers before St. Chrysostom."[71] He found 2630 quotations of the "Traditional Text" (Byzantine) and 1753 of the "Neologian" (critical text of Westcott and Hort), which is "in favor of the Traditional Text, being about 3:2."[72] In response, textual critics brush aside this weighty evidence, complaining that the citations are not "*distinctly* Byzantine." Yet some of Miller's citations are

---

[69] John Burgon dealt with all eight alleged conflations and noted that "after 30 years of laborious research, Dr. Westcott and [Hort] flatter themselves that they have succeeded in detecting *eight*" (John Burgon, *The Revision Revised* (1883), p.253, emphasis his). Wilbur Pickering searched contemporary publications and was able to find only four other examples that are clearly relevant (Wilbur Pickering, i (2014), p.29).
[70] Brooke Westcott and Fenton Hort, *The New Testament in the Original Greek*, Vol. 2 (1882), 114-115
[71] John Burgon and Edward Miller, *The Traditional Text* (1896), p.ix
[72] Ibid., p.99-101

distinctly Byzantine.[73] One example:

"They gave him vinegar to drink mingled with gall: and when he had tasted thereof, he would not drink." (Matt 27:34)

The word "vinegar" is in Byzantine, not Alexandrian manuscripts, and is considered a distinctively Byzantine reading. Those ancient Christian writers who used the word "vinegar" together with "gall" (to indicate a reference to Matt 27:34 rather than to Mark, Luke, or John) include the Epistle of Barnabas, Irenaeus, Tertullian, the Gospel of Peter, Origen, Gregory Nazianzus, Gregory of Nyssa, the Gospel of Nicodemus, the Apostolic Constitutions, and the Revelation of Esdras.[74]

3. Aleph and B – Westcott and Hort wrote that "it is our belief (1) that readings of Aleph and B should be accepted as the true readings until strong internal evidence is found to the contrary, and (2) that no readings of Aleph and B can safely be rejected absolutely."[75] They argued that Aleph and B should replace the *Textus Receptus* because they are the oldest. In reply, John Burgon constructed seven "Notes of Truth" (see below) to evaluate texts of scripture, a vastly superior method to the assumption that the oldest manuscripts are necessarily the best. Modern textual critics state that they no longer consider Aleph and B to be the "neutral text" and instead follow an "eclectic" approach whereby they look at all available manuscript readings and choose the ones that in their judgment seem best. However, they still systematically reject the Byzantine readings and most often choose the readings of Codices Aleph and B, referring to them as the "oldest and best manuscripts." Although newer theories have superseded much of what Westcott and Hort wrote, their rejection of "that vile *Textus Receptus*" and high estimation of Codices Aleph and B continue to be embraced by textual critics in the 21st century.[76]

---

[73] Wilbur Pickering, *The Identity of the New Testament Text IV* (2014), p.36

[74] List compiled by Pickering who concludes "...the reading 'vinegar' in Matthew 27:34 has second century attestation (or perhaps even first century in the case of Barnabas!)" (Wilbur Pickering, *The Identity of the New Testament Text IV* (2014), p.36 footnote 1).

[75] Brooke Westcott and Fenton Hort, *The New Testament in the Original Greek*, Vol 2 (1882), 225

[76] Wilbur Pickering, *The Identity of the New Testament Text IV* (2014), p.15

John Burgon's Seven Notes of Truth[77]

Review (highly simplified):
Byzantine Greek text -> *Textus Receptus* -> King James Bible
Alexandrian texts (mainly Aleph and B) -> Critical Greek text -> Modern translations

1. Antiquity or Primitiveness
"The worst corruptions to which the New Testament has ever been subjected, originated within a hundred years after it was composed."[78] Since Aleph and B were written some 200 years *after* deliberate corruptions were introduced, they are not sufficiently old to be confident they reflect non-corrupted scripture. The oldest *reading* might not be the one found in the oldest *document*.

"The woman saith unto him, Sir, thou hast nothing to draw with, and the well is deep: from whence then hast thou that living water?" (John 4:11)

29

P66 (AD 200): "the woman"
P75 (3rd century): phrase omitted
B (Codex Vaticanus, 4th century): phrase omitted
Aleph (Codex Sinaiticus, 4th century): "she"
All other Greek manuscripts (5th century onward): "the woman"
Critical Greek text (published as the United Bible Society and Nestle-Aland texts): "the woman" (thereby rejecting the readings of Aleph and B)
NASB: "She said to him" (following Aleph and rejecting B and the critical Greek text)
Conclusion: Aleph and B contradict each other and do NOT give the oldest reading.

"While Peter thought on the vision, the Spirit said unto him, Behold, <u>three men</u> seek thee." (Acts 10:19)
These "three men" (restated in Acts 11:11) are the two household servants and one devout soldier of Cornelius (Acts 10:7).

---

[77] John Burgon and Edward Miller, *The Traditional Text* (1896), p.40-68. Verses in bold text are from the King James Bible. Most manuscript references are from Nestle-Aland *Novum Testamentum Graece*, 28th edition (2012).
[78] Frederick Scrivener, *A Plain Introduction to the Criticism of the New Testament*, 4th edition, Vol. 2, (London, New York, and Cambridge 1894), p.265

B: "two men"
Aleph: "three men"
Byzantine Majority: "three men"
Critical Greek text: "three men" (thereby rejecting the reading of Codex B)
Conclusion: Aleph and B contradict each other and do NOT give a uniform, oldest reading.

"I must work the works of him that <u>sent me</u>, while it is day: the night cometh, when no man can work." (John 9:4)
King James Bible: "I ... sent me"
P66 and P75: "We ... sent us"
B: "We ... sent me"
Aleph: "We ... sent us"
Byzantine Majority: "I ... sent me"
Critical Greek text: "We ... sent me" (thereby rejecting the readings of P66, P75, and Aleph)
ISV: "I ... sent me" (matching the King James Bible)
NIV: "We ... sent me" (reflecting B and rejecting Aleph)
NLT: "We ... sent us" (reflecting Aleph and rejecting B)
GOD'S WORD® Translation: "We ... sent me wants us" (combining Aleph and B readings!)
Conclusion: Aleph and B contradict each other, and the critical text does NOT reflect the oldest reading.

2. Number of Witnesses

John Burgon wrote, "That 'witnesses are to be weighed – not counted,' – is a maxim of which we hear constantly... [Yet] the undeniable fact is overlooked that 'number' is the most ordinary ingredient of weight, and indeed in matters of human testimony, is an element which even cannot be cast away. Ask one of Her Majesty's Judges if it be not so. Ten witnesses (suppose) are called in to give evidence: of whom one resolutely contradicts what is solemnly deposed to by the other nine. Which of the two parties do we suppose the Judge will be inclined to believe?"[79]

The weight of numbers of the Byzantine manuscripts is especially striking when the Alexandrian manuscripts not only give a different reading but

---

[79] John Burgon and Edward Miller, *The Traditional Text* (1896), p.44

contradict each other on what the variant reading should be.

"And he departed thence, and entered into a certain man's house, named <u>Justus</u>, one that worshipped God, whose house joined hard to the synagogue." (Acts 18:7)
B: "Titius Justus" (six letters, "Titius")
Aleph: "Titus Justus" (five letters, "Titus")
Byzantine Majority: "Justus"
Critical Greek Text: "Titius Justus" (six letters, "Titius") reflecting Codex B and rejecting *every* other existing Greek manuscript
NASB, NIV, and most other modern versions follow the critical text: "Titius Justus" (six letters, "Titius")
Conclusion: Aleph and B contradict each other, and the critical text is based on ONE, SINGLE Greek manuscript

3. Variety of Evidence or Universality of Witness
"Witnesses of different kinds; from different countries; speaking different tongues – witnesses who can never have met, and between whom it is incredible that there should exist collusion of any kind – such witnesses deserve to be listened to most respectfully. Indeed, when witnesses of so varied a sort agree in large numbers, they must needs be accounted worthy of even implicit confidence."[80]

"It is precisely this consideration which constrains us to pay supreme attention to the combined testimony of the Uncials and of the whole body of the Cursive Copies [which as a whole support the *Textus Receptus*]. They are dotted over at least 1000 years ... they evidently belong to so many divers countries – Greece, Constantinople, Asia Minor, Palestine, Syria, Alexandria, and other parts of Africa, not to say Sicily, Southern Italy, Gaul, England, and Ireland ... they so clearly represent countless families of manuscripts, being in no single instance absolutely identical in their text ... that their unanimous decision I hold to be an absolutely irrefragable evidence of the Truth."[81]

"Variety helps us evaluate the independence of witnesses. If the witnesses

---

[80] Ibid., p.50
[81] Ibid., p.51

which share a common reading come from only one area, say Egypt, then their independence must be doubted. It seems quite unreasonable to suppose that an original reading should survive in only one limited locale."[82]

Mark 16:9-20. The last twelve verses of Mark are present in the King James Bible as scripture. However, the critical Greek text places them in double brackets to indicate they are doubtfully part of scripture.

Greek manuscripts:
Absent: Aleph and B (4th century) and 304 (12th century) are the only **three** that clearly end abruptly after Mark 16:8. However, the original text of Aleph is unavailable; only a replacement page exists. Codex B has an extra blank column after Mark 16:8, implying that the scribe knew of the 12 verses. Codex 304 is an "unusual manuscript which mingles the text with a commentary, and it is difficult to tell whether 304 is a valid witness against the inclusion of the long ending or not."[83]
Present: All other Greek manuscripts from the 5th century (Codices A, C, D, and W) onward.[84]

Non-Greek manuscripts:
Absent: Sinaitic Syriac manuscript (found in the same monastery as Aleph), one Latin manuscript, one Coptic (Sahidic) manuscript, some Armenian manuscripts, two Georgian manuscripts.
Present: most Old Latin manuscripts, Jerome's Latin Vulgate, Syriac (including the Peshitta), Coptic, Ethiopic[85], Gothic, most Armenian, some Georgian manuscripts.

Ancient Christian writers ("church fathers")
Evidencing omission: Eusebius, certain manuscripts referenced by Eusebius, and manuscripts referenced by Jerome
Evidencing inclusion: 24 writers from the **2nd century** onward.[86]

Summary: Out of **thousands** of Greek and non-Greek manuscripts, "the

---

[82] Wilbur Pickering, *The Identity of the New Testament Text*, 1st edition, p.102
[83] James Edward Snapp, Jr., "The Authenticity of Mark 16:9-20" (2007), p.4, 20, 22
[84] Ibid., chap. 2
[85] Ibid., footnote 5a
[86] Ibid., chap. 3

actual number of extant unmutilated early (pre-800 AD) manuscripts of Mark 16 in any language which clearly feature the abrupt or short ending [and lack the 12 verses] is **five**: Aleph, Codex B, Sinaitic Syriac, Latin Codex Bobiensis, and Coptic Codex 'P. Palau Rib. 182.'"[87] From ancient Christian writers there is a predominance of evidence supporting Mark 16:9-20.

4. Respectability of Witnesses or Weight

Individual manuscripts are "weighed" by comparing them to manuscripts showing features of good reliability. If "certain witnesses are found to range themselves continually on the side which is condemned by a large majority of others exhibiting other notes of truth entitling them to credence, those few witnesses must inevitably lose in respectability . . .[88] If they go wrong continually, their character must be low."[89] So when Aleph and B are observed to contradict each other over 3,000 times in the gospels alone,[90] the weight of their credibility is low.

Present in B but not Aleph:
"And he said, Lord, I believe. And he worshipped him." (John 9:38)

33

P66 (AD 200): verse is present
P75 (3rd century): absent
B (4th century): present
Aleph (4th century): absent
Byzantine Majority (5th century onward): present
Critical text: present (rejecting Aleph)
NET Bible: verse present, but bracketed to indicate doubt

"The beginning of the gospel of Jesus Christ, the <u>Son of God</u>;" (Mark 1:1)
"Son of God"
B: present
Aleph: absent
Byzantine Majority: present
Critical text: present (rejecting Aleph)
Today's NIV: absent (following Aleph and rejecting the Critical text)

---

[87] Ibid., footnote AP-8
[88] John Burgon and Edward Miller, *The Traditional Text* (1896), p.53-54
[89] Ibid., p.59
[90] H.C. Hoskier, *Codex B and its Allies* (London: Bernard Quaritch, 1914), II.1

<u>Present in Aleph but not B</u>:

"And there appeared an angel unto him from heaven, strengthening him. And being in an agony he prayed more earnestly: and his sweat was as it were great drops of blood falling down to the ground." (Luke 22:43-44)
"Then said Jesus, Father, forgive them; for they know not what they do. And they parted his raiment, and cast lots." (Luke 23:34)

P75: both passages absent
B: both passages absent
Aleph: the original included the passages; they were removed by one scribe, then restored by another scribe
Byzantine Majority: both passages present
Quoted by ancient Christian writers ("church fathers") from the **2ⁿᵈ century** onward[91]
Despite this evidence the Nestle-Aland critical text places these verses in double brackets, meaning they "are known not to be a part of the original text."[92]

34

<u>Absent in both B and Aleph</u>:

"Who shall separate us from the <u>love of Christ</u>? shall tribulation, or distress, or persecution, or famine, or nakedness, or peril, or sword?" (Romans 8:35)

B: "love of God in Christ Jesus"
Aleph: "love of God"
Byzantine Majority: "love of Christ"
Critical Text: "love of Christ" rejecting both Aleph and B
All modern Bible versions: "love of Christ"
Conclusion: BOTH Aleph and B readings are UNIVERSALLY rejected because the later manuscripts more accurately reflect the true reading.

5. Continuity or Unbroken Tradition

"When therefore a reading is observed to leave traces of its existence and of its use all down the ages, it comes with an authority of a peculiarly commanding nature."[93] On the other hand, "if a reading or tradition died

---

[91] John Burgon and Edward Miller, *The Traditional Text* (1896), p.110-111
[92] Nestle-Aland, *Novum Testamentum Graece*, 28th edition, Introduction
[93] John Burgon and Edward Miller, *The Traditional Text* (1896), p.50. Burgon adds, "Still

out in the fourth or fifth century we have the verdict of history against it."[94]

"And knew her not till she had brought forth her <u>firstborn</u> son: and he called his name JESUS." (Matt 1:25)
The word "firstborn" means Mary did not have a prior son (affirming the virgin birth), means that Jesus has pre-eminence in His birth family (and therefore no sibling with a right to the throne of David before Him), and hints at Christ's pre-eminence over all creation ("firstborn of every creature," Col 1:15).
"Firstborn" **absent**: Aleph and B (4th century) as well as three other Greek manuscripts (Z and 071 of the 6th century and 033 of the 9th century).
"Firstborn" **present**: All other existing Greek manuscripts (over 1500 manuscripts from the 5th century onward) other than the five noted above. Present in the ancient Syriac Peshitta. Absent in some old Latin copies but present in others including Jerome's Latin vulgate. Quoted by eighteen ancient Christian writers ("church fathers") from the 4th century onward.[95]
Conclusion: The reading "firstborn" shows continuity and unbroken textual tradition.[96] Most modern versions ignore the evidence for "firstborn son" and only write "son."

6. Evidence of the Entire Passage, or Context
Examining the context of a disputed verse within a given manuscript can be helpful because "the carelessness ... that leads a copyist to misrepresent one word is sure to lead him into error about another... So too on the other side. Clearness, correctness, self-collectedness, near to the moment in question, add to the authority of the evidence."[97]

"Howbeit this kind goeth not out but by prayer and fasting." (Matt 17:21)
Evidence against: Aleph and B (4th century), Theta (9th century), three other manuscripts (7th century onward)

---

more, when ... the transmission ceased after four centuries ... [and] engulfs not less than fifteen centuries in its hungry abyss ... it is evident that according to an essential Note of Truth, those [readings are to be rejected]."
[94] Wilbur Pickering, *The Identity of the New Testament Text*, 1st edition, p.103
[95] John Burgon, *The Revision Revised* (1883), p.123
[96] Ibid., p.124
[97] John Burgon and Edward Miller, *The Traditional Text* (1896), p.65

Evidence in favor: All other Greek manuscripts (from 5ᵗʰ century onward)
Discussion: The Codex Aleph in this passage has been corrected and "speaks uncertainly" and so "the case for rejection . . . rests such as it is upon [Codex] B . . . Now if we inspect verses 19, 20, 22, and 23, to go no farther, we shall discover that the entire passage in B is wrapped in a fog of error. It differs from the main body of the witnesses in ten places." In six of these places even the textual critics who champion Codex B reject the readings. The remaining four are each supported by no more than a half dozen manuscripts each. "Inspection of the Context therefore adds here strong confirmation" that Codices Aleph and B are in error.[98]

7. Internal Considerations or Reasonableness

Some readings may be "grammatically, logically, geographically, or scientifically impossible."[99]

"And when the <u>daughter of the said Herodias</u> came in, and danced, and pleased Herod and them that sat with him, the king said unto the damsel, Ask of me whatsoever thou wilt, and I will give it thee." (Mark 6:22)

The skillful young woman is named Salome; she is the daughter of Herodias by her former husband Philip, **not** by Herod.[100] After Salome's birth Herodias divorced Philip and married his step-brother Herod Antipas, which marriage John the Baptist condemned (Mark 6:17-18). This kinship is confirmed in Matt 14:6, ". . . the daughter of Herodias danced before them, and pleased Herod."

B and Aleph: "his [Herod's] daughter Herodias" which contradicts Matt 14:6

Byzantine Majority: indicate the daughter of Herodias

Critical text: "his [Herod's] daughter Herodias" which contradicts Matt 14:6

NLT: "Then his daughter, also named Herodias" which contradicts Matt 14:6 and contradicts the historical record that the girl is named Salome

God's Word Translation: "His daughter, that is, Herodias' daughter" which incorrectly implies that the young woman is the offspring of Herod and Herodias.

Conclusion: The critical text reading of B and Aleph is so unauthentic and

---

98 Ibid., p.62-63
99 Wilbur Pickering, *The Identity of the New Testament Text IV*, 1st edition, p.105
100 Josephus, *Antiquities of the Jews*, 18.5.4

misleading that most modern versions read "the daughter of Herodias" with the King James Bible.

"And Barnabas and Saul returned <u>from Jerusalem</u>, when they had fulfilled their ministry, and took with them John, whose surname was Mark." (Acts 12:25)
Barnabas and Saul first travel from Antioch to Jerusalem (Acts 11:26-30) and then return <u>from Jerusalem</u> to Antioch (Acts 12:25 - 13:1).
B (4th century) "to Jerusalem"
Aleph (4th century) "to Jerusalem"
A and D (5th century) "from Jerusalem"
Byzantine Majority "to Jerusalem"
Textus Receptus (underlying the King James Bible): "from Jerusalem"
Critical text: "to Jerusalem"
CSB, CEV, HCSB, NET: "to Jerusalem" (following the Critical text)
ESV, NASB, NIV, NLT: "from Jerusalem" (thereby rejecting the readings of B and Aleph as well as the Critical text)
Conclusion: Codices Aleph and B do NOT give the oldest reading and unreasonably contradict the narrative. The *Textus Receptus* contains the superior reading compared to the Byzantine Majority Text.

Summary:
The Masoretic text in the Old Testament and the *Textus Receptus* in the New Testament are based on the manuscripts preserved by God. The King James Bible was translated from these texts. God providentially worked through history to preserve His word in Hebrew, Greek, and English.

3. The Bible stands as absolute authority
"The grass withereth, the flower fadeth: but the word of our God shall stand for ever." (Isaiah 40:8)

"For all flesh is as grass, and all the glory of man as the flower of grass. The grass withereth, and the flower thereof falleth away: But the word of the Lord endureth for ever. And this is the word which by the gospel is preached unto you." (1 Peter 1:24-25)

Scripture is **words** that are rightly quoted with **absolute authority**.

1. Scripture stands as the unquestionable source of truth.
Even Satan, the enemy of truth (John 8:44), quoted scripture as the un-questionable source of truth to Jesus Christ ("for it is written," Matt 4:6 from Psalm 91:11-12). In turn, the One who is "the truth" (John 14:6) quoted scripture back to him ("it is written again," Matt 4:7 from Deut 6:16).

2. Scripture stands as the voice of God.
The author of Hebrews quoted the Old Testament as the voice of God, whether quoting words originally spoken by God to man (Heb 5:6 from Psalm 110:4), words spoken by man to God (Heb 1:10-12 from Psalm 102:25-27), or a combination of the two ("as the Holy Ghost saith" in Heb 3:7-11 quoting man's words in Psalm 95:7 and God's words in Psalm 95:8-11). Even the narrative statement of Gen 2:2 is written as the words of God (Heb 4:4).

3. Scripture stands for the authority of God.
"For <u>the scripture saith</u> unto Pharaoh, Even for this same purpose have I raised thee up, that I might shew my power in thee, and that my name might be declared throughout all the earth" (Rom 9.17). Paul quotes Exod 9:16 and substitutes "scripture" for the very name of God! He attributes to scripture the authority of God, Himself.

The King James Bible is the preserved word of God and stands as the source of absolute authority. No modern translation can be quoted with absolute authority since each publication is intended to be only a best-effort reflection of the original autographs, which no longer exist.

4. Conclusion

What is the Bible?

Biblical definition: An actual book based on the text (Hebrew Masoretic and Greek *Textus Receptus*) preserved by God that stands as absolute authority.
Non-biblical definition: The Bible is the word of God in the original writ-

ings, which no longer exist; extant (existing) manuscripts (hand-written copies) are the word of God insofar as they reflect the wording of the non-extant originals.

The King James Bible is the only book in the English language that meets this definition of the word "Bible."

An actual book:
King James Bible – yes, an actual book (whether physical or digital).
Modern versions – no, the originals no longer exist.

Text preserved by God:
King James Bible – yes, both in the Old and New Testament.
Modern versions – no, they do not exclusively use the Masoretic text in the Old Testament, and they do use corrupt manuscripts in the New Testament.

Stands as absolute authority:

King James Bible – yes; completely reliable from beginning to end and free of any error; read, quoted, memorized, and loved by humans and used by God for over 400 years.
Modern versions – no, the text is authoritative only so far as it reflects the original autographs, which no longer exist.

"God has preserved His Word through the centuries and continues in our century by providing for us His Word in a faithful translation in English. Today the Authorised Version is still the beloved standard by which other translations are judged. It stands as a faithful translation of the true texts of God's Word; it continues strong, proclaiming God's message to a lost and dying world. It has the blessing of God upon it, and has been the source of salvation and sanctification for many thousands of people throughout its history. Thus the Authorised Version stands as it did nearly four hundred years ago, as the Word of God in English and a monument to the God who gave it."[101]

---

[101] G. W. Anderson and D. E. Anderson, "The English Bible, Its Origin, Preservation and Blessing" (Trinitarian Bible Society, 2010)

40|

"Neither is there salvation in any other: for there is none other name under heaven given among men, whereby we must be saved."
Acts 4:12

Acts of the Apostles
Introduction

Theme Verse
"But ye shall receive power, after that the Holy Ghost is come upon you: and ye shall be witnesses unto me both in Jerusalem, and in all Judaea, and in Samaria, and unto the uttermost part of the earth" (Acts 1:8).

Overview
The *Acts of the Apostles* shows how Christ's followers, through the power of the Holy Ghost, fulfill His promise to spread the gospel from Jerusalem and Judea to Samaria and the greater Gentile world (Acts 1:8).

Luke's account focuses on the primarily Jewish ministry of Peter (Acts 1-12) and the primarily Gentile ministry of Paul (Acts 13-28). Both Peter and Paul will have a significant sermon recorded (Acts 2, 13), heal a lame individual (Acts 3, 14), heal persons from afar (Acts 5, 19), cast out unclean spirits (Acts 5, 16), receive a miraculous release from prison (Acts 12, 16), confront a sorcerer (Acts 8, 13), refuse to be worshiped (Acts 10, 14), receive heavenly visions (Acts 10, 16), lay on hands to impart the Holy Ghost (Acts 8, 19), raise the dead (Acts 9, 20), and be imprisoned for their faith (Acts 12, 21-28). Luke draws parallels between the two men to show that the same Holy Spirit empowers both apostles to do His work.

Transitions
Gospels: Old Testament to New Testament
Acts: Israel to the Church
Revelation: the Church to Israel

Outline
Luke gives a summary statement when the gospel is preached:
Acts 2:47 – initially at the temple
Acts 6:7   – throughout Jerusalem
Acts 9:31 – throughout Judea, Galilee, and Samaria

Acts 12:24   – into the Gentile world as far as Antioch in Syria
Acts 16:5   – into Asia Minor
Acts 19:20   – into Europe
Acts 28:30-31 – throughout the eastern half of the Roman Empire

Author

Acts is the second of Luke's two-volume series written to Theophilus. His first volume, the Gospel of Luke, bears the author's name. Luke first meets Paul at Troas during the apostle's second missionary journey and travels with him to Philippi (Acts 16:11-12), where he parts with Paul until rejoining him there toward the end of the third missionary journey (Acts 20:6). Luke then travels with Paul to Jerusalem (Acts 21:17), where the apostle is arrested. Luke is not continuously with Paul during the apostle's two-year confinement in Caesarea (Acts 24:27) but remains in the vicinity and subsequently travels with him to Rome (Acts 27:1). He is then present with Paul at the apostle's first imprisonment in Rome when Paul includes greetings from "Luke, the beloved physician" (Col 4:14, also Philem 24). Luke remains a faithful friend to Paul during the apostle's final imprisonment in Rome when Paul tells Timothy that "only Luke is with me" (2 Tim 4:11).

Reader

Luke writes Acts to Theophilus (Acts 1:1), whom he addresses in his first volume as "most excellent" (Luke 1:3). This title is used to show respect (like calling a judge "your honor"). Roman governors Felix (Acts 23:26, 24:3) and Festus (Acts 26:25) are also called "most excellent" or "most noble." Josephus writes *Against Apion* to "most excellent Epaphroditus," his patron (financial supporter).[102] So Theophilus might be a government official, Luke's patron, or another important individual.

Purpose

Primary purpose: Luke writes a narrative that shows how Christianity grows from a small group of believers in Jerusalem to a worldwide faith that extends to the capital of the Roman Empire. His primary purpose is to show how God accomplishes His desire to bring the gospel from Jerusa-

---

[102] Josephus, *Antiquities of the Jews*, preface.2

lem unto the "uttermost part of the earth" (Acts 1:8).

Secondary purposes: Luke emphasizes three issues. Three times he gives Paul's conversion testimony (Acts 9, 22, 26), three times Cornelius' conversion testimony (Acts 10, 11, 15), and then the last seven chapters he devotes to Paul's defense (Acts 22-28).

Paul's conversion – the Roman world believes that the Jewish religion (Judaism) is legitimate because it is ancient. Julius Caesar declared, "I permit this people to assemble and celebrate according to their ancestral customs and laws."[103] Emperor Claudius likewise decreed, "It will therefore be fit to permit the Jews ... to keep their ancient customs without being hindered so to do."[104] Luke intends to show that Christianity, from a judicial standpoint, is rightly considered an extension of Judaism and should be afforded the same legal protections. He illustrates this by showing that Paul, a devout Jew before his conversion, remains a devout Jew after his conversion. He emphasizes the genuineness of Paul's conversion by giving his testimony three times (Acts 9, 22, 26).

Cornelius' conversion – some would argue that Christianity cannot be consistent with Judaism because so many Gentiles have converted. Yet even the Jewish synagogue attracts Gentile God-fearers (meaning Gentiles who worship the God of Israel as Gentiles, Acts 13:16, 26). Luke illustrates this by showing that Cornelius is a God-fearing man (Acts 10:2, 22) both before and after his conversion. He emphasizes the genuineness of Cornelius' conversion by giving his testimony three times (Acts 10, 11, 15).

Paul's legal defense – while advocating the legitimacy of Christianity, Luke defends the record of Paul, the man who has done so much to spread Christianity. Luke shows Paul caught up in public upheavals of which he is not the cause (Acts 14:19, 16:19, 17:5, 13, 19:29, 21:30) and shows Paul being judged guiltless by Roman officials (Acts 16:36, 18:14, 19:37, 23:29, 25:25, 26:31). The last seven chapters of this volume (Acts 22-28) involve Paul's defense and could be helpful at his upcoming hearing before Caesar.

---

[103] Ibid., 14.10.8
[104] Ibid., 19.5.3

Date

The historical record indicates that Roman governor Festus replaces Felix (Acts 24:27) in AD 59.[105] Paul therefore arrives in Rome (Acts 28:16) about AD 60, where he stays for at least two years (Acts 28:30) until AD 62, awaiting his legal appeal to Caesar (Acts 25:11–12). Luke apparently finishes writing Acts during this time when the narrative catches up to current events.

The book of Acts ends without giving the outcome of Paul's hearing, but it appears that he is released from prison then later re-arrested and executed.[106] The subsequent Jewish rebellion against Rome begins in AD 66 and ends with the destruction of the Jerusalem temple in AD 70.[107]

The principal objection to an early date for Acts (circa AD 62) prior to the destruction of Jerusalem in AD 70 is that Luke shows that he already knows specific details about this very event (Luke 19:41-44, 21:5-6). Some therefore assume that Luke writes his account after AD 70 with the benefit of hindsight. However, although Luke cannot predict the future, God the Son knows "the end from the beginning" (Isa 46:10) and is the One who predicts the disastrous event of AD 70. Luke merely records the testimony of eyewitnesses (Luke 1:2) who heard Jesus' words.

45

Other factors that support a date of writing before the Jewish war of AD 66 – 70 include:

The temple – Jerusalem is still at peace at the end of the book of Acts. The temple is important to Luke (it is a frequent setting in his gospel and Acts), and he records Jesus' prediction of its destruction (Luke 21:5-6) but does not describe the actual event.

Paul – Luke gives an extensive account of Paul's legal hearings (Acts 23-26) and a riveting adventure story of his perilous journey to Rome (Acts

---

[105] William Ramsay, *St. Paul The Traveler and Roman Citizen* (1925), revised by Mark Wilson (Grand Rapids, MI: Kregel Publications, 2001), p.250
[106] See discussion at the end of Acts 28.
[107] "First Jewish Revolt." *Encyclopedia Britannica Online*, accessed 13 Nov 2019

27-28), then fails to tell of Paul's hearing before Caesar Nero, undoubtedly because the hearing has not yet taken place. Furthermore the apostle is still alive at the end of Acts. Luke records the martyrdom of Stephen (Acts 7:59) and James the son of Zebedee (Acts 12:2), but not of Paul. Also, Luke's lengthy legal defense of Paul is most relevant if the apostle is still alive.

Judaism – Luke argues that Christianity should be deemed acceptable to Roman authorities because it is an extension of Judaism (itself legitimate in Roman thought because it is an ancient religion). Luke's argument loses force and would be awkward to make after the Jewish rebellion against Rome of AD 66 – 70.

Paul's epistles – Luke shows no knowledge of Paul's letters that are preserved in the New Testament since, at this early date, they are not yet in broad circulation. For example, Luke was not with Paul at Corinth where his apostleship was under attack and had not read his letters (1 Cor 9:1-2, 15:7-9, 2 Cor 11:5, 11:22-28, 12:11-12); so nowhere in the book of Acts does Luke try to defend Paul's apostleship.

Gospel of Luke - the Apostle Paul in 1 Timothy 5:18 appears to quote Luke 10:7. Therefore Luke writes at least his first volume (the Gospel of Luke) before the apostle's death, which secular history teaches took place no later than AD 66.[108]

Open evangelism – in Acts the Roman government has no hostility towards Christians. Luke ends with a very positive statement about Paul preaching the gospel openly ("no man forbidding him," Acts 28:31) and does not seem aware of the future persecution under Nero.

Church history – Luke writes about church ordinances (such as baptism) and offices (such as elders) but never writes in a way that touches issues that become subjects of debate in the second century onward.

---

[108] "St. Paul the Apostle." *Encyclopedia Britannica Online*, accessed 7 Jan 2020

Sources

Luke writes from a firsthand perspective for part of the book ("we" sections in Acts 16:10-40, 20:5-21:18, 27:1-28:16) and elsewhere uses material he obtained directly from other observers (Luke 1:2). Whenever possible Luke documents two eyewitnesses because of the greater credibility they bring (Deut 19:15, Matt 18:16). Luke writes of two witnesses of the transfiguration (Luke 9:29-30), of the ministry of Jesus (Luke 10:1), of the end times (Luke 17:34-36), of the miraculous acquisition of the donkey (Luke 19:29-34), of the crucifixion (Luke 23:32), of the empty tomb (Luke 24:3-4), of the risen Christ (Luke 24:13-35), of the ascension (Acts 1:10), of the healing of the lame man (Acts 3:11), of the bold witness for Jesus (Acts 4:13), of the faithful witness of Stephen (Acts 7:56), of the conversion of the Samaritans (Acts 8:14), of the disciples' desire to resurrect Dorcas (Acts 9:38), of Cornelius' willingness to meet Peter (Acts 10:7), of Peter's miraculous release from prison (Acts 12:6), of the Jerusalem council's acceptance of Gentile believers (Acts 15:27), and of Paul's love for the Macedonian believers (Acts 19:22).

The record shows that Luke travels with Paul (indicated by the pronoun "we") across much of the known world, during which time he has access to many eyewitnesses. Luke most likely obtains information from:

Acts 1 - 5 – Luke visits Jerusalem with Paul (Acts 21:17) and may interview James and the church elders (Acts 21:18) and others in Jerusalem including believing priests (Acts 6:7) and Pharisees (Acts 15:5) as well as Mnason (a long-time disciple, Acts 21:16). Luke may learn of Gamaliel's closed-door speech (Acts 5:34-39) from Paul, who had been the rabbi's disciple (Acts 22:3).

Acts 6 - 8 – Philip (whom Luke meets at Caesarea, Acts 21:8) is a deacon (Acts 6:5) and an evangelist (Acts 8:5). Paul was also present at Stephen's stoning (Acts 7:58).

Acts 9 – Paul

Acts 10 - 12 – believers in Jerusalem (Acts 21:17), possibly John Mark's mother Mary or other surviving family members (Acts 12:12), and believers in Caesarea (Acts 21:8,16).

Acts 13 – Paul

Acts 14 – Paul and Timothy

Acts 15 – Paul and Silas

Acts 16 – Luke is an eyewitness.

Acts 17 - 19 – Paul, Silas, Timothy, Aristarchus (Acts 20:4, 27:2), and Tychicus (Acts 20:4, Col 4:7). Luke is not with Paul at Athens (Acts 17:16) but could visit later to review written records from the Areopagus about Paul's speech and interview Dionysius and Damaris (Acts 17:34).

Acts 20 - 21 – Luke is an eyewitness.

Acts 22 - 26 – Paul; Luke obtains Captain Lysias' written report (Acts 23:26-30); Luke likely collects records from legal hearings before the Jewish council (Acts 23:1), Governor Felix (Acts 24:1), Governor Festus (Acts 25:6), and King Agrippa II (Acts 26:1);[109] Luke no doubt interviews Paul's nephew to learn of his private conversation with Captain Lysias (Acts 23:16-22); Luke does not have a source for the private conversation between Governor Festus and his council (conversation not recorded, Acts 25:12), but does for the one between Governor Festus and King Agrippa II (conversation recorded, Acts 26:30-32).

Acts 27 - 28 – Luke is an eyewitness.

Luke is like the best historians of his day who take time to find and interview eyewitnesses. Herodian of Antioch wrote, "Unwilling to accept from others hearsay evidence and unsubstantiated information, I have collected, in my history, material that is still fresh in the minds of my intended readers."[110] Polybius wrote, "For as historical events take place in many different localities ... the only resource left is to ask questions of as many people as possible; and to believe those who are worthy of credit; and to show critical sagacity in judging of their reports."[111]

Luke is like the best historians of his day who travel long distances to collect facts. Appian wrote, "My history has often led me from Carthage to Spain, from Spain to Sicily or to Macedonia, or to join some embassy to foreign countries, or some alliance formed with them; thence back to Carthage or Sicily ... and again elsewhere, while the work was still unfin-

---

[109] The Roman courts apparently kept records of legal proceedings, such as those involving Paul in Judea. "The survival of some [legal] records ... [include] a small archive found in the Judean desert, dating to the late-1st/early-2nd century CE involving a woman named Babatha." Leanne Bablitz. "Roman Courts." *Oxford Classical Dictionary Online*, accessed 18 Nov 2021

[110] Herodian of Antioch, *History of the Roman Empire*, 1.1.3

[111] Polybius, *The Histories*, 12.4

ished."[112]

Luke understands that accuracy is of utmost importance because many eyewitnesses are still alive at the time of his writing. For example, King Agrippa II (Acts 25-26) will live until AD 93.[113] Josephus notes how carefully he must write of living witnesses, including "King Agrippa himself, a person that deserved the greatest admiration. Now all these men bore their testimony to me, that I had the strictest regard to truth. Who yet would not have … been silent, if I … had given false [accounts of] actions, or omitted any of them."[114]

Speeches

Luke gives a concise account of speeches by accurately recording selected portions. Speakers formally trained in Greco-Roman rhetoric (persuasive speech) include Hellenistic Jews such as Stephen (apparently a "Grecian" Jew, Acts 6:1, 5), Paul (from Tarsus, Acts 21:39), and Apollos ("born at Alexandria, an eloquent man, and mighty in the scriptures," Acts 18:24). Yet the strength behind these men is not "wisdom of words" (1 Cor 1:17), but the "power of God" (1 Cor 1:18) through the Holy Spirit (Acts 7:55, 13:9).

Selected speeches (Acts 7, 13, 17, 19, 20, 24, and 26) are outlined in the following manner:[115]
Introduction *(exordium)* – opening statement to build rapport with the audience
Narrative *(narratio)* – presentation of relevant facts
Thesis *(propositio)* – proposition for the audience to consider
Arguments *(probatio)* – proofs in support of the thesis statement
Refutation *(refutatio)* – a rebuttal of the opponent's allegations
Final appeal *(peroratio)* – closing words explaining why to consider the preceding arguments

Luke does shape the presentation of speeches by thoroughly examining source material and carefully choosing words to place in his record. Yet he

---

[112] Appian, *History of Rome*, preface.12
[113] "Herod Agrippa II." *Encyclopedia Britannica Online*, accessed 10 Nov 2021
[114] Josephus, *Against Apion*, 1.9
[115] Ben Witherington, *New Testament Rhetoric* (Eugene, OR: Cascade Books, 2009)

is always faithful to his sources. Consider Stephen's speech (Acts 7) to the Sanhedrin ("council," Acts 6:12), for which Luke undoubtedly has a transcript.[116] In Acts 7:15, Stephen mentions both Jacob and his sons; in the next verse, Stephen describes burial in Shechem, which actually applies only to Jacob's sons and not to Jacob (he is buried elsewhere). If Luke were merely fabricating a speech based on oral tradition, he certainly would have made the burial sequence much clearer. The fact that he writes Stephen's words (which are entirely true but perhaps confusing if not carefully studied) is a sign that Luke faithfully records rather than edits Stephen's Spirit-filled speech before Israel's leaders.

William Ramsay

Sir William Ramsay (1851-1939) was an Oxford professor when he began his research on the book of Acts. "From 1880 onwards he travelled widely in Asia Minor and rapidly became the recognized authority on all matters relating to the districts associated with St Paul's missionary journeys and on Christianity in the early Roman Empire."[117] Yet when he began his archeological investigations, he did not believe in the trustworthiness of the Bible. "On the contrary, I began with a mind unfavorable to it, as the ingenuity and apparent completeness of the [Bible-rejecting] Tübingen theory had at one time quite convinced me."[118]

Over time the evidence he discovered convinced him otherwise. "It was gradually borne in upon me that in various details the narrative showed marvelous truth."[119] "I set out to look for truth on the borderland where Greece and Asia meet, and found it here. You may press the words of Luke in a degree far beyond any other historian's, and they stand the keenest scrutiny and the hardest treatment."[120] "In short, this author should be

---

[116] "In the Great Sanhedrin ... there were also two secretaries, who were compensated for their services, and who kept a careful record of the proceedings of the court ..." Samuel Hirshberg (Dec 1926). "Jurisprudence Among Ancient Jews." *Marquette Law Review*, Vol. 11, Issue 1, p.26

[117] "William Mitchell Ramsay." *Encyclopaedia Britannica* (1911)

[118] William Ramsay, *St. Paul The Traveler* (1925), revised by Mark Wilson (2001), p.19

[119] Ibid.

[120] William Ramsay, *The Bearing of Recent Discovery on the Trustworthiness of the New Testament* (London: Hodder & Stoughton, 1915), p.89

placed along with the very greatest of historians."[121]

Marks of Authenticity

- Luke presents himself as an eyewitness only in the most obscure portions of his work ("we" sections in Acts 16:10-40, 20:5-21:18, 27:1-28:16), unlike a writer seeking glory who might interject himself into an important event such as the ascension (Acts 1:9). "[Acts] is a mere uncolored recital of the important facts in the briefest possible terms. The narrator's individuality and his personal feeling and preferences are almost wholly suppressed. He ... writes with the single aim to state the facts as he has learned them."[122]
- Luke confidently asserts that he is merely confirming facts to which other eyewitnesses can attest (Luke 1:1-4).
- Luke fails to embellish accounts that lack color. For example, the utterly plain report of the ascension (Acts 1:9-11) is evidence of its authenticity. Luke could add vivid details but chooses to write using only facts he has received from his sources.
- Luke accurately describes geographical locations and administrative regions. When he writes that Lystra and Derbe are cities of Lycaonia (Acts 14:6), he makes a precise statement that is "accurate at no other time except between AD 37 and 72."[123]
- Luke correctly gives official titles. "Every person is found just where he ought to be: proconsuls in senatorial provinces, asiarchs in Ephesus, [praetors] in Philippi, politarchs in Thessalonica, magicians and soothsayers everywhere."[124] Examples include proconsul[125] ("deputy," Acts 13:7, 18:12), praetors[126] ("rulers," Acts 16:19), politarchs[127] ("rulers," Acts 17:6), asiarchs[128] ("chief of Asia," Acts 19:31), town clerk[129] (Acts 19:35), and first man[130] (Acts 28:7).

51

---

[121] Ibid., p.222
[122] William Ramsay, *St. Paul The Traveler* (1925), revised by Mark Wilson (2001), p.27-28
[123] Ibid, p.100
[124] William Ramsay, *The Bearing of Recent Discovery*, p.96-97
[125] William Ramsay, *St. Paul The Traveler* (1925), revised by Mark Wilson (2001), p.74 and 198
[126] Ibid., p.174
[127] Ibid., p.183
[128] Ibid., p.216
[129] Ibid.
[130] Ibid., p.270

- Surviving records written in the first century are quite limited. However, when Luke's account overlaps available secular history, the Acts record is affirmed. The best example is the death of Herod Agrippa I, where the reports written by Luke (Acts 12:20-23) and Josephus[131] are thoroughly compatible with one another.[132]
- A writer of propaganda would not likely include material potentially embarrassing to Christians, such as the deceit of Ananias and Sapphira (Acts 5:1-11), the neglect of the Grecian widows (Acts 6:1), the shameful behavior of the convert Simon (Acts 8:18-24), Peter hesitating to obey God (Acts 10:14) and the brethren hesitating to accept Peter's story (Acts 11:1-3), Paul's slowness to begin evangelizing Gentiles (others beat him to it, Acts 11:19-20), Paul and Barnabas becoming objects of worship in Lystra (Acts 14:11-13), church dissension over circumcision (Acts 15:1, 5), the split-up of Paul and Barnabas (Acts 15:37-39), Paul's choosing to circumcise Timothy (Acts 16:1-3), Paul's lackluster success in Athens (Acts 17:32-34), Paul's long preaching leading to a young man's death (Acts 20:9), Paul's arrest in Jerusalem after being warned against it (Acts 21:33), and Paul's verbal abuse of the high priest (Acts 23:3-5). "Our hypothesis is that Acts was written by a great historian, a writer who set himself to record the facts as they occurred, a strong partisan indeed but raised above partiality by his perfect confidence that he had only to describe the facts as they occurred, in order to make the truth of Christianity and the honor of Paul apparent."[133]
- The cliffhanger ending of *Acts* fails to inform the reader of Paul's fate. A competent writer of fiction would not make such an obvious mistake.

Sevens

Seven summaries: Acts 2:47, 6:7, 9:31, 12:24, 16:5, 19:20, 28:30-31
Seven "Nazareth" references to Jesus: Acts 2:22, 3:6, 4:10, 6:14, 10:38, 22:8, 26:9
Seven references to both Peter and John (Acts 3:1, 3:3, 3:4, 3:11, 4:13, 4:19, 8:14)

---

[131] Josephus, *Antiquities of the Jews*, 19.8.2
[132] The Josephus narrative is provided in the notes at the end of Acts 12.
[133] William Ramsay, *St. Paul The Traveler* (1925), revised by Mark Wilson (2001), p.23

Introduction

Seven Roman provinces represented at Pentecost: Judea, Cappadocia, Pontus, Asia, Pamphylia, Egypt, and Cyrene (Acts 2:9-10)

Seven deacons of Jerusalem: Stephen, Philip, Prochorus, Nicanor, Timon, Parmenas, and Nicolas (Acts 6:5)

Seven angels: Liberator of the apostles (Acts 5:19), of Peter (Acts 12:7-11), and of Paul (Acts 27:23-24); the face of Stephen (Acts 6:15); instructor of Philip (Acts 8:26) and of Cornelius (Acts 10:3-7); and slayer of Herod (Acts 12:23)

Seven pagan gods: Moloch (Acts 7:43), Jupiter and Mercury (Acts 14:12), Mars (Acts 17:22), Diana (Acts 19:28), Castor and Pollux (Acts 28:11)

Seven pagan nations destroyed in Canaan: Acts 13:19

Seven sons of Sceva: Acts 19:14

Seven days waiting: at Troas (Acts 20:6), at Tyre (Acts 21:4), at the temple (Acts 21:27), and at Puteoli (Acts 28:14)

Seven delegates with Paul: Acts 20:4

Seven false teachers associated with the church at Ephesus (Acts 20:17, 30): Hymenaeus and Alexander (1 Tim 1:20), Phygellus & Hermogenes (2 Tim 1:15), Philetus (2 Tim 2:17), Diotrephes (3 John 9), and the Nicolaitans (Rev 2:6)

Seven devilish persons: Simon the sorcerer (Acts 8:9), Elymas the sorcerer (Acts 13:8), Herod Antipas (he receives worship, Acts 12:21-22), the priest of Jupiter (Acts 14:13), "damsel possessed with a spirit of divination" (Acts 16:16), Sceva the exorcist (Acts 19:13-14), and Demetrius the silversmith (Acts 19:24)

Fourteen (seven *twice*) speeches interrupted or prevented: by the crowd (Acts 2:37), the Sadducees (Acts 4:1), the council (Acts 7:54), the council again (Acts 7:57), the Holy Ghost (Acts 10:44), the angel of the Lord (Acts 12:21-23), the Areopagites (Acts 17:32), Gallio (Acts 18:14), the Ephesians (Acts 19:33-34), Eutychus (Acts 20:9), the crowd (Acts 22:22), Ananias (Acts 23:1-2), Felix (Acts 24:25), and Festus (Acts 26:24).

Teaching Questions

<u>True or False</u>? Consider Peter's sermons in Acts 2 and 3. Very few people can read or write, and Luke must rely on oral testimony passed down from person to person. Since important details are either omitted or become muddled through repeated re-telling of a story, Luke learns only the gist of the speeches and must reconstruct them based on what he thought Peter might have said.
<u>Answer</u>: False.

- Luke obtains oral testimony from eyewitnesses that give a "sure," "perfect," and "certain" (Luke 1:1-4) report of events.
- Literate persons such as priests (Acts 6:7) might take notes of Peter's sermons.
- During his extensive travels with the apostle Paul, Luke interviews individuals close to Peter (Acts 21:18), if not Peter himself.
- Luke typically highlights the main points of a sermon (using the speaker's own words) and does not need a transcript of the entire speech (see Luke's statement at Acts 2:40a). For example, Peter's sermon recorded in Acts 3 lasts over three hours (compare Acts 3:1 and 4:3). To write his report Luke needs a mere 15 verses of material (Acts 3:12-26), which is hardly a difficult task given the thousands of eyewitnesses (Acts 2:41, 4:4) and the momentous nature of the event.
- Peter making a statement that readers might find awkward ("and his name through faith in his name," Acts 3:16) is evidence that Luke has obtained and transcribed Peter's actual words.
- John the apostle is Peter's companion in Acts 3, 4, and 8, yet is never shown to speak words or perform actions apart from those of Simon Peter (Acts 3:4, 4:19, 8:14). This evidences Luke faithfully transcribing his source material without removing information (he could have left John out) or adding content (he could have put words in John's mouth).
- The same Holy Spirit whom Jesus said would help His apostles remember His words (John 14:26) can certainly help Peter's hearers remember his Spirit-inspired words.

Introduction

<u>True or False</u>? Luke could not have obtained an accurate account of Peter's sermons because only a tiny fraction of people can read and write. Only persons who receive formal religious training, such as the apostle Paul (who knew Hebrew, Acts 21:40; Greek, Acts 21:37; and Aramaic, 1 Cor 16:22) are literate.

<u>Answer</u>: False.

- Although the Levite priests are caretakers of written scripture (Deut 17:18, 31:9), God commanded all Israelites to teach their children both to recite from memory and to write the law (Deut 6:6-9). The importance of teaching scripture to one's children is affirmed in Psalm 78:5-7.
- "Moses therefore wrote this song [his final sermon, the book of Deuteronomy] the same day, and taught it the children of Israel" (Deut 31:22). He also commanded, "Now therefore write ye this song for you" (Deut 31:19a). Rabbis have interpreted this statement as a command for all Jewish men to write their own copy not only of Deuteronomy but of the entire law of Moses (a handwritten "Sefer Torah"). "Even if one's parents have left him a Sefer Torah, yet it is proper that he should write one of his own, as it is written: Now therefore write ye this song for you."[134]
- Jewish individuals are expected to read and write legal documents (Deut 24:1, Jer 32:44, Luke 16:5-7). The twelve spies submitted a written report (Joshua 18:9). The judicial pronouncement placed on Jesus' cross was "read [by] many of the Jews" (John 19:19-20).
- Timothy is a Jew who had a Greek father (Acts 16:1) and never received formal religious training (he wasn't even circumcised, Acts 16:3), yet he learned scripture from his Jewish mother and grandmother (2 Tim 1:5, 3:14-15). Jesus was a carpenter and never received formal religious training (John 7:15), yet He could read Hebrew (Luke 4:16-19). Jesus may have learned from His mother Mary, who also appears literate; she knew the psalm of Hannah (1 Sam 2:1-10) when she wrote her own (Luke 1:46-55). Peter is a fisherman who never received formal religious training (Acts 4:13); yet, he wrote one epistle aided by a scribe (1 Peter 5:12) and a second apparently on his own (2 Peter) in Greek (not his native language).
- Paul is an exception because he did receive formal religious train-

---

[134] *Babylonian Talmud*, Sanhedrin 21b

ing, being "... brought up in this city at the feet of Gamaliel, and taught according to the perfect manner of the law of the fathers" (Acts 22:3). Yet Paul was not the only one who received such instruction. "Rabbi Simeon [son of] Gamaliel [wrote of the] thousand youths who were in my father's house; five hundred of them learned Torah and the other five hundred learned Grecian Wisdom."[135]

- Many Jews from Asia Minor were visiting Jerusalem on the day of Pentecost (Acts 2:9-10). Some would certainly have been capable of taking notes of Peter's sermon (Acts 2:14-40) because "to limit the art of reading and writing in general to the urban notables [of Asia Minor] would be to disregard historical reality."[136]

Question: Can God still perform miracles today as He did in the Book of Acts?
Answer: Yes, God can perform miracles in any way He chooses.
Question: Well, of course, God can choose to perform **miracles** today, but does God anoint specific individuals with power to be **miracle-workers** who can perform supernatural wonders at will, as do Peter and Paul in the Book of Acts?

Answer: History of miracles in the Bible:
Genesis 1 to Exodus 3 – no miracle-workers reported
Exodus 4 to Deuteronomy 34 – Moses and Aaron are miracle-workers
Joshua 1 to 1 Kings 16 – no miracle-workers reported
1 Kings 17 to 2 Kings 13 – Elijah and Elisha are miracle-workers
2 Kings 14 to Malachi 4 – no miracle-workers reported
Matthew 1 to Acts 1 – Jesus Christ is a miracle-worker
Acts 2 to Acts 28 – Peter and Paul are miracle-workers
After Acts 28 – the reader is left to decide if miracle-workers on par with those listed above are among us today

---

[135] *Babylonian Talmud*, Baba Kamma 83a
[136] Christian Marek, *In the Land of a Thousand gods: A History of Asia Minor in the Ancient World* (Princeton University Press, 2016), chap. 9, Kindle edition.

Acts Chapter 1

[1] The former treatise have I made, O Theophilus, of all that Jesus began both to do and teach,

Luke's first volume ("former treatise"), his gospel, told of the earthly ministry of the Lord Jesus Christ (Luke 1:1–24:53). This second volume tells of the actions of the apostles who continue His work under the guidance of the Holy Spirit.

[2] Until the day in which he was taken up, after that he through the Holy Ghost had given commandments unto the apostles whom he had chosen:

- The Lord Jesus accomplished His earthly ministry in the power of the Holy Ghost (Luke 4:1). The disciples, like most Old Testament saints (1 Sam 16:13–14, Psalm 51:11), did not have the Spirit's continual indwelling and consequently had difficulty understanding spiritual matters (Matt 15:16, 16:8, 22, 1 Cor 2:14). After the resurrection a small group of disciples received God's Spirit (John 20:22) and can now understand Christ's teachings (Luke 24:45) "through the Holy Ghost." On the day of Pentecost all believers will receive the Holy Ghost for spiritual power (Acts 1:8, Rom 15:13), for sealing unto salvation (Eph 4:30), for spiritual baptism into the Church (Christ's body, 1 Cor 12:13), and as a Guide to the truth (John 16:13, 1 Cor 2:13).
- The Spirit's power is manifested throughout the book of Acts with specific mention of His work during Peter's preaching to the people (Acts 2:4) and the leaders of Jerusalem (Acts 4:8), during the believers' prayer (Acts 4:31), in the choosing of deacons (Acts 6:3), during Stephen's preaching at his trial (Acts 7:55), at the conversion of the Samaritans (Acts 8:15) and the Gentiles (Acts 10:44), at the healing of Saul (Acts 9:17), at the Jerusalem council (Acts 15:28), and during Paul's first (Acts 13:2, 4), second (Acts 16:6), and third missionary journeys (Acts 19:6).
- An "apostle" is a "sent one." God the Father sent the Son (called "the

57

Apostle," Heb 3:1), who then sent apostles of His own (John 20:21).

[3] To whom also he shewed himself alive after his passion by many infallible proofs, being seen of them forty days, and speaking of the things pertaining to the kingdom of God:

- The Lord Jesus appeared after His resurrection to Mary Magdalene (John 20:11–18) and other women (Matt 28:9–10, Luke 24:10), to Simon Peter (Luke 24:34, 1 Cor 15:5), to two men on the road to Emmaus (Luke 24:13–32), to the eleven apostles (John 20:19–29), to His half-brother James (1 Cor 15:7), and to disciples (John 21:1-2) and hundreds of other eyewitnesses (1 Cor 15:6). They spoke with Him, physically touched Him, and even ate with Him (Luke 24:41–43, John 21:12–14, Acts 10:41). The unmistakable evidence of Christ's resurrection is so overwhelming in its certainty (infallibility) that the disciples, who fled at His arrest (Matt 26:56), went into hiding (John 20:19), and disbelieved initial reports of His resurrection (Luke 24:11, John 20:25) have since completely changed course. They will turn the world upside down (Acts 17:6) for the witness of the gospel (Acts 20:24) and the advancement of God's kingdom (Acts 14:22).
- Christ had prepared for His earthly ministry with forty days of testing (Luke 4:2) and now readies the disciples for their ministry with forty days of scriptural instruction (as Moses, Exod 24:18) and spiritual renewal (as Elijah, 1 Kings 19:8).

[4] And, being assembled together with them, commanded them that they should not depart from Jerusalem, but wait for the promise of the Father, which, saith he, ye have heard of me.

The disciples saw the resurrected Lord first in Jerusalem (Luke 24:33), then in Galilee (Matt 28:16, Mark 16:7), and then again in Jerusalem (Luke 24:52), where they now wait as He commanded (Luke 24:49). He has told them of the Father's promise to send the Holy Ghost (John 14:26, 15:26) and how He must first depart in death, be resurrected, and then ascend into glory for the Spirit to come (John 7:39, 16:7).

Timeline to Pentecost (Acts 2:1):
1. Christ is crucified about the time of the Passover (Matt 26:17, John 19:14).
2. He is buried before the Sabbath (John 19:31).
3. He is resurrected on Sunday on the Feast of First Fruits (the day following the Sabbath after Passover, Lev 23:10-11).
4. He ascends forty days after the resurrection (Acts 1:3).
5. The Holy Ghost permanently indwells believers as promised (John 14:16) on the day of Pentecost, which is fifty days after the resurrection (which was on the Sabbath following Passover, Lev 23:15-16) and thus ten days after the ascension.

[5] For John truly baptized with water; but ye shall be baptized with the Holy Ghost not many days hence.

- Peter also quotes these words of Jesus in Acts 11:16, which reflect John's own words in Luke 3:16.
- John baptized his followers in water as an outward sign of inner repentance (Matt 3:6, 8). He spoke of the coming Messiah, who would spiritually baptize believers with the Holy Ghost at His first coming and physically baptize (immerse) unbelievers with fire (Matt 3:11) at His second coming (Joel 2:3, 2 Thes 1:8).
- The Savior's promise of the Holy Spirit will soon be fulfilled (Acts 2:4).

[6] When they therefore were come together, they asked of him, saying, Lord, wilt thou at this time restore again the kingdom to Israel?

[7] And he said unto them, It is not for you to know the times or the seasons, which the Father hath put in his own power.

- David's dynasty ended when Babylon conquered Judah (2 Kings 25). However, the Lord had promised David an everlasting kingdom (2 Sam 7:12–13) through his offspring, the Messiah (Zech 6:12–13). Over the last forty days, the Lord Jesus has taught the disciples the scriptures concerning His first coming as a suffering servant (Luke 24:26-27, 44-46) and future second coming (Acts 1:11) as a conquering King to rule the world from David's throne at Jerusalem (Luke

1:32–33, 69–74).

- On the road to Emmaus, Christ's disciples said, "we trusted that it had been he which should have redeemed Israel" (Luke 24:21). The resurrected Savior corrected their timing by stating, "Ought not Christ to have suffered these things, and to enter into his glory?" (Luke 24:26). Now again, the Lord Jesus accepts his disciples' understanding that His future dominion will be a literal, physical reign over Israel (Matt 25:31) and instructs them only in the matter of timing. Although God the Father had revealed the exact day of Christ's first coming (Dan 9:25), He has not revealed even to the Son the day of His return (Mark 13:32).

[8] But ye shall receive power, after that the Holy Ghost is come upon you: and ye shall be witnesses unto me both in Jerusalem, and in all Judæa, and in Samaria, and unto the uttermost part of the earth.

- God's Holy Spirit gives power for preaching the gospel (Acts 4:8, 7:55), manifesting spiritual gifts (1 Cor 12:7–11), living a holy life (Gal 5:16), and bringing forth spiritual fruit (Gal 5:22–23).
- Under the Spirit's guidance (John 16:13) the disciples will preach the gospel in Jerusalem (Acts 2–7); in Judea and Samaria (Acts 8–12); to people from Africa, Asia, and Europe (Acts 13–27); and will finally reach Rome (Acts 28), the gateway to the ends of the earth.
- Anyone can be a witness (Josh 24:22), but in scripture, only God uses the term "my witnesses" (Isa 43:10, 12, 44:8, Rev 11:3). The deity of Jesus Christ is therefore affirmed when He takes this phrase used only by God and applies it to His followers by calling them "witnesses unto me."

<u>Language</u>
Multiple ands (words conntected with ands instead of commas) – the Lord uses the word "and" four times to emphasize the importance of bringing the gospel to every group of people.[137]

---

[137] For further study of scriptural language see E. W. Bullinger, *Figures of Speech Used in the Bible* (1898).

[9] And when he had spoken these things, while they beheld, he was taken up; and a cloud received him out of their sight.

The Lord Jesus previously told the disciples that He would ascend to heaven (John 6:62, 20:17). They now witness His ascent (Mark 16:19, 1 Peter 3:22) and will soon receive God's Holy Spirit (Acts 2:4) as Elisha witnessed Elijah's ascent and received a "double portion" of his spirit (2 Kings 2:9–12). The Lord often presents Himself as partially veiled amid clouds (Exod 13:21, 24:16, Lev 16:2, Job 22:13–14, Psalm 18:11–12, 97:2, Matt 17:5, 1 Thes 4:17, Rev 1:7, 14:14).

[10] And while they looked stedfastly toward heaven as he went up, behold, two men stood by them in white apparel;

Two men in shining garments were also present at the empty tomb to announce Christ's resurrection (Luke 24:4); John identified them as angels (John 20:12). Angels may be challenging to identify (Heb 13:2) because they appear as men (Gen 19:1, 5).

[11] Which also said, Ye men of Galilee, why stand ye gazing up into heaven? this same Jesus, which is taken up from you into heaven, shall so come in like manner as ye have seen him go into heaven.

- Jesus was from Galilee (Matt 21:11), as were most of His disciples (Matt 4:25) and all of His apostles (Acts 2:7).
- The Lord Jesus has temporarily gone back to heaven (Acts 3:21, Heb 4:14) and will return in two phases. First, after the (primarily) Gentile Church is complete ("fullness of the Gentiles," Rom 11:25) He will **return for believers**, who "shall be caught up together with them in the clouds, to meet the Lord in the air" (1 Thes 4:13-18). Second, after Israel repents and turns to their Messiah (Hosea 5:15), He will return personally (Mal 3:1) amid the clouds in a manner **visible to all** (Dan 7:13-14, Luke 21:27, Rev 1:7) back here to the mount of Olives (Acts 1:12, Zech 14:4).

[12] Then returned they unto Jerusalem from the mount called Olivet, which is from Jerusalem a sabbath day's journey.

- The ascension took place on the south-eastern slope of the Mount of Olives near Bethany (Luke 24:50). The disciples now return to Jerusalem with great joy (Luke 24:52) because of the Lord's promise that they will one day see Him again (John 14:2-3).
- The "tradition of the elders" (Matt 15:2) limits an acceptable "Sabbath day's journey" to 2,000 cubits (0.6 miles or 1 km) based on their interpretation of Exodus 16:29 (apparently with Josh 3:4 and Num 35:5). "I have given you the Sabbath ... nor let any man go forth to walk beyond two thousand cubits on the sabbath day."[138] However, the "commandment of God" (Matt 15:3) does not actually prohibit walking on the Sabbath; the instruction to "abide ye every man in his place" (Exod 16:29) was a prohibition against going outside to gather manna.

[13] And when they were come in, they went up into an upper room, where abode both Peter, and James, and John, and Andrew, Philip, and Thomas, Bartholomew, and Matthew, James the son of Alphaeus, and Simon Zelotes, and Judas the brother of James.

- These eleven apostles escaped persecution the night of Jesus' trial as He had predicted (John 17:12, 18:9), but did so by shamefully fleeing at His arrest (Mark 14:50). Only John followed Him both to court and the cross (John 18:15, 19:26).
- Judas, the brother of James, the son of Alphaeus (Luke 6:14–16), is also called Thaddaeus (Matt 10:2–4, Mark 3:16–19).
- None of the apostles other than Peter, James, and John are mentioned again in the book of Acts. Matthew will go on to write the Gospel of Matthew.
- The upper room is the best one in the house (Matt 23:6). This upper room may be the location of the last supper before Christ's death (Mark 14:15), the place where He appeared to the disciples after the resurrection (John 20:19, 26), the home of Mary (the mother of John Mark, Acts 12:12), or another undisclosed location.

[14] These all continued with one accord in prayer and supplication, with the women, and Mary the mother of Jesus, and with his brethren.

---

[138] *Targum Pseudo Jonathan*, Exod 16:29

- Jesus' mother Mary and a group of faithful women (Luke 8:2-3) followed Him to the foot of the cross (John 19:25), went to His burial (Mark 15:47), and found the empty tomb on resurrection morning (Mark 16:1). Jesus' half-brothers (Mark 6:3) did not believe in Him (John 7:5) until He appeared to James after the resurrection (1 Cor 15:7). James' brother Jude also believes (Jude 1:1).
- The Lord Jesus had prayed faithfully (Mark 1:35) and taught His disciples to do the same (Luke 11:1-4). Their obedience to prayer leads to God's favorable response throughout the book of Acts. Their prayer now will lead to God's outpouring of blessing on the day of Pentecost (Acts 2:1-41). Stephen's prayer at his death (Acts 7:60) will inaugurate a wave of evangelism (Acts 8:4). Peter and John's prayer for the Samaritans will lead to their receiving the Holy Ghost (Acts 8:15-17). The prayers of Cornelius (Acts 10:2, 4) and Simon Peter (Acts 10:9) will lead to the gospel coming to the Gentiles (Acts 10:45). The prayers of the believers at Jerusalem (Acts 12:5) will lead to Peter's release from prison (Acts 12:11). The prayers of the church at Antioch will lead to Paul's first missionary journey (Acts 13:3). The prayers of the imprisoned missionaries at Philippi (Acts 16:25) will lead to the conversion of the jailer and his family (Acts 16:34).

[15] And in those days Peter stood up in the midst of the disciples, and said, (the number of names together were about an hundred and twenty,)

- Simon Peter did not hesitate to become a disciple when the Lord Jesus called him from his successful fishing business on the Sea of Galilee (Luke 5:1-11). He subsequently became part of the Lord's inner circle with James and John, sons of Zebedee (Mark 5:37, 9:2, 13:3, 14:33, Luke 22:8). Peter, under divine guidance, was one of the first to recognize Christ's true nature as the Son of God (Matt 16:16-17). Yet he often made rash statements (Matt 16:22, 17:4, 26:33, John 13:8) and showed erratic (Matt 14:28-30) and impulsive behavior (John 18:10). He failed as a disciple (Mark 16:7) when he denied knowing the Lord Jesus the night of His trial (Luke 22:60-62) but subsequently repented ("converted," Luke 22:32) and was restored (John 21:15-19).

- Peter demonstrates leadership now when speaking on behalf of the disciples as he previously did under the Lord's ministry (Matt 19:27, Luke 8:45, John 6:68). He will also show leadership on Pentecost (Acts 2:14), at the apostles' arrests (Acts 4:8, 5:29), in Samaria (Acts 8:14, 20), in Caesarea (Acts 10:34), and at the Jerusalem council (Acts 15:7–11). More importantly, Peter will demonstrate the transformative hand of God upon his life in his Spirit-filled sermon on the day of Pentecost (with 3,000 converts, Acts 2:41) and in the way that he exalts the Savior in his epistles (1 Peter 1:8, 2 Peter 1:16-17).
- These 120 disciples will soon receive an outpouring of God's Spirit as the 120 priests at the dedication of Solomon's temple received an outpouring of God's glory (2 Chron 5:12–14). Although 120 disciples gather here in Jerusalem, there are hundreds more in Galilee (1 Cor 15:6).

[16] Men and brethren, this scripture must needs have been fulfilled, which the Holy Ghost by the mouth of David spake before concerning Judas, which was guide to them that took Jesus.

[17] For he was numbered with us, and had obtained part of this ministry.

- Judas was an apostle (Mark 14:10) and even a friend of Jesus (Psalm 41:9), yet betrayed Him to the chief priests (Mark 14:43–46) in exchange for money (Matt 26:14–15).
- Peter affirms the inspiration of scripture (2 Tim 3:16) when explaining that God spoke through David (2 Peter 1:21) when he wrote words (Psalm 69:25, 109:8) concerning Judas (Acts 1:20). David actually wrote these words about his enemies; yet, the Holy Ghost moved David, who is a type of Christ (e.g., both David and Christ were anointed of God, 1 Sam 16:13, Acts 10:38), to write words that look beyond his adversaries to the enemy of Christ.
- Judas was falsely numbered with the true apostles (2 Cor 11:13) as Jesus was falsely numbered with the transgressors (Isaiah 53:12).

[18] Now this man purchased a field with the reward of iniquity; and falling headlong, he burst asunder in the midst, and all his bowels gushed out.

[19] And it was known unto all the dwellers at Jerusalem; insomuch as that field is called in their proper tongue, Aceldama, that is to say, The field of blood.

- Judas indirectly purchased when he returned the betrayal money to the chief priests (Matt 27:3), with which they bought a field for the burial of foreigners, thereby fulfilling scripture (Matt 27:6–10, Zech 11:12-13).
- Sisera (Judg 4:21), Abimelech (Judg 9:53), Goliath (1 Sam 17:49), and Judas (here) all received a deadly head wound, as will the "beast" (Rev 13:3) and eventually Satan at Christ's return (Gen 3:15, Psalm 74:14, Hab 3:13 Rom 16:20).
- The locals call the graveyard "the field of blood" because Judas spilled his blood there (Acts 1:18), but the chief priests do so because they purchased it with blood money (Matt 27:6–8).
- "Aceldama" is a word of the Aramaic language ("proper tongue"), which is spoken in Jerusalem alongside Hebrew.[139]

65

Language
Hebraism (a Hebrew manner of expression) – "this man purchased a field" is more vivid than "this man's actions facilitated the purchase of a field."

[20] For it is written in the book of Psalms, Let his habitation be desolate, and let no man dwell therein: and his bishoprick let another take.

[21] Wherefore of these men which have companied with us all the time that the Lord Jesus went in and out among us,

[22] Beginning from the baptism of John, unto that same day that he was taken up from us, must one be ordained to be a witness with us of his resurrection.

- Psalm 69:25 and Psalm 109:8 are quoted to show that the apostles obediently fulfill scripture (Acts 1:16) in choosing a replacement (Acts 1:26) for Judas, who proved himself to be the kind of wicked

---

[139] See notes on Acts 22:2.

man described in Psalms 69 and 109.
- "Bishoprick" is a bishop's area of authority and, in this case, means apostleship.
- They do not choose an apostle from among the recent converts because the Lord Jesus said the twelve apostles would be of those who have "followed me" (Matt 19:28) from the start of His earthly ministry (John 15:27).
- Christ's public ministry began when God the Father gave Him public approval at the baptism by John (Luke 3:22) and ended some three years later when He was witnessed ascending to heaven (Acts 1:9).

Language
- "Companied" means "accompanied."
- *Hebraism* (a Hebrew manner of expression) – "went in and out among us" describes unhindered fellowship.

[23] And they appointed two, Joseph called Barsabas, who was surnamed Justus, and Matthias.

[24] And they prayed, and said, Thou, Lord, which knowest the hearts of all men, shew whether of these two thou hast chosen,

- The Lord Jesus had chosen the original twelve apostles (Luke 6:13) from His larger group of disciples (Luke 10:1), and they now ask His direction in selecting a replacement. The current tally of eleven apostles is inadequate because twelve will be appointed as judges over the twelve tribes of Israel in the future kingdom age (Luke 22:30; also anticipated by the holy city with twelve gates and twelve foundations, Rev 21:12-14).
- Two candidates for apostleship meet the requirements of having been followers of Christ since the time of His baptism (Mark 1:9) and having seen Him alive after the resurrection (1 Cor 15:6). These two disciples both appear qualified outwardly, but only the Lord knows the heart (1 Sam 16:7, John 2:25).

[25] That he may take part of this ministry and apostleship, from which Judas by transgression fell, that he might go to his own place.

Judas, the "son of perdition" (John 17:12), deceived all the disciples and then expired to "his own place." He foreshadows the coming beast ("man of sin," 2 Thes 2:3), who shall ascend out of his place in the bottomless pit to go into perdition (Rev 9:11, 17:8) while deceiving the entire world (Rev 13:14). Absalom, who erected a pillar in his own name ("Absalom's place," 2 Sam 18:18) to honor himself (John 5:41-43), also foreshadows the coming beast who will erect an image in his own name (Rev 13:14) to receive worship from the entire world (Rev 13:8).

<u>Language</u>
"Perdition" means "ruin" or "utter destruction."

[26] And they gave forth their lots; and the lot fell upon Matthias; and he was numbered with the eleven apostles.

In the Old Testament, the Lord at times gave direction through seemingly random devices such as lots (1 Sam 14:41–42, 1 Chron 26:13-16, Jonah 1:7, Prov 16:33) and the Urim and Thummim (Exod 28:30, Num 27:21, 1 Sam 28:6). The disciples in this time of transition from the Old to the New Testament appropriately cast lots while praying for God's direction in choosing a new apostle.

67

Teaching Questions

<u>Question</u>: What is the difference between the "Holy Spirit" and the "Holy Ghost"?
<u>Answer</u>: None. Both English words are translated from the same Greek words, but the meanings have changed over time.
21st century: "Spirit" is an invisible essence, and "ghost" can mean a visible essence (apparition).
17th century: "Spirit" can mean a visible essence (Job 4:15–16, Matt 3:16, Luke 24:37-39), and "ghost" is an invisible essence (Gen 25:8, Matt 27:50). So the word "Ghost" informs the reader that the third Person of the Godhead is present with the believer invisibly. The two words (Acts 2:4, 1 Cor 12:3) refer to the same Person (compare Eph 4:30 and 2 Tim 1:14), and it is correct to use either one.

Question: What are some ways to reconcile the two different accounts of Judas' death?

Matt 27:5: Judas "... went and hanged himself."

Acts 1:18: "... and falling headlong, he burst asunder in the midst, and all his bowels gushed out."

Answer:

- Judas' attempted suicide by hanging goes terribly wrong when he falls and suffers blunt head trauma and penetrating abdominal injuries.
- Judas completes suicide by hanging; when the rope gives out (either the integrity of the cord fails or someone purposefully severs it to bring down the body), his corpse becomes mutilated while tumbling to the ground.
- Matthew's short statement that Judas "hanged himself" is an idiom for suicide (like saying "Judas kicked the bucket!"). Luke gives the gory details of Judas' suicide-by-falling to emphasize his divine judgment (as per Psalm 69:25, 109:8 and Christ's words in Mark 14:21).

Question: Are the disciples correct in choosing Matthias as the replacement apostle?

No: Matthias is man's choice, but Paul is God's choice (Rom 1:1).

Yes: The disciples are filled with the Spirit (John 20:22), base their actions on scripture (Acts 1:16-20), go to God in prayer (Acts 1:24), and use a legitimate Old Testament method of Divine guidance (i.e., lots, Prov 16:33). Furthermore, these twelve apostles minister primarily to the Jews and Paul primarily to the Gentiles (Gal 2:9).

Question: Does Luke, the author of Acts, view Paul as an apostle?

Answer: Paul does not meet Peter's criteria for a replacement apostle (Acts 1:21-22) because Paul was chosen later by God "as of one born out of due time" (1 Cor 15:8). However, the fact that Luke describes so many parallels between Peter and Paul (see Introduction, Overview section) implies that Luke would agree with Paul's affirmation that he is an apostle of Jesus Christ no less authoritative than Peter (2 Cor 11:5).

Question: Today a new apostle is chosen to replace Judas. Will more apostles continue to be selected to replace ones that die?
Answer: No. The church will not select a new apostle to replace James when he is martyred (Acts 12:2) because the requirement is not a running tally of twelve, but a permanent group of twelve who will one day rule over the twelve tribes of Israel (Luke 22:30).

Challenge Questions

1. What are the most significant events in Acts that describe how the gospel spreads throughout Jerusalem, Judea, Samaria, and "unto the uttermost part of the earth" (Acts 1:8)?
2. After the resurrection, why does Jesus ascend to heaven and not remain bodily on earth? Why could the Holy Spirit not come until after the ascension?
3. How can the two accounts of Judas' death (Matt 27:5, Acts 1:18) be reconciled?

Acts Chapter 2

[1] And when the day of Pentecost was fully come, they were all with one accord in one place.

- Pentecost is fifty days after the Sabbath following Passover (Lev 23:15-16) and is also known as the Feast of Harvest (Exod 23:16) and the Feast of Weeks (Deut 16:10). It is also called "the day of the firstfruits" (Num 28:26), which should not be confused with the Feast of First Fruits (Lev 23:10-11).
- Calculate the day of the week of Pentecost (Lev 23:15-16):
  Day 0: Saturday (Sabbath) after Passover
  Day 1: Sunday (Feast of First Fruits, Christ resurrected)
  Day 50: Sunday (day of Pentecost)
- New Testament events on the first day of the week (Sunday) include Christ's resurrection (Mark 16:9), His appearing to the disciples the first (John 20:19) and the second time (John 20:26), and the Holy Ghost's arrival on Pentecost.
- The disciples meet for prayer (Acts 1:14) on Sunday at 9 AM (Acts 2:15) fifty days after the resurrection in the "upper room" (Acts 1:13) or at some other unspecified location in Jerusalem (Luke 24:49).

[2] And suddenly there came a sound from heaven as of a rushing mighty wind, and it filled all the house where they were sitting.

[3] And there appeared unto them cloven tongues like as of fire, and it sat upon each of them.

- These Jewish disciples recognize wind and fire as evidence of God's presence, for both elements were seen by Ezekiel at his vision of God's glory (Ezek 1:4) and by Elijah at his commission on mount Sinai (1 Kings 19:11–12) and his parting into heaven (2 Kings 2:11). Divine wind breathes new life into Ezekiel's dry bones (Ezek 37:1-14). Fire may signify God's presence (Exod 3:2, 13:21, 24:17) and may also symbolize His judgment (Deut 4:24, Isa 10:17).

- Today the Lord fulfills the first half of John the Baptist's prophecy (Matt 3:11) as He baptizes the disciples with the Holy Ghost
  and gives a sign of fire. At His return the conquering Messiah will
  fulfill the second half of John's prophecy (Matt 3:12) as He baptizes
  (immerses in judgment) unbelievers with fire.
- Previously God's Spirit guided Israel as a whole but would indwell
  individuals only for distinct purposes (e.g., Num 11:25-29). Yet here
  a vision (Acts 2:17) of divided ("cloven") tongues like fire sits "upon
  each of them" to show that God's presence (the Holy Spirit) now
  indwells every believer (John 14:17).

**[4] And they were all filled with the Holy Ghost, and began to speak with
other tongues, as the Spirit gave them utterance.**

- Moses had shown miraculous signs to convince the people of Israel
  that the Lord sent him (Exod 4:1–9). The Jews therefore expect (1
  Cor 1:22) that the Messiah as the prophet "like unto Moses" (Deut
  18:15, Acts 3:22) will also show miraculous signs to demonstrate
  His authenticity. When they asked Jesus to do so, He pointed to the
  sign of the resurrection (Matt 12:38–40, John 2:18–22). God now
  gives the apostles the ability to speak ("utter") languages (Acts 2:6,
  8) that they have never learned to show that both they and the Holy
  Ghost indwelling them are sent from God and to authenticate the
  message they preach (1 Cor 14:22).
- The gift of tongues is demonstrated three times in the book of Acts,
  each time as a sign to Jews (1 Cor 1:22): that God gave the Holy
  Ghost (Acts 2:1-4), that God has brought salvation to the Gentiles
  (Acts 10:44-46), and that Paul preaches the same Savior as John the
  Baptist (Acts 19:1-7). The miracle of tongues does not universally
  accompany the Spirit's indwelling; tongues will not be mentioned
  among any other converts in the book of Acts, including the 3,000
  (Acts 2:41) and 5,000 converts in Jerusalem (Acts 4:4), the converts
  in Samaria (Acts 8:17), and the numerous converts of the Apostle
  Paul (Acts 13-28).
- Since the day of Pentecost, the Holy Ghost begins to indwell each
  believer at the moment of conversion with the exception of two
  other cases during this transitional time in the book of Acts: the
  converts in Samaria (Acts 8:17) and the disciples of John the Baptist

(Acts 19:6). Although Spirit baptism (1 Cor 12:13, Eph 4:4-6) occurs only once for a believer, he becomes filled with the Holy Spirit (Eph. 5:18) as he chooses to yield to the Spirit in the ways of righteousness rather than to fleshly human nature in the ways of sin (Gal 5:16–25).

Language

Metonymy (noun replaced by one related to it) – "tongues" is substituted for "languages."

[5] And there were dwelling at Jerusalem Jews, devout men, out of every nation under heaven.

All Jewish males are required to travel to Jerusalem for the Feast of Pentecost ("feast of weeks") and the feasts of Passover and Tabernacles (Deut 16:16). Several centuries ago, Jews were dispersed throughout the world following the defeat of Israel by Assyria and of Judah by Babylon (Ezek 36:19, Zech 2:6). Those who are profoundly religious return to Jerusalem to attend.

[6] Now when this was noised abroad, the multitude came together, and were confounded, because that every man heard them speak in his own language.

[7] And they were all amazed and marvelled, saying one to another, Behold, are not all these which speak Galilæans?

- The disciples move from their meeting place to a broad public area (apparently the temple grounds, Acts 2:46), where thousands of people gather to hear the apostles.
- The twelve apostles (Acts 2:14) of Galilee (Acts 1:11) are the ones fulfilling Christ's promise to miraculously speak in "new tongues" (Mark 16:17), meaning foreign languages they have not learned naturally.

[8] And how hear we every man in our own tongue, wherein we were born?

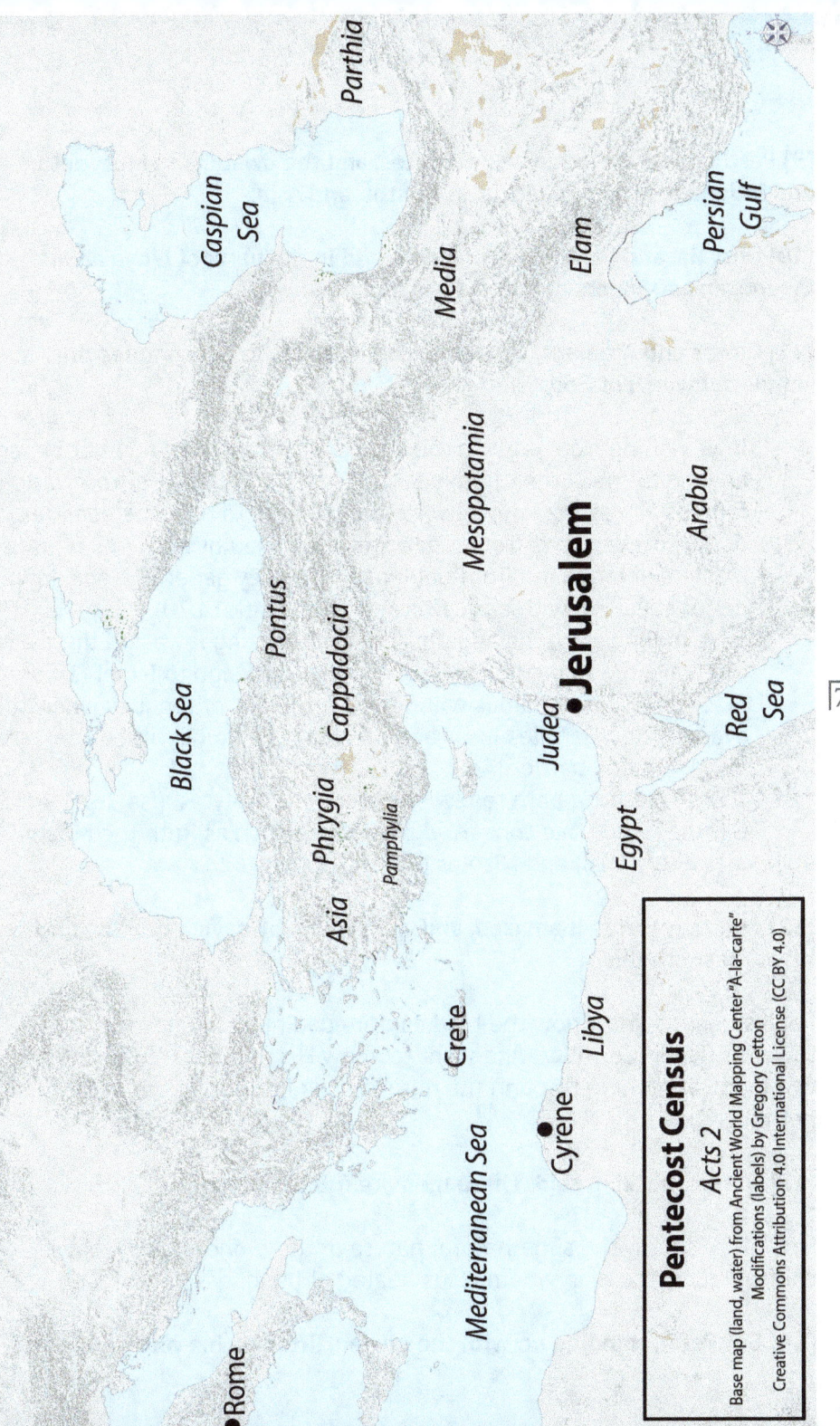

Pentecost Census

Acts 2

Base map (land, water) from Ancient World Mapping Center "A-la-carte"
Modifications (labels) by Gregory Cetton
Creative Commons Attribution 4.0 International License (CC BY 4.0)

73

[9] Parthians, and Medes, and Elamites, and the dwellers in Mesopotamia, and in Judæa, and Cappadocia, in Pontus, and Asia,

[10] Phrygia, and Pamphylia, in Egypt, and in the parts of Libya about Cyrene, and strangers of Rome, Jews and proselytes,

[11] Cretes and Arabians, we do hear them speak in our tongues the wonderful works of God.

- Jews visiting from outside the land of Israel (Acts 2:5) do not expect anyone to speak their native language here. Yet people from various regions across the known world are shocked to hear the apostles doing so. Even Jews from Judea are astonished by such (miraculous) mastery of language from Galileans, who they generally look down on for speaking with a provincial accent (Mark 14:70).
- Here in Jerusalem the apostles are evangelizing Jews and therefore have the miraculous gift of tongues as a sign to Israel (1 Cor 1:22). Paul and Barnabas will not have the gift of tongues when evangelizing Gentiles in Lycaonia and at one point will be confused by a language barrier (Acts 14:11-14).
- "Jews" are those born to Jewish parents. "Proselytes" (Isa 14:1) are Gentiles who have converted to Judaism, such as Ruth the Moabitess (Ruth 1:16) and Nicolas of Antioch (Acts 6:5).

[12] And they were all amazed, and were in doubt, saying one to another, What meaneth this?

Peter's hearers know how the Lord confounded human language at the tower of Babel (Gen 11:7) and want to know His purpose in unifying their communication here through the miraculous gift of tongues ("what meaneth this?").

[13] Others mocking said, These men are full of new wine.

Unbelievers deny the supernatural nature of this wonder, as did those confronted by the man whom Jesus healed of blindness (John 9:8-9).

[14] But Peter, standing up with the eleven, lifted up his voice, and said

unto them, Ye men of Judæa, and all ye that dwell at Jerusalem, be this known unto you, and hearken to my words:

[15] For these are not drunken, as ye suppose, seeing it is but the third hour of the day.

Peter opens his speech with humor. "How can they be drunk? Its only 9 AM!" It is mistaken to think them intoxicated this early since people usually abuse alcohol at night (1 Thes 5:7). The disciples' influence is not spirits of wine but the Holy Spirit (Eph 5:18).

[16] But this is that which was spoken by the prophet Joel;

[17] And it shall come to pass in the last days, saith God, I will pour out of my Spirit upon all flesh: and your sons and your daughters shall prophesy, and your young men shall see visions, and your old men shall dream dreams:

[18] And on my servants and on my handmaidens I will pour out in those days of my Spirit; and they shall prophesy:

[19] And I will shew wonders in heaven above, and signs in the earth beneath; blood, and fire, and vapour of smoke:

[20] The sun shall be turned into darkness, and the moon into blood, before that great and notable day of the Lord come:

[21] And it shall come to pass, that whosoever shall call on the name of the Lord shall be saved.

- "This is the sort of phenomenon that Joel spoke about." Peter quotes the prophet Joel (Joel 2:28–32) to explain ("what meaneth this?" Acts 1:12) that the outpouring of God's Spirit now in Jerusalem exemplifies the greater outpouring of the Holy Spirit in the kingdom age (Ezek 36:24-28).
- These celestial phenomena (Matt 24:29, Rev 8:12) will precede Christ's return and subsequent outpouring of God's Spirit during His thousand-year reign (Rev 20:4).

- Peter sees the outpouring of God's Spirit today on this small group of fellow believers (Acts 1:15) as the inauguration of "the last days" (2 Peter 3:3) and a prelude to the repentance of all Israel and Christ's imminent return (Acts 1:11, John 21:21-22). However, Israel will reject this offer to repent (Acts 7:57–60), and today's events will foreshadow rather than fulfill Joel's words.
- Joel described how the people of Israel would one day call on the Lord to save them from the judgments of the great tribulation (Matt 24:21) preceding Christ's return (Matt 24:27). Peter quotes Joel to explain how the people of Israel (Acts 2:5, 14, 22, 36) may now call on the Lord to save them from the judgment to come on their nation (temple destroyed, Luke 21:5-6; Jerusalem conquered, Luke 21:20–24; and the people scattered abroad, Ezek 22:15) for rejecting their Messiah (Acts 2:40).
- "I will pour out of my Spirit upon all flesh." Previously God's Spirit dwelled only within those specifically called by Him (e.g., 1 Sam 11:6, 16:13). Today Peter sees the Holy Spirit given not only to Jews from Jerusalem but also to Jews originating outside the land of Israel (Acts 2:9-10). Later Peter will see the Holy Spirit poured out not only upon Jews but upon Gentiles as well (Acts 10:45) because He now lives within all those who know God's Son (1 John 4:13). When Jesus Christ returns to vanquish Satan (Rev 20:2) and rule as King (in "the last days," Isa 2:2) He will give the Holy Spirit to all of humanity who are willing, for then everyone on earth will know Him (Heb 8:11).

Language
Synecdoche (the whole is given for the part) – "all flesh" meaning all people groups, not just Israelites.

[22] Ye men of Israel, hear these words; Jesus of Nazareth, a man approved of God among you by miracles and wonders and signs, which God did by him in the midst of you, as ye yourselves also know:

- Peter's sermon is to the Jewish people and refers to the Lord as "Jesus of Nazareth," a title that emphasizes Christ's earthly ministry as a prophet to Israel (Matt 21:11, Luke 24:19).
- It would be easy to imagine a Messiah originating from Jerusalem

(Psalm 137:5), but few would expect one from a place like Nazareth (John 1:46). Yet God the Father showed His approval ("approved of God among you") of the Son by giving Him the ability to perform miracles, which are yet well known to Peter's audience in Jerusalem (John 2:23). The disciples acknowledged these signs (John 2:11), as did ordinary people (John 6:2, 14), and both the believing (John 3:2) and unbelieving Pharisees (John 11:47). God's ultimate display of approval for the Son is the miracle of the resurrection (Rom 1:4).

[23] Him, being delivered by the determinate counsel and foreknowledge of God, ye have taken, and by wicked hands have crucified and slain:

Nobody was expecting a crucified Messiah (1 Cor 1:18). Yet Jesus' death was not a surprise to God because the Son's sacrificial death was part of the Father's plan (Gal 4:4-5). Even before the creation of the world, God the Father had determined to sacrifice His Son (1 Peter 1:19-20, Rev 13:8). He foretold His plan through prophecies (e.g., Isa 53) and typology (e.g., Abraham's near-sacrifice of Isaac, Gen 22:1-14). He also knew who would conspire to murder His Son (Acts 4:27) and holds those persons fully accountable (Luke 17:1).

Language
Synecdoche (the whole is given for the part, or the part is given for the whole) – wicked "hands" refers to those evil persons who slew Jesus.

[24] Whom God hath raised up, having loosed the pains of death: because it was not possible that he should be holden of it.

- Paul will call Jesus the one "whom God hath set forth" to die as part of His plan of redemption (Rom 3:25). Peter here calls Jesus the one "whom God hath raised up" from the dead.
- Death could not possibly hold Christ down in the grave. The just nature of God the Father demanded the resurrection of the Son both because of Christ's righteous work (Isa 53:12, Heb 10:12, 1 John 4:10) and because of Christ's lack of sin (1 Peter 2:22).

[25] For David speaketh concerning him, I foresaw the Lord always before my face, for he is on my right hand, that I should not be moved:

David wrote of his fellowship with God (Psalm 16:8-11). His words to an even greater degree describe the Lord Jesus, who lived in constant fellowship with His Father (John 5:19–20). Likewise, each believer is to spiritually behold God's face (2 Cor 3:18) as he walks with Him (Eph 5:2).

Language
"Foresaw" means "saw beforehand."

[26] Therefore did my heart rejoice, and my tongue was glad; moreover also my flesh shall rest in hope:

[27] Because thou wilt not leave my soul in hell, neither wilt thou suffer thine Holy One to see corruption.

- David knew that his body would not lie forever decomposed ("corrupted") in the grave because God would resurrect him one day (Psalm 16:10). David's words look beyond his own future and speak of God's Son, who endured the cross knowing that his body would not decay because after three days the Father would resurrect and exalt Him (Acts 5:31, Phil 2:9, Heb 12:2). Similarly, each believer can confidently expect God to resurrect him one day to receive a glorified body like Christ's (Phil 3:21).
- "Hell" in scripture can refer in a general sense to the "grave" (1 Cor 15:55) of souls, the abode of the dead (Psalm 139:8, Jonah 2:2) within the heart of the earth (Matt 12:40) containing a fiery place of punishment for the wicked and formerly (before Christ's resurrection, contrast 2 Cor 5:8, Phil 1:23) a place of comfort for the righteous (called "Abraham's bosom," Luke 16:22–26 or "paradise," Luke 23:43). It can also refer in a limited sense to only the fiery place of punishment (Psalm 9:17, 55:15, Luke 16:23). The general sense of the word is used here when God the Father promised to resurrect the Son from the dead. The Lord Jesus did not suffer after death; He suffered only once for sins on the cross (1 Peter 3:18, Heb 10:12), departed at death to paradise (Luke 23:43), and rose to life the third day (Luke 24:46).

[28] Thou hast made known to me the ways of life; thou shalt make me

full of joy with thy countenance.

David's future tense statement ("thou wilt show me the path of life," Psalm 16:11a) is given here as a past tense statement ("hast made known") because the Son fulfilled this prophecy when the Father raised Him to life again (Rom 6:4) and set Him at His right hand (Psalm 16:11b).

[29] Men and brethren, let me freely speak unto you of the patriarch David, that he is both dead and buried, and his sepulchre is with us unto this day.

The location of David's tomb (1 Kings 2:10) is still known since the return from exile (Neh 3:16), and more recently, Herod the Great "built a splendid and expensive memorial of white stone at the mouth of the burial vault."[140] The grave is referenced by Simon Peter today to show that David's resurrection prophecy (Psalm 16:10) cannot refer merely to David since he is still entombed.

79

[30] Therefore being a prophet, and knowing that God had sworn with an oath to him, that of the fruit of his loins, according to the flesh, he would raise up Christ to sit on his throne;

[31] He seeing this before spake of the resurrection of Christ, that his soul was not left in hell, neither his flesh did see corruption.

[32] This Jesus hath God raised up, whereof we all are witnesses.

- An Israelite cannot be both a priest and a king, as priests are from the tribe of Levi (Josh 18:7), and kings are from the tribe of Judah (Gen 49:10). King David (2 Sam 5:3), who here is described as a prophet, had acted as a priest when he took the showbread from Ahimelech (1 Sam 21:1–6, Matt 12:3–4) and when he sacrificed before the ark of the Lord while wearing a priestly ephod (2 Sam 6:12–14). David is therefore a type of Christ who is a Prophet (Luke 24:19), Priest (Psalm 110:4), and King (2 Tim 4:1).
- The Lord promised that the Messiah would be David's physical

---

[140] Josephus, *Antiquities*, 16.7.1

offspring (Psalm 132:11, 2 Sam 7:12-13) and fulfilled this promise in Jesus Christ (Matt 1:1–17, Rom 1:3), who one day will reign from David's throne in Jerusalem (Luke 1:31-33).

- David foresaw the resurrected Messiah (Psalm 16:8–11, 49:15), as did Job (Job 19:25–26), Isaiah (Isa 53:10–12), and Zechariah (Zech 12:10). Christ's resurrection was also foreshadowed by the sign of Jonah (Matt 12:40) and in the typology of Abraham's offering of Isaac (Heb 11:17–19).
- God has raised up Jesus as prophesied by David (Psalm 16:8–11a), and Peter boldly proclaims that "we standing among you have seen Him alive!"

Language

Hebraism (a Hebrew manner of expression) – "flesh" can mean edible meat (Isa 22:13), the human body (Gen 2:21, Acts 2:26, 2:31), a kinsman (Gen 29:14, Acts 2:30), humankind (Isa 40:5, Acts 2:17), or all created beings (Gen 7:21). The New Testament usage of "flesh" as "sinful human nature" (Gal 5:24, Eph 2:3) is not a Hebraism.

80

[33] Therefore being by the right hand of God exalted, and having received of the Father the promise of the Holy Ghost, he hath shed forth this, which ye now see and hear.

- Jesus promised the disciples that they would receive the Holy Spirit (Acts 1:4-5, Luke 24:49, John 15:26). The fact that Christ's words are now fulfilled (as witnessed by Peter's audience, Acts 2:6-12) confirms that He is exalted at God's right hand (Rom 8:34, Eph 1:20, Col 3:1).
- John the Baptist stated that Jesus "shall baptize you with the Holy Ghost and with fire" (Luke 3:16). Sending the Holy Ghost is something that only God can do (Ezek 39:29 and also Joel 2:28-29 quoted by Peter in Acts 2:17-18). Therefore the deity of Jesus Christ is affirmed when He is identified as the One who has sent forth the Holy Ghost.
- The three persons of the Godhead are noted to work in harmony (1 John 5:7-8) when Peter describes how God the Son has been exalted at the right hand of God the Father (as prophesied by David in Psalm 16:11b) and has sent forth God the Spirit (as promised in

John 14:16, 26, 15:26).

[34] For David is not ascended into the heavens: but he saith himself, The LORD said unto my Lord, Sit thou on my right hand,

[35] Until I make thy foes thy footstool.

- Peter quotes another Messianic prophecy (Psalm 110:1) in which David calls his descendant his Lord, a confusing statement in this patriarchal culture in which David would always be considered greater than his offspring. This statement cannot be understood unless David's descendant is Jesus, the resurrected and exalted Messiah (Matt 22:41-46).
- This scripture (Psalm 110:1) also indicates a waiting period between the first advent of Christ, after which He now sits at the Father's right hand, and the second advent of Christ, after which He will reign from David's throne in Jerusalem (Acts 2:30).

81

<u>Language</u>
Hebraism (a Hebrew manner of expression) – to "make thine enemies thy footstool" (Psalm 110:1) is to subjugate one's enemies.

[36] Therefore let all the house of Israel know assuredly, that God hath made that same Jesus, whom ye have crucified, both Lord and Christ.

- The Gentile nation of Rome is responsible for the death of Christ through the decisions of its governors, Herod Antipas and Pontius Pilate (Acts 4:27). Israel is responsible for the death of Christ through the actions of its leaders who persuaded Pilate to execute Him (Acts 3:13, 13:28). Every human is responsible for the death of Christ through his own sinful actions because Jesus died to save sinners (Rom 5:8). Peter here focuses on Israel's guilt, for whom the Savior asked forgiveness (Luke 23:34) and to whom Peter preaches the need for repentance to receive such forgiveness (Acts 3:19).
- Peter proclaims that Jesus is both Lord (Phil 2:10-11) and Christ. The Greek word "Christ" is the equivalent of the Hebrew word "Messiah" (Dan 9:25-26). The Messiah is the descendant of David who will rule forever over Israel and the whole earth (Isa 9:6-7, Jer 23:5-6).

The Lord Jesus is the Messiah, as previously announced by the angel Gabriel (Luke 1:31-33) and now confirmed by Simon Peter.

[37] Now when they heard this, they were pricked in their heart, and said unto Peter and to the rest of the apostles, Men and brethren, what shall we do?

- They are convicted by the Holy Spirit (John 16:8) as the preaching (1 Cor 1:21) of God's word (a sword, Heb 4:12) pricks (Acts 9:5) their hearts.
- The Jews of Jerusalem ask what they should do now that they have crucified their Messiah (Acts 2:23, 36).

[38] Then Peter said unto them, Repent, and be baptized every one of you in the name of Jesus Christ for the remission of sins, and ye shall receive the gift of the Holy Ghost.

- Repentance is a change of heart and mind, which leads to a change of action. John the Baptist preached that every Israelite must repent as an individual, undergo water baptism as a sign of his repentance (Matt 3:6), and bring forth fruit (good works) that demonstrates repentance (Matt 3:8). Had they done so, the entire nation of Israel would have been prepared to receive the Messiah (Matt 3:3) at His first coming as a Servant and His second coming as King (Matt 3:2). Peter now preaches that "every one of you" (every Israelite, Acts 2:14, 22, 36) must repent of murdering their Messiah (Acts 2:23, 36), undergo water baptism as a sign of repentance, and bring forth spiritual fruit through the Holy Ghost (Gal 5:22-23). In so doing the entire nation of Israel will be ready to receive the Messiah when He returns as King (Rom 11:26).
- "Remission" means "payment is applied, debt is forgiven." See the end of this chapter for a discussion on forgiveness of sins.
- The Holy Ghost is given in different ways during this transitional period in the book of Acts. Here He is promised to Jews who undergo water baptism to emphasize the importance of Israel's repentance. To the Samaritans He will be given by laying on of the apostles' hands to emphasize their apostolic authority (Acts 8:17). To the disciples of John the Baptist in Ephesus, He will be given after

the laying on of hands of Paul to confirm that Jesus is the Messiah of whom John had spoken (Acts 19:6). To the Gentiles He will be given at the moment of conversion (Acts 10:44), the usual way seen otherwise throughout the New Testament (Eph 4:30).

[39] For the promise is unto you, and to your children, and to all that are afar off, even as many as the Lord our God shall call.

Peter again quotes Joel's prophecy ("the remnant whom the Lord shall call," Joel 2:32b). He explains that this forgiveness of sins is not only for Jews (Acts 5:31) in Jerusalem but for Jews scattered throughout the whole world ("far off," Dan 9:7, James 1:1) who worship "the Lord our God" (i.e., the God of Israel, Deut 6:4). Later Peter will also see God call to salvation Samaritans (Acts 8:14) and Gentiles (Acts 10:45), "who sometimes were far off [but now] are made nigh by the blood of Christ" (Eph 2:13).

The numerous fonts throughout Jerusalem built for Jewish baptism are undoubtedly used for baptism by those turning to Jesus the Messiah.

LevT / Shutterstock.com

[40] And with many other words did he testify and exhort, saying, Save yourselves from this untoward generation.

The disobedient generation of Israel that rejected God's plan under Moses did not enter the promised land (Num 32:13). Peter preaches that this present generation of Israel will likewise miss God's promise for their nation if they continue to reject the Messiah (Heb 3:7-11).

Language
"Untoward" here means "stubborn and perverse."

[41] Then they that gladly received his word were baptized: and the same day there were added unto them about three thousand souls.

- At the giving of the law, 3000 died (Exod 32:28). At the giving of the Holy Ghost, 3,000 are saved.
- "Within the [temple] enclosure is an ever-flowing spring; in the hills are subterraneous excavations, with pools and cisterns for holding rainwater."[141] Numerous pools of water throughout the Jerusalem temple area that are used for ceremonial cleansing can now be used for the baptism of new believers.
- Peter, who had been an ignorant fisherman, has now graduated from Christ's school and become a fisher of men as the Lord promised (Matt 4:19). He is now better equipped than any scribe to preach the word of God because of the power of the Holy Spirit (John 14:26).
- Peter exercises the authority given to him by Christ when he uses spiritual "keys" (Matt 16:18-19) to open the door (1 Cor 16:9) of the kingdom of God by bringing the gospel to the Jews as he will to the Samaritans (Acts 8) and the Gentiles (Acts 10).

[42] And they continued stedfastly in the apostles' doctrine and fellowship, and in breaking of bread, and in prayers.

- The apostles' evangelism does not lead people to make superficial and impulsive professions resulting in only a temporary change of life that quickly regresses (like seed sown on stony ground, Matt

---

[141] Tacitus, *Histories*, 5.12

13:5−6). Instead, the gospel leads to a permanent change of life with fruit that remains (Matt 3:8, John 15:16).

- The apostles' doctrine includes Old Testament scripture (Prov 4:2) and the commandments of the Lord Jesus (Matt 7:28, 28:20, 1 Tim 6:3). It will eventually include new revelation given by God to the apostles (Gal 1:12, 2 Peter 3:15, Jude 17).
- Sharing a meal for nutrition and fellowship (Luke 24:30, 35) is a practice going back at least to the days of Abraham (Gen 14:18−20). Devout Jews say a prayer as they break off a piece of bread at the start of a meal to thank God for His provision (Matt 14:19, Acts 27:35). The Lord Jesus gave new meaning to an old practice when He asked His disciples to remember Him (Matt 26:26−29) when praying over the bread and the cup (1 Cor 10:16). Now the disciples with their deep love for the Lord Jesus will seek to remember Him in this way whenever breaking bread at the start of a meal, whether in private homes (Acts 2:46) or larger groups (Acts 20:7, 11). As the church grows to include Gentiles, and local assemblies of believers eat together ("feasts of charity," Jude 12), there will be abuses, and the apostle Paul will admonish them to leave the banqueting at home (1 Cor 11:20-22). So eventually "breaking of bread" will come to mean a simple remembrance of the Savior through the bread and cup without an associated meal and will be synonymous with the terms "communion" (1 Cor 10:16) and "Lord's supper" (1 Cor 11:20).

[43] And fear came upon every soul: and many wonders and signs were done by the apostles.

- Fear is the emotion commonly felt when experiencing the super-natural. For example, the soldiers who saw the resurrection felt fear (Matt 28:4), whereas the disciples felt both "fear and great joy" (Matt 28:8). Here Luke describes the emotion felt by those under the apostles' ministry to substantiate the reality of their supernatural experience.
- God confirms that the apostles are sent by Him when he gives them the ability to perform miracles, as He did with the Lord Jesus (Acts 2:22, Heb 2:3−4).

<u>Language</u>
Hebraism (a Hebrew manner of expression) – "every soul" (Lev 17:15) means "everybody."

[44] And all that believed were together, and had all things common;

[45] And sold their possessions and goods, and parted them to all men, as every man had need.

- These Spirit-filled believers demonstrate genuineness in their natural outpouring of love for each other. The intense infilling of God's presence makes them aware of others and their needs. They live their lives with the conviction that Christ may return at any moment. They fulfill His commandment to love one's neighbor (Luke 10:27, 18:22), and their selfless fellowship gives a foretaste of heaven.
- They give willingly of their belongings to be used by those in need (Acts 4:32, Heb 13:16), but do not abolish individual ownership of property (Acts 5:4) such as land and houses (Acts 2:46, 12:12).

[46] And they, continuing daily with one accord in the temple, and breaking bread from house to house, did eat their meat with gladness and singleness of heart,

[47] Praising God, and having favour with all the people. And the Lord added to the church daily such as should be saved.

- The believers meet in the temple (Acts 3:1, 5:42) and house churches (Rom 16:5, Col 4:15, Philem 2).
- Luke gives the first of seven summary statements in the book of Acts now that the gospel has been preached first in Jerusalem.

Teaching Questions

<u>Question</u>: Peter speaks of both baptism and forgiveness in Acts 2:38. What are some ways to interpret his words?

Answer:
1. Repent and be baptized, **then** your sins will be forgiven, and you will receive the Holy Ghost.
2. Repent and be baptized; **because** your sins are forgiven (by grace, not baptism), you will receive the Holy Ghost.
3. Repent and be baptized, then you will receive the gift of the Holy Ghost; when all Jews do so, **Israel's sins** will be forgiven, and the Messiah will return (Acts 3:19-20).

Question: How would you explain these three views?
Answer:
1. Repent and be baptized, **then** your sins will be forgiven, and you will receive the Holy Ghost.
Discussion: This interpretation is not consistent with the whole of Peter's teaching. He elsewhere preaches that an individual can receive God's grace unto salvation through faith alone in Jesus Christ (Acts 4:12, 15:9, 11). He teaches not that one is saved by water baptism but saved by that which baptism represents ("the like figure," 1 Peter 3:21), meaning the death, burial, and resurrection of Jesus Christ (Rom 6:3–10). He will also see God give the Holy Ghost to new believers at the moment of spiritual conversion before they undergo water baptism (Acts 10:44).

2. Repent and be baptized; **because** your sins are forgiven (by grace, not baptism), you will receive the Holy Ghost.
Discussion: "...for the remission of sins" can mean "[because] the remission of sins [has been accomplished]." This interpretation is consistent with the whole of Peter's teaching described above.

3. Repent and be baptized, then you will receive the gift of the Holy Ghost; when all Jews do so, **Israel's sins** will be forgiven, and the Messiah will return (Acts 3:19-20).
Discussion: Peter looks beyond individual conversions and imagines what it would look like for the entire nation to turn to Jesus the Messiah (as they will one day, Hosea 5:15, Matt 23:37-39). In Acts 3:19, Peter asks the Jews (there are no Gentiles in his audience) to repent and be converted so their nation as a whole may turn to God, at which time the Messiah will return and purge Israel's sins (Rom 11:26-27). Peter similarly in Acts 2:38 asks the Jews to repent and be baptized not to effect the forgiveness

of their sins as individuals, but as a nation (he says "every one of you" to emphasize this). Therefore Peter's exhortation to "repent and be baptized … for the remission of sins" is his instruction on how Israel can "repent … and be converted" (Acts 3:19) to receive forgiveness as a nation at Christ's second coming ("that your sins may be blotted out when the times of refreshing shall come from the presence of the Lord," Acts 3:19).

<u>Question</u>: Where did water baptism come from?
<u>Answer</u>: God gave the rite of baptism in the Old Testament as a ceremony done upon one's self ("bathe himself in water," Num 19:19). The Bible does not explain why, but John the Baptist introduced a new form of baptism, whereby a baptizer immerses a participant in water (John 3:22). When Jesus asked for baptism, He gave only the short explanation that "it becometh us to fulfil all righteousness" (Matt 3:15). Christ subsequently taught baptism to His disciples, including Peter (John 4:1-2).

<u>Question</u>: Here believers "had all things common" (Acts 2:44, 4:32). How does this differ from communism?
<u>Answer</u>:
1. Communists take by force, whereas the believers give voluntarily (Acts 2:45, 4:35, 4:37, 5:2).
2. Communists abolish private ownership, whereas the believers continue to own property such as land and houses (Acts 2:46, 5:4, 12:12).
3. Communists (falsely) claim to divide things equally, whereas the believers give according to need (Acts 2:45, 4:35).
4. Communists seek forced unity through class warfare, whereas the believers seek true unity through the Person of Jesus Christ (Acts 2:42, 4:24-31).

Challenge Questions

1. Why does Peter quote Joel's Old Testament prophecy (Acts 2:16-21)? Was Joel's prophecy fulfilled on Pentecost?
2. What does it mean that they "began to speak with other tongues" (Acts 2:4)?

Acts Chapter 3

[1] Now Peter and John went up together into the temple at the hour of prayer, being the ninth hour.

- John and his brother James, the sons of Zebedee (Matt 4:21), called the "sons of thunder" (Mark 3:17), had been called by Jesus to be disciples along with their fishing partner Simon Peter (Luke 5:10). The three had been with Jesus at His transfiguration (Mark 9:2), the raising of Jairus' daughter (Mark 5:37-43), the private instruction on the end times (Mark 13:3-37), and the garden of Gethsemane (Matt 26:36-37). The mother of James and John asked Jesus to give them a place of status in His kingdom, but He promised them only suffering for His name (Matt 20:20-23). John, "the disciple whom Jesus loved" (John 21:7), was the only disciple to follow Him to court and to the foot of the cross, where the Lord made him caretaker of His mother Mary (John 18:15, 19:26). James will be executed by Herod Agrippa I (Acts 12:2), but John will later move to Ephesus (near Patmos, Rev 1:9) and write the Gospel of John, three epistles preserved as scripture (1st, 2nd, and 3rd John), and the Revelation.
- Devout Jews pray three times a day (Psalm 55:17, Dan 6:10), and it is for the 3 PM prayer that the disciples enter the "house of prayer" (Matt 21:13, Psalm 5:7). The apostles continue to observe Jewish traditions while they follow Jesus the Messiah, the One who fulfills all the promises made to the people of Israel (Matt 5:17).
- Peter and John go "up" into the temple, which stands both physically and spiritually higher than the city.

[2] And a certain man lame from his mother's womb was carried, whom they laid daily at the gate of the temple which is called Beautiful, to ask alms of them that entered into the temple;

[3] Who seeing Peter and John about to go into the temple asked an alms.

[4] And Peter, fastening his eyes upon him with John, said, Look on us.

- The author, Luke the physician (Col 4:14), describes 40 years of disability (Acts 4:22) originating from birth rather than from a recent injury that might heal spontaneously.
- The Lord Jesus taught His followers to be kind to the disabled (Luke 14:13). Job exemplified such behavior, saying "I was eyes to the blind, and feet was I to the lame" (Job 29:15).
- The Beautiful Gate is not mentioned by name in any other ancient literature. It may be the Nicanor Gate which opens eastward and facilitates westward entrance into the inner temple area; it is "much larger" than the other temple gates and is made "of Corinthian brass ... [and] adorned after a most costly manner, as having much richer and thicker plates of silver and gold upon them than the other [gates]."[142] Or the Beautiful Gate may be one of the gates on the temple's outer wall since they proceed to "the porch that is called Solomon's" (Acts 3:11), which is just inside the eastern outer wall.[143] Other possible locations include the Shushan Gate on the east (opening to the Mount of Olives) or the Double Gate on the south (opening to the city of Jerusalem).

Devotional
- The lame man who never enters the temple is a picture of a man born in sin (Job 25:4, Psalm 51:5) who lives outside God's dwelling place (Rev 22:15, unlike Psalm 27:4).
- He asks for a financial gift because he does not know to ask for the spiritual gift (John 4:10) of faith unto salvation (Acts 3:16).
- The helpless man looking to Peter pictures a man looking to Jesus. To receive new life as a repentant sinner or to receive blessings from God as a Christian, one must look into the face of Christ (2 Cor 4:6). While He can do anything He wills to do, He most often requires the believer to look to Him in humble prayer and expectancy.

Language
"Alms" means charitable gifts to the poor.

---

[142] Josephus, Jewish War, 5.5.3
[143] Ibid., 5.5.1

[5] And he gave heed unto them, expecting to receive something of them.

[6] Then Peter said, Silver and gold have I none; but such as I have give I thee: In the name of Jesus Christ of Nazareth rise up and walk.

[7] And he took him by the right hand, and lifted him up: and immediately his feet and ancle bones received strength.

[8] And he leaping up stood, and walked, and entered with them into the temple, walking, and leaping, and praising God.

[9] And all the people saw him walking and praising God:

[10] And they knew that it was he which sat for alms at the Beautiful gate of the temple: and they were filled with wonder and amazement at that which had happened unto him.

[11] And as the lame man which was healed held Peter and John, all the people ran together unto them in the porch that is called Solomon's, greatly wondering.

- Peter has no money because he has charitably given away his possessions to those in need, as have other believers (Acts 2:44-45).
- "In the name of" means "by the authority of" and "by the power of." One could act under the authority of David (1 Sam 25:5, 9), God the Father (John 5:43, 10:25), or Jesus (1 Cor 5:4). One could appeal to the power of the Lord (Prov 18:10, 2 Kings 2:24) or Jesus (Acts 4:10, 9:34).
- Peter says, "**In the name of Jesus Christ** of Nazareth rise up and walk" (Acts 3:6) because he must appeal to a higher authority (i.e., to Jesus; see John 14:13-14). God the Son, however, had no such need and simply said, "Rise, take up thy bed, and walk" (John 5:8).
- Peter heals in the name of Jesus, who had previously healed in the temple (Matt 21:14), substantiating that this miracle is done in the power of the One "greater than the temple" (Matt 12:6).
- The Lord Jesus healed a lame man to show that His power and authority are from God (Luke 5:18-26). Scripture also records the healing of a lame man both by Peter (Acts 3:1-11 and Acts 9:32-

34) and Paul (Acts 14:8-10) to show that the same God who healed through Jesus Christ also heals through these apostles who work in His name.

- This healing foreshadows the time of Christ's return when "the lame man [shall] leap as an hart" (Isa 35:6), and all with disease shall be made whole (Mal 4:2).
- Solomon's porch is a double colonnade (row of columns) that runs the length of the inside of the eastern, outer temple wall.[144]

Devotional
- The disabled man has no strength to save himself (Rom 5:6) yet receives salvation immediately upon trusting in the Name of the Savior (Acts 3:16) and henceforth walks with Him (Col 2:6).
- He now walks for the first time through the Beautiful Gate, which is a picture of Christ. All the world lies spiritually crippled at the Beautiful Gate, not realizing that by a look of faith into the face of the Savior, they can leap up and enter in.
- He is full of joy because of what Jesus Christ did for him (John 15:11, 1 Peter 1:8).
- His changed life is a powerful testimony to others (Gal 1:23-24).
- Riches cannot save one's soul (1 Peter 1:18–19, Prov 11:28); only the name of (i.e., the Person of) Jesus Christ can save (Acts 4:12, 1 Cor 6:11).

Language
Metonymy (noun replaced by one related to it) – "silver and gold" is substituted for "money."

[12] And when Peter saw it, he answered unto the people, Ye men of Israel, why marvel ye at this? or why look ye so earnestly on us, as though by our own power or holiness we had made this man to walk?

- Peter opens his speech with humor. "Why are you looking at us? We didn't do anything!" He refuses to take any credit for the miraculous healing and will also show humility when meeting Cornelius (Acts 10:26).

---

[144] Josephus, *Antiquities*, 8.3.2

- The people are surprised because they do not know God's promise to work miracles through the Holy Ghost (Mark 16:17–18, John 5:20).
- God previously showed His approval of the Son by granting Him miracles (Acts 2:22). God now shows approval of the (resurrected and ascended) Son by granting the apostles miracles.

[13] The God of Abraham, and of Isaac, and of Jacob, the God of our fathers, hath glorified his Son Jesus; whom ye delivered up, and denied him in the presence of Pilate, when he was determined to let him go.

- When Moses first met the Lord at the burning bush, He identified Himself as "the God of Abraham, the God of Isaac, and the God of Jacob" (Exod 3:6), which is to say the God of the forefathers (patriarchs) of the Israelites.
- Pilate tried to release Jesus several times (John 18:38-39, 19:4-6, 19:12).

The Western Wall is the only remaining portion of the original enclosure around the Jerusalem temple, where Peter and the early believers preach the gospel (Acts 3:1).   Yevgenia Gorbulsky / Shutterstock.com

- The resurrected Christ is now glorified in heaven (John 7:39, Luke 24:26, Rev 1:13-18) and will one day reign gloriously on the earth (Isa 24:23, Matt 25:31).

Language

The Greek word *paida* can be translated as either "son" or "servant" for Christ is both God's Son (Isa 7:14, 16) and Servant (Isa 42:1). The rendering of "Son" is correct here and its use affirms Christ's deity (John 5:18). Also, Peter's statement that God glorified "his Son Jesus" when He "raised [Him] from the dead" (Acts 3:15) is consistent with Paul's statement that God's "Son Jesus Christ our Lord ... [was] declared to be the Son of God .. . by the resurrection from the dead" (Rom 1:3–4). The resurrection shows God's approval of Jesus not merely as a servant (like Elijah, 2 Kings 10:10), but as His Son.

[14] But ye denied the Holy One and the Just, and desired a murderer to be granted unto you;

The people of Jerusalem rejected the righteous Jesus (Psalm 16:10, 1 John 2:20) and asked pardon for the murderer Barabbas (Mark 15:7, 15).

Language

Hendiadys (two words for one idea) – "ye denied the Holy One, i.e., the Righteous Holy One, and desired an unrighteous murderer."

[15] And killed the Prince of life, whom God hath raised from the dead; whereof we are witnesses.

It is a great contradiction (Heb 12:3) that sinful humanity would kill the One who created life (John 1:3–4). Yet Jesus died not because He was compelled (Matt 26:52-53) but because He voluntarily laid down His life as a sacrifice (1 Cor 5:7) and took up His life again (John 10:17–18).

[16] And his name through faith in his name hath made this man strong, whom ye see and know: yea, the faith which is by him hath given him this perfect soundness in the presence of you all.

- Peter's audience knows the disabled man and witnessed his healing,

so the miracle will not be disputed (Acts 4:7).
- The name of (i.e., the Person of) Jesus Christ ("his name") brought healing to the disabled man because he trusted in (had faith in) Jesus. His faith in Jesus ("faith in his name") was given to him by God ("which is by him").
- Luke demonstrates his commitment to accuracy when he faithfully transcribes (rather than simplifies) Peter's complicated phrase "his name through faith in his name."

<u>Language</u>
Metonymy (a noun is replaced by one related to it) – "his name" is substituted for "Jesus Christ" (also Acts 4:12, 5:41, 10:43).

[17] And now, brethren, I wot that through ignorance ye did it, as did also your rulers.

Neither the ordinary people (Eph 4:18) nor the leaders (1 Cor 2:8) of Israel expected a Messiah who suffers death (1 Cor 1:23, Matt 16:21–23). Peter preaches that Christ's sacrifice was planned by "the determinate counsel and foreknowledge of God" (Acts 2:23). Although they acted sinfully and are fully responsible for their actions, the people of Jerusalem thought they were eliminating a threat to Israel (John 11:48) and were unaware that they were killing the Messiah. Therefore Peter graciously charges the people of Jerusalem with a crime of ignorance (Luke 23:34, Acts 13:27) for which the law of Moses may grant forgiveness (Num 15:22-29), unlike a crime done knowingly, for which the law does not offer forgiveness (Num 15:30-31). Peter's audience knows that the law of Moses provides no remedy for the crime of premeditated murder. For manslaughter, however, the law provides "cities of refuge" for which "the slayer that killeth any person unawares and unwittingly may flee thither" (Josh 20:2-3). The refugee then lives under the protection of that city "until the death of the high priest" (Josh 20:6). Since the Lord Jesus is now the high priest who lives forever (Heb 6:20), all those who turn to Him are safe from all charges of sin forever (Rom 8:33-34).

<u>Language</u>
"Wot" means "to know."

[18] But those things, which God before had shewed by the mouth of all his prophets, that Christ should suffer, he hath so fulfilled.

- Peter has charged the people of Jerusalem with the horrendous sin of killing their Messiah (Acts 3:13-15). He now wants to give them room to repent by removing any feelings of hopelessness. In the previous verse, Peter told the people that their lack of understanding ("ignorance") means that forgiveness is available. Now he shows how their negligent acts unwittingly (1 Cor 2:8) furthered God's plan of redemption (Rom 3:7-8). Peter's words parallel Joseph's words, "But as for you, ye thought evil against me; but God meant it unto good" (Gen 50:20).
- "All his prophets" without exception spoke of a coming Messiah (from Gen 3:15 to Mal 4:2). Peter uses this phrase to refer to the subset of those prophets who foretold what the Messiah would suffer (Gen 3:15, Psalm 22:1-21, Isa 53:3-12, Dan 9:26, Zech 12:10, 13:7).
- The prophecies of Christ's sacrifice for sin have been fulfilled (Luke 24:26-27), but those of His future earthly reign (Isa 11:10) have not.

Language
- "Wot" means "to know."
- *Metonymy* (a noun is replaced by one related to it) – "by the mouth of" is substituted for "by the preaching of."
- *Synecdoche* (the whole refers to the part) – Peter says "all his prophets" (as in Acts 10:43) to refer to those prophets who foretold the sufferings of Christ ("all the prophets who foretold Christ's suffering give a consistent message").

[19] Repent ye therefore, and be converted, that your sins may be blotted out, when the times of refreshing shall come from the presence of the Lord;

[20] And he shall send Jesus Christ, which before was preached unto you:

- The people of Israel must repent (a change of heart and mind which leads to a change of action) and be converted (change from acting according to their own reasoning and submit to the purposes of

God) for Him to forgive their sin of rejecting the Messiah. The Lord Jesus will not return to establish His kingdom until they experience this change of heart (Matt 23:37-39, Hosea 5:15).

- Peter exhorts the people to repent, as did John the Baptist, who preached that Israel must repent of its sins as a nation to prepare for God to bring in His kingdom (Matt 3:2).
- Peter does not ask his fellow Jews to "be converted" in the sense of changing from their religion to Christianity (a term which is not yet conceived and will initially describe Gentiles who follow the Jewish Messiah, Acts 11:26). Instead, he asks them as Jews to follow Jesus, the Savior of Israel (Acts 4:12).
- When the people of Israel as a nation acknowledge their guilt and recognize Jesus as their Messiah, He will forgive their crimes against Him (Isa 44:21-22, Jer 50:20, Rom 11:15, 25-27). The Lord will then send the spiritual renewal ("times of refreshing") that precedes Christ's return as foretold by Joel (Joel 2:28-29 "pour out my spirit," quoted in Acts 2:16-21), Ezekiel (Ezek 37:1-14 "shall put my spirit in you"), and Zechariah (Zech 12:10a "the spirit of grace"). 97
- Subsequently the Lord "shall [again] send Jesus Christ," who will physically and publicly (Rev 1:7) descend onto the Mount of Olives as foretold by the two witnesses (Acts 1:10-11) and by Zechariah (Zech 14:4).
- At His return (accompanied by visual signs, Joel 2:30-31), the Lord Jesus will destroy His enemies (Joel 2:31b, Zech 12:9, Rom 11:26), restore full fellowship to Israel (Ezek 37:14, Amos 9:14-15, Heb 8:10-12), and reign for a thousand years (Rev 20:6).

<u>Language</u>
Redundancy (words beyond those needed to convey the message) – "refreshing shall come from the Lord" is sufficient, but "presence of" is added to emphasize His physical return.

[21] Whom the heaven must receive until the times of restitution of all things, which God hath spoken by the mouth of all his holy prophets since the world began.

- The Lord Jesus ascended to heaven and is seated at the Father's right hand (Acts 2:33-34), where He remains until Israel repents

(Hosea 5:15–6:3, Matt 23:37-39). He will then return to establish His millennial kingdom (Acts 1:6, Matt 19:28, Rev 20:6) and restore the earth ("times of restitution of all things") to a state of harmonious peace (Isa 11:6–9, 35:1-10, 40:4–5) as He removes the curse upon the earth brought about by humanity's fall (Gen 3:17, Rom 8:20–23).

- The "times of restitution" are foreshadowed in Israel by the year of Jubilee (Lev 25:8-9), in which land is returned to its original owner, families are reunited, indentured servants are released, and debts are forgiven (Lev 25:8–55, Deut 15:1–2).
- Our Savior's feet will not touch the ground (Zech 14:4) again until He returns to restore Israel (Amos 9:14-15). Before this, however, He will make an appearance in the air (the "rapture") to take away His saints (1 Cor 15:51–57, 1 Thes 4:13–18).

Language

Repetition (words repeated for emphasis) – "mouth of" in both Acts 3:18 and 3:21.

[22] For Moses truly said unto the fathers, A prophet shall the Lord your God raise up unto you of your brethren, like unto me; him shall ye hear in all things whatsoever he shall say unto you.

[23] And it shall come to pass, that every soul, which will not hear that prophet, shall be destroyed from among the people.

- Peter now connects with his Jewish audience by preaching on Abraham (the father of the Israelite people, Acts 3:25), Moses (the father of the Israelite nation), Samuel (the founder of the Israelite monarchy, Acts 3:24), and by implication, David (Israel's beloved king, anointed by Samuel).
- Moses and the Messiah are alike (Deut 18:15, 18) in that both were Israelites (Exod 2:1–2, Matt 1:1-2), were nearly the victims of murder by evil rulers as young children (Exod 1:22, Matt 2:16), spent some early years in Egypt (Acts 7:22, Matt 2:14–15), willingly abandoned wealth to serve God (Heb 11:24–26, Phil 2:6–7), were raised up by God to deliver Israel (Acts 7:35, Rom 11:26), were faithful in their commissions (Heb 3:1–2), were rejected by their brethren

(Exod 2:13–14, John 1:11), performed great miracles (Deut 34:10–11, Acts 2:22), had power over wind and sea (Exod 14:21, Matt 8:27), freed slaves from bondage (Acts 7:36, John 8:36), fed their people with bread (Exod 16:15, John 6:11), were men of prayer (Num 11:2, Luke 6:12) and fasting (Exod 34:28, Matt 4:2), asked forgiveness for Israel (Num 14:19, Luke 23:34), had their authority challenged (Num 16:3, Matt 21:23), were nearly stoned (Exod 17:4, John 8:59), initiated a blood covenant (Exod 24:8, Heb 12:24), chose a group of 12 (Deut 1:23, Mark 3:14) and 70 (Num 11:16, Luke 10:1), offered themselves to die in their people's stead (Exod 32:32, Heb 7:27), and had people doubt their return (Exod 32:23, 2 Peter 3:4). Both acted in the role of a servant (Psalm 105:26, Matt 12:18), prophet (Deut 18:15, John 6:14), priest (Psalm 99:6, Heb 6:20), shepherd (Exod 3:1, John 10:14), mediator (Exod 33:8–9, 1 Tim 2:5), intercessor (Num 21:7, Rom 8:34), and judge (Exod 18:13, John 5:27). Moses delivered Israel from Pharaoh and led the nation to the promised land; the Messiah will deliver Israel from Satan's forces during the great tribulation (Matt 24:21) and liberate the promised land (Zech 14:1-11).

- The people of Israel have been anticipating the appearance of a prophet like Moses (John 1:21, "that prophet"). Peter quotes Moses' words (Deut 18:15) which instruct the people of Israel to follow that prophet (whom Peter preaches is Jesus the Messiah) and warn them of the consequences of rejecting Him (Lev 23:29b).
- The Messiah ("that prophet" like Moses) will rule "with a rod of iron" during His future reign on earth (Psalm 2:6-12, Deut 18:19).

Language
- *Redundancy* (words beyond those needed to convey the message) – "it shall come to pass" is not grammatically necessary but is added to emphasize that judgment will surely come to those who choose to ignore God's words.
- *Metonymy* (noun replaced by one related to it) – "soul" is substituted for "human."

[24] Yea, and all the prophets from Samuel and those that follow after, as many as have spoken, have likewise foretold of these days.

- Moses (Acts 3:22) and Samuel (Acts 3:24) are two of the greatest figures in Israel's history (Jer 15:1). Moses founded the *nation* of Israel (Num 33:2-3) and Samuel founded the *kingdom* of Israel (1 Sam 10:25).

- Samuel, who anointed Israel's first king (Saul, 1 Sam 10:1), was different than the prophets before him because he (and prophets after him) proclaimed God's word directly to Israel's kings.
- Samuel faithfully performed his part in establishing the Messianic line (after Saul was rejected, 1 Sam 16:1) by anointing David as king over Israel (1 Sam 16:13). God subsequently promised David a descendant who would reign forever (2 Sam 7:12-13; identified as Jesus in Luke 1:31-33). David foretold the Messiah (e.g., Psalm 2, 16, 22, 69) as did other prophets (e.g., Isa 53).

[25] Ye are the children of the prophets, and of the covenant which God made with our fathers, saying unto Abraham, And in thy seed shall all the kindreds of the earth be blessed.

- Peter tells his audience that they are "children of the prophets," meaning that they are heirs to the promises made by God through prophets such as Moses, who spoke of the Messiah (Acts 3:22).
- Peter's listeners are likewise inheritors of the covenant (agreement) that God made when He promised Abraham a descendant who would bless all peoples of the earth (Gen 12:3; "thy seed" in Gen 22:18, 26:4). David also received a promise to his offspring ("thy seed" in 2 Sam 7:12). God fulfilled His promises to Abraham and David in their physical descendant, Jesus Christ (Matt 1:1-17, Gal 3:16, Rom 1:3), whose blessings are offered not only to the house of Israel (Acts 2:36) but to all humankind (Gal 3:14).

[26] Unto you first God, having raised up his Son Jesus, sent him to bless you, in turning away every one of you from his iniquities.

- "Raised up" indicates Jesus was "raised unto Israel a Saviour" (Acts 13:23) and was "raised ... from the dead" (Acts 13:30).
- Abraham rejoiced to foresee "these days" (Acts 3:24) of the advent of the Messiah (John 8:56). Abraham's descendants hearing Peter's sermon can celebrate that they are the "first" to have lived to see "these days" wherein God has "raised up his Son Jesus" (as He raised

up Moses) to be a blessing to Israel by giving them a chance to repent (Acts 5:31).

- The news of the Messiah has been sent to the Jews first (Rom 1:16) because their acceptance of Him will lead to the establishment of God's earthly kingdom (Acts 3:19–21), at which time God's blessings will flow to the Gentiles through Israel in the kingdom age (Isa 60:1-3, Amos 9:11-12, Zech 8:22-23). However, even in this present age, God will direct Peter to bring the gospel to Gentiles (Acts 10) as He takes "out of them a people for his name" (Acts 15:14).

Teaching Question

Question: How is Peter's sermon in Acts 2 like his sermon in Acts 3?
Answer: In each case Peter speaks to a crowd amazed by a miracle (Acts 2:12, 3:10) and attributes the miracle to the power of God (Acts 2:16, 3:12, 16). He begins each speech with humor (Acts 2:15, 3:12). In both sermons Peter speaks to individuals but addresses them as a nation ("ye men of Israel," Acts 2:22, 3:12) and calls them to repentance as a nation (Acts 2:38, 3:19). In both sermons Peter accuses the people of murder (Acts 2:23, 3:15), proclaims Christ's resurrection (Acts 2:24, 3:15), shows Jesus in heaven (Acts 2:33, 3:21) temporarily (Acts 2:34b-35, 3:21), teaches that God showed approval of the Son (by miracles, Acts 2:22; by glorification, Acts 3:13), appeals to the patriarchs (David, Acts 2:29; Moses and Samuel, Acts 3:22, 24) who functioned as prophets (Acts 2:30, 3:22, 24), quotes from Psalm 16:10 written by David (Acts 2:27, 3:14), references prophesies about Jesus being raised up like David (Acts 2:30) and Moses (Acts 3:22) and declares fulfillment of those prophecies (Acts 2:32, Acts 3:26), preaches repentance and forgiveness of sins (Acts 2:38, 3:19), promises Spiritual renewal (Acts 2:17, 3:19), and issues a timely warning (Acts 2:40, 3:23). Both sermons lead to thousands of new believers (Acts 2:41, 4:4) who practice charity (Acts 2:45, 4:32) and are committed to prayer and fellowship (Acts 2:42, 4:24).

Challenge Questions

1. When Peter says, "Repent ... that your sins may be blotted out" (Acts 3:19), to what sins is he referring? Compare this verse with Acts 2:38.
2. What are the "times of refreshing" and what must happen for it to "come from the presence of the Lord" (Acts 3:19)?
3. Now (within Acts 2 – 7) the gospel message is given exclusively to Jews in a way that addresses them as a nation. Only after Acts 7 will the apostles preach to other people groups such as Samaritans (Acts 8), Ethiopians (Acts 8), Romans (Acts 10), Galatians (Acts 14), and Greeks (Acts 17). If Israel, as a nation, accepts Jesus as their Messiah (between now and Acts 7), will He return immediately to establish His kingdom? Or is it inevitable that the nation of Israel will reject their Messiah now and must wait some 2,000 years to have another opportunity to receive Him?

Acts Chapter 4

[1] And as they spake unto the people, the priests, and the captain of the temple, and the Sadducees, came upon them,

[2] Being grieved that they taught the people, and preached through Jesus the resurrection from the dead.

- The Sadducees do not believe in the resurrection (Mark 12:18, Acts 23:8). They are outraged by the disciples' testimony now as they previously were by the testimony of the resurrected Lazarus (John 12:9-11). The teaching of the risen Savior troubles them because it both contradicts their doctrine and bolsters the apostles' charge against them of murder (Acts 3:13). Most Jews believe in only one general resurrection at the "last day" (Dan 12:2, John 11:24, Rev 20:12), and even Christ's followers were perplexed by His teaching that He would rise from the dead (Mark 9:9–10, John 11:24–26) before anyone else (1 Cor 15:20).
- Paul will explain that one day believers, because they have been made righteous by Christ's work on the cross (1 Peter 2:24), will be resurrected *before* the final gathering of the dead for the last judgment (1 Cor 15:51–57, 1 Thes 4:13–18, Rev 20:4–6). Non-believers envision the final judgment as a time when all will argue their own relative merits before God (Prov 20:6). So the teaching that a group of righteous persons will be resurrected "from the dead" beforehand is offensive to them because it implies that people are not all on an equal footing before God.

[3] And they laid hands on them, and put them in hold unto the next day: for it was now eventide.

[4] Howbeit many of them which heard the word believed; and the number of the men was about five thousand.

- Peter's sermon had started after the healing of the lame man at 3

PM (Acts 3:1), and they now wait under arrest (Acts 5:18) until the council convenes in the morning.

- There were 3,000 converts on the day of Pentecost (Acts 2:41), and apparently the total has now risen to 5,000.

[5] And it came to pass on the morrow, that their rulers, and elders, and scribes,

[6] And Annas the high priest, and Caiaphas, and John, and Alexander, and as many as were of the kindred of the high priest, were gathered together at Jerusalem.

Moses appointed Aaron as the first high priest (1 Chron 6:48-49). When the children of Israel entered the promised land, there were a series of high priests to minister at the tabernacle. During this era of the Judges (about 400 years), the government was supposed to be a theocracy (ruled by God) but fell to anarchy (lawlessness) during times of national sin (Judg 17:6). Repeated wars with foreign invaders and a devastating civil war (Judg 20:46) led to the appointment of a king (1 Sam 8:6-7) with the Davidic monarchy lasting over 400 years (Ezek 4:4-6) until the fall of Jerusalem in 586 BC to Babylon. Babylonians, Persians, and then Greeks (the Seleucid Empire) ruled Israel. Under Seleucid rule the office of high priest for the first time was given not to a rightful descendant of Aaron but to whoever offered the most substantial payment. "When Antiochus, called Epiphanes, took the kingdom, Jason the brother of Onias [then current high priest] laboured underhand to be high priest, promising unto the king by intercession three hundred and threescore talents of silver . . ." (2 Maccabees 4:7b-8a).[145] Jason's bribe was accepted and he was appointed as high priest, but not long after that, he was betrayed by his own steward. "Three years afterward Jason sent Menelaus ... to bear the money unto the king ... but he being brought to the presence of the king ... got the priesthood to himself, offering more than Jason by three hundred talents of silver." (2 Maccabees 4:23-24). Later in 140 BC the Maccabeans under "Simon, the high priest, the governor and leader of the Jews" (1 Maccabees 13:42) led a successful revolt against the Seleucids. Once

---

[145] The Book of Maccabees is part of the Apocrypha, which is *not* considered scripture and is quoted only as a historical source.

again, the Jews were able to govern their nation. This Simon was the first high priest to wield both religious authority and national political power.

The Roman General Pompey subjugated Judea in 63 BC. This event began with a quarrel between Simon's great-grandsons Aristobulus and Hyrcanus, two brothers who each wanted to be king of Judea. "While Pompeius (Pompey) was staying near Damascus in Syria, he was approached by Aristobulus the king of the Jews and his brother Hyrcanus, who were in dispute over who should be king." At the same time a group went to the General to argue that neither brother should be king, but rather the high priest should continue to govern Judea. "The most eminent of the Jews, more than two hundred in number, met the imperator [Pompey] and explained that their ancestors, when they rebelled from [the Greek empire], had sent envoys to the [Roman] senate. In response, the senate granted them ... to be free and autonomous, under the leadership not of a king but of a high priest." The envoy argued (deceptively) that "the Jews have never had any king; but that the leadership of the people has always been entrusted to a priest, who excels all the rest in prudence and virtue. They call him the chief priest, and they regard him as the messenger and interpreter of the mind and commands of God."[146] Pompey asked the two brothers to go home until he could visit them and make a decision. Aristobulus returned to Judea but rejected Pompey's instructions and prepared to fight against the Romans. "At this behavior Pompey was angry; and taking with him ... Roman legions which he had with him, he made an expedition against Aristobulus"[147] and conquered the city of Jerusalem. With this the Jewish nation "lost [their] liberty and became subject to the Romans." A high priest descended from Aaron no longer governs them because "the royal authority, which was a dignity formerly bestowed on those that were high priests by the right of their family, became the property of private men" appointed by Rome.[148] Hyrcanus was appointed as high priest by Pompey and later as ethnarch by Julius Caesar, who also appointed Antipater I (the father of Herod the Great) as the Roman governor.[149] Israel has since been governed by a Roman-appointed administrator who chooses the high priest, the nation's highest-ranking non-Roman

---

[146] Diodorus Siculus, *The Library of History*, 40.2-3
[147] Josephus, *Antiquities*, 14.3.4
[148] Ibid., 14.4.5
[149] Ibid., 14.8.5

who holds religious authority and limited civil authority.

The Roman governor Cyrenius (Quirinius) appointed Annas (Ananus) as high priest after the death of Herod the Great and subsequent exile of Herod's son Archelaus.[150] Annas has five sons and one daughter who married Caiaphas; all seven men will subsequently serve as the high priest. Annas' last son (also named Annas) will plot to murder James, the half-brother of Jesus.[151] The current governor of Judea, Pontius Pilate, was appointed by Tiberius Caesar.[152] The present high priest, Caiaphas (son-in-law of Annas, John 18:13), was appointed by the former governor Valerius Gratus.[153] Although Annas has been officially removed from the office of high priest, he is the head of the family and still acts as high priest alongside Caiaphas (Luke 3:2, Acts 4:6). Annas appears to be the primary decision-maker; when Jesus was arrested He was brought first before Annas who interrogated Him (John 18:13, 19-21), ordered him to be slapped across the face (John 18:22-24, like Acts 23:2), sentenced Him to death (Mark 14:60-64), and sent Him "bound unto Caiaphas" (John 18:24). Jesus answered freely before Annas but subsequently said almost nothing before Caiaphas (Matt 26:57, 62-63) and the Sanhedrin (Mark 15:1, Luke 22:66-71) as if the first hearing (by Annas) was the only one that really mattered. Here in Acts 4 the patriarch Annas is shown as the *de facto* high priest attended by family members, including his sons Caiaphas (the *formal* high priest) and John (Jonathan will be high priest after Caiaphas[154]).

[7] And when they had set them in the midst, they asked, By what power, or by what name, have ye done this?

- Their question is legitimate, for the council must determine if the apostles are using this healing (Acts 4:14) to turn people away from the Lord (Deut 13:1-5).
- The healed man has been known to temple attendees for several decades (Acts 4:22). Therefore the leaders do not try to deny the miracle (contrast John 9:8-9) but recognize it as genuine (Acts 4:16).

---

[150] Ibid., 18.2.1
[151] Ibid., 20.9.1
[152] Luke 3:1; Josephus, *Jewish War*, 2.9.2
[153] Josephus, *Antiquities*, 18.2.2
[154] Ibid., 18.3

[8] Then Peter, filled with the Holy Ghost, said unto them, Ye rulers of the people, and elders of Israel,

In the book of Acts the Holy Ghost fills (indwells and empowers) believers for speaking (Acts 2:4, 4:8, 31), serving (Acts 6:3), teaching (Acts 11:24), discerning (Acts 7:55, 13:9), and rejoicing (Acts 13:52). Peter's answer is given to him by God through the Spirit (Luke 21:12-15).

[9] If we this day be examined of the good deed done to the impotent man, by what means he is made whole;

[10] Be it known unto you all, and to all the people of Israel, that by the name of Jesus Christ of Nazareth, whom ye crucified, whom God raised from the dead, even by him doth this man stand here before you whole.

- Peter notes that he is ironically on trial (being "examined") for the "crime" of healing, which is an act of charity and not a crime. Paul will similarly confess to a non-crime (Acts 24:14).
- Peter furthermore explains that the one "guilty" of the "crime" of healing is Jesus Christ of Nazareth. By adding "whom ye crucified," Peter turns the tables and accuses them of wrongdoing. By adding "whom God raised from the dead," Peter accuses them of resisting God, as will Stephen (Acts 7:51).

Language
"Impotent" means "powerless" or "disabled."

[11] This is the stone which was set at nought of you builders, which is become the head of the corner.

- Not long ago the Lord Jesus was asked by the chief priests and the elders at the temple to explain "by what authority doest thou these things?" (Matt 21:23). He quoted Psalm 118:22 and answered that He is the "stone which the builders rejected" (Matt 21:42). They have now asked Peter "by what name" he has performed the healing (Acts 4:7); he reminds them of Christ's words that He is the Stone which they have rejected (1 Peter 2:4, 7).

- Four Old Testament passages use a stone to create a metaphor of the Messiah: foundation stone of Isa 28:16 (quoted in Rom 9:33, 10:11, Eph 2:20 and 1 Peter 2:6, 7), once-rejected cornerstone of Psalm 118:22 (quoted in Matt 21:42, Mark 12:10, Luke 20:17, Acts 4:11, and 1 Peter 2:4, 7), stumbling stone of Isa 8:14 (quoted in Rom 9:33 and 1 Peter 2:8), and stone not cut by human hands of Dan 2:34 (quoted in Matt 21:44 and Luke 20:18).

[12] Neither is there salvation in any other: for there is none other name under heaven given among men, whereby we must be saved.

- Peter's greatest words ever spoken are written here. Previously he failed to understand God's plan (Matt 16:21-23), but now Peter boldly proclaims that one "must" come to God *only* through Jesus Christ.
- Jesus the Messiah is the only "hope of Israel" to save them as a nation (Acts 28:20, Jer 14:8, Joel 3:16). Israel as a whole will one day "acknowledge their offence" and turn to Him (Hosea 5:15).
- Peter's message of hope is also a word of warning. The Savior warned that saved Gentiles will enter God's kingdom while Israel-ites who reject Him will be forever excluded (Luke 13:28-29).
- Jesus is also God's only way of salvation for each individual (John 3:36, 1 John 5:12). "Jesus saith unto him, I am the way, the truth, and the life: no man cometh unto the Father, but by me" (John 14:6). Since Jesus is the only way to God, His followers will be called people of the "way" (Acts 9:2, 19:9, 23, 22:4, 24:14, 22).
- Jesus is not just the exclusive Savior, but also the only man worthy of dedicating one's entire life to. Paul will therefore teach believers, "And whatsoever ye do in word or deed, do all in the name of the Lord Jesus, giving thanks to God and the Father by him" (Col 3:17).

Language
Hebraism (a Hebrew manner of expression) – "under heaven" (Gen 1:9) means "on earth."

[13] Now when they saw the boldness of Peter and John, and perceived that they were unlearned and ignorant men, they marvelled; and they took knowledge of them, that they had been with Jesus.

- The bewildered elders and rulers are not used to being spoken to in such a frank manner (2 Cor 3:12), especially by fishermen (Luke 5:10) lacking formal religious training (John 7:15), who would generally be uncomfortable challenging their authority (John 9:22-23, 12:42). The boldness of Peter and John contrasts with the demeanor of the more typical defendant. "Every one, whosoever he be, that comes to be tried by this Sanhedrin, presents himself in a submissive manner, and like one that is in fear of himself, and that endeavors to move us to compassion, with his hair disheveled, and in a black and mourning garment."[155]
- Peter and John stand with boldness for the truth and with no care for their lives. In contrast, Herod the Great stood with pride and self-preservation when once on trial before the Sanhedrin. "This admirable man Herod, who is accused of murder, and called to answer so heavy an accusation, stands here clothed in purple, and with the hair of his head finely trimmed, and with his armed men about him, that if we shall condemn him by our law, he may slay us, and by overbearing justice may himself escape death."[156]
- Peter and John remind them of Jesus by the way they unflinchingly speak with moral authority (Mark 1:22). Boldness stems from confidence (Acts 28:31) in the word of God (Psalm 119:160), unlike arrogance, which is the result of pride (Prov 8:13).
- The apostles' speech is not compelling because they possess education in religion and rhetoric, but because the Holy Ghost (Acts 4:8) moves their hearts as they speak (2 Peter 1:21). The epistles of Peter (1 and 2 Peter) and John (1, 2, and 3 John) will confirm that their spiritual insight is far greater than the rulers' (Psalm 119:100).

[14] And beholding the man which was healed standing with them, they could say nothing against it.

One can debate points of doctrine but cannot dispute the reality of a changed life (Luke 8:35). Likewise, the religious leaders never challenge the truth of Christ's resurrection (Acts 5:34-39) against the testimony of

---

[155] Josephus, *Antiquities*, 14.9.4
[156] Ibid.

hundreds of eyewitnesses (1 Cor 15:6).

[15] But when they had commanded them to go aside out of the council, they conferred among themselves,

- A "council" is an authoritative assembly, and in the context of the temple, refers to the Sanhedrin, which acts both as Israel's highest governing body and supreme court. "The Great Sanhedrin was composed of seventy-one judges"[157] (seventy plus the high priest) to reflect the precedent of Moses appointing seventy elders (Num 11:16). The members include **elders, chief priests, and scribes** (Mark 14:43, 14:53, 15:1, Luke 9:22, 20:1, 22:66, Acts 4:5), most of whom are either Sadducees or Pharisees (Acts 23:6).
- The **elders** are senior family or tribal leaders recognized because of their age and expected wisdom. Moses first to the elders presented God's plan of deliverance from Egypt (Exod 4:29-31), gave instructions for the Passover (Exod 12:21), introduced God's law from Mount Sinai (Exod 19:7), and called for participation in the initial consecration of Aaron at the tabernacle (Lev 9:1). Joshua called the elders to hear his last farewell messages (Josh 23:2, 24:1). Boaz called the elders of Bethlehem to effect his redemption of Ruth at the city gates (Ruth 4:1-2, Prov 31:23). The elders asked Samuel to appoint a king over Israel (1 Sam 8:4), and later Abner convinced the elders of Israel to recognize David as king (2 Sam 3:17, 1 Chron 11:3). The elders went with David to bring the ark of the Lord into Jerusalem (1 Chron 15:25) then went with Solomon to bring the ark into the temple (2 Chron 5:2). The elders of Israel were complicit in Absalom's *coup d'état* against David (2 Sam 17:4). King Rehoboam disastrously ignored the advice of the elders who served his father Solomon (1 Kings 12:6-19). Jezebel infamously manipulated the elders to slay the innocent Naboth (1 Kings 21:11). When Israel was exiled in Babylon, the elders sought to receive the word of the Lord from Ezekiel (Ezek 20:1), and when returned from exile, the elders received authority to rebuild the temple (Ezra 6:7,14).
- The **chief priests** form a group that apparently includes the current high priest, former high priests, and their influential family mem-

---

[157] *Mishna*, Sanhedrin 2a

bers (implied from a comparison of passages such as John 18:13,24 with John 18:3,35; and Acts 4:6 with Acts 4:23, 5:24).

- **Scribes** are experts of the law, the writings, and the prophets of the Old Testament (Luke 24:44). King Herod asked the scribes where the Messiah would be born (Matt 2:4). The scribes correctly taught that an appearance of Elijah would precede the arrival of the conquering Messiah (Mal 4:5, Matt 17:10). They were correct in reasoning that only God can forgive sins (Mark 2:6-7). Jesus warned the scribes who accused Him of working miracles by the power of Satan (Mark 3:22) of their great spiritual danger (Mark 3:29-30). The scribes correctly teach that the Messiah is a descendant of David (Mark 12:35). Jesus condemned hypocritical scribes (Mark 12:38-40) but commended those scribes who understand the heart of God (Mark 12:28-34).

[16] Saying, What shall we do to these men? for that indeed a notable miracle hath been done by them is manifest to all them that dwell in Jerusalem; and we cannot deny it.

They should not ask, "What shall we do to these men?" Instead, they should ask, "What shall I do then with Jesus which is called Christ?" (Matt 27:22).

[17] But that it spread no further among the people, let us straitly threaten them, that they speak henceforth to no man in this name.

The members of the Sanhedrin hold power because they control the Jerusalem temple, which is the most important place of worship in the world for Jews. They are opposed to any movement that might threaten the delicate balance of power they have achieved with Rome (John 11:48). They wish to punish Peter and John, who have undermined their authority by convincing the people of Jerusalem that they are guilty of murder (Acts 4:10, 5:28). However, they know the apostles have not broken any law and know the people view the apostles favorably due to the miraculous healing (Acts 3:7). They worry about the apostles' growing influence yet are concerned that a sentence of punishment would be very unpopular (Acts 4:21, 5:26; as with Jesus, Matt 21:26,46), so they will let them go with only a warning.

<u>Language</u>
"Straitly threaten" means "strictly threaten."

[18] And they called them, and commanded them not to speak at all nor teach in the name of Jesus.

They cannot punish Peter and John for violating principles of formal religious training that they have not received (Acts 4:13), so the rulers choose to warn them now. Later they will punish the apostles when they violate these instructions (Acts 5:40).

[19] But Peter and John answered and said unto them, Whether it be right in the sight of God to hearken unto you more than unto God, judge ye.

Likewise the Hebrew midwives obeyed God rather than Pharaoh (Exod 1:17).

[20] For we cannot but speak the things which we have seen and heard.

They want to speak of Jesus Christ because they are filled with the Holy Ghost (Acts 4:8), whose ministry it is to glorify the Savior (John 16:13–14).

[21] So when they had further threatened them, they let them go, finding nothing how they might punish them, because of the people: for all men glorified God for that which was done.

Apparently anyone who is not wealthy (like Herod) or popular (like the apostles) should expect swift punishment from these powerful rulers who threaten anyone they see as rivals, even those not guilty of any crime.

[22] For the man was above forty years old, on whom this miracle of healing was shewed.

[23] And being let go, they went to their own company, and reported all that the chief priests and elders had said unto them.

[24] And when they heard that, they lifted up their voice to God with one accord, and said, Lord, thou art God, which hast made heaven, and earth,

and the sea, and all that in them is:

Quoting Psalm 146:6. The disciples serve the Creator of the universe. Anyone opposing their preaching the gospel (like the high priest and his allies, Acts 4:6) will futilely "be found even to fight against God" (Acts 5:39), the Creator of all.

[25] Who by the mouth of thy servant David hast said, Why did the heathen rage, and the people imagine vain things?

[26] The kings of the earth stood up, and the rulers were gathered together against the Lord, and against his Christ.

- These words of David (Psalm 2:1-2) depict opposition to Christ by *Gentile* leaders at the time of His future return. It is sadly ironic that the words of this Psalm also fit the opposition to Christ by *Jewish* leaders now experienced by the disciples. During His earthly ministry the Savior was opposed by the high priest and his allies (Mark 14:53), and now the same rulers oppose the disciples.
- The disciples' statement that "God ... [spoke] by the mouth of thy servant David" (Acts 4:24-25) is consistent with Peter's that "the Holy Ghost [spoke] by the mouth of David" (Acts 1:16). The very words of the Old Testament (as well as the New) are God's own words because "holy men of God spake as they were moved by the Holy Ghost" (2 Peter 1:21).

[27] For of a truth against thy holy child Jesus, whom thou hast anointed, both Herod, and Pontius Pilate, with the Gentiles, and the people of Israel, were gathered together,

[28] For to do whatsoever thy hand and thy counsel determined before to be done.

- Their prayer designates those responsible for Christ's death as the Roman-appointed Jewish leader Herod Antipas (Luke 23:11), the Gentile leader Pontius Pilate (Acts 3:13), and the people of Israel present at Jerusalem (specified in Acts 2:23, 3:17, Luke 13:33-34). A charge of murder is never leveled at Jews outside Jerusalem (e.g.,

Paul speaking in Asia Minor, Acts 13:27-28).
- Jesus was not "unexpectedly killed" by Jews and Gentiles in Jerusalem. Rather He laid down His life for sinful humankind (John 10:15-18, 15:13, Rom 5:8) as part of God's plan (Rom 3:25, Gal 4:4). Any individual may choose whether or not to serve God, but either way, His pre-determined plan is accomplished (Acts 2:23–24).

Language
- The Greek word *pais* can be translated as either "child" or "servant" for Christ is both God's Son (Isa 9:6) and Servant (Isa 52:13). The rendering of "child" is correct here because its use affirms Christ's deity (John 19:7) and because the quoted scripture (Psalm 2) presents the Messiah as God's Son (Psalm 2:7) in contrast to the believers who are His servants (Acts 4:29).
- *Gradual ascent* – the list of offenders ascends from Herod to Pilate to the Gentiles to the people of Israel.

[29] And now, Lord, behold their threatenings: and grant unto thy servants, that with all boldness they may speak thy word,

[30] By stretching forth thine hand to heal; and that signs and wonders may be done by the name of thy holy child Jesus.

- Peter and John were threatened "not to speak at all nor teach in the name of Jesus" (Acts 4:17-18). Yet the disciples continue to pray in His name, the name at which every knee shall bow (Phil 2:10). They no longer pray based on the merits of the forefathers (Exod 32:13; Deut 9:27, 2 Chr 6:16-17), but only on the righteousness of Jesus Christ (1 Cor 1:30).
- The disciples pray for boldness of witness (Phil 1:20, Jer 20:9) rather than for personal safety. At the cost of his life, the martyr Stephen will give a bold witness (Acts 7) that will lead to the spread of the gospel outside Jerusalem (Acts 8:1, 11:19-20) and will inspire believers for many generations to come.
- God has now granted miracles to facilitate evangelism (Acts 8:6).

[31] And when they had prayed, the place was shaken where they were assembled together; and they were all filled with the Holy Ghost, and they

spake the word of God with boldness.

- An earthquake indicated God's presence to Moses at Sinai (Exod 19:18) and Isaiah at his vision (Isa 6:4) and will to Paul and Silas at Philippi (Acts 16:26).
- The disciples are filled with the Holy Ghost in contrast to the Sadducees, who are filled with resentment (Acts 4:2).
- God answers their prayer to proclaim His word boldly (Acts 4:29).

[32] And the multitude of them that believed were of one heart and of one soul: neither said any of them that ought of the things which he possessed was his own; but they had all things common.

[33] And with great power gave the apostles witness of the resurrection of the Lord Jesus: and great grace was upon them all.

[34] Neither was there any among them that lacked: for as many as were possessors of lands or houses sold them, and brought the prices of the things that were sold,

115

[35] And laid them down at the apostles' feet: and distribution was made unto every man according as he had need.

- The message of the resurrected Savior has the power to transform the lives of sinners who repent (1 Tim 1:15). God gives believers grace to give of themselves sacrificially to meet each other's needs (1 John 3:23). They still own private property (Acts 5:4) but share it selflessly.
- The believers' actions demonstrate their love and concern for each other (Acts 2:45). Church leaders such as James, Peter, and John will continue to encourage charitable giving (Gal 2:9-10). The apostle Paul will twice bring a gift to the Jerusalem saints from international believers (Acts 11:29–30, 24:17).

[36] And Joses, who by the apostles was surnamed Barnabas, (which is, being interpreted, The son of consolation,) a Levite, and of the country of Cyprus,

[37] Having land, sold it, and brought the money, and laid it at the apostles' feet.

- Joses Barnabas' relative Mary will host a church in her Jerusalem home (Acts 12:12), and her son John Mark (Col 4:10) will accompany Paul and Barnabas on their first missionary journey, starting at Barnabas' home island of Cyprus (Acts 13:4-5).
- Barnabas will live up to his name by being an encouragement ("consolation") to Paul when vouching for him before the apostles who will not believe he has truly changed (Acts 9:26–27) and when vouching for John Mark when Paul does not believe he has truly changed (Acts 15:37–38).
- Levites such as Barnabas can rightfully own land under the law, for although Moses did not give them tribal territory (Deut 18:1–2), the Levites were allocated individual cities and suburbs under Joshua (Num 35:7, Josh 21:3).
- Barnabas is identified as a Levite but is not shown acting as a priest because the Old Testament Levitical priesthood (Deut 21:5) has been replaced in this age by the priesthood of all believers (1 Peter 2:9) under the High Priest Jesus Christ (Heb 3:1).

Teaching Question

Question: Peter in Acts 4:11 quotes Psalm 118:22, "The stone which the builders refused is become the head stone of the corner." Where would a builder place "the head stone of the corner"?
Answer: A Jewish writer of this era gives a fictional account of Solomon finishing the temple. "And there was a stone, the end stone of the corner lying there, great, chosen out, one which I desired lay in the head of the corner of the completion of the Temple... And I Solomon, beholding the stone raised aloft and placed on a foundation, said: 'Truly the Scripture is fulfilled, which says: 'The stone which the builders rejected on trial, that same is become the head of the corner.'"[158]

---

[158] *The Testament of Solomon*, 118 and 123

Challenge Questions

1. Why are the religious authorities so upset by the preaching of Christ's resurrection (Acts 4:1-2)?
2. Who is Peter thinking about when he says, "we must be saved" (Acts 4:12)?
3. How does the charity expressed by these believers differ from communism?
4. Which events (both "good" and "bad") from the time of Christ's arrest (Luke 22:54) until now (Acts 4:37) have occurred due to God's pre-determined plan (Acts 4:28) and which have occurred due to the choices of individuals?

Acts Chapter 5

[1] But a certain man named Ananias, with Sapphira his wife, sold a possession,

[2] And kept back part of the price, his wife also being privy to it, and brought a certain part, and laid it at the apostles' feet.

[3] But Peter said, Ananias, why hath Satan filled thine heart to lie to the Holy Ghost, and to keep back part of the price of the land?

[4] Whiles it remained, was it not thine own? and after it was sold, was it not in thine own power? why hast thou conceived this thing in thine heart? thou hast not lied unto men, but unto God.

- The couple does not sin when not donating all the proceeds but does wrong in making the false appearance of doing so to impress others with their generosity (Matt 6:1). They yield (Rom 6:16) their hearts to Satan, the father of lies (John 8:44b), rather than to the Spirit of truth (John 16:13).
- Peter affirms the deity of the Spirit of the Lord (Acts 5:9) when he states that lying to the Holy Ghost (Acts 5:3) is lying to God.

Language
"Privy to" means "privately knowing."

[5] And Ananias hearing these words fell down, and gave up the ghost: and great fear came on all them that heard these things.

The Lord at times in the Old Testament would deliver sudden judgment on sinners by the few (Gen 38:7, 10, Lev 10:1-2, 2 Sam 6:7) or the many (Num 14:36-37, 16:35, 21:6, 25:9, Josh 7:24-25, 1 Sam 6:19, 2 Kings 1:10-12, 19:35), but He mercifully does not in the New Testament (excepting here and Acts 12:23). Yet the character of God has not changed, as evidenced by Ananias' punishment. God's holiness and hatred of sin are unvarying, and it is only His present longsuffering (patience) that holds back judgment to allow sinners to repent (Rom 2:4, 2 Peter 3:9).

[6] And the young men arose, wound him up, and carried him out, and buried him.

They cover the body to preserve its dignity before carrying it away for burial.

[7] And it was about the space of three hours after, when his wife, not knowing what was done, came in.

[8] And Peter answered unto her, Tell me whether ye sold the land for so much? And she said, Yea, for so much.

[9] Then Peter said unto her, How is it that ye have agreed together to tempt the Spirit of the Lord? behold, the feet of them which have buried thy husband are at the door, and shall carry thee out.

- Ananias and Sapphira report the same sale price, indicating collusion rather than a mistake.
- The couple "tempt the Lord" by challenging God to overlook their sinful deceit. Peter does not determine a sentence of death; he simply proclaims the judgment of God (1 Tim 5:20, 1 Peter 4:17).
- Peter's substitution of "Spirit of the Lord" for "Lord your God" (Deut 6:16, Matt 4:7) affirms the deity of the Holy Spirit.

[10] Then fell she down straightway at his feet, and yielded up the ghost: and the young men came in, and found her dead, and, carrying her forth, buried her by her husband.

[11] And great fear came upon all the church, and upon as many as heard these things.

- The tragic story of Ananias and Sapphira (Acts 5:1-11) serves as a sobering warning to the early church, as did the story of Achan to the Israelites (Joshua 7:1-26).
- The Holy Spirit is grieved by sin in a believer's life (Eph 4:30). Sin

may lead to suffering and death (Rom 8:13, 1 Cor 11:30) since the Father deals with believers as with sons (Heb 12:5-11).

[12] And by the hands of the apostles were many signs and wonders wrought among the people; (and they were all with one accord in Solomon's porch.

The Lord Jesus taught "in the temple in Solomon's porch" (John 10:23). The disciples now meet in this sheltered area inside the eastern outer wall.[159] Here on the temple grounds their preaching (Acts 5:42) is confirmed by miracles.

[13] And of the rest durst no man join himself to them: but the people magnified them.

- Ananias and Sapphira wanted to be part of the church while following a Satan-inspired agenda of deceit (Acts 5:1-4). The Lord brought swift judgment upon them (Acts 5:5-10), an event which has made a frightening impression on those who have heard (Acts 5:11).
- The people of Jerusalem esteem the apostles, who have worked signs and wonders (Acts 5:12), but also fear them, given the supernatural deaths of Ananias and Sapphira. Only those genuinely committed to following Christ dare to join the believers.

[14] And believers were the more added to the Lord, multitudes both of men and women.)

The Lord continues to add "to the church daily such as should be saved" (Acts 2:47).

[15] Insomuch that they brought forth the sick into the streets, and laid them on beds and couches, that at the least the shadow of Peter passing by might overshadow some of them.

The outpouring of the Holy Ghost on Simon Peter is so overflowing that even those with indirect contact are healed, as they were with the Lord

---

[159] Josephus, *Antiquities*, 15.11.3

Jesus (Mark 6:56, Luke 7:7-10, 8:43-44) and will be with the Apostle Paul (Acts 19:12).

[16] There came also a multitude out of the cities round about unto Jerusalem, bringing sick folks, and them which were vexed with unclean spirits: and they were healed every one.

The fact that the apostles miraculously heal everyone without fail, as did the Lord Jesus (Luke 4:40), confirms that their ministry is under His divine authority (Mark 16:18).

[17] Then the high priest rose up, and all they that were with him, (which is the sect of the Sadducees,) and were filled with indignation,

[18] And laid their hands on the apostles, and put them in the common prison.

The Sadducees arrest the apostles now as they previously did (Acts 4:1). They do not consider the witness of God (2 Chron 24:19) through miracles (Acts 5:15-16) but contemplate only how the apostles' persuading of the people affects their positions of power (John 11:48).

Language
Hebraism (a Hebrew manner of expression) – "the high priest rose up ... and [was] filled with indignation" corresponds with "Cain rose up ... and slew" (Gen 4:8). The words "rose up" are redundant but highlight the emotional fervor.

[19] But the angel of the Lord by night opened the prison doors, and brought them forth, and said,

The angel of the Lord (i.e., a visible appearance of the Lord, Exod 3:2,4) will also release Peter from prison when Herod arrests him (Acts 12:7–11) and will later appear to comfort Paul (Acts 27:23).

[20] Go, stand and speak in the temple to the people all the words of this life.

The Lord Jesus is "the life" (John 14:6) and gives spiritual life to His followers (John 5:24, 10:10). Peter correctly told Him, "thou hast the words of eternal life" (John 6:68).

Language
Interchange (word order reversed) – "the words of this life" are "these life-giving words."

[21] And when they heard that, they entered into the temple early in the morning, and taught. But the high priest came, and they that were with him, and called the council together, and all the senate of the children of Israel, and sent to the prison to have them brought.

[22] But when the officers came, and found them not in the prison, they returned, and told,

[23] Saying, The prison truly found we shut with all safety, and the keepers standing without before the doors: but when we had opened, we found no man within.

[24] Now when the high priest and the captain of the temple and the chief priests heard these things, they doubted of them whereunto this would grow.

The temple authorities are perplexed by the news of the missing prisoners and wonder what this will lead to.

[25] Then came one and told them, saying, Behold, the men whom ye put in prison are standing in the temple, and teaching the people.

[26] Then went the captain with the officers, and brought them without violence: for they feared the people, lest they should have been stoned.

They also "feared the people" when plotting to kill Jesus (Luke 20:19, 22:2).

Language
Irony (unexpected outcome or event) – when the apostles are arrested

then miraculously released, they return to the temple where they can easily be re-arrested.

[27] And when they had brought them, they set them before the council: and the high priest asked them,

[28] Saying, Did not we straitly command you that ye should not teach in this name? and, behold, ye have filled Jerusalem with your doctrine, and intend to bring this man's blood upon us.

- The council disregards the miraculous exit from prison (Acts 5:19), the healing of the lame man (Acts 3:6-8), and the miracle of Christ's resurrection (Acts 4:33).
- The leaders try to deflect their guilt for the Messiah's death (Matt 27:25) by scolding God's messengers. King Ahab did the same when confronted by the prophet Elijah (1 Kings 18:17).
- The council unintentionally praises the success of the apostles in saying they have "filled Jerusalem" with the gospel message. Paul's critics will do the same of him (Acts 17:6, 19:26, 21:28).
- The council's flippant reference to the Creator of the universe as "this man" shows that they do not know Him (Festus will speak likewise, Acts 25:19).

[29] Then Peter and the other apostles answered and said, We ought to obey God rather than men.

The apostles have continued to preach despite threats (Acts 4:17) because they have been commanded to by the Lord Jesus (Acts 1:8, Matt 28:19-20, Luke 24:47) and by His angel who miraculously released them from prison (Acts 5:20).

[30] The God of our fathers raised up Jesus, whom ye slew and hanged on a tree.

- Like in Acts 3:26, "God ... raised up Jesus" to be a Savior to Israel (Acts 13:23) and also raised Him from the dead (Acts 13:30).
- Peter accuses the Jewish leaders of two evils: they murdered their Messiah (Acts 2:23, 5:30) and concurrently declared Him accursed by

hanging Him on the cross (Deut 21:22–23, Gal 3:13).

[31] Him hath God exalted with his right hand to be a Prince and a Saviour, for to give repentance to Israel, and forgiveness of sins.

God wants each individual Jew (Acts 3:25–26) to repent (a change of heart and mind which leads to a change of action) and turn to Jesus Christ (Acts 20:21). When Israel as a whole repents, He will forgive the national sins of Israel, and the Messiah will return to reign over them (Acts 3:19–21).

[32] And we are his witnesses of these things; and so is also the Holy Ghost, whom God hath given to them that obey him.

The Holy Ghost is not merely an indistinct force, but a Person, who is a witness of the resurrection because He raised Jesus from the dead (Rom 8:11). The Lord has given the Spirit to those who have followed Peter's exhortation to repent (Acts 2:38, 3:19) and turn to the Savior (Acts 5:31).

[33] When they heard that, they were cut to the heart, and took counsel to slay them.

- Peter is brash by nature (Matt 16:22, John 13:8), and now, with the Spirit's filling (Acts 4:8), his words effectively pierce the hearts (Heb 4:12) of his listeners. The council is angry with Peter's refusal to submit to their authority (Acts 5:29), his affirmation of the resurrection (Acts 5:31, Acts 4:2), the repeated charge of murder (Acts 5:30), and the implication that God's Spirit does not indwell them because they disobey God (Acts 5:32).
- The high priest and the council portray themselves as wise judges free of hostility, unlike the apostles, who "intend to bring this man's blood upon us" (Acts 5:28). The malicious intent of the high priest and council is now unmasked when they plan to slay the apostles.

[34] Then stood there up one in the council, a Pharisee, named Gamaliel, a doctor of the law, had in reputation among all the people, and commanded to put the apostles forth a little space;

[35] And said unto them, Ye men of Israel, take heed to yourselves what ye intend to do as touching these men.

[36] For before these days rose up Theudas, boasting himself to be somebody; to whom a number of men, about four hundred, joined themselves: who was slain; and all, as many as obeyed him, were scattered, and brought to nought.

[37] After this man rose up Judas of Galilee in the days of the taxing, and drew away much people after him: he also perished; and all, even as many as obeyed him, were dispersed.

- Herod the Great at his death (Matt 2:19) willed rulership of the province of Judea to his son Archelaus.[160] Before Caesar Augustus could formally execute Herod's will, Archelaus was responsible for a violent incident at the Jerusalem temple that led to the death of 3,000 Jews. When Archelaus traveled to Rome to seek the rulership of Judea willed to him by his late father, he found that a separate delegation of Jews arrived from Israel to ask Caesar to deny the office to Archelaus and instead appoint a Roman governor.[161] Caesar sided with Archelaus and appointed him as ruler of Judea (Matt 2:22). However, Archelaus continued to rule in a "barbarous and tyrannical" manner,[162] so Caesar had him banished to Gaul and stripped of his wealth.[163] The emperor also granted the Jews their request by making Judea a Roman province (underneath the territory of Syria) and by appointing a Roman governor, rather than a Jewish king such as Herod had been.

125

- Around AD 6 Caesar gave Cyrenius (Quirinius) authority in the province of Syria and Judea to dispose of the possessions of the disgraced Archelaus while taking a census for taxation. Most citizens of Judea followed the counsel of the High Priest Joazar and cooperated, but Judas of Galilee stirred his followers to violent opposition. "A certain Galilean, whose name was Judas, prevailed with his countrymen to revolt, and said they were cowards if they would endure

---

[160] Matt 2:22; Josephus, *Antiquities*, 17.8.1
[161] Josephus, *Antiquities*, 17.11.2
[162] Ibid., 17.8.2
[163] Ibid., 17.13.2

to pay a tax to the Romans."[164] Although Judas of Galilee perished, his offspring Manahem and Eleazar[165] will take part in the disastrous rebellion against Rome that will lead to the destruction of the Jerusalem temple.

- Luke reports both a *first* census taken while Cyrenius (Quirinius) was governor of Syria at the time of Jesus' birth (Luke 2:1-2) and this *second* census taken a decade later (Acts 5:37); the historian Josephus mentions only the more recent tally. Luke writes of a malcontent named Theudas, who arose *before* Judas of Galilee, and Josephus writes of an instigator named Theudas, who appeared *after* Judas of Galilee.[166]

[38] And now I say unto you, Refrain from these men, and let them alone: for if this counsel or this work be of men, it will come to nought:

- Gamaliel, the grandson of the famous rabbi Hillel,[167] commands great respect among the Jews and is addressed not merely with the usual title "Rabbi" ("my master"), but with the honorific title "Rabban" ("our master"). He will be so greatly mourned at his death that his admirers will write, "when Rabban Gamaliel the elder died, the glory [ascribed to] the Torah ceased, and purity and separateness perished."[168] Saul of Tarsus is a former student of Gamaliel (Acts 22:3).
- Gamaliel believes not that Jesus is the Messiah, but only a popular teacher of the likes of Theudas and Judas of Galilee. Nevertheless, Israel has a history of killing God's prophets and later realizing their grievous error (Matt 23:29-31, 37, Acts 7:52), so Gamaliel suggests a policy that will avoid any possibility of repeating this regrettable pattern. He argues that if the apostles are false teachers, both they and their followers will ultimately fail (Matt 15:14).

[39] But if it be of God, ye cannot overthrow it; lest haply ye be found even to fight against God.

---

[164] Josephus, *Jewish War*, 2.8.1
[165] Ibid., 2.17.8 and 7.8.1
[166] Josephus, *Antiquities*, 20.5.1
[167] *Babylonian Talmud*, Shabbat 15a
[168] *Mishnah*, Sotah 9:15

"...you might happen to find yourself fighting against God."

[40] And to him they agreed: and when they had called the apostles, and beaten them, they commanded that they should not speak in the name of Jesus, and let them go.

- The Sadducees hold key positions of power. The temple captain is their ally (Acts 4:1), as is the high priest and others who initiate today's proceedings against the apostles (Acts 5:17). "The Sadducees are able to persuade none but the rich, and have not the populace [loyal] to them, but the Pharisees have the multitude on their side."[169] Although the Pharisees have little political power, they hold the greater moral authority among the common people. The Pharisees "are able greatly to persuade the body of the people; and whatsoever they do about Divine worship, prayers, and sacrifices, [the people] perform them according to [the Pharisees'] direction... [this is] on account of [the Pharisees'] virtuous conduct, both in the actions of their lives and their discourses also."[170]
- "The sect of the Sadducees, whose notions are quite contrary to those of the Pharisees," initially asked for the death penalty for the apostles (Acts 5:33). In a prior case a Sadducee named Jonathan asked for a death sentence against a criticizer named Eleazar. "The Pharisees made answer, that he deserved stripes and bonds, but that it did not seem right to punish reproaches with death. And indeed the Pharisees, even upon other occasions, are not apt to be severe in punishments"[171] in contrast to the "Sadducees, who are very rigid in judging offenders, above all the rest of the Jews."[172]
- The Sadducees have greater affluence (wealthy citizens are their allies) and political prominence (the high priest is a Sadducee) than the Pharisees. Yet the Sadducees' call for severe punishment does not stand against the words of the Pharisee Gamaliel, who has greater moral influence among ordinary people. The council orders the apostles beaten for disobeying the prior order not to speak in the name of Jesus (Acts 4:18). The punishment is still unjust

---

[169] Josephus, *Antiquities*, 13.10.6
[170] Ibid., 18.1.3
[171] Ibid., 13.10.6
[172] Ibid., 20.9.1

because the apostles' teaching of Jesus as the promised Messiah violates no law.

[41] And they departed from the presence of the council, rejoicing that they were counted worthy to suffer shame for his name.

They rejoice for their sufferings as was foretold by the Savior (Luke 6:22-23) and as will be written by Peter (1 Peter 2:19–21).

<u>Language</u>
Oxymoron (a foolish-sounding statement that is actually wise) – only a true servant of God welcomes suffering in service to Him.

[42] And daily in the temple, and in every house, they ceased not to teach and preach Jesus Christ.

They will continue to evangelize without interference until the persecution brought by Saul after the death of Stephen (Acts 8:1–4).

Teaching Question

The ancient historian Josephus also writes of a Theudas,[173] but his story occurs *after* Judas of Galilee and Luke's *before*. Therefore Luke and Josephus write of two *different* revolutionaries, both named Theudas.
<u>Question</u>: Is it possible that there is really only *one* revolutionary named Theudas and that Luke acquired his information for Acts 5:36 from the writings of Josephus (rather than from eyewitnesses) and confused the dates?
<u>Answer</u>: No.
- Josephus will publish *Antiquities of the Jews* in AD 93,[174] whereas Luke writes in the early AD 60's.[175] Since Luke writes at an earlier time than Josephus, he is closer to the actual events and is therefore less likely to confuse the dates.

---

[173] Ibid., 20.5.1
[174] "Flavius Josephus." *Encyclopedia Britannica Online*, accessed 28 Apr 2020
[175] See "Introduction" to Acts for discussion.

- Luke undoubtedly has eyewitnesses (Luke 1:2) of Gamaliel's speech since "a great company of the priests were obedient to the faith" (Acts 6:7). Furthermore, Gamaliel is a Pharisee (Acts 5:34), and members of his religious sect will also believe (Acts 15:5).
- The more verbose account of Josephus[176] contrasts significantly with Luke's brief record, which suggests that they write about two different men: "Just seven years ago [Luke: 'before these days'] arose Theudas boasting that he was a prophet and magician [Luke: 'to be somebody'] and persuaded thousands [Luke: 'about 400'] to leave their homes with their belongings in order to leave Judea by way of the Jordan river which he would miraculously part [Luke: 'joined themselves']. Before they got very far, Governor Fadus set his soldiers upon them [Luke: no mention of soldiers or of Governor Fadus since he was not appointed until decades later]. Theudas was beheaded [Luke: 'was slain'] and many of his followers were killed or captured [Luke: 'were scattered']."

129

Challenge Questions

1. Peter says, "We ought to obey God rather than men" (Acts 5:29). Under what circumstances is it appropriate for a believer to disobey the government?
2. Does Gamaliel give sound advice when he says, "And now I say unto you, Refrain from these men, and let them alone: for if this counsel or this work be of men, it will come to nought: But if it be of God, ye cannot overthrow it; lest haply ye be found even to fight against God" (Acts 5:38-39)?

---

[176] Josephus, *Antiquities*, 20.5.1

Acts Chapter 6

[1] And in those days, when the number of the disciples was multiplied, there arose a murmuring of the Grecians against the Hebrews, because their widows were neglected in the daily ministration.

- Alexander the Great brought his army into Asia Minor to overthrow the Persian empire. He victoriously entered the land of Israel in 332 BC. "The Greek language became a common language for nearer Asia, and with the language went Greek culture, Greek art, and Greek thought... [However, devout Jews] regarded it as their chief task to preserve their religion uncontaminated, a task that required the strict separation of the congregation both from all foreign peoples [Ezra 10:11, Neh 9:2] and from the Jewish inhabitants of Palestine who did not strictly observe the Law [Ezra 6:21, Neh 10:30]."[177]

- The word "Grecian" means "Hellenist" and refers to those whose language and culture are Greek. In the context of Jerusalem (here and in Acts 9:29), the term means Jews born outside of Israel ("Hellenistic" Jews) whose language and culture are Greek, in contrast to Jews born inside the promised land ("Hebrews") whose language and culture is Hebrew. In the context of Antioch (Acts 11:20), the term refers to Greek-speaking Gentiles of Syria.

- Jews in Jerusalem who are native-born speak Hebrew and Aramaic. They are determined to live in the ways of their forefathers. They may look down on the foreign-born Grecian ("Hellenistic") Jews whose language and culture are Greek. "Among us there is no welcome for people who learn the languages of other nations so as to think like them. We regard this as no proper task for a free man but rather as one that should be left to slaves who choose to learn them, whereas we deem as wise the one who fully understands our own laws and can interpret their meaning."[178] The apostle Paul will bridge both groups. He was born in Tarsus and understands Greek

---

[177] Carl Siegfried, Richard Gottheil. "Hellenism." *Jewish Encyclopedia*, 1906
[178] Josephus, *Antiquities*, 20.11.2

language (Acts 21:37) and thought (Acts 17:22-31). He was also raised in Jerusalem and understands Hebrew language (Acts 22:2) and thought, having been taught by Gamaliel (Acts 22:3).

- Two factors have led to the neglect of the Grecian widows. First is the tremendous growth of believers in Jerusalem. So far the disciples are all Jewish believers (Acts 2:5). The church was counted at 3,000 on Pentecost (Acts 2:41) and subsequently grew to 5,000 (Acts 4:4). The church now multiplies further, and some 20 years from now the apostle Paul will meet in Jerusalem with James who will declare that there are "many thousands of Jews ... which believe" (Acts 21:20). This rapid growth has created unanticipated difficulties with distributing food to needy widows.
- The second factor leading to the neglect of the Grecian widows is the cultural differences between the native-born and foreign-born Jews, which has resulted in the former (apparently unintentionally) neglecting the widows of the latter.

[2] Then the twelve called the multitude of the disciples unto them, and said, It is not reason that we should leave the word of God, and serve tables.

[3] Wherefore, brethren, look ye out among you seven men of honest report, full of the Holy Ghost and wisdom, whom we may appoint over this business.

[4] But we will give ourselves continually to prayer, and to the ministry of the word.

- The twelve apostles are the original eleven (Acts 1:13) plus Matthias (Acts 1:26). They are certainly not above feeding the hungry (Paul will in Acts 11:28-30) or caring for widows (Peter will in Acts 9:36-41). However, their time is best spent on ministry and prayer. The task of reforming their charitable distribution system can be delegated to others, and even Jesus delegated food-serving to His disciples (Luke 9:13-16).
- Daniel's continual devotion to prayer (Dan 6:10, 9:3) brought him the revelation of God's word (Dan 9:23, 12:4).

[5] And the saying pleased the whole multitude: and they chose Stephen, a man full of faith and of the Holy Ghost, and Philip, and Prochorus, and Nicanor, and Timon, and Parmenas, and Nicolas a proselyte of Antioch:

- The church selects seven men to act as deacons (1 Tim 3:8-13) and minister to the widows (1 Tim 5:2-16). Each of the seven men must have a good reputation ("be proved ... being found blameless," 1 Tim 3:10). They must have both the Holy Ghost and wisdom, unlike Solomon, who had wisdom (1 Kings 4:29-30) but not the filling of the Holy Ghost to lead a righteous life (1 Kings 11:4-6).
- The disciples show their commitment to unity (1 Cor 1:10) by choosing seven apparently Grecian Jews (they all have Greek names) to ensure that all the widows' needs are met.
- Stephen will be a martyr (Acts 7:59) and Philip an evangelist (Acts 8:5-40, 21:8).
- Antioch is where the disciples will first be called Christians (Acts 11:26) and will be the origin of Paul's three missionary journeys (Acts 13:1-3, 15:35-36, 18:22-23).

[6] Whom they set before the apostles: and when they had prayed, they laid their hands on them.

- The church members chose the seven men (Acts 6:5), and the apostles now commission them to serve.
- Prayer is a central theme in Acts and is made individually (Acts 9:11, 10:9), as a group (Acts 1:14, 4:31), with fasting (Acts 10:30, 14:23), to facilitate healing (Acts 9:40, 28:8), during travel (Acts 20:36, 21:5), amid persecution (Acts 12:5, 16:25), and before important decisions (Acts 1:24, 13:2-3).
- Laying on of hands in Acts is variously used to confer blessings (Acts 6:6, 13:3), the Holy Ghost (Acts 8:17, 19:6), miracles (Acts 9:17-18, 14:3, 28:8), and spiritual gifts (1 Tim 4:14, 2 Tim 1:6).

[7] And the word of God increased; and the number of the disciples multiplied in Jerusalem greatly; and a great company of the priests were obedient to the faith.

- Hundreds of years ago, in the days of Nehemiah, there were over

1,000 priests in Jerusalem (Neh 11:10-14). With population growth, there certainly must be many more now in the 1st century AD.
- The chief rulers of the synagogue at Corinth, Crispus (Acts 18:8) and Sosthenes (Acts 18:17, 1 Cor 1:1), will also believe.
- Luke gives the second of seven summary statements in the book of Acts now that the gospel has spread throughout Jerusalem.

[8] And Stephen, full of faith and power, did great wonders and miracles among the people.

Miracles are performed in Acts by Jesus (Acts 1:9, 2:22), the apostles (Acts 2:43, 5:12), Peter (Acts 3:6), Stephen (Acts 6:8), Philip (Acts 8:6), Barnabas (Acts 14:3), and Paul (Acts 19:11).

[9] Then there arose certain of the synagogue, which is called the synagogue of the Libertines, and Cyrenians, and Alexandrians, and of them of Cilicia and of Asia, disputing with Stephen.

- This synagogue consists of freed slaves ("libertines") from North Africa (province of Cyrene and city of Alexandria, Egypt) and Asia Minor (provinces of Cilicia and Asia).
- Jews originating outside Israel presumably migrate here intending to live a more religiously-focused life, yet native-born Hebrews might naturally suspect outsiders of bringing religiously liberal ideas. Therefore these foreign-born men welcome the opportunity to demonstrate their orthodoxy by debating vigorously with Stephen, who is (apparently, Acts 6:1, 5) also a foreign-born Jew.
- Saul is a foreign-born Jew from Cilicia (Acts 21:39). He will take part in Stephen's stoning (Acts 7:58) and eventually perform greater persecution of believers (Acts 8:1-4) than any of his peers (Gal 1:14).

[10] And they were not able to resist the wisdom and the spirit by which he spake.

Sometimes "spirit" can refer to the Holy Spirit (Acts 2:4, 8:29) and other times to one's own spirit (Acts 7:59, 17:16, Isa 57:15, 1 Cor 14:32).

[11] Then they suborned men, which said, We have heard him speak blasphemous words against Moses, and against God.

Stephen's opponents cannot beat him in open debate, so they seek to frame him with criminal charges. Stephen's trial is like Jesus' in that his arguments are unanswerable (Acts 6:10, Matt 22:46), so his enemies stir up the people (Acts 6:12, Matt 27:20) and suborn (unlawfully induce) perjury (Acts 6:11, Matt 26:59). They falsely accuse him of blasphemy (Acts 6:13, Matt 26:65), lawlessness (Acts 6:13, Matt 12:2), and seeking the destruction of the temple (Acts 6:14, Matt 26:61).

[12] And they stirred up the people, and the elders, and the scribes, and came upon him, and caught him, and brought him to the council,

[13] And set up false witnesses, which said, This man ceaseth not to speak blasphemous words against this holy place, and the law:

[14] For we have heard him say, that this Jesus of Nazareth shall destroy this place, and shall change the customs which Moses delivered us.

[15] And all that sat in the council, looking stedfastly on him, saw his face as it had been the face of an angel.

- The word "council" in the New Testament refers to a committee, a governing body, or a court. In the context of Stephen's trial at Jerusalem, it relates to the highest Jewish judicial council, the Sanhedrin, which judges according to Jewish law (Acts 18:15, 24:6).
- They primarily accuse Stephen of speaking against the man-made temple and only secondarily against God's holy law. The Lord Jesus rebuked men for such spiritual confusion (Matt 23:16-22).
- The people had misinterpreted Jesus' words describing the temple of His body, which was to be crucified and resurrected (John 2:18-22). They also misunderstood His criticism of their manner of following the law of Moses, as He taught that one's attitude toward God and toward others is of the highest importance (Mark 12:28-34). Stephen doubtless echoes Christ's teachings (Mark 2:23-3:6) and receives the same false charges (Mark 14:57-58).
- Stephen's countenance reveals a man who spiritually beholds the

face of his Lord (Heb 12:2, 2 Cor 3:18, Acts 7:55), as did David (Acts 2:25, 28), and as do the angels (Matt 18:10).

Teaching Questions

Question: The Sanhedrin (the Jerusalem "council") will bring Stephen to trial for a capital crime (i.e., a crime that may be punished by death). Do they have authority under **Jewish law** to pronounce a sentence of death?
Answer: Yes. The law of Moses appoints the death penalty for certain crimes such as blasphemy (Lev 24:16). Therefore, the Sanhedrin has given a death sentence to specific individuals judged guilty of blasphemy, such as Jesus Christ (Matt 26:59-66), and will do the same to Stephen (Acts 7:1-60).

Question: Does the Sanhedrin have authority under **Roman law** to enforce a sentence of death?

Answer: No. The Roman authorities recognize the prerogative of the Sanhedrin to enforce religious law (John 18:31, Acts 18:15, 24:6). However, only the Roman governor may lawfully order an execution. "And now ... Judea was reduced into a province, and Coponius ... was sent as a procurator, having the power of [life and] death put into his hands by Caesar."[179] One day the Roman governor will rebuke the high priest Ananus when he seeks to execute religious rivals because "it was not lawful for Ananus to assemble a sanhedrin [to judge a capital crime] without his consent."[180]

Question: So the Jewish leadership cannot apply the death penalty, but is there an exception to this rule regarding the temple?
Answer: Yes. The one exception involves Gentiles who violate the sanctity of the temple. General Titus will ask, "Have not you ... by our permission, put up this partition-wall [separating Jews and Gentiles] before your sanctuary? Have not you been allowed to put up the pillars ... and on it to engrave in Greek, and in your own letters, this prohibition, that no foreigner should go beyond that wall? Have not we given you leave to kill such

---

[179] Josephus, *Jewish War*, 2.8.1
[180] Josephus, *Antiquities*, 20.9.1

as go beyond it, though he were a Roman?"[181] Paul will be falsely accused (Acts 24:18) of bringing a Gentile into the temple (Acts 21:29); a mob will try to kill Paul, but Roman soldiers will stop the assault (Acts 21:30-32).

Challenge Questions

1. Who are the Grecians (Acts 6:1)?
2. How might Stephen's enemies twist his words to frame him as somebody who speaks "blasphemous words against Moses, and against God" (Acts 6:11)?

---

[181] Josephus, *Jewish War*, 6.2.4

Acts Chapter 7

[1] Then said the high priest, Are these things so?

The high priest directs Stephen to answer the charges against him (Acts 6:11-14). Caiaphas is the high priest officially appointed by Rome, and Annas (father-in-law of Caiaphas, John 18:13) is the former high priest who still holds considerable power.[182]

[2] And he said, Men, brethren, and fathers, hearken; The God of glory appeared unto our father Abraham, when he was in Mesopotamia, before he dwelt in Charran,

Abraham's first call by "The God of glory" (Psalm 29:3) is not explicitly stated in the Genesis account but is hinted at when they set out "to go into the land of Canaan" (Gen 11:31) from Ur of the Chaldees in Mesopotamia (Gen 15:7, Neh 9:7).

137

[3] And said unto him, Get thee out of thy country, and from thy kindred, and come into the land which I shall shew thee.

[4] Then came he out of the land of the Chaldæans, and dwelt in Charran: and from thence, when his father was dead, he removed him into this land, wherein ye now dwell.

- Abraham's second call (Gen 12:1-3, Heb 11:8) occurred when he was in Haran (Gen 11:32). When his father Terah died, Abraham moved his family to Canaan (Gen 12:4-5, Heb 11:9-10).
- Terah fathered a series of three sons (Abram, Nahor, and Haran, Gen 11:26) starting at age 70. Although Abram's name is first on the list (Gen 11:26), he is not the firstborn, as with Jacob and Esau (Esau was older, Gen 25:25-26), Ephraim and Manasseh (Manasseh was older, Gen 48:1), and Moses and Aaron (Aaron was older, Exod

---

[182] See comments on Acts 4:6.

7:7). Since Abraham left Haran at age 75 (Gen 12:4) when his father Terah died at age 205 (Gen 11:32), Abraham would have been born when his father Terah was 130 years old.

- Jesus likewise called His followers to leave people and possessions to follow Him. Those who do so receive "manifold more in this present time, and in the world to come life everlasting" (Luke 18:29-30).

Language
"Haran" translated from Hebrew is equivalent to "Charran" translated from Greek.

[5] And he gave him none inheritance in it, no, not so much as to set his foot on: yet he promised that he would give it to him for a possession, and to his seed after him, when as yet he had no child.

Abraham received the promise of inheritance (Gen 12:7) before the births of Ishmael (Gen 16:15) and Isaac (Gen 21:3). In Canaan he purchased a burial plot (Gen 23:13-20), but his extended family never secured a permanent homeland (Heb 11:9) until the conquest of Joshua (Heb 11:30). The ultimate promise of the entire land grant (Gen 15:18) is yet to be fulfilled (Heb 11:13).

Language
Amplification (a phrase is added at the end of the sentence for emphasis) – "no, not so much as to set his foot on."

[6] And God spake on this wise, That his seed should sojourn in a strange land; and that they should bring them into bondage, and entreat them evil four hundred years.

Four hundred thirty years of sojourning from the Abrahamic covenant in Haran (Gen 12:1) until the Exodus (Exod 12:40-41) and giving of the law (Gal 3:17). Four hundred years of affliction (Gen 15:13) from Isaac first being recognized as Abraham's promised seed (the beginning of hostility, Gen 21:8-10) until the Exodus.

[7] And the nation to whom they shall be in bondage will I judge, said God: and after that shall they come forth, and serve me in this place.

Ur of the Chaldees

Mesopotamia

Euphrates River

Nineveh

Babylon

Tigris River

Haran (Charran)

Damascus

Shechem (Sychem)

Bethel

Hebron

Canaan

Mediterranean Sea

Egypt

Red Sea

Abraham's Journey
Genesis 11-13, Acts 7

Base map (land, water) from Ancient World Mapping Center "A-la-carte"
Modifications (labels, routes) by Gregory Cetton
Creative Commons Attribution 4.0 International License (CC BY 4.0)

God judged Egypt with plagues, which brought deliverance to the Israelites (Exod 6:6), who worshiped God at Mount Sinai ("this place" refers to "this mountain," Exod 3:12) and now at the Jerusalem temple ("the place which the Lord thy God hath chosen," Deut 12:21, 16:11).

[8] And he gave him the covenant of circumcision: and so Abraham begat Isaac, and circumcised him the eighth day; and Isaac begat Jacob; and Jacob begat the twelve patriarchs.

- Circumcision is a sign (indication or "token," Gen 17:11) of the covenant of a people set-apart unto God (Gen 17:10-14), which symbolizes purity (Isa 52:1) and righteousness (Rom 2:25-29, 4:11).
- Those said to be circumcised on the eighth day include Isaac (Gen 21:4), Israelite children (Lev 12:3), John the Baptist (Luke 1:59), Jesus (Luke 2:21), and Paul (Phil 3:5).
- Jacob's sons are called the twelve patriarchs (here), fathers (Acts 7:11, 12, 15), and tribes (Gen 49:28, Acts 26:7, James 1:1).

[9] And the patriarchs, moved with envy, sold Joseph into Egypt: but God was with him,

Jesus' enemies were also moved with envy (Gen 37:11, Mark 15:10, Prov 27:4) and sold him for the price of a slave (Gen 37:28, Matt 26:15).

[10] And delivered him out of all his afflictions, and gave him favour and wisdom in the sight of Pharaoh king of Egypt; and he made him governor over Egypt and all his house.

Gen 41:39-44. Jesus likewise was delivered (Acts 2:31-36) and exalted at the right hand of Authority (1 Peter 3:22).

[11] Now there came a dearth over all the land of Egypt and Chanaan, and great affliction: and our fathers found no sustenance.

[12] But when Jacob heard that there was corn in Egypt, he sent out our fathers first.

Jacob turning to Joseph during the "great affliction" of this famine (Gen 42:1-3) anticipates Israel turning to Jesus during the great tribulation (Matt 24:21), also known as the time of Jacob's trouble (Jer 30:7).

Language
- "Canaan" (Gen 42:5) translated from Hebrew is equivalent to "Chanaan" translated from Greek.
- "Corn" encompasses all edible grains, such as wheat, rye, oats, barley, and maize.

[13] And at the second time Joseph was made known to his brethren; and Joseph's kindred was made known unto Pharaoh.

Joseph was not received by his brothers (who initially failed to recognize the divine import of his dreams, Gen 37:5-11) until the second time (Gen 50:17-18). Israel's Messiah likewise will not be received (Luke 9:22, 17:25) until the second time at the revival of Israel in the great tribulation (Zech 12:10-14, 2 Cor 3:16, Rev 7:3-8).

[14] Then sent Joseph, and called his father Jacob to him, and all his kindred, threescore and fifteen souls.

The tallies of "75" (here), "70" (Gen 46:27), and "66" (Gen 46:26) vary depending on which names are included. See the explanation at the end of this chapter.

[15] So Jacob went down into Egypt, and died, he, and our fathers,

[16] And were carried over into Sychem, and laid in the sepulchre that Abraham bought for a sum of money of the sons of Emmor the father of Sychem.

Three tombs in Genesis:
- Tomb of Shechem. When Abraham came to Shechem (Sychem, here; Sichem, Gen 12:6-7) he built an altar to the Lord, who promised the land to his descendants. There in Shechem he bought a sepulcher (crypt or tomb) from the Hamor (Emmor) family. Later Jacob bought "a parcel of a field," also from the Hamor family (Gen 33:19),

probably surrounding the sepulcher. "Our fathers," apparently the twelve patriarchs (Jacob's sons, Acts 7:8-9), are the ones buried in "the sepulcher that Abraham bought" in Shechem. Joseph is among those buried there (Gen 50:24-26, Heb 11:22, Josh 24:32). Although in verse 15 Stephen mentions Jacob, in verse 16 he reports only the burial of his twelve sons (Jacob was buried elsewhere).

-   Tomb of Hebron. Abraham also bought a cave and surrounding field in Machpelah (Hebron, Gen 23:16-20), where he was later buried (Gen 25:8-9) as were Sarah (Gen 23:19), Isaac, Rebekah, and Leah (Gen 49:30-31). Jacob left Canaan for Egypt due to famine (Gen 47:4), and then at his death (Gen 49:33, Heb 11:21) his body was brought back to Canaan and entombed in the cave in Hebron (Machpelah, Gen 50:13-14).
-   Tomb of Rachel. Rachel died and was buried between Bethel and Bethlehem (Gen 35:16, 19).

Language

"Shechem" and "Hamor" (Gen 34:18) translated from Hebrew are equivalent to "Sychem" and "Emmor" translated from Greek.

[17] But when the time of the promise drew nigh, which God had sworn to Abraham, the people grew and multiplied in Egypt,

-   Israel would be delivered as promised after four hundred years (Gen 15:13-14).
-   The people multiplied greatly (Exod 1:7, Neh 9:23) as the Lord promised Abraham (Gen 22:17). The 75 individuals who entered Egypt (Acts 7:14) grew to 600,000 men plus women and children at the time of the Exodus (Exod 12:37).

[18] Till another king arose, which knew not Joseph.

Joseph had saved Egypt from seven years of deadly famine and brought vast wealth to Pharaoh's household (Gen 47:13-26). Yet the new Pharaoh had no respect for Joseph or his people (Exod 1:8), and enslaved them (Exod 1:9-14).

[19] The same dealt subtilly with our kindred, and evil entreated our

fathers, so that they cast out their young children, to the end they might not live.

- Exod 1:16. Pharaoh had ordered the Hebrew midwives to slay all male infants, but they refused (Exod 1:17-21).
- Herod also ordered the murder of children (Matt 2:16).

[20] In which time Moses was born, and was exceeding fair, and nourished up in his father's house three months:

Exod 2:1-2. Moses' parents Amram and Jochebed (Num 26:59) courageously hid him for the first three months of his life because "they were not afraid of the king's commandment" (Heb 11:23).

[21] And when he was cast out, Pharaoh's daughter took him up, and nourished him for her own son.

- Exod 2:3-10. Moses' sister Miriam (Exod 15:20) hid him on the river, where he was found and adopted by Pharaoh's daughter.
- Pharaoh's genocidal plan of murdering all male infants (Exod 1:16) was resisted by the midwives (Exod 1:17-21), Moses' mother and sister (Exod 2:2-4), and finally Pharaoh's own daughter (Exod 2:5-10).

[22] And Moses was learned in all the wisdom of the Egyptians, and was mighty in words and in deeds.

[23] And when he was full forty years old, it came into his heart to visit his brethren the children of Israel.

- Moses was willing to forsake everything to save his people from bondage. He "refused to be called the son of Pharaoh's daughter; Choosing rather to suffer affliction with the people of God, than to enjoy the pleasures of sin for a season" (Heb 11:24-27).
- Moses was 40 years old when he left Egypt (age recorded only here), 80 years old when he returned to Egypt (Exod 7:7), and 120 years old when he died (Deut 34:7).
- The Lord Jesus left the glories of heaven to lay down his life for lost sinners (Phil 2:5-8).

[24] And seeing one of them suffer wrong, he defended him, and avenged him that was oppressed, and smote the Egyptian:

Exod 2:11-12. Moses killed an Egyptian who was beating a Hebrew slave. Moses then buried the body in the sand, thinking nobody saw him.

[25] For he supposed his brethren would have understood how that God by his hand would deliver them: but they understood not.

While living in Pharaoh's household Moses revealed himself to his people as their deliverer. Yet they rejected him, causing him to flee into the desert for 40 years until God called him back again (compare Acts 7:23 and Exod 7:7). Israel's failure to understand Moses' role in God's plan of deliverance cost them 40 extra years of bondage to Egypt. Israel's failure to recognize Jesus as their Messiah will cost them some 2,000 years of bondage to sin (Luke 19:44, John 1:11, Rom 11:25).

[26] And the next day he shewed himself unto them as they strove, and would have set them at one again, saying, Sirs, ye are brethren; why do ye wrong one to another?

Exod 2:13. Moses wanted to mediate between two angry Israelites and reconcile them ("set them at one again").

[27] But he that did his neighbour wrong thrust him away, saying, Who made thee a ruler and a judge over us?

[28] Wilt thou kill me, as thou diddest the Egyptian yesterday?

- Exod 2:14. Moses' own people rejected him and apparently reported him to the Egyptian authorities (Exod 2:15a).
- Jesus was also rejected at His first coming (Matt 21:23, 42).

[29] Then fled Moses at this saying, and was a stranger in the land of Madian, where he begat two sons.

Exod 2:15. Pharaoh wanted to kill Moses for slaying the Egyptian, so he fled from Egypt (Heb 11:27) to Midian. There he met Jethro and married the man's daughter Zipporah (Exod 2:15-21). They had two children, Gershom (Exod 2:22) and Eliezer (Exod 18:2-4).

Language
"Midian" (Exod 2:15,16) translated from Hebrew is equivalent to "Madian" translated from Greek.

[30] And when forty years were expired, there appeared to him in the wilderness of mount Sina an angel of the Lord in a flame of fire in a bush.

- Exod 3:1-2. "And the angel of the Lord appeared unto him in a flame of fire out of the midst of a bush: and he looked, and, behold, the bush burned with fire, and the bush was not consumed" (Exod 3:2).
- Thorns from a bramble bush (Luke 6:44) symbolize the curse (Gen 3:18, Isa 32:13, Matt 27:29), fire symbolizes judgment (Isa 10:17, 33:12, Heb 6:8), and "not consumed" symbolizes mercy (Lam 3:22, Mal 3:6). Moses is attracted not by God's judgment, but by His mercy.

145

Language
Scripture uses "Mount Sinai" (here "Mount Sina") interchangeably with "Mount Horeb" (Exod 3:1).

[31] When Moses saw it, he wondered at the sight: and as he drew near to behold it, the voice of the Lord came unto him,

Exod 3:3-4. The voice of God spoke to Moses "out of the midst of the bush" (Exod 3:4, Mark 12:26).

[32] Saying, I am the God of thy fathers, the God of Abraham, and the God of Isaac, and the God of Jacob. Then Moses trembled, and durst not behold.

Exod 3:6, also quoted in Luke 20:37. The Lord Jesus revealed that His is the voice of God that spoke from the burning bush (Exod 3:14, John 8:58).

[33] Then said the Lord to him, Put off thy shoes from thy feet: for the place where thou standest is holy ground.

Exod 3:5. Moses was told he was standing on holy ground because he was in God's presence (Psalm 114:7). The ground is cursed (Gen 5:29), but God's presence (Lev 11:45, Isa 6:3) makes a place holy (Josh 5:15, 1 Kings 8:10-11).

[34] I have seen, I have seen the affliction of my people which is in Egypt, and I have heard their groaning, and am come down to deliver them. And now come, I will send thee into Egypt.

- Exod 3:7-8a, 10. The Lord promised to bring the children of Israel out of Egypt and into Canaan, "a land flowing with milk and honey" (Exod 3:8b).
- Suffering people may feel that God has forgotten them. Still, He always has a timeline for deliverance, as seen in bringing Israel out from Egypt (after four hundred years of affliction, Acts 7:6), in sending forth His Son (Dan 9:25, Mark 1:15, Gal 4:4), in restoring the nation of Israel (Luke 21:24, Acts 1:6-7), and in returning to establish His kingdom (Matt 24:36, 44).

<u>Language</u>
Duplication (a word is repeated for emphasis) – "I have seen" is given twice to underscore how God never forgets His suffering people.

[35] This Moses whom they refused, saying, Who made thee a ruler and a judge? the same did God send to be a ruler and a deliverer by the hand of the angel which appeared to him in the bush.

"This Moses," the very man commissioned by God at the burning bush (Exod 3), was rejected by Israel at his first appearance, as was Christ (Luke 19:14). Moses was then accepted by Israel the second time, as will be Christ (Isa 11:10-12, Rom 11:25-27).

[36] He brought them out, after that he had shewed wonders and signs in the land of Egypt, and in the Red sea, and in the wilderness forty years.

- God punished Egypt with plagues (Exod 4-12) then blessed Israel with the miraculous crossing of the Red Sea (Exod 14, Heb 11:29).
- Miracles ("wonders and signs") during the forty years of wilderness

wanderings (Num 32:13) include the provision of food (Exod 16:35, Num 11:21) and water (Exod 15:25, 17:6, Num 20:11), a pillar of cloud and a pillar of fire (Exod 13:21), signs at Mount Sinai (Exod 20:18), miraculous victories in battle (Exod 17:11-13), giving and curing of Miriam's leprosy (Num 12:10-13), Korah's rebels swallowed up by the earth (Num 16:31-33), budding of Aaron's rod (Num 17:5-8), healing through a brass serpent (Num 21:8-9), and clothing that never wore out (Deut 29:5).

[37] This is that Moses, which said unto the children of Israel, A prophet shall the Lord your God raise up unto you of your brethren, like unto me; him shall ye hear.

- Stephen quotes Deut 18:15 to show Israel's leaders that Moses had predicted the very Person they are rejecting (John 5:46). Simon Peter quoted these same words (Acts 3:22) and declared that they are fulfilled in Jesus the Messiah (Acts 3:26). Many who saw Christ's miracles recognized Him as "that prophet" like Moses (John 6:14).
- Moses was first rejected by Israel then later accepted (Acts 7:35). Christ likewise was first rejected by Israel and later will be accepted by them. For a list of many other ways in which Jesus and Moses are alike, see comments on Acts 3:22-23.

147

[38] This is he, that was in the church in the wilderness with the angel which spake to him in the mount Sina, and with our fathers: who received the lively oracles to give unto us:

- "Church" can refer to any assembly of people, such as that of Israel (present verse), Christians (Acts 9:31), or even pagans (Acts 19:37).
- Moses was at Mount Sinai ("Sina") with the assembly of Israelites, who were the forefathers of Stephen's audience today. Through the angel of the Lord (as in Exod 3:2) Moses received God's spoken law ("oracles" in Rom 3:1-2), which he wrote down (Exod 24:4) and is said to be alive ("lively" here, "quick" in Heb 4:12).

Language
- "Oracles" means "spoken words of scripture."
- "Lively oracles" means "living words."

[39] To whom our fathers would not obey, but thrust him from them, and in their hearts turned back again into Egypt,

- The children of Israel asked, "Were it not better for us to return into Egypt? And they said one to another, Let us make a captain, and let us return into Egypt" (Num 14:3b-4).
- Israel, likewise, by not obeying the gospel (Rom 10:16), has turned from spiritual freedom back to the bondage of the law (Gal 5:1), which has no power to free from sin (Rom 7:5-11).

[40] Saying unto Aaron, Make us gods to go before us: for as for this Moses, which brought us out of the land of Egypt, we wot not what is become of him.

Exod 32:1. Moses was with God on Mount Sinai "forty days and forty nights" (Exod 24:18). He gave Moses the precious gift of His word, "two tables of testimony, tables of stone, written with the finger of God" (Exod 31:18). Yet the people became impatient while Moses was away and asked his brother Aaron to construct idols for them to worship.

[41] And they made a calf in those days, and offered sacrifice unto the idol, and rejoiced in the works of their own hands.

- Exod 32:4a and Jer 1:16. The people convinced Aaron to make a golden calf. Despite **God** delivering them miraculously from Egypt, they looked to the idol **they** had made "and they said, These be thy gods, O Israel, which brought thee up out of the land of Egypt" (Exod 32:4b).
- The Lord forgave their sin, yet the children of Israel continued to rebel. The last straw was when Joshua and Caleb brought a favorable reconnaissance report from the land of Canaan (Num 14:6-9), yet the people rejected them and "all the congregation bade stone them with stones" (Num 14:10). The Lord then "sware in my wrath that they should not enter into my rest" (the promised land; Psalm 95:10-11, quoted in Heb 3:7-11) and condemned everyone except Joshua and Caleb to die during 40 years of wandering in the desert (Num 14:30-33).

- Like a good preacher, Stephen reminds Israel of their sin. By focusing on Israel's guilt rather than greatness, he undoubtedly makes his audience uncomfortable.[183] Yet Stephen plans only to increase the intensity of his message further. Here he preaches that *ancient* Israel rejected God and "rejoiced in the works of their own hands." Soon he will preach that *present-day* Israel rejects God, who "dwelleth not in temples made with [their own] hands" (Acts 7:48-50).

<u>Language</u>
Hebraism (a Hebrew manner of expression) – "works of the hands" can refer to the product of human labor (such idols, 2 Kings 19:18, Psalm 135:15) or of God's (such as creation, Psalm 8:6, 102:25).

[42] Then God turned, and gave them up to worship the host of heaven; as it is written in the book of the prophets, O ye house of Israel, have ye offered to me slain beasts and sacrifices by the space of forty years in the wilderness?

- Quoting Amos 5:25. The prophet Amos told how Israel during the forty years of wilderness wanderings (and repeatedly afterward) offered sacrifices to God, but then turned from Him and worshiped idols representing bulls (1 Kings 18:26, 2 Kings 17:16, Neh 9:18) and planets (2 Kings 23:5, Jer 19:13, Ezek 8:16). When Israel obstinately persisted, God "gave them up" to their sin as He did to pagan Gentiles (Rom 1:24, 26, 28).
- Stephen previously spoke of Israel's sin of idolatry (Acts 7:41) and now turns up the heat by describing God as being so disgusted with Israel's idolatry that He gave them up to their sin. Stephen implies that Israel now offers temple sacrifices, but rejects Jesus as their Messiah, so God will likewise turn from them and give them up to their sin and subsequent judgment as He did in the wilderness (Exod 32:20, 27-28, 35, Psalm 81:12).

[43] Yea, ye took up the tabernacle of Moloch, and the star of your god Remphan, figures which ye made to worship them: and I will carry you

---

[183] The golden calf incident is so scandalous that the ancient historian Josephus conspicuously omits it when writing Israel's history in *Antiquity of the Jews*.

away beyond Babylon.

- Quoting Amos 5:26-27 to show that Israel was to worship the Lord through the tabernacle (the precursor of the temple) but made an idol of it by worshipping pagan gods. So too Israel now makes an idol of the temple by counting it more important than Jesus their Messiah.
- The northern kingdom of Israel had gone into "captivity beyond Damascus" (Amos 5:27) when judged for its sin and conquered by Assyria (2 Kings 17:21-23). The southern kingdom of Judah later went into captivity "beyond Babylon" (2 Chron 36:20); they subsequently returned (books of Ezra and Nehemiah), and Stephen speaks to their descendants today. Stephen changes the Amos quotation from "Damascus" to "Babylon" as a sharp reminder to his listeners that the people of Judah were conquered too, not just the people of Israel. They were once the recipients of God's judgment and will receive His judgment again if they do not repent.
- The use of the word "Babylon" also foreshadows Babylon's future wickedness and judgment in the great tribulation (Rev 17-18).
- Stephen is a defendant on trial but chooses to act like a preacher. He wants his audience to feel the weight of their sin and repent.

[44] Our fathers had the tabernacle of witness in the wilderness, as he had appointed, speaking unto Moses, that he should make it according to the fashion that he had seen.

The tabernacle was a sacred worship center designed by God and built under Moses (Exod 25:9, 25:40, 26:1-31:18), even though sometimes people wrongfully used it for idolatry.

[45] Which also our fathers that came after brought in with Jesus into the possession of the Gentiles, whom God drave out before the face of our fathers, unto the days of David;

- Joshua led the Israelite forefathers to conquer the land of Canaan as described in the book of Joshua (summarized in Acts 13:19). He made a semi-permanent home for the tabernacle in Shiloh (Josh 18:1), where it remained for several hundred years (1 Sam 1:3) until

it was eclipsed by Solomon's temple (1 Kings 7:51).
- "Jesus" is the Greek equivalent of the Hebrew word "Joshua." The name "Jesus" is transliterated (rather than translated as "Joshua") to attest that His return is foreshadowed by Joshua, who attacked an accursed city (Josh 6:17, Rev 17-18); was preceded by two witnesses (Josh 2:1 and Heb 11:31, Rev 11:3); after seven days (Josh 6:15 and Heb 11:30, Dan 9:27); accompanied by celestial signs (Josh 10:12-13, Matt 24:29); to ultimately subdue the land (Deut 31:3-8, Rev 19:6); and to establish a theocracy (Judg 8:23, Psalm 2:6-9).

Language
- "Fashion" means "pattern."
- "Drave out" means "drove out."

[46] Who found favour before God, and desired to find a tabernacle for the God of Jacob.

Quoting Psalm 132:5, which refers to 2 Sam 6:17 and 1 Chron 15:1 , when David brought the ark of the covenant to Jerusalem and placed it inside a tent ("tabernacle").

[47] But Solomon built him an house.

- Solomon built David a "house" both by erecting the temple planned by his father David (2 Sam 7:5-11) and by establishing the family line promised by God (2 Sam 7:12-16).
- God performs His will throughout the world (including Mesopotamia, Haran, Canaan, Egypt, Midian, and Babylon), and cannot be confined to any one location. Turning the mobile tabernacle that God designed (Acts 7:44) into an immobile temple of human design hints at people trying to manage God by confining Him to one place. David proposed a temple (2 Sam 7:1-2), but the Lord never asked for one and only reluctantly agreed (2 Sam 7:5-11) to allow Solomon to build one (1 Kings 6:1-38).

[48] Howbeit the most High dwelleth not in temples made with hands; as saith the prophet,

- Stephen here speaks to a Jewish audience. The apostle Paul at Athens will preach the same message to pagan Gentiles, saying "God ... dwelleth not in temples made with hands (Acts 17:24).
- When Solomon dedicated the first temple, God filled it with His presence (1 Kings 8:1-11, 2 Chron 5:13-14, 7:1-3). However, He did not accept sacrifices offered with a rebellious attitude (Acts 7:39, 1 Sam 15:22, Jer 7:22-23), a disobedient form of worship (Acts 7:42, 2 Chron 33:3-5, Hosea 8:14), or a stiff-necked heart (Acts 7:51, Isa 1:11-15, Jer 7:11).
- That first temple was destroyed, and a second temple was built (Ezra 3:12, 6:15) and recently expanded (John 2:20). However, there has been no recorded manifestation of God's presence there.
- The Lord Jesus was accused of saying, "I will destroy this temple that is made with hands, and within three days I will build another made without hands" (Mark 14:58). His words were misunderstood and twisted, for He spoke of his body being crucified and resurrected (John 2:18-22) and foresaw the temple's destruction by war (Matt 24:1-2).

- Stephen's words have also been twisted and he has been accused of saying, "Jesus of Nazareth shall destroy this place" (Acts 6:14). He could favorably rebut the charges by praising the beauty of the temple (Luke 21:5). Instead, he offends his judges by preaching that they have made an idol of the temple by desiring it more than God. Indeed, Isaiah preached that temple sacrifices made with an impure heart are like idolatry because empty rituals do not connect one to God (Isa 66:3; Stephen will next quote Isa 66:1-2).
- Stephen was brought before the council to answer the (false) charge that he speaks against the temple (Acts 6:13). His statement in this verse has not helped his case. Yet Stephen has been called by God to preach (Acts 6:10) and will not let even his own life stand in the way of fulfilling his calling. The apostle Paul will live the same way, and state "neither count I my life dear unto myself, so that I might finish my course with joy, and the ministry, which I have received of the Lord Jesus, to testify the gospel of the grace of God" (Acts 20:24).
- God's temple is no longer a manmade building (2 Cor 5:1). Since Pentecost His Holy Spirit dwells within the body of each believer (1 Cor 3:17, 6:19).

[49] Heaven is my throne, and earth is my footstool: what house will ye build me? saith the Lord: or what is the place of my rest?

[50] Hath not my hand made all these things?

- Quoting Isa 66:1 – 66:2a.
- Stephen does not criticize the temple. God the Son taught at the temple and defended its sanctity (Luke 19:45-47). God the Holy Spirit has been working through the apostles' preaching on the temple grounds (Acts 2:46, 3:1, 5:12, 5:42) to save thousands of souls (Acts 2:41, 4:4). Instead, Stephen preaches against those who would make an idol of the temple by trying to shut up God there. The first temple's builder, Solomon, knew that the Creator of the universe is too great to be confined within a building (1 Kings 8:27). Rather, His temple is all of creation (Isa 40:12).
- Humans do God no favor by building temples, for God made the physical universe (Col 1:16-17) and gave people the ability to create (1 Cor 3:10); therefore God is the actual Builder (Heb 3:3-4, 11:10). What God truly desires is "him that is poor and of a contrite spirit, and trembleth at my word" (Isa 66:2b).

Language
Anthropomorphism (God condescends to describe Himself in human terms) – God does not have a human hand, although His creative ability can be likened to one.

[51] Ye stiffnecked and uncircumcised in heart and ears, ye do always resist the Holy Ghost: as your fathers did, so do ye.

- With impure ("uncircumcised," Isa 52:1) hearts (Lev 26:41, Deut 10:16, Jer 9:26) and ears (Jer 6:10), the leaders of Israel stubbornly (Exod 33:3-5) resist (Acts 7:57) the Holy Ghost.
- An ordinary, self-preserving man would flatter his judges and deflect the charges against him. Stephen, however, is filled with the Holy Ghost (Acts 7:55) and preaches as God moves him.

[52] Which of the prophets have not your fathers persecuted? and they have slain them which shewed before of the coming of the Just One; of whom ye have been now the betrayers and murderers:

Stephen deliberately provokes his hearers to either acknowledge Israel's sin or publicly show themselves to be no different than their predecessors ("your fathers," John 8:44), who rebelled against God and Moses and who murdered the prophets (2 Chron 36:15-16, Neh 9:26, Jer 2:30, Luke 13:34). Stephen baits them with sarcasm by asking, "can you name any prophet your fathers didn't persecute?" He adds that they murdered both the Messiah (1 Thes 2:15) and the prophets who foretold Him.

[53] Who have received the law by the disposition of angels, and have not kept it.

- Moses received the law through the "angel of the Lord" (Acts 7:30, 35, Gal 3:19, Heb 2:2).
- Stephen holds his audience to a high level of accountability because of the special revelation they have received (Rom 2:17-27, contrast Acts 4:13a).

Language
"Disposition" here means "direction."

[54] When they heard these things, they were cut to the heart, and they gnashed on him with their teeth.

- Stephen, acting as a preacher rather than a defendant, has accelerated his powerful exhortation by making a personal attack against his listeners' moral integrity (Acts 7:51-53); at this they are overcome with maddening fury (contrast James 1:19-20). If they were not guilty of Stephen's accusations, they would not respond so angrily.
- They grind their teeth in anger at Stephen, but ultimately, they rage against God. In so doing, they make a horrific foreshadowing of the eternal condition of the lost (Matt 8:12).

[55] But he, being full of the Holy Ghost, looked up stedfastly into heaven, and saw the glory of God, and Jesus standing on the right hand of God,

Stephen has lived his brief life in communion with the Lord Jesus, beholding Him spiritually (2 Cor 3:18, Heb 12:2), and now seeing His very face (Psalm 11:7, 1 Cor 13:12). **Stephen is God's temple** (His presence indwells Stephen) and they will tear him down as they did Christ (John 2:19-21).

[56] And said, Behold, I see the heavens opened, and the Son of man standing on the right hand of God.

- Other prophets have likewise received visions of God's throne (Isa 6, Ezek 1, Rev 4). Yet it is Daniel who specifically proclaims the "Son of man" as the One with direct access to God's presence, unto whom God will one day give rule over the entire world (Dan 7:9-10, 13-14).
- Stephen stands accused of blaspheming the "holy temple" (Acts 6:13), where God once dwelt (Isa 37:16, 2 Kings 19:15) and had ordained priests to mediate between Him and the people (Heb 5:1). In Stephen's vision Jesus (Matt 12:6) is not seated (Psalm 110:1, Mark 16:19) but standing in the priest's role (Heb 10:11) as a Mediator (1 Tim 2:5). The temple is no longer needed because the believer can enter God's presence directly through Christ (Heb 10:19-20).

[57] Then they cried out with a loud voice, and stopped their ears, and ran upon him with one accord,

[58] And cast him out of the city, and stoned him: and the witnesses laid down their clothes at a young man's feet, whose name was Saul.

- Stephen's words identify Jesus Christ as the Son of man and imply that God approves of Stephen and his message and disapproves of his opponents, the Sanhedrin; this fills them with violent rage (Prov 4:17).
- Previously the high priest accused Jesus of blasphemy and sentenced Him to death when He indicated that He is the Son of Man (Matt 26:64-66) described by Daniel the prophet (Dan 7:9-10, 13-14). So too now they equate Stephen's words envisioning Jesus as the Son of Man (Acts 7:56) with blasphemy and believe they now

> have reason to slay him. They refuse to listen further (Prov 15:32, Zech 7:11) and punish Stephen with death (Deut 17:6-7).
- Saul fully approves (Acts 22:20) of this stoning (Lev 24:16, 23), which is unlawful under Roman law (John 18:31). Today's execution also violates Jewish law because "in capital cases a verdict of acquittal may be reached on the same day, but a verdict of conviction not until the following day."[184]
- Saul is a "young man" now. By the time he is converted (Acts 9), completes three missionary journeys (Acts 13-27), and reaches Rome (Acts 28), he will (in one letter) call himself "Paul the aged" (Philem 9).

[59] And they stoned Stephen, calling upon God, and saying, Lord Jesus, receive my spirit.

[60] And he kneeled down, and cried with a loud voice, Lord, lay not this sin to their charge. And when he had said this, he fell asleep.

- Stephen prays as Jesus did, although in the opposite order of Christ, who prayed first for others (Luke 23:34) and then for Himself (Luke 23:46).
- Stephen prays for forgiveness for the nation of Israel in rejecting their Messiah at His first appearance that they might receive Him at His second, as they had done with Joseph (Acts 7:13) and Moses (Acts 7:35).
- Stephen is "faithful unto death" (Rev 2:10). Although his body "sleeps" in death (John 11:13, 1 Cor 15:20, 1 Thes 4:14), his soul is with Christ (2 Cor 5:8, Phil 1:23).

Language
Irony (unexpected outcome or event) – Stephen's unjust execution proves his point that Israel's leaders are "uncircumcised in heart" (Acts 7:51).

Correspondence (parallel words and ideas):
Acts 7:1-43:   Mesopotamia -> Abraham -> Joseph -> Moses -> Resistance
Acts 7:44-50: Wilderness -> Joshua -> David -> Solomon -> Resistance

---

[184] *Mishna*, Sanhedrin 4.1

Persuasive Speech

Stephen's Spirit-filled sermon shows a mastery of persuasive speech (rhetoric).

Introduction *(exordium)* – "And he said, Men, brethren, and fathers, hearken" (Acts 7:2a).

Narrative *(narratio)* – Stephen lays the groundwork needed to appeal to Israel's leaders to recognize Jesus the Messiah. He contrasts those of Israel's past who made God-honoring choices with those who made self-serving choices. He points to Moses and Joseph, who were rejected at their first appearance and accepted at their second appearance (Acts 7:2b - 7:34).

Thesis *(propositio)* – rather than submitting to God's messengers, Israel has rejected those sent by God, as they did Moses with the words "who made thee a ruler and a judge?" (Acts 7:35).

Arguments *(probatio)* – after rejecting God's messenger Moses, Israel went from bad to worse by worshipping the golden calf and other false deities until the Lord punished them with exile into Babylon. Israel's leaders, in rejecting God's messenger Jesus, technically do not worship false gods, yet have made an idol of the temple. Like Israel of old they will also face God's judgment (Acts 7:36-50).

Final appeal *(peroratio)* – Stephen makes a passionate appeal to Israel's leaders to acknowledge their role in the nation's disobedience through their disastrous mistreatment of their Messiah, Jesus (Acts 7:51-53).

Teaching Questions

<u>Question</u>: What are the themes of Stephen's speech?
<u>Answer</u>:

1. The great men of Israel's history are those who responded to God's call to take courageous action, such as Abraham (Acts 7:4), Jacob (Acts 7:15), Moses (Acts 7:36), and Joshua (Acts 7:45). Contrasted are those who promoted their own ambitions, such as Jacob's first ten sons selling Joseph (Acts 7:9), Moses killing the Egyptian (Acts 7:24), Aaron and the Israelites wandering in the wilderness (Acts 7:39-41), those who value the temple above God (Acts 7:48-50), and all who stubbornly resist the words of God's prophets (Acts 7:51-52).

2. The people failed to recognize God's servants when they appeared the **first time**, such as with Joseph (Acts 7:9), Moses (Acts 7:23-29), and Jesus (Acts 7:52). Yet the people recognized God's servants when they appeared the **second time**, such as with Joseph (Acts 7:13), Moses (Acts 7:35), and now (Stephen hopes) with Jesus (Heb 9:28).

Question: Many of Stephen's Old Testament quotations do not precisely match the associated Hebrew text because Stephen, under the guidance of the Holy Spirit, cites these verses in an interpretive rather than a direct manner. Yet some people teach that instead of quoting the Hebrew Old Testament, Stephen quotes the Greek Septuagint. Does the manuscript evidence support this idea?
Answer: No. "The text of the Septuagint is contained in a few early, but not necessarily reliable, manuscripts ... from the 4th century and ... from the 5th century" AD.[185] There are no existing Septuagint manuscripts written before the time of Christ that contain any text quoted anywhere in the New Testament.[186]

Question: Do Stephen's quotations consistently match the Greek Septuagint?
Answer: No. Stephen changes "Damascus" to "Babylon" (Acts 7:43) under the guidance of the Holy Spirit (Acts 6:5), and his quotation does **not** match the Septuagint text of Amos 5:27.

Challenge Questions

1. Why does Stephen take so much time reciting Israel's history to men who are experts in Israel's history?
2. Abraham is first called when in Mesopotamia (Acts 7:2) and responds by traveling to Haran (Charran, Acts 7:4). He does not actually leave for Canaan until his second calling (Gen 12:1-4) after his father dies (Gen 11:32). Does Abraham sin in delaying his journey?
3. Why is the Lord Jesus "standing on the right hand of God" (Acts 7:55) when he is usually described as seated at God's right hand (Acts 2:34)?

---

[185] "Septuagint." *Encyclopedia Britannica Online*, accessed 29 Nov 2019
[186] Floyd Nolan Jones, *The Septuagint: A Critical Analysis*, 6th edition (The Woodlands, TX: KingsWord Press, 2000), p.21

The following is referred to in the comments for Acts 7:14.

Genesis 46:5-27
[5] And Jacob rose up from Beer-sheba: and the sons of Israel carried Jacob their father, and their little ones, and their wives, in the wagons which Pharaoh had sent to carry him.
[6] And they took their cattle, and their goods, which they had gotten in the land of Canaan, and came into Egypt, Jacob, and all his seed with him:
[7] His sons, and his sons' sons with him, his daughters, and his sons' daughters, and all his seed brought he with him into Egypt.
[8] And these are the names of the children of Israel, which came into Egypt, Jacob and his sons: Reuben, Jacob's firstborn.
[9] And the sons of Reuben; Hanoch, and Phallu, and Hezron, and Carmi
[10] And the sons of Simeon; Jemuel, and Jamin, and Ohad, and Jachin, and Zohar, and Shaul the son of a Canaanitish woman.
[11] And the sons of Levi; Gershon, Kohath, and Merari.
[12] And the sons of Judah; Er, and Onan, and Shelah, and Pharez, and Zerah: but Er and Onan died in the land of Canaan. And the sons of Pharez were Hezron and Hamul.
[13] And the sons of Issachar; Tola, and Phuvah, and Job, and Shimron.
[14] And the sons of Zebulun; Sered, and Elon, and Jahleel.
[15] These be the sons of Leah, which she bare unto Jacob in Padan-aram, with his daughter Dinah: all the souls of his sons and his daughters were thirty and three.
[16] And the sons of Gad; Ziphion, and Haggi, Shuni, and Ezbon, Eri, and Arodi, and Areli.
[17] And the sons of Asher; Jimnah, and Ishuah, and Isui, and Beriah, and Serah their sister: and the sons of Beriah; Heber, and Malchiel.
[18] These are the sons of Zilpah, whom Laban gave to Leah his daughter, and these she bare unto Jacob, even sixteen souls.
[19] The sons of Rachel Jacob's wife; Joseph, and Benjamin.
[20] And unto Joseph in the land of Egypt were born Manasseh and Ephraim, which Asenath the daughter of Poti-pherah priest of On bare unto him.
[21] And the sons of Benjamin were Belah, and Becher, and Ashbel, Gera, and Naaman, Ehi, and Rosh, Muppim, and Huppim, and Ard.
[22] These are the sons of Rachel, which were born to Jacob: all the souls were fourteen.

[23] And the sons of Dan; Hushim.
[24] And the sons of Naphtali; Jahzeel, and Guni, and Jezer, and Shillem.
[25] These are the sons of Bilhah, which Laban gave unto Rachel his daughter, and she bare these unto Jacob: all the souls were seven.
[26] All the souls that came with Jacob into Egypt, which came out of his loins, besides Jacob's sons' wives, all the souls were threescore and six;
[27] And the sons of Joseph, which were born him in Egypt, were two souls: all the souls of the house of Jacob, which came into Egypt, were threescore and ten.

Three different ways to add this list of names:
Seventy sons and grandchildren - The number 70 is commonly reported in scripture (Gen 46:27 above, Exod 1:5, Deut 10:22) and contains all of Jacob's sons and grandchildren. Subtotals for each of his four wives: 33 for Leah (vs. 15), 16 for Zilpah (vs. 18), 14 for Rachel (vs. 22), and 7 for Bilhah (vs. 25), totaling 70.
Sixty-six travelled to Egypt - The list of those who journeyed to Egypt with Jacob totals 66 (Gen 46:26 above). Starting with the 70 above, add Dinah (vs. 15, not included in the sum of 70), subtract Er and Onan who died in the land of Canaan (vs. 12), and subtract Joseph, Ephraim, and Manasseh, who were already in Egypt (vs. 20).
Seventy-five wives, children, and grandchildren - The names of all of Jacob's household listed above totals 75 (Acts 7:14), although not everyone took the trip to Egypt. Starting with the 70 above, add Dinah (vs. 15, not in the sum of 70) and Jacob's four wives, Leah (vs. 15), Zilpah (vs. 18), Rachel (vs. 22), and Bilhah (vs. 25) for a total of 75. This sum matches Stephen's description in Acts 7:14 of "Jacob … and all his kindred, threescore and fifteen souls" (although only 66 of these went with him to Egypt).

Acts Chapter 8

[1] And Saul was consenting unto his death. And at that time there was a great persecution against the church which was at Jerusalem; and they were all scattered abroad throughout the regions of Judæa and Samaria, except the apostles.

- Saul is a most zealous Pharisee (Phil 3:5-6) as well as a Roman citizen (Acts 16:37). He was born in Tarsus and educated in the Greek language (Acts 21:37) and culture (Acts 17:28) but raised in Jerusalem, where he was taught the law of Israel by the Pharisee Gamaliel (Acts 22:3). Saul had approved of Stephen's death (Acts 7:58, 22:20), thereby placing himself among those who murder God's prophets (Luke 11:47-48). He now brings furious persecution (Acts 8:3), which unintentionally results in believers bringing the gospel to Judea (1 Thes 2:14), Samaria (Acts 8:5), and regions beyond (Acts 11:19).
- The disciples go forth as Jesus did (John 20:21), leaving their homes (Matt 19:29, Luke 9:58), forsaking family (Matt 10:37), sowing spiritual seed (Matt 13:3-9), performing miracles (Mark 16:17-18), enduring persecution (Matt 5:11-12), baptizing converts (Matt 28:19), and working by the power of the Lord (Matt 28:18).

[2] And devout men carried Stephen to his burial, and made great lamentation over him.

- Burial is very important to Jewish people (Acts 7:16), and a lack of burial is dreadful (Isa 14:20, Jer 14:16). The rich man was buried, but poor Lazarus was not (Luke 16:22). Moses was buried by God (Deut 34:5-6), but Jezebel's body was eaten by dogs (2 King 9:33-35). The Philistines disrespectfully displayed King Saul's body on a wall (1 Sam 31:8-10), but courageous men retrieved and buried it (1 Sam 31:12-13). Jesus' body was buried by devout men (Joseph of Arimathea and Nicodemas, John 19:38-40), as is now Stephen's body.

- Condemned criminals at their death "shall not be lamented,"[187] but Stephen's friends know that he suffered a martyr's death (Acts 7:59-60). That men committed to the ways of God ("devout men") are memorializing Stephen means that he lived his life in a praiseworthy manner.
- Devout men here make lamentation as had been made for Jacob (Gen 50:10), Jephthah's daughter (Judg 11:40), the smitten of Beth-shemesh (1 Sam 6:19), Samuel (1 Sam 25:1), Saul and Jonathan (2 Sam 1:17-27), Abner (2 Sam 3:33), Josiah (2 Chron 35:25), Zedekiah (Jer 34:5), Jerusalem (book of Lamentations), the slain children of Bethlehem (Jer 31:15, Matt 2:18), and Jesus (Luke 23:27). Such lamentation had not been made for Jehoiakim (Jer 22:18) or those slain at the fall of Jerusalem (Jer 16:4), will not rightly be made for Babylon the great (Rev 18:9), nor made at all for the slain at Christ's second coming (Jer 25:33).

[3] As for Saul, he made havock of the church, entering into every house, and haling men and women committed them to prison.

- Saul's misdirected zeal (Rom 10:2; see also King Saul in 2 Sam 21:1-2) leads him to use imprisonment (Acts 22:19), torture (Acts 26:11), and murder (Acts 22:4). His destructive actions go beyond those of "many my equals in mine own nation" because he is "more exceedingly zealous of the traditions of my fathers" (Gal 1:14).
- Saul will later lament how "beyond measure I persecuted the church of God, and wasted it" (Gal 1:13). Despite God's merciful forgiveness at conversion (1 Tim 1:13), Saul will never forgive himself (1 Cor 15:9).

Language
"Hale" means to haul or to drag away by force.

[4] Therefore they that were scattered abroad went every where preaching the word.

Saul's persecution is meant to destroy, but instead (Phil 1:12-13) it

---

[187] *Babylonian Talmud*, Sanhedrin 46b

produces a harvest of souls (Acts 8:6) as the disciples are scattered like seed (Luke 8:5-8). From this torrent of affliction the Lord calls Philip the evangelist (Acts 8:5-40).

[5] Then Philip went down to the city of Samaria, and preached Christ unto them.

- The Israelites conquered Canaan under Joshua (Acts 7:45), who granted the hilly region of Samaria ("mount Ephraim," Josh 17:15) to his tribe Ephraim (Num 13:8). There he established a temporary national capital at Shechem (Josh 24:1) and placed the tabernacle at Shiloh (Josh 18:1). Samaria's prominence was later lost when the ark of the covenant was captured by the Philistines and subsequently brought by King David to Jerusalem, the new national capital. When the nation divided after the death of Solomon, Ephraim separated from Judah and joined the northern kingdom, where the city of Samaria later became the capital (1 Kings 16:29).
- Hundreds of years later the conquering Assyrians exiled most Ephraimites living in the region of Samaria and replaced them with Gentiles (2 Kings 17:24) who, over time, intermarried with local Israelites and were considered half-Jews. These people, called "Samaritans" (2 Kings 17:29), learned Judaism but mixed it with idolatry (2 Kings 17:24-41). The Jews refused to allow the Samaritans to help them rebuild the temple (Ezra 4:1-3) and condemned mixed marriages with them (Ezra 9:1-3). These rejected people built their own temple at Mount Gerizim (John 4:20) and were regarded as loathsome (John 8:48) foreigners (Luke 17:18) by Jews.
- Philip's evangelism of Samaria is very significant, given the long-standing hostility between Jews and Samaritans. Philip was previously chosen to act as a deacon and is apparently a Hellenistic or "Grecian" Jew (Acts 6:1-6) born outside of Jerusalem; as such he is naturally more comfortable reaching out to a group such as the Samaritans. Philip wants to tell others because he is grateful for what Jesus has done for him, as the Samaritan cleansed of leprosy (Luke 17:16-19). Philip's compassion follows the example of the "good Samaritan" (Luke 10:29-37).
- This Philip goes forth as an evangelist (Acts 21:8), whereas Philip the apostle (Acts 1:13) stays in Jerusalem with the other apostles

(Acts 8:1). Two apostles (Peter and John) will soon visit Samaria (Acts 8:14).

[6] And the people with one accord gave heed unto those things which Philip spake, hearing and seeing the miracles which he did.

[7] For unclean spirits, crying with loud voice, came out of many that were possessed with them: and many taken with palsies, and that were lame, were healed.

[8] And there was great joy in that city.

- The Holy Ghost works through Philip the evangelist in Samaria, as He did through the apostles in Jerusalem (Acts 5:12,14). Not only does he heal, but he also casts out unclean spirits (Mark 16:17), as did the apostles (Acts 5:16) and as will Paul (Acts 16:16, 19:12).
- The Samaritans who have faith in Christ are filled with joy (1 Peter 1:8), as will be the Gentile believers (Acts 13:52).
- In Jerusalem the disciples met in the temple (Acts 2:46, 5:42), but since the persecution will be meeting in house churches (Acts 12:12, 1 Cor 16:19, Col 4:15, Philem 2).

[9] But there was a certain man, called Simon, which beforetime in the same city used sorcery, and bewitched the people of Samaria, giving out that himself was some great one:

[10] To whom they all gave heed, from the least to the greatest, saying, This man is the great power of God.

[11] And to him they had regard, because that of long time he had bewitched them with sorceries.

- Simon the sorcerer promotes himself as a demigod through Satanic power, as did the Egyptian magicians (Exod 7:11, 22, 8:7, 2 Tim 3:8) before they were thwarted by God's power (Exod 8:19, 9:11). Promoters of witchcraft such as the witch of Endor (1 Sam 28:7-25), Jezebel (2 Kings 9:22), Elymas (Acts 13:6,8), and the sorcerers of Babylon (Rev 18:23) will be eternally condemned (Rev 21:8, 22:15).

- Simon the sorcerer is like Philip the Evangelist in that both men work wonders (Acts 8:9,11 and 8:6,13) that amaze (8:10 and 8:6,13) crowds (8:9-10 and 8:6) who "gave heed" to their message (8:10 and 8:6) and attribute their power to God (8:10 and 8:12). The two men are not alike in that Simon seeks his own glory (8:9,19), whereas Philip works to bring glory to Christ (8:12).
- Simon the sorcerer foreshadows the one "whose coming is after the working of Satan with all power and signs and lying wonders" (2 Thes 2:9), whose false miracles deceive the whole world (Matt 24:24, Rev 13:3-4, 11-15, 18:23).

[12] But when they believed Philip preaching the things concerning the kingdom of God, and the name of Jesus Christ, they were baptized, both men and women.

The kingdom of God is spiritual (Rom 14:17) until Christ returns to establish His physical kingdom on earth (Acts 1:6-7, Rev 11:15).

[13] Then Simon himself believed also: and when he was baptized, he continued with Philip, and wondered, beholding the miracles and signs which were done.

Only God (Psalm 44:21, Acts 15:8) and Simon (2 Cor 13:5, 2 Peter 1:10) know if Simon's belief is genuine faith (Rom 3:22, 1 Peter 1:9) or not (James 2:19).

[14] Now when the apostles which were at Jerusalem heard that Samaria had received the word of God, they sent unto them Peter and John:

- Before His resurrection, Christ gave the apostles (including Peter and John) a very focused commission. "These twelve Jesus sent forth, and commanded them, saying, Go not into the way of the Gentiles, and into any city of the Samaritans enter ye not: But go rather to the lost sheep of the house of Israel" (Matt 10:5-6). Therefore the original disciples and the converts on Pentecost are all Jews (Acts 2:5).
- After His resurrection, Christ gave His followers an entirely new commission. "And ye shall be witnesses unto me both in Jerusalem,

and in all Judaea, and in Samaria, and unto the uttermost part of the earth" (Acts 1:8b). Philip has followed Christ's instructions regarding Samaria and many Samaritans have responded to the gospel. The apostles now send a delegation to investigate this significant new development.

[15] Who, when they were come down, prayed for them, that they might receive the Holy Ghost:

[16] (For as yet he was fallen upon none of them: only they were baptized in the name of the Lord Jesus.)

[17] Then laid they their hands on them, and they received the Holy Ghost.

- Although for hundreds of years the "Jews have [had] no dealings with Samaritans" (John 4:9b), the apostles now work directly to fulfill Christ's commission (Acts 1:8) by bringing them the gospel.

- The Holy Ghost so far has been given to those baptized under the apostles' ministry to the Jews in Jerusalem (Acts 2:38) but not yet under Philip's ministry to the Samaritans (Acts 8:12).
- The Samaritans and the disciples of John the Baptist (Acts 19:6) receive the Holy Ghost through the laying on of hands. The Jews (Acts 2:1-4) and the Gentiles (Acts 10:44) receive the Holy Ghost without the laying on of hands.
- The Samaritans' receiving the Holy Ghost through the actions of the Jewish apostles shows the Samaritans the authority of the apostles (2 Peter 3:2) and indicates to the apostles God's acceptance of the believing Samaritans (Rom 3:22).
- Peter exercises the authority given to him by Christ when he uses spiritual "keys" (Matt 16:18-19) to open the door (1 Cor 16:9) of the kingdom of God by bringing the gospel to the Samaritans as he had to the Jews (Acts 2) and will to the Gentiles (Acts 10).

[18] And when Simon saw that through laying on of the apostles' hands the Holy Ghost was given, he offered them money,

[19] Saying, Give me also this power, that on whomsoever I lay hands, he may receive the Holy Ghost.

Simon, who was called "the great power of God" (Acts 8:10) before Philip's arrival (Acts 8:6), now lusts after the apostles' power to use for his selfish desires (James 4:3). The sons of Sceva, with similar motives, will misuse the Apostle Paul's name when improperly seeking divine power (Acts 19:13-16).

[20] But Peter said unto him, Thy money perish with thee, because thou hast thought that the gift of God may be purchased with money.

[21] Thou hast neither part nor lot in this matter: for thy heart is not right in the sight of God.

[22] Repent therefore of this thy wickedness, and pray God, if perhaps the thought of thine heart may be forgiven thee.

[23] For I perceive that thou art in the gall of bitterness, and in the bond

Philip the evangelist brings the gospel to the Samaritans (Acts 8:5), whose genuine faith is confirmed by Peter and John (Acts 8:14-17).

Pavel Bernshtam / Shutterstock.com

of iniquity.

- Simon the sorcerer lost his former place of prominence in Samaria (Acts 8:9). Rather than partaking of the "great joy in that city" (Acts 8:8) he becomes cynical and resentful (bitter, Rom 3:14, Eph 4:31). He chooses sin (iniquity, Psalm 66:18, Matt 23:28) rather than the righteousness of Christ.
- Peter is familiar with both reprimand (Matt 16:23) and the corruptive influence of money (Acts 5:1-11, also Mark 11:15, 14:10-11, Matt 28:12-15,) when he sharply rebukes Simon for his disgraceful financial proposition (Prov 13:11, 1 Tim 6:10).
- The Holy Ghost, working through Peter, knows the actual state of Simon's heart (1 Sam 16:7, Acts 1:24, Luke 16:15).
- God's forgiveness (1 John 1:9) is available to those who genuinely desire to turn from sin (2 Tim 2:25-26).

<u>Language</u>

Reprimand (sharp rebuke rather than a simple statement of fact) – Peter shames the evil sorcerer (as will Paul on Cyprus, Acts 13:10).

[24] Then answered Simon, and said, Pray ye to the Lord for me, that none of these things which ye have spoken come upon me.

Only God and Simon know if he makes true repentance (Rev 3:19) or requests prayer merely because he fears punishment (like the evil King Jeroboam, 1 Kings 13:6; 2 Cor 7:10).

[25] And they, when they had testified and preached the word of the Lord, returned to Jerusalem, and preached the gospel in many villages of the Samaritans.

- Peter and John present the gospel to Samaritans while traveling back to Jerusalem. Whereas the disciples previously sought to destroy the Samaritans with fire from heaven (Luke 9:51-56), the disciples now bring them the good news of the Savior (2 Cor 5:18).
- John is not mentioned further in the book of Acts. He will meet Paul when the latter visits Jerusalem (Gal 2:9), apparently when the church of Antioch sends relief during the famine (Acts 11:27-

30). John will eventually move to Ephesus and write his gospel and three epistles preserved as scripture (1st, 2nd, and 3rd John). He will later be exiled to the island of Patmos (Rev 1:9), where he will receive and put into writing the Revelation of Jesus Christ (Rev 1:1).

[26] And the angel of the Lord spake unto Philip, saying, Arise, and go toward the south unto the way that goeth down from Jerusalem unto Gaza, which is desert.

[27] And he arose and went: and, behold, a man of Ethiopia, an eunuch of great authority under Candace queen of the Ethiopians, who had the charge of all her treasure, and had come to Jerusalem for to worship,

[28] Was returning, and sitting in his chariot read Esaias the prophet.

- Philip is obedient (Acts 26:19) when he sets out by faith (Heb 11:8), leaving the multitudes of Samaria to seek a solitary sinner (Luke 15:4-7). Philip meets a man from Ethiopia who is Queen Candace's treasurer.
- The Ethiopians (Psalm 68:31) are the black (Jer 13:23) descendants of Cush, who was Ham's son and Noah's grandson (Gen 10:6-7). The descendants of all three of Noah's sons will receive the gospel: Shem (the peoples of Asia, Gen 10:21-31) in Acts 2, Ham (the peoples of Africa, Gen 10:6-20) in Acts 8:27-39, and Japheth (the peoples of Europe, Gen 10:2-5) in Acts 10.
- "Candace" is a title for the queen of Ethiopia, as is "Pharaoh" for the king of Egypt (compare "Pharaoh-hophra" of Jer 44:30 and "Pharaoh-necho" of Jer 46:2) and "Caesar" for the emperor of Rome (compare "Caesar Augustus" of Luke 2:1 and "Tiberius Caesar" of Luke 3:1). "[Ethiopia] was subject to a Queen named Candace, a name that for many years already hath passed in succession from one Queen to another."[188]

Language
"Isaiah" translated from Hebrew is equivalent to "Esaias" translated from Greek.

---

[188] Pliny, *Natural History*, 6.29

[29] Then the Spirit said unto Philip, Go near, and join thyself to this chariot.

[30] And Philip ran thither to him, and heard him read the prophet Esaias, and said, Understandest thou what thou readest?

[31] And he said, How can I, except some man should guide me? And he desired Philip that he would come up and sit with him.

- Philip runs to obey God's will, unlike Jonah, who ran from God's will (Jonah 1:3). Philip finds the Ethiopian man reading from Isaiah 53.
- The Lord Jesus taught the disciples of Himself from scripture (Luke 24:45). The Savior quoted Isaiah 53:12 (Luke 22:37) as the fulfillment of His impending arrest and crucifixion. The Gospel of Mark also quotes Isaiah 53:12 (Mark 15:28) when explaining His crucifixion amongst thieves. The Gospel of Matthew quotes Isaiah 53:4 (Matt 8:17) to explain Christ's healing ministry (Matt 8:13-16). Both the Gospel of John (John 12:37-38) and Paul (Rom 10:16) quote Isaiah 53:1 when describing Israel's rejection of the Messiah. Peter will quote Isaiah 53:5 and 53:9 (1 Peter 2:21-25) when telling how the Savior patiently endured wrongful suffering.
- The Ethiopian treasurer may have heard believers at the Jerusalem temple (Acts 5:42) applying Isaiah 53 to Jesus Christ. He will now ask Philip about Isaiah 53:7-8.

[32] The place of the scripture which he read was this, He was led as a sheep to the slaughter; and like a lamb dumb before his shearer, so opened he not his mouth:

Quoting Isaiah 53:7. Anyone treated unjustly would naturally protest, but Jesus willfully suffered the punishment deserved by others (Heb 12:3). He endured affliction as a lamb led to the slaughter (John 1:29, 1 Cor 5:7, 1 Peter 1:19, Rev 5:12) and uttered not a word of protest (Mark 15:3-5, Luke 23:8-9, 1 Peter 2:23).

[33] In his humiliation his judgment was taken away: and who shall declare his generation? for his life is taken from the earth.

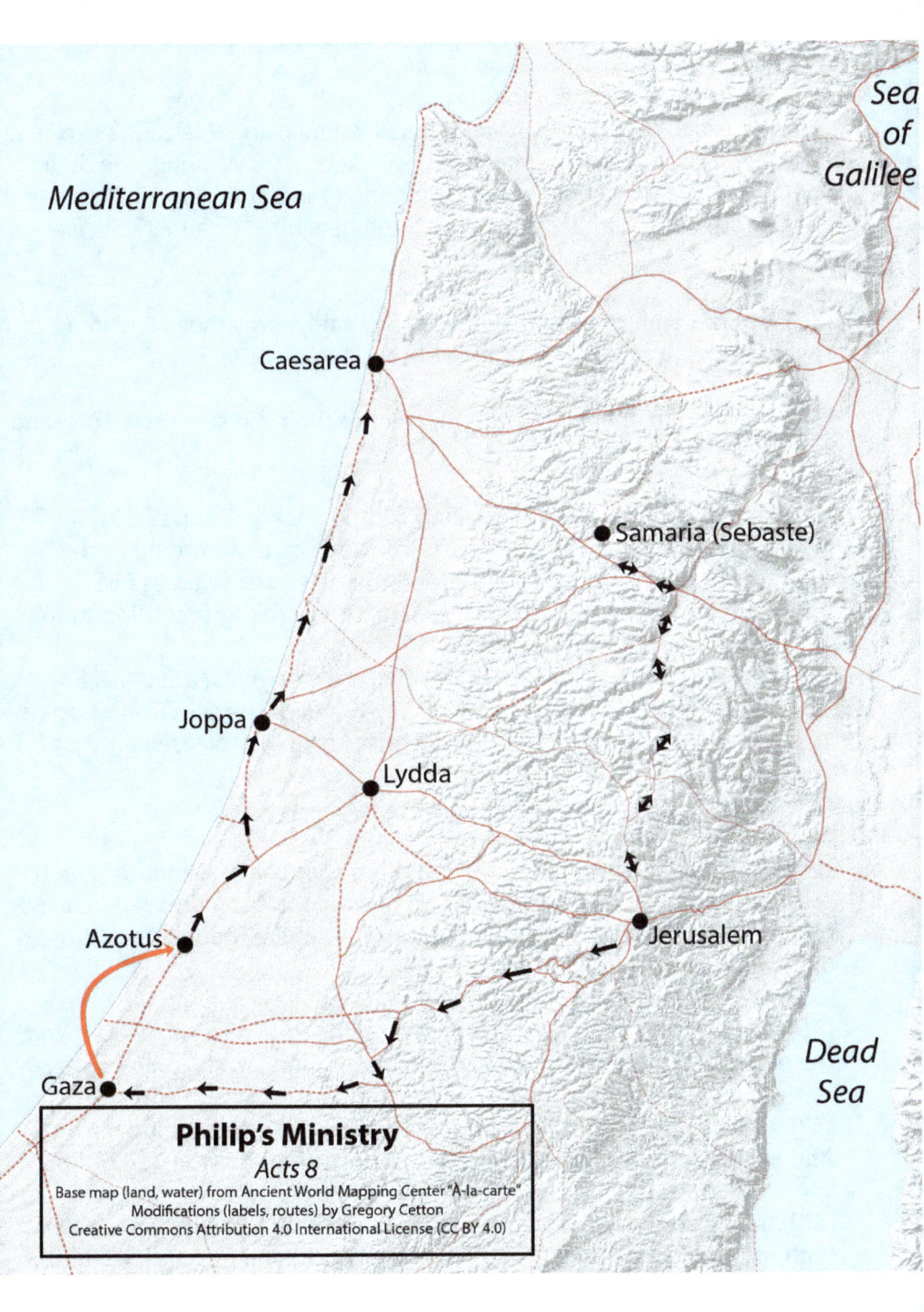

Mediterranean Sea

Sea
of
Galilee

Caesarea

Samaria (Sebaste)

Joppa

Lydda

Azotus

Jerusalem

Gaza

Dead
Sea

Philip's Ministry

Acts 8

Base map (land, water) from Ancient World Mapping Center "À-la-carte"
Modifications (labels, routes) by Gregory Cetton
Creative Commons Attribution 4.0 International License (CC BY 4.0)

Quoting Isaiah 53:8. The Lord Jesus received mocking (Matt 27:29, 41-43, Luke 23:11) and injustice (Matt 26:59-60, Acts 3:13). Although He died young without leaving a physical offspring (generation, Isa 53:8), Christ has begotten a spiritual seed through the new birth (Psalm 22:30, Isa 53:10, John 3:3-8, 1 Peter 1:3, 23).

[34] And the eunuch answered Philip, and said, I pray thee, of whom speaketh the prophet this? of himself, or of some other man?

[35] Then Philip opened his mouth, and began at the same scripture, and preached unto him Jesus.

- Philip continues reading Isaiah 53 and shows (1 Cor 15:3-4) that Christ died (Isa 53:10) for our sins (Isa 53:5-6) according to the scriptures ("report," Isa 53:1), and that He was buried (Isa 53:9) and that He rose again (Isa 53:10b) the third day according to the scriptures.
- He also teaches (Rom 5:1) that therefore being justified (Isa 53:11) by faith ("believed," Isa 53:1), we have peace (Isa 53:5) with God (Isa 53:10) through our Lord Jesus Christ ("my righteous servant," Isa 53:11).

Language
Hebraism (a Hebrew manner of expression) – "opened his mouth ... and preached" corresponds with "after this opened Job his mouth, and cursed his day" (Job 3:1). The words "opened his mouth" are redundant, but they underscore the profound words spoken.

[36] And as they went on their way, they came unto a certain water: and the eunuch said, See, here is water; what doth hinder me to be baptized?

[37] And Philip said, If thou believest with all thine heart, thou mayest. And he answered and said, I believe that Jesus Christ is the Son of God.

[38] And he commanded the chariot to stand still: and they went down both into the water, both Philip and the eunuch; and he baptized him.

[39] And when they were come up out of the water, the Spirit of the Lord caught away Philip, that the eunuch saw him no more: and he went on his way rejoicing.

- The book of Acts is a transitional period in which God shifts the focus of His dealings from Israel to the Church. He uses varying and transitory means to bring this about. Sometimes He uses phenomena such as tongues (Acts 2:4) or healing (Acts 8:7) to help spread the gospel message. At other times He uses baptism (Acts 2:38) or laying on of hands (Acts 8:17) to impart His Holy Ghost. The case of the Ethiopian treasurer is significant because his testimony of salvation is a simple example of Romans 10:9-10, which becomes the New Testament pattern God uses to save lost sinners (Acts 16:30-31).
- Baptism is provided after his profession of faith in Christ and is performed soon after conversion (Acts 16:30-33). Isaiah 53 does not mention baptism, so the Ethiopian treasurer may have learned of this from believers at the Jerusalem temple (Acts 2:41).
- Going "down both into the water" and then coming "up out of the water" (here and Matt 3:16) demonstrates immersion as the mode of baptism.
- The Ethiopian man rejoices in the gift of salvation through Jesus Christ (Psalm 35:9, Isa 61:10). His conversion fulfills Bible prophecy (Psalm 68:31).

173

[40] But Philip was found at Azotus: and passing through he preached in all the cities, till he came to Cæsarea.

- Philip is caught away as were Elijah (1 Kings 18:12a, 2 Kings 2:16) and Ezekiel (Ezek 11:1). He is miraculously transported to Azotus (Ashdod, 1 Sam 5:1).
- The evangelist preaches as he travels through various cities (Luke 4:43). Philip settles in Caesarea where Paul will visit him some twenty years later (Acts 21:8).

Teaching Questions

<u>Question</u>: Is the Ethiopian treasurer a Jew or a Gentile?
<u>Answer</u>:
- **Gentile**: He is a Gentile "God-fearer" (Acts 10:2) who worships the God of the Bible but has not converted to Judaism. He cannot become a Jew because eunuchs are excluded under Moses' law (Deut 23:1).
- **Jew**: Luke portrays Cornelius as the first Gentile convert (Acts 11:18) and the treasurer as an Ethiopian Jew visiting Jerusalem to worship. The Mosaic law banning eunuchs (Deut 23:1) was written to prevent Jews from castrating their children like pagans might; the Lord accepts all those who choose Him, including eunuchs (Isa 56:3-5).

<u>Question</u>: The Ethiopian treasurer is called a "eunuch." Does this mean he was physically mutilated to make him sterile?
<u>Answer</u>:

- **Yes**: The term "eunuch" includes men who serve the queen (2 Kings 9:30-32) or manage the king's harem (Esther 2:3). Princes taken captive from foreign lands, like Daniel and his friends (Dan 1:7), were involuntarily "made eunuchs [by the cruel actions] of men" (Matt 19:12). Emperor Nero's paramour Sporus will be called a eunuch when castrated.[189] Plutarch describes the humiliating implications of this label: "... they all laughed at Demetrius, except Lysimachus; he was incensed that Demetrius considered him a eunuch (it was the general practice to have eunuchs for treasurers)."[190]
- **No**: "Eunuch" can be the honorific title of a high governmental military or political official (Jer 52:25 and Acts 8:27, respectively). "In ancient Egypt, a court officer was called eunuch whether or not he had castration."[191] The term can also refer to a birth defect or voluntary celibacy (Matt 19:12).

<u>Question</u>: The Lord brings the gospel to the people of Africa in Acts 8:26-39. Under many circumstances of world history, an international conflict

---

[189] Cassius Dio, *Roman History*, 62.28.2-3
[190] Plutarch, *The Life of Demetrius*, 25.5
[191] "Eunuch." *LookLex Encyclopedia*, http://i-cias.com/e.o/eunuch.htm, accessed 23 Feb 2019

Ethiopian Treasurer
Acts 8
Base map (land, water) from Ancient World Mapping Center "À-la-carte"
Modifications (labels, routes) by Gregory Cetton
Creative Commons Attribution 4.0 International License (CC BY 4.0)

Judea

Jerusalem

Gaza

Alexandria

Memphis

Egypt

Thebais

Parva (Premnis)

Syene

Pselchis

Red Sea

Nile River

Ethiopia

Napata

Meroë
(Ethiopian Capital)

would preclude an official from one nation (such as Ethiopia) from traveling freely across borders to another (such as Judea, part of the Roman Empire). Yet God loves to work in ways that confound the purposes of human power and bring Him glory (1 Cor 1:27-29). How did Rome and Ethiopia achieve peace in 22 BC in a very unusual manner that subsequently allowed people such as the Ethiopian treasurer to travel freely to Jerusalem and back?

Answer: Egypt is a critically important province due to the enormous supplies of grain it sends to Rome[192] since being annexed in 31 BC. Therefore, a successful attack by Ethiopian raiding parties into Roman-occupied Egypt in 27 BC brought a swift military response ordered by Caesar Augustus. The Roman troops sent to secure Egypt readily defeated the Ethiopians. Still, the tenacity of Queen Candace and her warriors brought Ethiopia a favorable position at the negotiating table in 27 BC that led to Ethiopia's exemption from Roman tribute as a condition of peace.

"But the Ethiopians, emboldened by the fact that a part of the Roman force in Egypt had been drawn away with Cornelius Gallus when he was carrying on war against the Arabians, attacked the Thebaïs and the garrison of the three cohorts at Syenê, and by an unexpected onset took Syenê and Elephantinê and Philae, and enslaved the inhabitants and also pulled down the statues of Caesar. But Petronius, setting out with less than ten thousand infantry and eight hundred cavalry against thirty thousand men, first forced them to flee back to Pselchis, an Ethiopian city, and sent ambassadors to demand what they had taken, as also to ask the reasons why they had begun war; and when they said that they had been wronged by the Nomarchs he replied that these were not rulers of the country, but Caesar; and when they had requested three days for deliberation, but did nothing they should have done, he made an attack and forced them to come forth to battle; and he quickly turned them to flight, since they were badly marshaled and badly armed...Among these fugitives were the generals of Queen Candace, who was ruler of the Ethiopians in my time – a masculine sort of woman, and blind in one eye...After this he set out for Napata. This was the royal residence of Candace; and her son was there, and she herself was residing at a place near by. But though she

---

[192] Africa supplies "fruits of the earth, which maintain the multitude of the Romans for eight months in the year" (Josephus, *Jewish War*, 16.4).

sent ambassadors to entreat for friendship and offered to give back the captives and the statues brought from Syenê, Petronius attacked and captured Napata too, from which her son had fled, and razed it to the ground; and having enslaved its inhabitants, he turned back again with the booty, having decided that the regions farther on would be hard to traverse. But he fortified Premnis better, threw in a garrison and food for four hundred men for two years, and set out for Alexandria...Meantime Candace marched against the garrison with many thousands of men, but Petronius set out to its assistance and arrived at the fortress first; and when he had made the place thoroughly secure by sundry devices, ambassadors came, but he bade them go to Caesar; and when they asserted that they did not know who Caesar was or where they should have to go to find him, he gave them escorts; and they went to Samos, since Caesar was there . ..And when the ambassadors had obtained everything they pled for, he even remitted the tributes which he had imposed."[193]

Challenge Questions

1. Why do the Samaritans not receive the gift of the Holy Ghost until the apostles lay hands on them (Acts 8:17)?
2. Is Simon a true believer who makes a wrong decision or a non-believer who made a false profession?

---

[193] Strabo, Geography, 17.1.54

Acts Chapter 9

[1] And Saul, yet breathing out threatenings and slaughter against the disciples of the Lord, went unto the high priest,

[2] And desired of him letters to Damascus to the synagogues, that if he found any of this way, whether they were men or women, he might bring them bound unto Jerusalem.

- Saul[194] acts with the religious fervor of Jehu, who rid Israel of Baal worship (2 Kings 10:18-28), but fails spiritually (2 Kings 10:31) when he imprisons and murders disciples (Acts 8:3, 22:4-5, 19-20, 26:10-11).
- The high priest had previously abused the power of his office in the unjust executions of Jesus (Matt 26:3-4, John 11:49-53) and Stephen (Acts 7:1, 57-60). He subsequently authorized the persecution of saints in Jerusalem (Acts 26:10). Saul now asks for authority to do the same in Damascus and receives his desired warrants (Acts 9:14, 22:5). He intends to use the authority of the synagogues to imprison believers, as predicted by Christ (Luke 21:12).
- The disciples preach Jesus Christ as the only way (Matt 7:14, John 14:6) of salvation (Acts 16:17), and they call this belief the "way" (Acts 19:9, 23, 22:4, 24:14, 22).

Language
Hendiadys (two words for one idea) – "breathing out threatenings and slaughter," i.e., murderous threats.

[3] And as he journeyed, he came near Damascus: and suddenly there shined round about him a light from heaven:

[4] And he fell to the earth, and heard a voice saying unto him, Saul, Saul, why persecutest thou me?

---

[194] See biographical comments at Acts 8:1.

- Saul is not following the right spiritual path (Acts 8:27-28) but the wrong one (Num 22:31) when at noontime (Acts 22:6), he sees God's glory in a light (Rev 21:23) brighter than the sun (Acts 26:13).
- The Lord calls Saul's name twice as He did at critical times in the lives of other men such as Abraham (Gen 22:11), Moses (Exod 3:4), and Samuel (1 Sam 3:10).
- No one can see God and live (Exod 33:20). Therefore God will show Himself to someone in a form the individual can safely see yet unmistakably identify as Him. Such an appearance of God is called a "theophany." God appeared as a theophany to Abraham (Gen 15:17) and Moses (Exod 3:2, 34:5-8). God the Son appeared as a theophany to Peter, James, and John (the transfiguration, Mark 9:2-3); to Stephen (Acts 7:55-56); and now to Saul.
- Saul falls to the earth before the Lord Jesus, as had the wise men (Matt 2:11), Simon Peter (Luke 5:8), Mary of Bethany (John 11:32), Jairus (Luke 8:41), the woman with the issue of blood (Luke 8:47), the Syrophoenician woman (Mark 7:25), the Samaritan (Luke 17:16), the leper (Luke 5:12), unclean spirits (Mark 3:11, Luke 8:28), men and officers of the chief priests (John 18:6), our resurrected Lord's disciples (Matt 28:9), and as will John (Rev 1:17) and ultimately everyone (Phil 2:10).

179

[5] And he said, Who art thou, Lord? And the Lord said, I am Jesus whom thou persecutest: it is hard for thee to kick against the pricks.

- "*I am* Jesus" reminds the reader of Moses at the burning bush (Exod 3:1-3) hearing, "I am the God of thy father, the God of Abraham, the God of Isaac, and the God of Jacob" (Exod 3:6). Furthermore, "God said unto Moses, I AM THAT I AM" (Exod 3:14). Subsequently, John recorded the words of God the Son: "Jesus said unto them, Verily, verily, I say unto you, Before Abraham was, I am" (John 8:58).
- Since believers are members of Christ's body, Saul attacks Jesus when persecuting them (1 Cor 12:26-27, Luke 10:16).
- A cow will kick against the pricks of a cattle goad. Saul strives to follow God's law (Phil 3:6) righteously but wanders (Lam 4:14) from the true path, so God uses painful circumstances to "prick" (Judg 8:16) him back to the right way.

<u>Language</u>
Proverb (a widely-used saying) – "kick against the pricks" is a widely-used saying. Seneca (the brother of Gallio, Acts 18:12) wrote, "The human mind is naturally self-willed, kicks against the goad, and sets its face against authority."[195]

[6] And he trembling and astonished said, Lord, what wilt thou have me to do? And the Lord said unto him, Arise, and go into the city, and it shall be told thee what thou must do.

- Saul is called amidst his occupation as were Moses (Exod 3:1-10), Matthew (Matt 9:9), and Peter (Luke 5:3-11).
- Saul is immediately willing to follow God's call (Acts 26:19) as were Samuel (1 Sam 3:10), Isaiah (Isa 6:8), Peter and Andrew (Matt 4:19-20), and Levi (Luke 5:27-28).
- God calls on every believer to walk in the good works He has ordained for them (Eph 2:10).

[7] And the men which journeyed with him stood speechless, hearing a voice, but seeing no man.

- They first fell (Acts 26:14), then stood up again.
- Saul comprehends the Hebrew-speaking voice (Acts 26:14). His companions hear but do not understand the words from heaven (John 12:28-29, Acts 22:9).

[8] And Saul arose from the earth; and when his eyes were opened, he saw no man: but they led him by the hand, and brought him into Damascus.

[9] And he was three days without sight, and neither did eat nor drink.

- When Moses met God on Mount Sinai (Exod 34:5-8), his face reflected God's glory (Exod 34:29-30), and the veil with which he covered himself symbolizes Israel's spiritual blindness toward Christ (Isa

---

[195] Seneca, *Of Clemency*, 1.24

6:10, 2 Cor 3:13-15). Saul's spiritual blindness is lifted (Acts 9:6) even as he becomes physically blind. Temporary blindness and spiritual enlightenment also occur in stories about Elisha and the Syrians (2 Kings 6:17-20) and Sergius Paulus and Elymas (Acts 13:6-12).

- Jesus had likened Jonah's three-day wait in the whale to His three-day wait in the earth (Jonah 1:17, Matt 12:40). God's divine plan was also manifest during other three-day pauses: Abraham when Isaac was dead to him (Gen 22:1-4, Heb 11:17-19), the Egyptians during the plague of darkness, (Exod 10:22), Joshua's army preparing to cross Jordan (Josh 1:11), Esther's people fasting before her petition (Esther 4:16), and Jesus' parents searching for Him (Luke 2:46). Future Israel will wait three days while expecting Christ to return (Hosea 5:15-6:3).

[10] And there was a certain disciple at Damascus, named Ananias; and to him said the Lord in a vision, Ananias. And he said, Behold, I am here, Lord.

[11] And the Lord said unto him, Arise, and go into the street which is called Straight, and enquire in the house of Judas for one called Saul, of Tarsus: for, behold, he prayeth,

[12] And hath seen in a vision a man named Ananias coming in, and putting his hand on him, that he might receive his sight.

- Ananias is a Jewish believer in Jesus the Messiah, who lives a life consistent with God's law and thus has a good testimony before all Jews (Acts 22:12).
- As an unsaved Pharisee Saul has *said* prayers (Luke 18:11), but now he prays in the Spirit (Eph 6:18), with joy (Phil 1:4), with thanksgiving (Phil 4:6), with remembrance (2 Tim 1:3), with faith (James 5:15), with enthusiasm (James 5:16), with earnest (James 5:17), night and day (1 Thes 3:10), for all people (1 Tim 2:1), and without ceasing (1 Thes 5:17).
- Saul and Ananias receive corresponding visions, as will Peter and Cornelius (Acts 10:1-16).

[13] Then Ananias answered, Lord, I have heard by many of this man, how much evil he hath done to thy saints at Jerusalem:

[14] And here he hath authority from the chief priests to bind all that call on thy name.

- Ananias knows of Saul's relentless persecution of Christians (Acts 22:19-20, 26:9-11) and apparently word of his intentions here in Damascus has preceded his arrival (Acts 9:21). Ananias does not refuse God's command; he simply asks for clarification, as will Peter (Acts 10:13-14).
- The chief priests had forbidden the disciples to speak in Jesus' name (Acts 4:18, 5:40), but they never cease to call on Him (Acts 7:59, 1 Cor 1:2, Eph 5:20).

[15] But the Lord said unto him, Go thy way: for he is a chosen vessel unto me, to bear my name before the Gentiles, and kings, and the children of Israel:

- Unconverted Saul had been a dishonorable vessel (Hosea 8:8, 2 Tim 2:20) worthy of destruction (Rom 9:22, Rev 2:27), but is now an honorable vessel (2 Tim 2:21) ready to be filled with God's power and bring glory to Him (2 Cor 4:7).
- Although Saul's commission (Acts 26:16-18) will send him to preach the gospel initially to Jews ("the people," Acts 26:17), he will most often evangelize Gentiles (Rom 11:13). Saul will preach before kings such as Agrippa (Acts 26:2), other high officials such as Sergius Paulus (Acts 13:7), Governor Felix (Acts 24:25), Governor Festus (Acts 26:23-24), and to Caesar Nero (Acts 27:24).

[16] For I will shew him how great things he must suffer for my name's sake.

Saul will endure (2 Tim 2:3) great suffering (2 Cor 11:23-28) and ultimately be put to death (2 Tim 4:6) for the cause of Christ. All believers are likewise called to suffer for Him (Phil 1:29-30, 1 Peter 2:21).

[17] And Ananias went his way, and entered into the house; and putting his hands on him said, Brother Saul, the Lord, even Jesus, that appeared unto thee in the way as thou camest, hath sent me, that thou mightest

receive thy sight, and be filled with the Holy Ghost.

At his recent conversion (Acts 9:6), Saul had been sealed with the Holy Ghost, as are all believers (Eph 1:13). With the laying on of hands, he now (in this unique circumstance) becomes filled with the Holy Ghost (Eph 5:18), as are potentially all believers who live their lives in fellowship with God through His Spirit (Gal 5:16-25). Saul also receives healing by the laying on of hands and will later heal others in like manner (Acts 14:3, 28:8-9).

[18] And immediately there fell from his eyes as it had been scales: and he received sight forthwith, and arose, and was baptized.

Saul had already been spiritually "born again" (1 Cor 15:8, John 3:3) when he saw the Lord Jesus (1 Cor 9:1) three days ago and now receives baptism only after salvation (Acts 10:44-47, 16:31-33).

Saul is converted on the road to Damascus (Acts 9:1-6) then meets Ananias at a house on Straight Street (shown in photo with old Roman arch).

John Wreford / Shutterstock.com

[19] And when he had received meat, he was strengthened. Then was Saul certain days with the disciples which were at Damascus.

Saul will visit Arabia (Gal 1:15-17) sometime between now and verse 24.

[20] And straightway he preached Christ in the synagogues, that he is the Son of God.

- Saul's heart is for his people Israel (Rom 10:1), so his custom (Acts 17:1-2) is to preach in synagogues whenever possible (Acts 13:5, 14:1, 17:10, 18:4,19, 19:8).
- The Holy Ghost's ministry is to glorify the Lord Jesus Christ (John 16:13-14). Therefore Saul, being filled with the Holy Ghost (Acts 9:17), preaches that Jesus Christ is the Son of God. Saul knows the title "Son of God" is consistent with the Old Testament (Psalm 2:7) and will quote Psalm 2 in his sermon at Antioch in Pisidia (Acts 13:33). Furthermore, Saul knows that Jesus in not just **a** son of God (like Adam, Luke 3:38, or angels, Job 38:7), but Jesus is **the** Son of God (Matt 16:16-17, John 20:31). Peter (Acts 3:13, 3:26) and Philip (Acts 8:37) also preach that Jesus Christ is the Son of God.

184

[21] But all that heard him were amazed, and said; Is not this he that destroyed them which called on this name in Jerusalem, and came hither for that intent, that he might bring them bound unto the chief priests?

[22] But Saul increased the more in strength, and confounded the Jews which dwelt at Damascus, proving that this is very Christ.

Saul shows scripture prophesying that Christ would be born of a virgin (Isa 7:14) in Bethlehem (Micah 5:2) and raised in Nazareth (Matt 2:23). He describes how Christ would remain silent at His trial (Isa 53:7), suffer mocking (Isa 50:6), be crucified (Isa 53:4-6, Zech 12:10) without broken bones (Psalm 22:16-17), be placed in an appointed tomb (Isa 53:9), and be gloriously resurrected (Psalm 16:9-11). Saul explains the specific time the Messiah would come (Dan 9:25, Luke 19:44). His listeners agree that Christ must be a descendant of King David (2 Sam 7:12-13, Isa 11:1, Matt 22:42), and Saul points to Jesus' verifiable lineage (Matt 1, Luke 3:23-38).

[23] And after that many days were fulfilled, the Jews took counsel to kill him:

Saul describes the "many days" as three years in Gal 1:18. He, like Stephen, becomes the target of murder (Acts 6:11-14) by those who cannot refute his arguments (Acts 6:9-10).

[24] But their laying await was known of Saul. And they watched the gates day and night to kill him.

[25] Then the disciples took him by night, and let him down by the wall in a basket.

Governor Aretas instructs the city garrison to apprehend Saul, but they are watching the gates and not the entire city wall (2 Cor 11:32-33). Saul escapes through a window and down the wall, as did the two spies (Josh 2:15) and David (1 Sam 19:12).

[26] And when Saul was come to Jerusalem, he assayed to join himself to the disciples: but they were all afraid of him, and believed not that he was a disciple.

Saul seeks ("assays") to assemble with other disciples, as should all believers (Heb 10:25). They have certainly heard of Saul's conversion (which occurred three years ago, Gal 1:18), but do not trust him yet.

[27] But Barnabas took him, and brought him to the apostles, and declared unto them how he had seen the Lord in the way, and that he had spoken to him, and how he had preached boldly at Damascus in the name of Jesus.

Barnabas has been a long-time, faithful disciple (Acts 4:36-37). He vouches for Saul's authentic conversion (Acts 9:1-8) and zealous ministry in Damascus (Acts 9:22). The two men will travel together on the first missionary journey (Acts 13:2).

[28] And he was with them coming in and going out at Jerusalem.

Saul is now accepted and can freely interact with the disciples. He might lodge with his sister in Jerusalem (Acts 23:16). He also stays with Peter for fifteen days and sees James, the half-brother of Jesus, but none other of the twelve apostles (Gal 1:18-19).

Language
Hebraism (a Hebrew manner of expression) – "coming in and going out" describes unhindered fellowship (as also in 1 Sam 29:6).

[29] And he spake boldly in the name of the Lord Jesus, and disputed against the Grecians: but they went about to slay him.

- Grecians ("Hellenists") are those whose language and culture are Greek; in the context of Jerusalem (here and in Acts 6:1), the term refers to Jews born outside of Israel ("Hellenistic" Jews). These foreign-born men welcome the opportunity to demonstrate their religious zeal by debating vigorously with Saul, as they did with Stephen (Acts 6:9-10).
- Saul had approved of Stephen's death by stoning (Acts 7:58-8:1) and now becomes a target of murder as he fills Stephen's former role of disputing with the Grecians.

[30] Which when the brethren knew, they brought him down to Cæsarea, and sent him forth to Tarsus.

Saul wisely leaves Jerusalem for the port city of Caesarea. From there he travels northward, preaching the gospel while passing through Judea (Acts 26:20) without seeking out existing believers since some might still be afraid to meet with him (Gal 1:22-23). He returns home to Tarsus (Acts 22:3) via Syria and Cilicia (Gal 1:21), where he undoubtedly preaches the gospel (Gal 1:23) while awaiting God's future calling (Acts 11:25-26).

[31] Then had the churches rest throughout all Judæa and Galilee and Samaria, and were edified; and walking in the fear of the Lord, and in the comfort of the Holy Ghost, were multiplied.

- The persecution of Christians has ceased now that Saul has become one of them. In the future, Saul will suffer persecution, possibly by some of his former associates (1 Thes 2:14-16).

- The brethren show their fear of God (Heb 12:28-29) by acknowledging His hatred of and judgment for sin in the lost (Luke 12:5, Heb 10:31) and in the lives of believers (Heb 12:5-11). They determine to live each day seeking personal holiness by walking (Gal 5:16) in the comfort (John 14:26) and power (Rom 15:13) of the Holy Ghost.
- Luke gives the third of seven summary statements in the book of Acts now that the gospel has spread throughout Judea, Galilee, and Samaria.

Language

Hebraism (a Hebrew manner of expression) – one who recognizes God for who He is has an attitude toward God ("fear of the Lord") that affects his thinking about right and wrong (Prov 8:13, 19:23, 23:17).

When Paul's life is threatened in Jerusalem, believers there send him back to Tarsus (Acts 9:28-30), his home city (Acts 21:39).

OlhaPro / Shutterstock.com

[32] And it came to pass, as Peter passed throughout all quarters, he came down also to the saints which dwelt at Lydda.

[33] And there he found a certain man named Æneas, which had kept his bed eight years, and was sick of the palsy.

[34] And Peter said unto him, Æneas, Jesus Christ maketh thee whole: arise, and make thy bed. And he arose immediately.

[35] And all that dwelt at Lydda and Saron saw him, and turned to the Lord.

- The plain of Sharon ("Saron") lies north of Lydda (1 Chron 5:16), which is also called "Lod" (1 Chron 8:12).
- Peter heals a lame man as previously both he (Acts 3:6-8) and Jesus did (Matt 9:6-7, John 5:8-9).

Language
Hyperbole (facts are exaggerated to describe feelings) – "so many people have come to Christ through Peter's preaching that it feels like everyone has!"

[36] Now there was at Joppa a certain disciple named Tabitha, which by interpretation is called Dorcas: this woman was full of good works and almsdeeds which she did.

[37] And it came to pass in those days, that she was sick, and died: whom when they had washed, they laid her in an upper chamber.

[38] And forasmuch as Lydda was nigh to Joppa, and the disciples had heard that Peter was there, they sent unto him two men, desiring him that he would not delay to come to them.

[39] Then Peter arose and went with them. When he was come, they brought him into the upper chamber: and all the widows stood by him weeping, and shewing the coats and garments which Dorcas made, while she was with them.

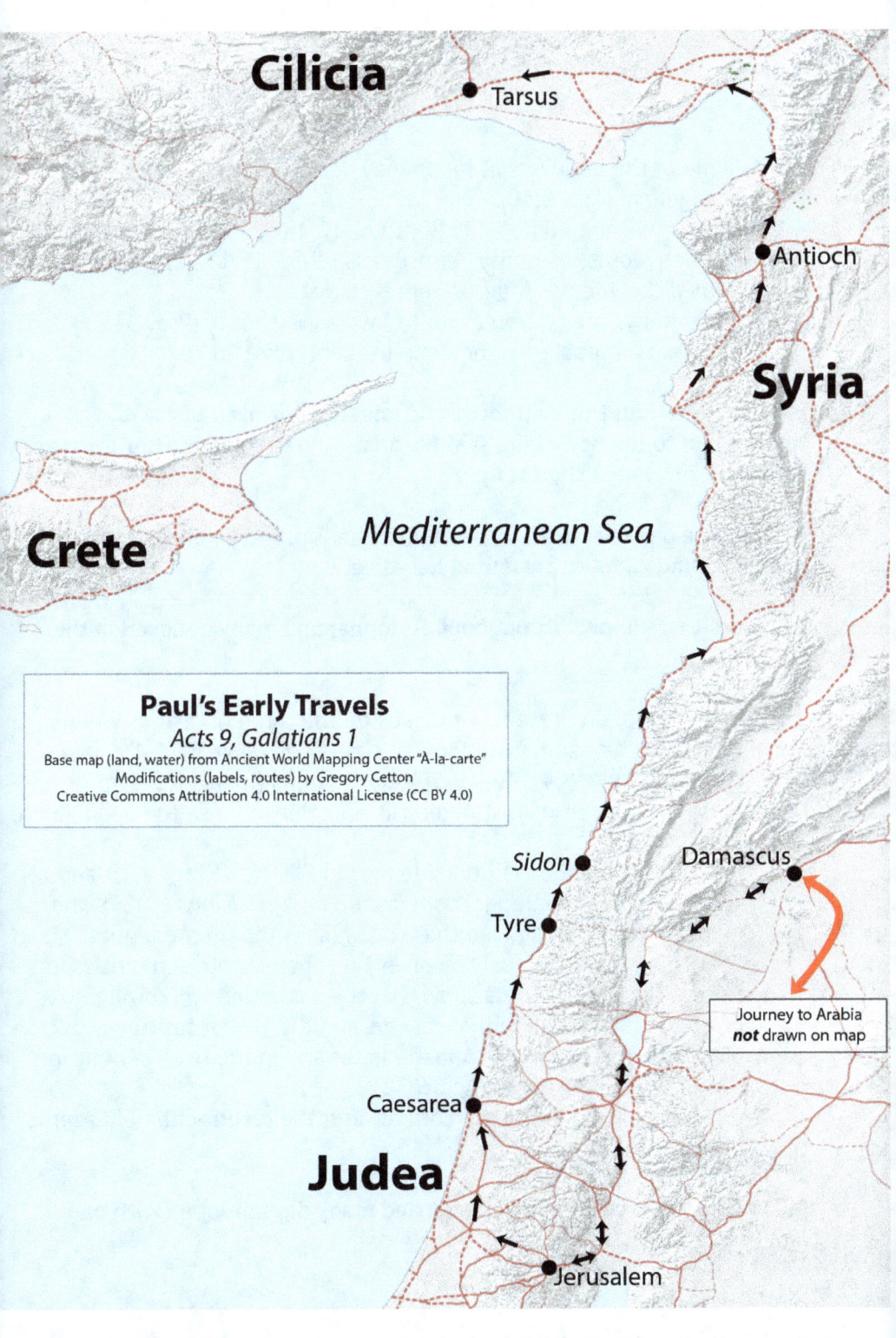

Cilicia

● Tarsus

Antioch ●

Syria

Crete

Mediterranean Sea

Paul's Early Travels

Acts 9, Galatians 1

Base map (land, water) from Ancient World Mapping Center "À-la-carte"
Modifications (labels, routes) by Gregory Cetton
Creative Commons Attribution 4.0 International License (CC BY 4.0)

Sidon ●

Damascus ●

Tyre ●

Journey to Arabia
not drawn on map

Caesarea ●

Judea

● Jerusalem

- Some of the believers at Joppa may be converts of Philip's earlier evangelism (Acts 8:40).
- Dorcas has helped (Prov 31:20, 1 Cor 12:28) the widows of Joppa through works of charity ("almsdeeds," 1 Cor 13:13), as others have helped the widows in Jerusalem (Acts 6:1).
- The widows praise Dorcas for her works of charity (Prov 31:31) and pray that a miracle will be done for her (Prov 19:17).

[40] But Peter put them all forth, and kneeled down, and prayed; and turning him to the body said, Tabitha, arise. And she opened her eyes: and when she saw Peter, she sat up.

[41] And he gave her his hand, and lifted her up, and when he had called the saints and widows, presented her alive.

[42] And it was known throughout all Joppa; and many believed in the Lord.

- Peter had been present with Jesus on the three occasions when He raised the dead: the widow of Nain's son (Luke 7:11-16), Jairus' daughter (Luke 8:41-42, 49-56), and Lazarus (John 11:1-45). Furthermore the Lord Jesus instructed His apostles to "raise the dead" (Matt 10:8).
- Peter has everyone wait outside (as did Elisha, 2 Kings 4:33, and Jesus, Luke 8:54) the upper room (as did Elijah, 1 Kings 17:19) where he prays over Dorcas' (Tabitha's) body (as with Jairus' daughter, Mark 5:41), which miraculously receives life. The notable similarities between the four accounts show that the same God who brought resurrection life through Elijah, Elisha, and the Lord Jesus now works in like manner through the Apostle Peter and in the lives of believers through His Holy Ghost (Acts 9:31).
- Believers are added to the Lord as after the resurrection of Lazarus (John 12:9-11).

[43] And it came to pass, that he tarried many days in Joppa with one Simon a tanner.

A tanner of animal skins is considered ceremonially unclean due to contact with dead animals (Lev 5:2). A man of that profession is so looked down upon in Jewish society that women, who usually do not hold the right of divorce (only men do, Deut 24:1), are given an exception. "The following are compelled to divorce [their wives]: a man who is afflicted with boils ... or gathers [of dogs' excrement] ... or a tanner."[196] Peter does not hesitate to stay with Simon the Tanner because Peter is learning that God's grace (John 1:17) supersedes the law (Acts 10:28).

Current Events

1. Pontius Pilate and the High Priest Caiaphas are removed from office
Pontius Pilate ordered the execution of Jesus Christ after pronouncing Him not guilty (Matt 27:22-24). Caiaphas conspired against Jesus (John 11:49-51), sentenced Him to death (Matt 26:65-66), then subsequently directed persecution against the apostles (Acts 4:1-6 and likely Acts 5:26-28, Acts 7, and Acts 9:1-2).

"But the nation of the Samaritans did not escape without tumults. The man who excited them to it ... bid them to get together upon Mount Gerizzim, which is by them looked upon as the most holy of all mountains, and assured them, that when they were come thither, he would show them those sacred vessels which were laid under that place, because Moses put them there. So they came thither armed ... and desired to go up the mountain in a great multitude together; but Pilate prevented their going up, by seizing upon roads with a great band of horsemen and foot-men, who fell upon those that were gotten together in the village .. . some of them they slew, and others of them they put to flight, and took a great many alive, the principal of which, and also the most potent of those that fled away, Pilate ordered to be slain."

"But when this tumult was appeased, the Samaritan senate sent an embassy to Vitellius ... who was now president of [the Roman province of] Syria, and accused Pilate of the murder of those that were killed; for that they did not go to Tirathaba in order to revolt from the Romans, but to

---

[196] *Babylonian Talmud*, Kethuboth 77a

escape the violence of Pilate. So Vitellius ... ordered Pilate to go to Rome, to answer before the emperor to the accusations of the Jews. So Pilate, when he had tarried ten years in Judea, made haste to Rome ... but before he could get to Rome Tiberius was dead... [Vitellius] also deprived ... Caiaphas [Luke 3:2] of the high priesthood, and appointed Jonathan [John, Acts 4:6] the son of Ananus [Annus, Luke 3:2], the former high priest, to succeed him."[197]

2. Emperor Tiberius dies and names Caligula as his successor

Tiberius was emperor during the earthly ministry of Jesus Christ (Luke 3:1) and had appointed Pilate to be governor of Judea.[198] "When the Romans understood that Tiberius was dead, they rejoiced at the good news ... For this Tiberius had brought a vast number of miseries on the best families of the Romans, since he was easily inflamed with [anger] in all cases, and ... had taken a hatred against men without reason; for he was by nature fierce in all the sentences he gave, and made death the penalty for the lightest offenses; insomuch that the Romans heard ... about his death gladly... Tiberius had at this time appointed Caius [Caligula] to be his successor."[199]

3. Herod Antipas is exiled and Herod Agrippa I is promoted

Herod Antipas is the son of Herod the Great (who murdered the young children of Bethlehem, Matt 2:16). He was given rulership over the fourth part of his late father's kingdom (hence the title "tetrarch," Luke 3:1). Antipas married Herodias after she had been married to his brother Philip. John the Baptist condemned the adulterous relationship (Exod 20:14), so Herod had John imprisoned. Antipas briefly met Jesus Christ and treated Him shamefully (Luke 23:8-11).

Herodias is the granddaughter of Herod the Great and sister of Herod Agrippa I. She married Herod Antipas after she had been married to his brother Philip. She hated John the Baptist for condemning their relationship as adulterous but could not convince her husband Herod Antipas to

---

[197] Josephus, *Antiquities*, 18.4.1-3
[198] Ibid., 18.2.2
[199] Ibid., 18.6.10

execute John (Mark 6:18-20). She ultimately had her revenge when she manipulated Antipas through her daughter Salome (who danced well) into beheading John the Baptist (Matt 14:3-11).

Herod Agrippa I is the grandson of Herod the Great, nephew of Herod Antipas, and sister of Herodias. He was raised in Rome with the son of the emperor Tiberius and eventually received an inheritance from his late grandfather Herod the Great. However, "he spent a great deal extravagantly in his daily way of living ... insomuch that he was, in a little time, reduced to poverty, and could not live at Rome any longer ... and sailed to Judea ... because he had not wherewithal to pay his creditors, who were many in number." He contemplated suicide, but his wife contacted his sister Herodias who was married to Herod Antipas and persuaded the couple to take them in. Antipas readily agreed "and allotted him Tiberias for his habitation, and appointed him some income of money for his maintenance, and made him a magistrate of that city, by way of honor to him." It was not long until Agrippa complained to his brother-in-law that the money "was not sufficient for him" and left on ill terms. Agrippa next went to Flaccus, who "had been a very great friend to him at Rome formerly, and was now president of [the Roman province] of Syria." However, Agrippa was soon dismissed when caught accepting a bribe. He returned penniless to Rome, where he came into great friendship with Caligula, the great-nephew of emperor Tiberius, through personal devotion and a large gift of (borrowed) money. When Agrippa behaved indiscreetly, the emperor had him arrested until Tiberius' death six months later. Caligula then became emperor and freed his friend Agrippa and "put a diadem upon his head, and appointed him to be king of the tetrarchy of Philip [Luke 3:1]."[200]

Herod Antipas and his wife **Herodias** then experienced a change in circumstances quite the opposite of Agrippa's. "Herodias, Agrippa's sister, who now lived as wife to that Herod [Antipas] ... took this authority of her brother in an envious manner, particularly when she saw that he had a greater dignity bestowed on him than her husband [Antipas] had; since, when he ran away, it was because he was not able to pay his debts; and now he was come back, he was in a way of dignity, and of great good fortune. She was therefore grieved and much displeased at so great a [trans-

---

[200] Ibid., 18.6.1-11

formation] of his affairs and ... was not able to conceal how miserable she was, by reason of the envy she had towards him; but she [agitated] her husband [Antipas], and desired him that he would sail to Rome, to court honors equal to [Agrippa's]; for she said that she could not bear to live any longer, while Agrippa ... now returned a king ... [she said to Herod Antipas] 'nor do thou esteem it other than a shameful thing to be inferior to one who, the other day, lived upon thy charity. But let us go to Rome, and let us spare no pains nor expenses, either of silver or gold, since they cannot be kept for any better use than for the obtaining of a kingdom ...' But for Herod, he opposed her request at this time ... having a suspicion of the trouble he should have at Rome ... but the more she saw him draw back, the more she pressed him to it ... and at last she left not off till she engaged him, whether he would or not, to be of her sentiments, because he could not otherwise avoid her importunity. So he ... went up to Rome, and took Herodias along with him. But Agrippa, when he was made sensible of their intentions and preparations, he also prepared to go thither; and as soon as he heard they set sail, he sent Fortunatus, one of his freedmen, to Rome, to carry presents to the emperor, and letters against Herod, and to give Caligula a particular account of those matters ... Now Caligula [greeted] Herod [Antipas], for he first met with him, and then looked upon the letters which Agrippa had sent him, and which were written in order to accuse Herod [Antipas]; wherein he accused him [of treason against Rome] and as a demonstration of which he alleged, that he had armor sufficient for seventy thousand men ready in his armory. Caligula was moved at this information, and asked Herod [Antipas] whether what was said about the armor was true; and when he confessed there was such armor there, for he could not deny the same, the truth of it being too [well-known], Caligula took that to be a sufficient proof of the accusation, that he intended to revolt. So he took away from him his [kingdom], and gave it by way of addition to Agrippa's kingdom; he also gave Herod's money to Agrippa, and, by way of punishment, [condemned] him [to] a perpetual banishment, and appointed Lyons, a city of Gaul, to be his place of [exile]. But when [Caligula] was informed that Herodias was Agrippa's sister, he ... prevented her being put under the same calamity with her husband. But she made this reply: 'Thou, indeed, O emperor! actest after a magnificent manner ... but the kindness which I have for my husband hinders me from partaking of the favor of thy gift; for it is not just that I, who have been made a partner in his prosperity, should forsake him in his misfortunes.'

Hereupon Caligula was angry at her, and sent her with Herod into banishment, and gave her estate to Agrippa."[201]

Teaching Questions

Question: Explain the words "it is hard for thee to kick against the pricks" (Acts 9:5).
Answer: This phrase reflects a well-known Greek proverb about fighting against a god. The playwright Euripides wrote, "I would rather do him sacrifice than in a fury kick against the pricks; thou a mortal, he a god."[202]
Question: Why would Jesus, speaking to Saul out of heaven, quote a Greek proverb?
Answer: The Lord Jesus seeks daily fellowship with His believers (John 15:5). During His earthly ministry He spoke to the Jewish disciples using familiar phrases that they would readily understand (e.g., "this proverb, Physician, heal thyself," Luke 4:23). Although now resurrected and glorified, the Lord Jesus speaks to Saul as if he were casually sitting across the table from him, conversing as a companion who readily uses figures of speech commonly known to Greek-educated Jews such as Saul.

Question: Why did the Lord raise Dorcas from the dead? Was she worthy? Her friends thought she was worthy. What does God think?
Answer: Dorcas was not raised from the dead because of her merits. She was raised because of the merits of Christ. Peter is preaching Christ's gospel, and God grants miracles to affirm the apostle's message and glorify the Savior.

Challenge Questions

1. What aspects of Saul's story point to a genuine conversion?
2. Why did Dorcas' friends at Joppa believe that Peter could raise her from the dead (Acts 9:38)?

---

[201] Ibid., 18.7.1-2
[202] Euripides, *The Bacchantes*

Acts Chapter 10

[1] There was a certain man in Cæsarea called Cornelius, a centurion of the band called the Italian band,

- A Roman centurion such as Cornelius commands a "century" of nominally 100 men; the actual number is between 60 and 100 men depending on the unit configuration. A legion (army) is made up of about 6000 men, including heavy infantry, light infantry, and cavalry. Each legion is comprised of 10 cohorts ("bands"), and each cohort has six centuries of 100 men. Julius Caesar had about 3600 heavy infantry per legion of 6000 men and therefore 360 men per heavy infantry cohort and 60 men per heavy infantry century.[203]
- Centurion Cornelius' cohort ("band") is named the "Italian," as Julius' is called "Augustus" (Acts 27:1).
- "They wish the centurions not so much to be venturesome and daredevil as to be natural leaders, of a steady and sedate spirit. They do not desire them so much to be men who will initiate attacks and open the battle, but men who will hold their ground when worsted and hard-pressed and be ready to die at their posts."[204]
- Centurions in the Bible are depicted as honorable men of good character (Matt 8:5-10, Mark 15:39, Acts 21:32, 22:25-26, 27:43).

[2] A devout man, and one that feared God with all his house, which gave much alms to the people, and prayed to God alway.

- Israel had made a covenant with God (Exod 24:7-8, Deut 5:1-3) to keep the written law of Moses (Lev 18:5, Mal 4:4). The Gentiles of the Old Testament did not receive this revelation (Psalm 147:19-20) and were not held accountable to it (Rom 2:12). God held a Gentile responsible for whatever light of truth he received (Rom 1:19-20), such as a voice from heaven (Gen 8:15), dreams (Gen 20:3), visions

---

[203] "Legion" and "Centurion." *Encyclopedia Britannica Online*, accessed 2 Dec 2019
[204] Polybius, *Histories*, 6.24

(Job 33:14-15), miracles (Josh 2:10, Luke 4:25-27), prophetic messages (Jonah 3:1-10), scripture (Gen 9:1-7, Acts 8:27-28), conscience
(Rom 2:14-15), or the witness of creation around him (Rom 1:20).
- Cornelius is a devout Gentile who worships God according to the
  light (Psalm 43:3, 1 John 1:5) given to him (Micah 6:8). He knows to
  fear God (Josh 4:24, Dan 6:26), give alms (Job 36:6,15), and pray (Job
  33:26, Jonah 3:8).
- Cornelius is not the only Gentile who worships the God of Israel
  without converting to Judaism. The synagogue at Antioch in Pisidia
  also has Gentile "God-fearers" (Acts 13:16, 13:26). The centurion at
  Capernaum (Luke 7:1) was judged by the local Jews to be a worthy
  man (Luke 7:4-5) but he insisted that only Jesus is worthy (Luke 7:7),
  and the Savior healed the man's servant (Luke 7:9-10).

Language
Metonymy (a noun is replaced by one related to it) – "house" is substituted
for "household."

**[3] He saw in a vision evidently about the ninth hour of the day an angel
of God coming in to him, and saying unto him, Cornelius.**

**[4] And when he looked on him, he was afraid, and said, What is it, Lord?
And he said unto him, Thy prayers and thine alms are come up for a
memorial before God.**

- Cornelius observes the Jewish hour of prayer (Acts 3:1) at 3 PM.
- The prayers and righteous acts of Cornelius (Acts 10:31) are come
  up before God as would the sweet savor (Gen 8:21, Psalm 141:2)
  of an acceptable sacrifice (Psalm 20:3, Phil 4:18). His actions are a
  memorial (Lev 2:2) in that they lead God to remember (Acts 10:31)
  Cornelius as He remembered saints such as Noah (Gen 6:9, 8:1) for
  whom He provided deliverance (2 Peter 2:5).
- Cornelius is not saved (Acts 11:14), his good works notwithstanding
  (Titus 3:5), so God responds to his devoutness by allowing him to
  hear the gospel (Acts 10:34-43).

Language
An "evident vision" is clear and unmistakable.

[5] And now send men to Joppa, and call for one Simon, whose surname is Peter:

[6] He lodgeth with one Simon a tanner, whose house is by the sea side: he shall tell thee what thou oughtest to do.

Peter lodges at Joppa with Simon, a professional tanner of animal skins (Acts 9:43). Jonah sailed out of Joppa (Jonah 1:3) on a mission to Gentiles in Nineveh (Jonah 3:3) and soon Peter will leave Joppa on a mission to Gentiles in Caesarea (Acts 10:24).

[7] And when the angel which spake unto Cornelius was departed, he called two of his household servants, and a devout soldier of them that waited on him continually;

Cornelius' unnamed soldier is a faithful messenger (Prov 25:13), as was Abraham's servant, who worked faithfully to find his son Isaac a wife (Gen 24, in which narrative he is likewise unnamed and is a type of the Holy Spirit).

[8] And when he had declared all these things unto them, he sent them to Joppa.

[9] On the morrow, as they went on their journey, and drew nigh unto the city, Peter went up upon the housetop to pray about the sixth hour:

[10] And he became very hungry, and would have eaten: but while they made ready, he fell into a trance,

[11] And saw heaven opened, and a certain vessel descending unto him, as it had been a great sheet knit at the four corners, and let down to the earth:

[12] Wherein were all manner of fourfooted beasts of the earth, and wild beasts, and creeping things, and fowls of the air.

- Around noon (Psalm 55:17), as Cornelius' party approaches, Peter

goes to the flat rooftop (Matt 24:17, Mark 2:4) to pray (1 Peter 4:7).
- Peter is "very hungry" as were Esau (Gen 25:30-32) and Jonathan (1 Sam 14:24-27).
- A "trance" is a state between waking and sleeping in which the individual appears awake though transfixed to observers.
- During the wilderness wanderings God had opened the windows of heaven (Mal 3:10) and sent down food to the Israelites (Psalm 78:23-25).
- "All manner," meaning both ceremonially clean and unclean animals (Lev 11) together in one vessel (Mark 11:16) representing Jews and Gentiles together in one body (Eph 3:6).

[13] And there came a voice to him, Rise, Peter; kill, and eat.

[14] But Peter said, Not so, Lord; for I have never eaten any thing that is common or unclean.

[15] And the voice spake unto him again the second time, What God hath cleansed, that call not thou common.

[16] This was done thrice: and the vessel was received up again into heaven.

- Peter was apparently raised as a devout Jew and has strictly followed Old Testament dietary laws (Lev 11). Therefore he is appalled at the idea of eating ceremonially unclean food, as would any Jew (Ezek 4:14, Dan 1:8).
- The Old Testament ordinances in general (Col 2:14-16) and dietary regulations in specific (1 Tim 4:1-6) have been abolished in the New Testament.
- A wise man fears God and is afraid to disobey Him (1 Kings 13:20-24), but Peter has been quite comfortable saying "no" to the Lord when he judges it right to do so (Matt 16:22, John 13:8). Here, however, Peter has reason to believe God is testing him (Gen 22:1, James 1:2,12) by asking him to eat food that is common (unsanctified, 1 Sam 21:4-5) and unclean (ritually unapproved, Lev 11).
- For the believer, food is blessed by God (1 Tim 4:4-5) and cannot harm him spiritually (Mark 7:14-23, Rom 14:14).

- The vision is shown three times in correlation with the three approaching Gentiles (Acts 10:7-8). Peter may recall how the Lord Jesus had thrice repeated his admonition (John 21:15-17).

[17] Now while Peter doubted in himself what this vision which he had seen should mean, behold, the men which were sent from Cornelius had made enquiry for Simon's house, and stood before the gate,

[18] And called, and asked whether Simon, which was surnamed Peter, were lodged there.

[19] While Peter thought on the vision, the Spirit said unto him, Behold, three men seek thee.

[20] Arise therefore, and get thee down, and go with them, doubting nothing: for I have sent them.

Peter is to have no doubts (Rom 14:23) about God allowing him to eat all foods (Acts 10:14) and likewise to have no uncertainty that God is directing him to go with these Gentiles (Acts 10:28).

[21] Then Peter went down to the men which were sent unto him from Cornelius; and said, Behold, I am he whom ye seek: what is the cause wherefore ye are come?

[22] And they said, Cornelius the centurion, a just man, and one that feareth God, and of good report among all the nation of the Jews, was warned from God by an holy angel to send for thee into his house, and to hear words of thee.

Jews affirm the devoutness of the Gentile Cornelius (Acts 10:2) as Jews had affirmed the devoutness of the centurion of Capernaum (Luke 7:2-5).

[23] Then called he them in, and lodged them. And on the morrow Peter went away with them, and certain brethren from Joppa accompanied him.

- Before His resurrection, Christ had told His disciples to evangelize other Jews, not the Gentiles or Samaritans (Matt 10:5-6). More recently, Peter saw (Acts 8:14) Philip fulfill Christ's post-resurrection commission to bring the gospel to Samaritans (Acts 1:8). Now Peter is sent to Caesarea to fulfill Christ's commission to bring the gospel to Gentiles (Acts 1:8).

- Peter considers the vision and understands that he can travel with Gentiles because "God hath shewed me that I should not call any man common or unclean" (Acts 10:28). However, not until the outpouring of God's Spirit tomorrow (Acts 10:44-47) will he understand that the vision indicates that God is placing Jews and Gentiles together into one body.
- Peter and six brethren (Acts 11:12) form a traveling party of seven, the Biblical number of perfection (Gen 2:2). These seven plus three Romans (Acts 10:7) form a traveling party of ten, the number of witnesses present when Boaz redeemed his Gentile bride (Ruth 4:2).

[24] And the morrow after they entered into Cæsarea. And Cornelius waited for them, and had called together his kinsmen and near friends.

[25] And as Peter was coming in, Cornelius met him, and fell down at his feet, and worshipped him.

[26] But Peter took him up, saying, Stand up; I myself also am a man.

- Cornelius took the vision seriously and invited family and friends to meet Peter with him.
- Cornelius, who is from the West, doubtless understands that in the East, obeisance is made as a show of respect (Exod 18:7) and prostrates himself before Peter.
- Peter likewise knows that in the Roman world, such posturing is reserved for worship, which is due only to God (Luke 5:8, Rev 1:17, 19:10, 22:8-9), and Peter does not allow worship any more than will Paul and Barnabas (Acts 14:11-15).
- Herod will not show humility (Acts 12:20-23) like Peter does (1 Peter 5:5-6).

[27] And as he talked with him, he went in, and found many that were come together.

[28] And he said unto them, Ye know how that it is an unlawful thing for a man that is a Jew to keep company, or come unto one of another nation; but God hath shewed me that I should not call any man common or unclean.

[29] Therefore came I unto you without gainsaying, as soon as I was sent for: I ask therefore for what intent ye have sent for me?

- God called Israel to be separated unto Him (Deut 14:2), but the laws regarding clean and unclean (Lev 11) have been applied in such a rigorous manner that almost any contact with Gentiles is potentially defiling (Acts 11:2-3).
- Christ's accusers said, "This man receiveth sinners, and eateth with them" (Luke 15:2). The Lord Jesus welcomes fellowship with those who recognized their need for His mercy and grace (Luke 5:32).
- When Peter meets Cornelius and observes his devoutness, he understands God's message to "go with them doubting nothing" (Acts 10:20), in that he no longer needs to shun Gentiles as he would avoid unclean animals. Despite professing insight, he is yet to fully understand the rooftop vision's (Acts 10:11-16) meaning (Jews and Gentiles together in one body) and will be astonished (Acts 10:45) when he does (Acts 10:47).

Language
To "gainsay" is to speak against or oppose (Luke 21:15).

[30] And Cornelius said, Four days ago I was fasting until this hour; and at the ninth hour I prayed in my house, and, behold, a man stood before me in bright clothing,

- Cornelius had seen the vision the afternoon of the first day of this account (Acts 10:3), his men met Peter about noon on the second day (Acts 10:9), they left to travel back the third day (Acts 10:23), and now meet on the fourth day (Acts 10:24).
- The angel at the empty tomb wore bright clothing ("raiment white as snow," Matt 28:3).

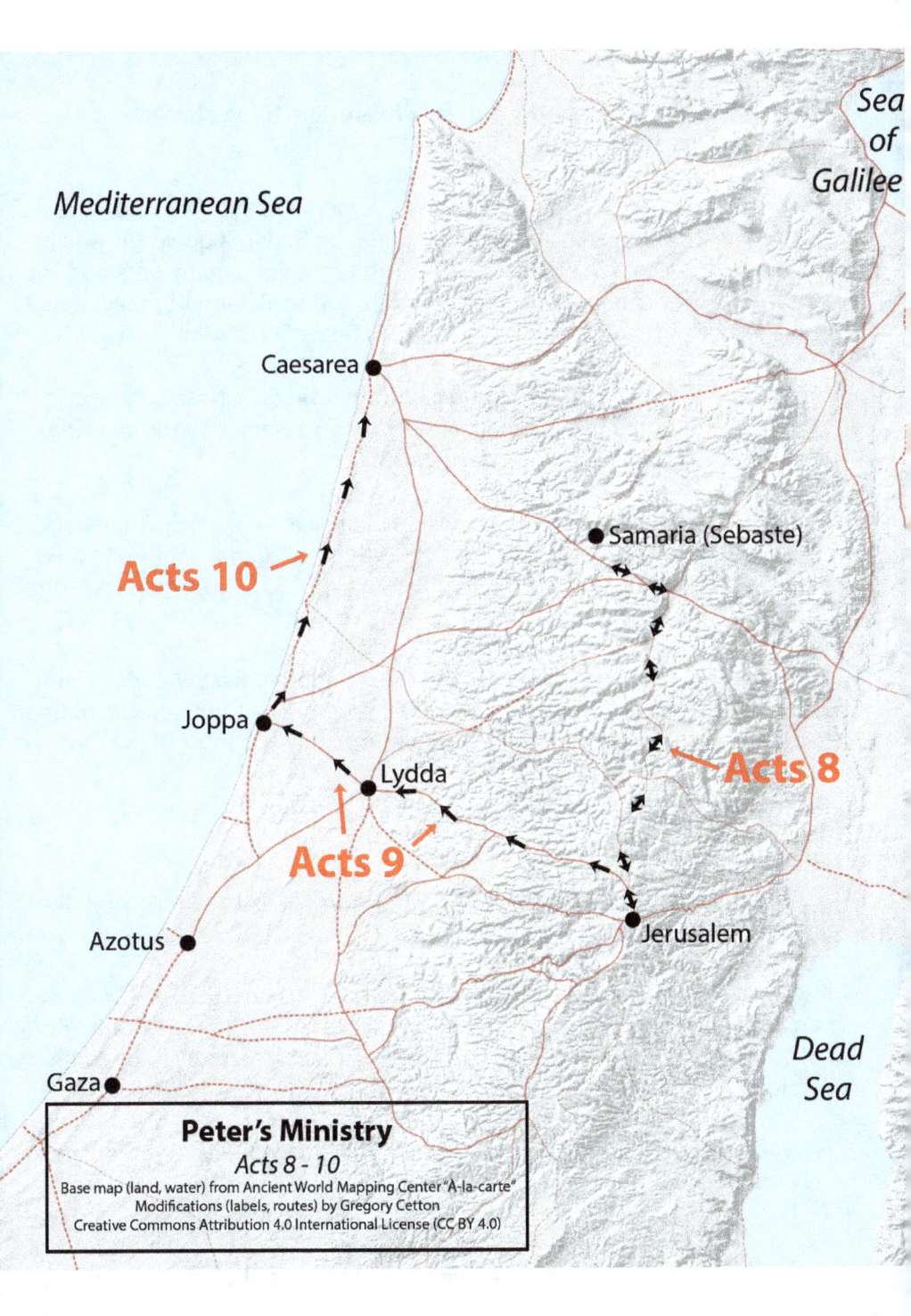

Mediterranean Sea

Sea of Galilee

Caesarea

Acts 10

Samaria (Sebaste)

Joppa

Lydda

Acts 8

Acts 9

Azotus

Jerusalem

Gaza

Dead Sea

Peter's Ministry
Acts 8 - 10
Base map (land, water) from Ancient World Mapping Center "A-la-carte"
Modifications (labels, routes) by Gregory Cetton
Creative Commons Attribution 4.0 International License (CC BY 4.0)

[31] And said, Cornelius, thy prayer is heard, and thine alms are had in remembrance in the sight of God.

As Cornelius speaks, Peter undoubtedly remembers his visit to Dorcas, whose charitable deeds were remembered by God in a powerful way (Acts 9:36-43). He also perceives that although Cornelius' good works got God's attention, they cannot earn him salvation, and so Peter will preach forgiveness of sins through faith in the Lord Jesus Christ (Acts 10:36-43).

[32] Send therefore to Joppa, and call hither Simon, whose surname is Peter; he is lodged in the house of one Simon a tanner by the sea side: who, when he cometh, shall speak unto thee.

The Lord Jesus has promised that He will always be with His followers (Matt 28:20). Here the reader is given but a small glimpse of God's all-encompassing presence with the believer (Psalm 139:7-10) when the angel describes Peter's exact location.

[33] Immediately therefore I sent to thee; and thou hast well done that thou art come. Now therefore are we all here present before God, to hear all things that are commanded thee of God.

Cornelius obeyed immediately (Matt 4:22) and now listens attentively (Prov 1:5).

[34] Then Peter opened his mouth, and said, Of a truth I perceive that God is no respecter of persons:

God does not alter His righteous requirements (Deut 10:17-19) because an individual is rich or poor (Job 34:19, James 2:1-4), Jew or Gentile (Rom 10:12, Luke 3:8). God measures an individual's character by judging his actions (Col 3:25, 1 Peter 1:17).

[35] But in every nation he that feareth him, and worketh righteousness, is accepted with him.

- God chose the nation of Israel to be His "special people" (Deut 7:6) and decreed them acceptable to receive His word and plan of salvation. Gentiles are outside the covenant (Eph 2:12), so Jews tend to believe that only they are acceptable to God and Gentiles are not (Gal 2:15). Yet there have been individual Gentiles whom God deemed acceptable to receive light from Him, such as Melchizedek (Gen 14:18-20), Job (Job 1:8), Rahab (Josh 6:25), and Ruth (Ruth 2:12).

- Peter knows that the gospel originally "was sent unto the children of Israel" (Acts 10:36) and not to the Gentiles (Matt 15:24). However, Cornelius reminds Peter of righteous, God-fearing Gentiles of the Old Testament. Peter therefore believes that Cornelius is acceptable to receive God's word and plan of salvation.

- Paul was saved when not working righteousness (he was persecuting Jesus' followers, Acts 9:1-6). He in turn will bring the gospel not merely to "acceptable" Gentiles such as Cornelius but even to "unacceptable" pagan Gentiles such as the jailor at Philippi (Acts 16:30), Greek philosophers like Dionysius (Acts 17:34), and practitioners of witchcraft at Ephesus (Acts 19:19).

Centurion Cornelius is on military assignment in Caesarea when God graciously sends Peter to him with the gospel (Acts 10).

GOR Photo / Shutterstock.com

[36] The word which God sent unto the children of Israel, preaching peace by Jesus Christ: (he is Lord of all:)

- Peter preaches Jesus' earthly ministry now as he did at Pentecost (Acts 2:22-24). The gospel went first to Jews and now to Gentiles (Rom 1:16).
- Christ is "The Prince of Peace" (Isa 9:6, Luke 2:14) and provides to believers "peace with God" (Rom 5:1).
- "Lord of all" means He Lord of both Jews and Gentiles (Rom 3:29) and offers the gift of salvation to all who will receive it. "For the same Lord over all is rich unto all that call upon him" (Rom 10:12).

[37] That word, I say, ye know, which was published throughout all Judæa, and began from Galilee, after the baptism which John preached;

Cornelius knows of the former public ministries of both John the Baptist (as do Jews as far away as Asia Minor, Acts 13:24) and the Lord Jesus (as do other devout Gentiles, Luke 7:1–9).

[38] How God anointed Jesus of Nazareth with the Holy Ghost and with power: who went about doing good, and healing all that were oppressed of the devil; for God was with him.

- "God anointed Jesus" means that He is the "Messiah" (Hebrew word for "anointed") and "Christ" (Greek word for "anointed").
- The Savior was filled with the Holy Ghost (Luke 4:1,18) and always worked to the benefit of others (Matt 13:37). His miracles included healings and exorcisms (Luke 4:40-41).

[39] And we are witnesses of all things which he did both in the land of the Jews, and in Jerusalem; whom they slew and hanged on a tree:

- Jesus "went about doing good" (Acts 10:38) yet was shamefully executed (1 Peter 3:18) by crucifixion "on a tree" (1 Peter 2:24).
- Peter previously (Acts 5:30) accused the Jewish leaders of two evils: they murdered their Messiah (Acts 2:23) and concurrently declared Him accursed by hanging Him on the cross (Deut 21:22–23, Gal

3:13).

[40] Him God raised up the third day, and shewed him openly;

Christ had predicted that His resurrection would be on the third day (Luke 18:33, 24:6-7).

[41] Not to all the people, but unto witnesses chosen before of God, even to us, who did eat and drink with him after he rose from the dead.

Jesus presented infallible proofs (Acts 1:3) of His resurrection when He privately showed Himself to His disciples (including Peter) and ate with them (Luke 24:34-43, John 21:12-14). After He rose from the dead, He was seen and touched (Matt 28:9, John 20:27, 1 John 1:1) only by those who loved Him (1 John 4:19).

[42] And he commanded us to preach unto the people, and to testify that it is he which was ordained of God to be the Judge of quick and dead.

- Peter was commanded by Jesus to preach the gospel (Acts 1:8, Matt 28:19-20, Luke 24:47), which Peter has done despite threats (Acts 4:17), beating (Acts 5:40), and imprisonment (Acts 5:18, 12:5).
- God the Father has appointed Jesus to one day judge the world (John 5:22, 1 Peter 4:5), both those persons who are living ("quick") and dead. The Father has confirmed this by raising the Son from the dead (Acts 17:31).

[43] To him give all the prophets witness, that through his name whosoever believeth in him shall receive remission of sins.

- "All the prophets" without exception spoke of a coming Messiah (from Gen 3:15 to Mal 4:2; Rom 1:1-2, 3:21), and Peter uses this phrase to refer to the subset of those prophets who linked the Messiah to forgiveness of sins (Isa 53:4-12, Jer 31:34, Dan 9:24).
- Peter preaches that this foretold Messiah is Jesus and that all who believe on Him (whether Jew or Gentile, Rom 10:12) receive forgiveness of sins (Acts 13:38).
- "Remission" means "payment is applied, debt is forgiven." God for-

gives sins, not through leniency, but because Christ paid the penalty that is due (Rom 3:25, 2 Cor 5:21).

Language
Synecdoche (the whole refers to the part) – Peter says "all the prophets" (as in Acts 3:18) to refer to those prophets who foretold the saving work of Christ ("all the prophets who foretold Christ's atonement give a consistent message").

[44] While Peter yet spake these words, the Holy Ghost fell on all them which heard the word.

Peter's listeners obey from the heart (Rom 6:17) the gospel message (1 Cor 15:3-4) by believing on the Lord Jesus Christ (Acts 16:31). They receive salvation and the gift of the Holy Ghost without verbal confession (Rom 10:9-10), laying on of hands (Acts 8:17), or water baptism (Mark 16:16, Acts 2:38).

[45] And they of the circumcision which believed were astonished, as many as came with Peter, because that on the Gentiles also was poured out the gift of the Holy Ghost.

In the Old Testament, the Holy Spirit was promised only to the people of Israel (Isa 44:1-3, Ezek 36:26-27). Therefore the Jewish believers are astonished that these Gentiles are given God's gift without first converting to Judaism through customary rights such as circumcision (Exod 12:48, Acts 15:1).

[46] For they heard them speak with tongues, and magnify God. Then answered Peter,

The Jewish believers miraculously hear their language spoken (Acts 2:8) by these European Gentiles (Acts 10:1).

[47] Can any man forbid water, that these should not be baptized, which have received the Holy Ghost as well as we?

- These Gentiles are saved (Acts 11:14) and have received the gift

of the Holy Ghost and may therefore undergo water baptism (Acts 11:17).
- Peter will later explain (Acts 11:16) that at this point he recalled the words of Jesus, who said, "John truly baptized with water; but ye shall be baptized with the Holy Ghost" (Acts 1:5). Therefore if God baptized these Gentiles with the Holy Ghost, it would be wrong for Peter to withhold water baptism.
- Peter finally understands the meaning of the rooftop vision, which showed "all manner" of animals together (Acts 10:11-16): Jews and Gentiles can be united in Christ through the gospel (Acts 15:9, Gal 3:28, Eph 2:11-22).

[48] And he commanded them to be baptized in the name of the Lord. Then prayed they him to tarry certain days.

- Peter directs the baptism but apparently does not perform it himself, mirroring the practice of Jesus (John 4:2) and Paul (1 Cor 1:14-17).
- They are baptized in the name of the Lord (Matt 28:19-20), which is the Father (Matt 11:25), the Son (Phil 2:11), and the Holy Spirit (Acts 21:11, 2 Cor 3:17).
- Like the Ethiopian treasurer (Acts 8:35-37), these Gentiles receive salvation by simple faith in Jesus Christ (Rom 10:9-10), receive the Holy Spirit at the moment of conversion without laying on of hands, and are baptized only after conversion. God's work in the lives of Cornelius and company is the New Testament pattern He uses to save lost sinners (Acts 16:30-33).
- Peter exercises the authority given to him by Christ when he uses spiritual "keys" (Matt 16:18-19) to open the door (1 Cor 16:9) of the kingdom of God by bringing the gospel to the Gentiles as he had to the Jews (Acts 2) and the Samaritans (Acts 8).
- Peter now lodges with Cornelius and eats with the Gentile new believers (Acts 11:3).

Current Events

- Emperor Caligula (Gaius) rules for just over four years. He is described as "one that had arrived at the utmost pitch of wickedness . . . a slave to his pleasures . . . of a very murderous disposition . . . enjoyed his exorbitant power to this only purpose, to injure those who least deserved it . . . and got his wealth by murder and injustice."[205] While building a reputation for "cruelty and licentiousness" towards the people of Rome he orders "temples to be erected and sacrifices to be offered to himself as to a god."[206]
- Caligula is considered such a brutal tyrant that he is assassinated in a plot formed by two of his "tribunes in the praetorian guard," which is supported by "practically all his courtiers . . . and those who did not take part in the conspiracy . . . were glad to see a plot formed against him."[207]
- The Roman people remember both Caligula and Tiberius (the emperor during Jesus' earthly ministry, Luke 3:1) for their cruelty. "Hence the name of Gaius [Caligula] does not occur in the list of emperors whom we mention in our oaths and prayers any more than does that of Tiberius."[208]
- Claudius, the nephew of the late Tiberius, becomes emperor and decrees, "It will therefore be fit to permit the Jews, who are in all the world under us, to keep their ancient customs without being hindered so to do."[209]
- Herod Agrippa I has a fortuitous part in bringing the new Emperor Claudius to power[210] and is rewarded with rule over all the territory "over which Herod [the Great], who was his grandfather, had reigned, that is, Judea and Samaria."[211]

---

[205] Josephus, *Antiquities*, 19.2.5
[206] Cassius Dio, *Roman History*, 59.24:1 and 59.4:4
[207] Ibid., 59.29.1
[208] Ibid., 60.30.6
[209] Josephus, *Antiquities*, 19.5.3
[210] Ibid., 19.4.1-2
[211] Ibid., 19.5.1

Teaching Question

<u>Question</u>: Peter initially is quite fearful of eating with Gentiles. What is the thinking of his day regarding Gentiles in the context of clean and unclean food rules?

<u>Answer</u>: "They and theirs were defiled; their houses unclean, as contain-ing idols or things dedicated to them; their feasts, their joyous occasions, their very contact, was polluted by idolatry ... if a heathen were left alone in a room he might in wantonness or by carelessness defile the wine or meat on the table, or the oil or wheat in the store. Under such circum-stances, everything must be regarded as having been rendered unclean. Three days before a heathen festival every business transaction with them was prohibited, for fear of giving either help or pleasure. Jews were to avoid passing through a city where there was an idolatrous feast – nay, they were not even to sit down within the shadow of a tree dedicated to idol-worship. Its wood was polluted; if used in baking the bread was un-clean... Milk drawn by a heathen, if a Jew had not been present to watch it, bread and oil prepared by them, were unlawful. Their wine was wholly interdicted – the mere touch of a heathen polluted a whole cask; nay, even to put one's nose to heathen wine was strictly prohibited!"[212]

Challenge Questions

1. Why does God choose Cornelius to hear the gospel and not some other Gentile?
2. What is the meaning of Peter's statement that "... in every nation he that feareth him, and worketh righteousness, is accepted with him" (Acts 10:35)?

---

[212] Alfred Edersheim, *The Life and Times of Jesus the Messiah*, chap. 7

Acts Chapter 11

[1] And the apostles and brethren that were in Judæa heard that the Gentiles had also received the word of God.

The gospel came first to Jews (Acts 2:5) and later to Samaritans (Acts 8:14). Gentiles had been considered ineligible for God's blessing (Eph 2:11–12), and this new development comes as a surprise (Acts 10:45).

Language
"Brethren" was originally used to refer to fellow Jews (Acts 2:29, 7:2, Rom 9:3, Heb 7:5), but in the New Testament is used to refer to fellow believers in Christ (Acts 15:1, 23, Rom 1:13).

[2] And when Peter was come up to Jerusalem, they that were of the circumcision contended with him,

[3] Saying, Thou wentest in to men uncircumcised, and didst eat with them.

- God sent Peter to preach the gospel to Cornelius in Caesarea (Acts 10:19-43). Peter's Gentile hearers responded to the gospel and were saved (Acts 10:44-47). Cornelius then invited Peter to stay in his home for a few days (Acts 10:48), where he ate meals as any guest would. Peter followed Christ's instructions to missionaries, "in the same house remain, eating and drinking such things as they give" (Luke 10:7).
- Jews ("the circumcision") believe that God's blessings flow through Abraham to his descendants (Rom 4) via Isaac and Jacob. Although God promised Abraham that "in thee shall all families of the earth be blessed" (Gen 12:3), so far Israel's experience generally has been one of God blessing Jews, not Gentiles. For well over 1,000 years Jews have taught that for a Gentile to be worthy before God, he must undergo the rite of circumcision and convert to Judaism. The thinking was, "Except ye be circumcised after the manner of Moses,

ye cannot be saved" (Acts 15:1).

- Therefore, Peter's actions appear reckless to his peers. Eating with Gentiles ("men uncircumcised") has been condemned (Acts 10:28) because their food does not conform to Moses' dietary laws (Lev 11). More importantly, by dining together, Peter seems to show acceptance (Luke 15:2, 1 Cor 5:11) of sinful Gentiles (Gal 2:15) and appears to disregard the importance of circumcision (Acts 21:21). They rebuke Peter and demand an answer.
- Peter's detractors would do better to recall that Jesus did "eat and drink with publicans and sinners" (Luke 5:30). Christ even spent two days with the Samaritans (John 4:40), a seemingly scandalous choice since devout "Jews have no dealings with the Samaritans" (John 4:9). The Savior also dined with His beloved disciples (John 21:12) and will one day eat with His beloved Church (Rev 19:9).

[4] But Peter rehearsed the matter from the beginning, and expounded it by order unto them, saying,

Peter will now summarize Acts 10.

[5] I was in the city of Joppa praying: and in a trance I saw a vision, A certain vessel descend, as it had been a great sheet, let down from heaven by four corners; and it came even to me:

[6] Upon the which when I had fastened mine eyes, I considered, and saw fourfooted beasts of the earth, and wild beasts, and creeping things, and fowls of the air.

[7] And I heard a voice saying unto me, Arise, Peter; slay and eat.

[8] But I said, Not so, Lord: for nothing common or unclean hath at any time entered into my mouth.

[9] But the voice answered me again from heaven, What God hath cleansed, that call not thou common.

[10] And this was done three times: and all were drawn up again into heaven.

[11] And, behold, immediately there were three men already come unto the house where I was, sent from Cæsarea unto me.

[12] And the Spirit bade me go with them, nothing doubting. Moreover these six brethren accompanied me, and we entered into the man's house:

[13] And he shewed us how he had seen an angel in his house, which stood and said unto him, Send men to Joppa, and call for Simon, whose surname is Peter;

[14] Who shall tell thee words, whereby thou and all thy house shall be saved.

Despite his good works (Acts 10:2), Cornelius was not saved (Titus 3:5), for though he had *heard* of Jesus Christ (Acts 10:37-38), he did not *know* Jesus Christ as his Savior (John 17:3).

214

[15] And as I began to speak, the Holy Ghost fell on them, as on us at the beginning.

As Peter began to speak his following phrase after "remission of sins" (Acts 10:43), the Gentiles (in response to their faith, Acts 11:18) suddenly received the Holy Ghost (Acts 10:44) as had the Jews at Pentecost (Acts 2:1-4).

[16] Then remembered I the word of the Lord, how that he said, John indeed baptized with water; but ye shall be baptized with the Holy Ghost.

Peter quotes Christ's words, recorded in Acts 1:5. John's words are recorded in Luke 3:16.

[17] Forasmuch then as God gave them the like gift as he did unto us, who believed on the Lord Jesus Christ; what was I, that I could withstand God?

Peter explains that since the Gentiles had received the baptism of the Holy Ghost (Acts 10:44), which is performed by God, he would have been resisting God's direction by withholding water baptism (Acts 10:47), which is a rite performed by mere humans.

[18] When they heard these things, they held their peace, and glorified God, saying, Then hath God also to the Gentiles granted repentance unto life.

- Until now, the saved have all been persons born as Jews or converts to Judaism, such as the proselytes attending Pentecost (Acts 2:10) and (possibly) the Ethiopian treasurer (Acts 8:27). The apostles at Jerusalem now recognize that the Gentiles as a nation (Gen 10:1-32, Rom 11:11-24) have access to eternal life (John 3:16) by repenting (a change of heart and mind which leads to a change of action, Acts 20:21) and turning to Jesus Christ, even as do the Jews (Acts 5:31, 10:47b). The recognition of God's new plan has no doubt been difficult for Jews to accept, and here in Acts 11, the author (Luke) repeats much of the narrative of Acts 10 to emphasize the gravity of this subject.
- Now that "the apostles and brethren" (Acts 11:1) understand Peter's explanation, they glorify God for His work and fully accept His plan. However, some staunch advocates of circumcision will remain unconvinced, and the Jerusalem church will hold a council to settle the matter (Acts 15:1-21).

215

[19] Now they which were scattered abroad upon the persecution that arose about Stephen travelled as far as Phenice, and Cyprus, and Antioch, preaching the word to none but unto the Jews only.

[20] And some of them were men of Cyprus and Cyrene, which, when they were come to Antioch, spake unto the Grecians, preaching the Lord Jesus.

- The region of Phoenicia (Phenice) includes Tyre and Sidon (Matt 15:21). The Lord Jesus preached in (Luke 6:17-49) and performed "mighty works" in Tyre and Sidon (Luke 10:13), including the healing of the Syrophoenician woman's son (Mark 7:24-30). Disciples have evangelized this area and Paul will later meet believers there (Acts 15:3, 21:3-4, 27:3). Cyprus is the home island of Barnabas (Acts 4:36).
- Jewish believers fleeing persecution in Jerusalem (Acts 8:1,4) went

to Phoenicia, Cyprus, and Antioch. Being from Jerusalem, they were naturally most comfortable interacting with other Jews and brought the gospel only to other Jews.

- Jews originally from Cyprus and the North-African city of Cyrene had received the gospel at Pentecost (Acts 2:10). They are ethnically Jewish but their language and culture are Greek, so they are called "Hellenistic Jews." In contrast to other Jewish believers who brought the gospel only to other Jews, these from Cyprus and Cyrene are comfortable interacting with other Greek-speakers and therefore bring the gospel to "Grecians" (Hellenists) in Damascus, meaning Hellenistic Syrian Gentiles, whose language and culture are Greek.
- Evangelists from Cyrene may include Lucius (Acts 13:1) and possibly Simon, whose family is known to Mark (Mark 15:21).
- The efforts of both groups of missionaries (native and foreign-born Jews) will lead to a united Jewish-Gentile church at Antioch in Syria that will eventually send Paul on three missionary journeys (Acts 13:1-14:26, 15:40–18:22, 18:23–21:17).

216

Grecian = Hellenist = one whose language and culture are Greek
Acts 6:1:   Grecians are Greek-speaking Jews of Jerusalem
Acts 9:29:   Grecians are Greek-speaking Jews of Jerusalem
Acts 11:20: Grecians are Greek-speaking Syrian Gentiles of Damascus

Luke writes the Greek word *Hellēnistōn* each time (Acts 6, 9, and 11), which is consistently translated as "Grecians" in the King James Bible. Modern English versions typically translate *Hellēnistōn* as one word in Acts 6 and 9 and then a different word in Acts 11, such as "Hellenistic Jews" and "Greeks,"[213] or "Greek-speaking believers" and "Gentiles."[214] The King James Bible consistently translates *Hellēnistōn* as "Grecians" to reflect what Luke wrote and to allow the reader to consider the meaning of these words in their context.

[21] And the hand of the Lord was with them: and a great number believed, and turned unto the Lord.

---

[213] *New International Version*
[214] *New Living Translation*

The hand of the Lord can be with a believer for a blessing (Ezra 7:6) or against an unbeliever for a curse (Acts 13:11).

Language
Anthropomorphism (God condescends to describe Himself in human terms) – God does not have a human hand, but one is attributed to Him to describe His mercy and judgment.

[22] Then tidings of these things came unto the ears of the church which was in Jerusalem: and they sent forth Barnabas, that he should go as far as Antioch.

[23] Who, when he came, and had seen the grace of God, was glad, and exhorted them all, that with purpose of heart they would cleave unto the Lord.

[24] For he was a good man, and full of the Holy Ghost and of faith: and much people was added unto the Lord.

217

- The gospel came first to Jews (Acts 2:5), later to Samaritans (Acts 8:14), and finally to Gentiles (Acts 11:18). Each group has had its own separate places of worship, so the church at Antioch is unique because Jews and Gentiles worship together.
- The apostles previously sent Peter and John to investigate the unique development in Samaria. They now investigate this new situation at Antioch by sending Barnabas, a long-time disciple from the early days of the Jerusalem church (Acts 4:36-37).
- Barnabas knows that for hundreds of years, Gentiles have been "strangers from the covenants of promise, having no hope, and without God in the world" (Eph 2:12). Therefore when he observes Gentiles who are now saved, he sees the grace of God at work. Some Jews, when seeing Gentiles brought into the faith without circumcision (Acts 15:1,5), are "filled with envy" (Acts 13:45). Barnabas, however, is a "good man" and therefore glad to see what Jesus has done for them.
- Barnabas is filled with the Holy Ghost, so his goodness is not his own (Matt 19:17) but is a fruit of the Spirit (Gal 5:22).
- One cleaves unto the Lord by following and obeying Him (Josh 23:8,

2 Kings 18:6).

[25] Then departed Barnabas to Tarsus, for to seek Saul:

[26] And when he had found him, he brought him unto Antioch. And it came to pass, that a whole year they assembled themselves with the church, and taught much people. And the disciples were called Christians first in Antioch.

- Barnabas had been the first to introduce Saul to the church at Jerusalem (Acts 9:27). There Saul's fervent witness brought him into serious conflict with unbelieving Jews, and the brethren sent him home to Tarsus to preserve his life (Acts 9:29-30). However, the situation in Antioch is very different than Jerusalem. Barnabas knows that Saul's zeal and knowledge of scripture (Acts 22:3) will be of great benefit here. He doubtless knows of Saul's calling by Christ to "bear my name before the Gentiles" (Acts 9:15). Therefore Barnabas now invites Saul to the church at Antioch.
- Early in the book of Acts, the believers were all of Jewish background (Acts 2:14, 36) and considered themselves the truest of all Jews because they believe God's promise of the Messiah (Luke 24:26-27, Acts 24:14-15). As they grew, they referred to their doctrine simply as the "way" (Acts 9:2, 19:9, 23, 22:4, 24:14,22). Now that the followers of Jesus Christ include persons who are no longer pagan Gentiles yet have not become Jews, a new term is needed, and this mixed group is given the name "Christians" (Acts 26:28, 1 Peter 4:16).

[27] And in these days came prophets from Jerusalem unto Antioch.

[28] And there stood up one of them named Agabus, and signified by the Spirit that there should be great dearth throughout all the world: which came to pass in the days of Claudius Cæsar.

- Agabus the prophet (Eph 4:11) uses his gift (Rom 12:6) for foretelling the future (Acts 21:10-11). Other prophets such as Judas and Silas are shown forth-telling through words of exhortation (Acts 15:32, 1 Cor 14:3).

- The prophecy will come to pass: "for whereas a famine did oppress them at that time, and many people died for want of what was necessary to procure food ..."[215]

[29] Then the disciples, every man according to his ability, determined to send relief unto the brethren which dwelt in Judæa:

[30] Which also they did, and sent it to the elders by the hands of Barnabas and Saul.

- Israel has always had elders in a leadership role (Exod 3:18, 1 Sam 8:4-5). The early Church also ordains elders (1 Tim 3:1-7), the first ones being selected by apostles (Acts 14:23) or those under them (Titus 1:5).
- Saul has a heart for giving (Gal 2:10), which prompts him to take this journey. Later he will take another collection for the poor saints of Judea (1 Cor 16:1-4, 2 Cor 8:1-9:15) and with his future companions (Acts 20:4) will deliver that charitable gift (Rom 15:25-27, 31) to Jerusalem (Acts 21:17, 24:17).
- This journey of Barnabas and Saul to Jerusalem is described in Gal 2:1-10. While there Saul meets with Simon Peter, James the half-brother of Jesus, and John the Apostle (Gal 2:9). Their meeting is a private matter (Gal 2:2) unrecorded by Luke.
- Saul and Barnabas will later return from their charitable mission along with John Mark (Acts 12:25), "sister's son to Barnabas" (Col 4:10).

219

Challenge Question

With whom does Peter speak in Acts 11:2-18?

---

[215] Josephus, *Antiquities*, 20.2.5

Acts Chapter 12

[1] Now about that time Herod the king stretched forth his hands to vex certain of the church.

King Herod Agrippa I[216] is the grandson of Herod the Great, who murdered the young children of Bethlehem (Matt 2:16) and nephew of Herod Antipas, who beheaded John the Baptist (Matt 14:6-10) and mocked the Lord Jesus (Luke 23:11). Paul will preach before his son, Herod Agrippa II (Acts 26:1-29).

[2] And he killed James the brother of John with the sword.

- Herod Agrippa I now rules Judea and Samaria[217] but knows that he must have the cooperation of the populace to govern effectively. Although he is a Jew he has lived his life as a man of the world. So he now puts on a new face to improve his reputation. "He also came to Jerusalem, and offered all the sacrifices that belonged to him, and omitted nothing which the law required."[218] "The flute would play before them, until they reached the Temple Mount. When they reached the Temple Mount even King Agrippa would take the basket and place it on his shoulder and walk as far as the Temple Court. When he got to the Temple Court, the Levites would sing …"[219]
- Herod calculates that he can further improve his standing as a righteous Jew and gain the loyalty of zealous Israelites by murdering James the apostle, the brother of John (both are sons of Zebedee, Matt 4:21).

[3] And because he saw it pleased the Jews, he proceeded further to take Peter also. (Then were the days of unleavened bread.)

---

[216] For the story of Agrippa's rise to power, see notes at the end of Acts 9.
[217] Josephus, *Antiquities*, 19.5.1
[218] Ibid., 19.6.1
[219] *Mishna*, Bikkurim 3.4

- Executing James was popular with Herod's allies in Jerusalem, so he now intends to kill Peter.
- Seven days of eating unleavened bread (Exod 12:15, Lev 23:6) follow the annual sacrifice of the Passover (Exod 12:5-6, 21).

[4] And when he had apprehended him, he put him in prison, and delivered him to four quaternions of soldiers to keep him; intending after Easter to bring him forth to the people.

Peter is imprisoned for the third time. He had previously been arrested by temple authorities (Acts 4:3) and released (Acts 4:23), then re-arrested and miraculously escaped (Acts 5:18-20). Now the Romans confidently assign a group of sixteen soldiers (four quads) and make the prison as secure as they can (Matt 27:65).

<u>Language</u>
The early Church celebrated the resurrection of Christ at the time of the Jewish Passover. The word *pascha* (in both ancient and contemporary Greek) can refer to either Easter or Passover, depending on the context. Around 1530, William Tyndale sought a new English word to differentiate the Old Testament feast from the New Testament era holiday and coined the term "Passover" for his English translation. In 1611, *pascha* was translated with the newer word "Passover" for pre-resurrection settings and the traditional "Easter" for the post-resurrection context of Acts 12.

[5] Peter therefore was kept in prison: but prayer was made without ceasing of the church unto God for him.

The power of Herod is contrasted with the power of prayer during an all-night prayer meeting at Mary's house (Acts 12:12).

[6] And when Herod would have brought him forth, the same night Peter was sleeping between two soldiers, bound with two chains: and the keepers before the door kept the prison.

The night before his execution, Peter apparently remembers Jesus' words (John 21:18) and sleeps well (Psalm 4:8).

[7] And, behold, the angel of the Lord came upon him, and a light shined in the prison: and he smote Peter on the side, and raised him up, saying, Arise up quickly. And his chains fell off from his hands.

Their security arrangements prove ineffective (Prov 21:31) as the angel of the Lord brings light (Rev 21:23) to the prison and incapacitates the soldiers (Matt 28:4, 1 Sam 26:12).

[8] And the angel said unto him, Gird thyself, and bind on thy sandals. And so he did. And he saith unto him, Cast thy garment about thee, and follow me.

[9] And he went out, and followed him; and wist not that it was true which was done by the angel; but thought he saw a vision.

Peter recalls his former vision (Acts 10:9-16).

222

[10] When they were past the first and the second ward, they came unto the iron gate that leadeth unto the city; which opened to them of his own accord: and they went out, and passed on through one street; and forthwith the angel departed from him.

David wrote, "Let the wicked fall into their own nets, whilst that I withal escape" (Psalm 141:10).

[11] And when Peter was come to himself, he said, Now I know of a surety, that the Lord hath sent his angel, and hath delivered me out of the hand of Herod, and from all the expectation of the people of the Jews.

Peter is the picture of a sinner imprisoned by the devil (2 Tim 2:26), bound by sin (Prov 5:22), spiritually asleep (Eph 5:14), appointed to die (Heb 9:27), and without hope of deliverance (Eph 2:12). He is visited (Luke 1:68), receives light (1 Peter 2:9), is raised up (Eph 2:6), is set free from bondage (Gal 5:1), puts on the armor of God (Eph 6:11-18), and follows Christ (1 Peter 2:21). Now, like the prodigal son, he comes to himself (Luke 15:17), is reconciled to God (Col 1:21), acknowledges the Lord's deliverance (Col 1:13), and goes to tell others what Jesus Christ has done for him (Acts 12:17).

[12] And when he had considered the thing, he came to the house of Mary the mother of John, whose surname was Mark; where many were gathered together praying.

Mary is a relative of Barnabas (Col 4:10) and the mother of John Mark (Acts 12:25).

[13] And as Peter knocked at the door of the gate, a damsel came to hearken, named Rhoda.

[14] And when she knew Peter's voice, she opened not the gate for gladness, but ran in, and told how Peter stood before the gate.

[15] And they said unto her, Thou art mad. But she constantly affirmed that it was even so. Then said they, It is his angel.

Peter is scheduled for execution this morning (Acts 12:6), and they can hardly believe he is alive. As at Christ's resurrection, they first disbelieve the report (Luke 24:10-11) then imagine they see his "angel" (i.e., his spirit, Luke 24:36-37, Acts 23:8).

<u>Language</u>
Dramatic Irony (the character is unaware of the inconsistency) – Rhoda is so shocked to see Peter that she leaves him standing at the door.

[16] But Peter continued knocking: and when they had opened the door, and saw him, they were astonished.

[17] But he, beckoning unto them with the hand to hold their peace, declared unto them how the Lord had brought him out of the prison. And he said, Go shew these things unto James, and to the brethren. And he departed, and went into another place.

- "James the Lord's brother" (Gal 1:19) is a leader in the church at Jerusalem (see Acts 21:18 and comments on Acts 15:13).
- Peter leaves (Matt 10:23) Agrippa's jurisdiction and will visit the church at Antioch in Syria (Gal 2:9) before returning to Jerusalem

after Herod's death (Acts 15:7-11).

[18] Now as soon as it was day, there was no small stir among the soldiers, what was become of Peter.

[19] And when Herod had sought for him, and found him not, he examined the keepers, and commanded that they should be put to death. And he went down from Judæa to Cæsarea, and there abode.

Herod's plans failed (Psalm 33:10) when the Lord answered the fervent prayers of His saints (James 5:16). Herod shows no mercy (James 2:13) when taking empty vengeance (Rom 12:19) by enforcing the Roman policy of death to guards of escaped prisoners (Acts 16:27, 27:42). He will soon receive recompense (Prov 11:31) of his own misdeeds (Acts 12:23).

[20] And Herod was highly displeased with them of Tyre and Sidon: but they came with one accord to him, and, having made Blastus the king's chamberlain their friend, desired peace; because their country was nourished by the king's country.

Tyre and Sidon, the chief cities of Phoenicia (Phenice, Acts 11:19), receive food supply from Judea (1 Kings 5:1,11, Ezra 3:7, Ezek 27:2,17). They ask Blastus, Herod's personal aide or *valet de chambre*, to help settle the dispute (Matt 5:25).

[21] And upon a set day Herod, arrayed in royal apparel, sat upon his throne, and made an oration unto them.

Herod proudly (James 4:6) makes his final speech, which does not please God (Prov 6:16-17).

[22] And the people gave a shout, saying, It is the voice of a god, and not of a man.

The people enthusiastically honor Herod (Jude 16), who foreshadows the coming "beast" who will speak great blasphemies and be worshiped by all the people of the earth (Rev 13:4-8).

[23] And immediately the angel of the Lord smote him, because he gave not God the glory: and he was eaten of worms, and gave up the ghost.

Although he behaved like a religious Jew while at Jerusalem, Herod Agrippa I is now in a Greco-Roman setting and reverts to his usual behavior. He does not give God the glory (Rom 1:21) when he accepts (Prov 25:27) rather than refuses (Acts 10:26) the people's worship and is therefore smitten (2 Kings 19:35, Mal 4:6) unto death (Psalm 49:20).

[24] But the word of God grew and multiplied.

Luke gives the fourth of seven summary statements in the book of Acts now that the gospel has spread into the Gentile world as far as Antioch in Syria.

"It is the voice of a god, and not of a man"! The crowd blasphemously praises the evil King Herod Agrippa I during his public speech. "And immediately the angel of the Lord smote him, because he gave not God the glory" (Acts 12:19-23).   Lindasj22 / Shutterstock.com

[25] And Barnabas and Saul returned from Jerusalem, when they had ful-filled their ministry, and took with them John, whose surname was Mark.

- Barnabas and Saul return to Antioch after their charitable mission to Jerusalem (Acts 11:27-30).
- Peter and brethren sent from James may visit Antioch at this time (Gal 2:11-14).
- John Mark is the son of Mary (Acts 12:12) and "sister's son to Barnabas" (Col 4:10). He will author the second gospel under Simon Peter's influence (1 Peter 5:13). Mark comes from a family of means, as his mother has at least one servant (Acts 12:13) and owns a home in Jerusalem large enough to hold prayer meetings (Acts 12:12). He will initially accompany Barnabas and Saul on the first missionary journey (Acts 13:1-5) but will abandon the trip early on (Acts 13:13). For this, Saul will deem him unreliable and refuse him company on his second missionary journey (Acts 15:37-39), but Mark will later regain Saul's complete favor (Col 4:10, 2 Tim 4:11, Philem 24).

Teaching Question

Question: What is the relationship between Barnabas and John Mark?
Answer: "... Marcus, sister's son [*anepsios*] to Barnabas ..." (Col 4:10).

The Greek word *anepsios* is defined in dictionaries of modern Greek as "nephew" and biblical dictionaries of ancient Greek as "cousin." Secular experts of ancient Greek, however, explain that in "Classical Greek terminology ... *anepsios* varies between cousin-German and nephew."[220] So, on the one hand, examples in ancient literature can be found of *anepsios* referring to cousins, such as the ancient Greek translation of Numbers 36:11. On the other hand, a funerary monument from the "Roman imperial period" at an excavation in Cilicia (the Apostle Paul's home province, Acts 21:39) bears a Greek inscription in which *anepsios* appears to indicate nephews.[221]

---

[220] M. Miller (1953). "Greek kinship terminology." *The Journal of Hellenic Studies*, 73, p.46
[221] Emanuela Borgia (2005). "A new funerary cippus from Elaiussa Sebaste." *Adalya, VIII,*

In conclusion, *anepsios* "must be regarded as a general 'descendant,' referred to those persons who share a common grandparent... Thus the term *anepsios* could be used indifferently in ancient sources to indicate either a nephew or a cousin."[222] Modern versions typically translate *anepsios* as "cousin," but the King James Bible more precisely translates *anepsios* as "sister's son," an antiquated term derived from the German word *geschwisterkind* which carries the meaning of either nephew or cousin.

Challenge Questions

The ancient historian Flavius Josephus writes in the same time period as Luke, but their material rarely overlaps. One exception is the death of Herod Agrippa I, which both historians record. Is the following account given by Josephus compatible with or contradictory to Luke's account? What is the significance of your answer?

"Now when Agrippa had reigned three years over all Judea he came to the city Caesarea, which was formerly called Strato's Tower; and there he exhibited spectacles in honor of Caesar, for whose well-being he'd been informed that a certain festival was being celebrated. At this festival a great number were gathered together of the principal persons of dignity of his province. On the second day of the spectacles he put on a garment made wholly of silver, of a truly wonderful texture, and came into the theater early in the morning. There the silver of his garment, being illuminated by the fresh reflection of the sun's rays, shone out in a wonderful manner, and was so resplendent as to spread awe over those that looked intently upon him. Presently his flatterers cried out, one from one place, and another from another (though not for his good), that he was a god; and they added, 'Be thou merciful to us; for although we have hitherto reverenced thee only as a man, yet shall we henceforth own thee as superior to mortal nature.' Upon this the king neither rebuked them nor rejected their impious flattery. But he shortly afterward looked up and saw an owl sitting on a certain rope over his head, and immediately

p.135-150
[222] Ibid., p.139

understood that this bird was the messenger of ill tidings, just as it had once been the messenger of good tidings to him; and fell into the deepest sorrow. A severe pain arose in his belly, striking with a most violent intensity. He therefore looked upon his friends, and said, 'I, whom you call a god, am commanded presently to depart this life; while Providence thus reproves the lying words you just now said to me; and I, who was by you called immortal, am immediately to be hurried away by death. But I am bound to accept what Providence allots, as it pleases God; for we have by no means lived ill, but in a splendid and happy manner.' When he had said this, his pain became violent. Accordingly he was carried into the palace ... and when he had been quite worn out by the pain in his belly for five days, he departed this life, being in the fifty-fourth year of his age, and in the seventh year of his reign."[223]

---

[223] Josephus, *Antiquities*, 19.8.2

Acts Chapter 13

[1] Now there were in the church that was at Antioch certain prophets and teachers; as Barnabas, and Simeon that was called Niger, and Lucius of Cyrene, and Manaen, which had been brought up with Herod the tetrarch, and Saul.

- Barnabas is from Cyprus (Acts 4:36). He previously brought Saul[224] from Tarsus to teach at Antioch (Acts 11:25-26).
- Simeon has a Jewish name but is called "Black."
- Lucius of Cyrene may have been among the first evangelists to Antioch (Acts 11:20).
- Manaen (the Greek name for Menahem, 2 Kings 15:14) was raised with Herod Antipas, who had ruled over the fourth part of his father Herod the Great's kingdom (hence "tetrarch") and beheaded John the Baptist (Matt 14:6-10) and mocked Jesus (Luke 23:11).
- Some prophets (Eph 4:11) have a gift (Rom 12:6) of foretelling the future, such as Agabus (Acts 11:28, 21:10-11). Other prophets such as Judas and Silas are shown forth-telling through words of exhortation (Acts 15:32, 1 Cor 14:3).
- Church members at Antioch have various spiritual gifts (1 Cor 12) and work together in unity (Psalm 133:1, Eph 4:3).

[2] As they ministered to the Lord, and fasted, the Holy Ghost said, Separate me Barnabas and Saul for the work whereunto I have called them.

- Old Testament saints were set apart for God's service ("separated," Lev 20:24b), and so too Barnabas and Saul are "separated unto the gospel of God" (Rom 1:1).
- The Holy Ghost speaks directly to these believers as He did to Philip (Acts 8:29) and Peter (Acts 10:19) and will to others (Acts 16:6-7, 20:23, 21:11). The Spirit works to glorify the Lord Jesus Christ (John 16:13-14) by separating these two men unto a gospel mission (Rom

229

---

[224] See biographical comments at Acts 8:1.

1:1) that will bring glory to God's Son by winning souls to Him (Acts 13:12, 43, 48, 14:1, 23).

[3] And when they had fasted and prayed, and laid their hands on them, they sent them away.

- Saints shown fasting and praying include Samuel (1 Sam 7:6), David (2 Sam 12:16), Elijah (1 Kings 19:8), Jehoshaphat (2 Chron 20:3), Ezra (Ezra 8:23), Nehemiah (Neh 1:4), and the disciples of John the Baptist (Luke 5:33). God has at times given special revelation to those occupied in fasting and prayer, such as to Moses, who received the law (Deut 9:9), Daniel, who received visions of the last days (Dan 9:3, 10:2-3), and Cornelius, who received the gospel (Acts 10:30). Esther's people were delivered from death after she fasted (Esther 4:16). Anna's many years of commitment to fasting and prayer were rewarded by seeing the Christ child when she was 84 years old (Luke 2:36-38). The Lord Jesus triumphed over temptation following His forty-day fast (Matt 4:2).
- Christ taught his disciples fasting with prayer (Matt 6:5-18), and this practice is considered a normal part of the Christian life by the Apostle Paul (2 Cor 6:5, 11:27) and other believers (Acts 13:2, 14:23).

[4] So they, being sent forth by the Holy Ghost, departed unto Seleucia; and from thence they sailed to Cyprus.

Saul and Barnabas begin the first missionary journey, which will end at Acts 14:26.

[5] And when they were at Salamis, they preached the word of God in the synagogues of the Jews: and they had also John to their minister.

- Saul's great desire of the heart is to see the salvation of his people Israel (Rom 9:1-5, 10:1), and he works to bring them the gospel by preaching in synagogues first (Acts 9:20). Jews know the Old Testament and will readily understand the gospel message of Jesus the Messiah.

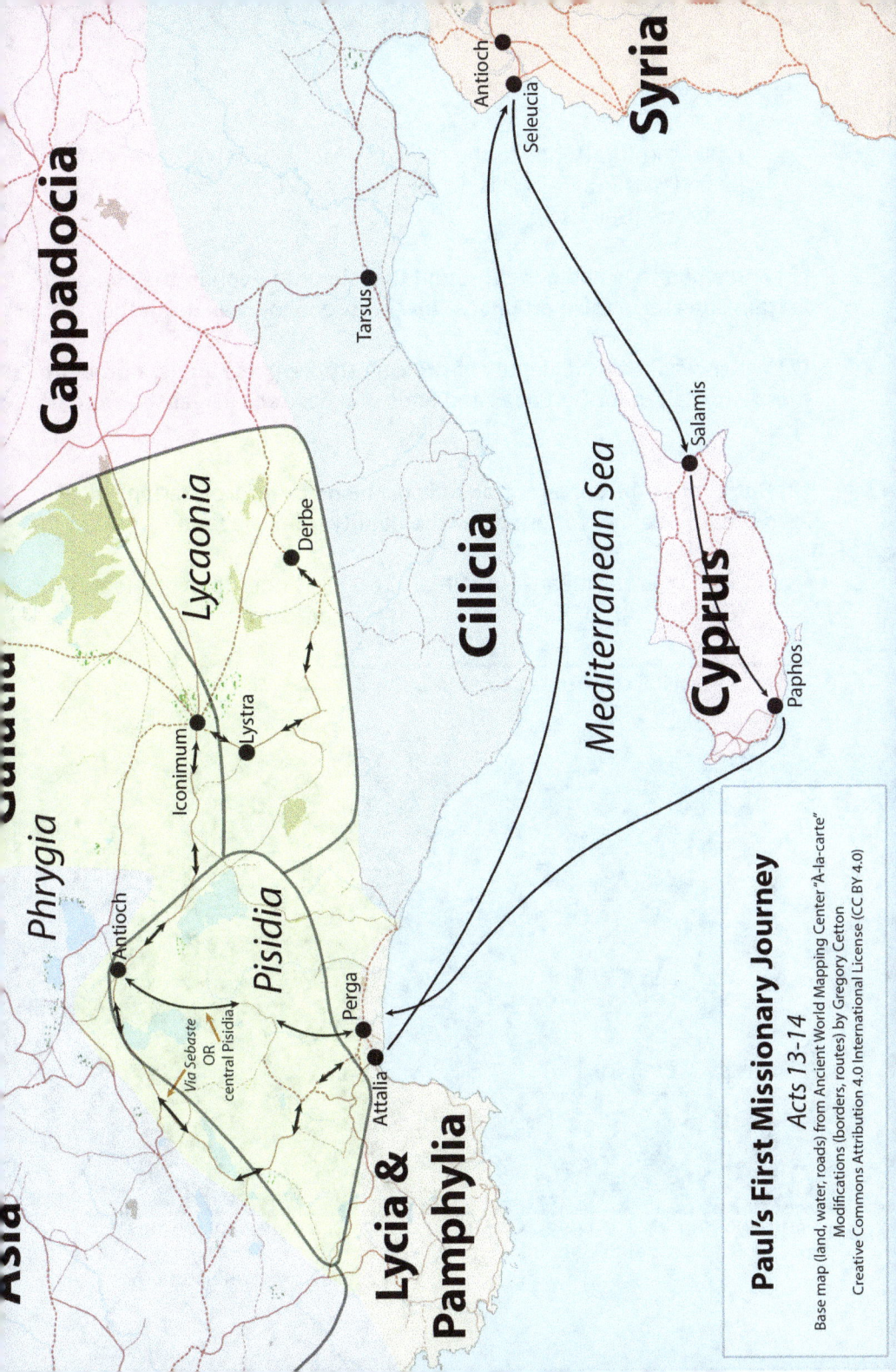

Cappadocia

Syria

Antioch
Seleucia

Tarsus

Cilicia

Mediterranean Sea

Salamis

Cyprus

Paphos

Galatia

Lycaonia

Derbe

Phrygia

Iconium

Lystra

Antioch

Pisidia

Via Sebaste
OR
central Pisidia

Perga

Attalia

Lycia &
Pamphylia

Asia

Paul's First Missionary Journey

Acts 13-14

Base map (land, water, roads) from Ancient World Mapping Center "A-la-carte"
Modifications (borders, routes) by Gregory Cetton
Creative Commons Attribution 4.0 International License (CC BY 4.0)

- John Mark[225] attends to their needs (Matt 27:55) with a servant's heart (Matt 20:26-27), as did Christ (Matt 20:28) and as should all believers (Gal 5:13).

[6] And when they had gone through the isle unto Paphos, they found a certain sorcerer, a false prophet, a Jew, whose name was Bar-jesus:

[7] Which was with the deputy of the country, Sergius Paulus, a prudent man; who called for Barnabas and Saul, and desired to hear the word of God.

[8] But Elymas the sorcerer (for so is his name by interpretation) withstood them, seeking to turn away the deputy from the faith.

- "Bar" in Greek means "son" (Matt 16:17), as does "ben" in Hebrew (Gen 35:18). So "Bar-jesus" means "son of Jesus."

[225] See biographical comments at Acts 12:25.

Paul and Barnabas travel to Cyprus on their first missionary journey and preach the gospel at Salamis (Acts 13:4-5).

sadullahkisi / Shutterstock.com

- Governor Paulus is "prudent" (Prov 16:21, 18:15), meaning he is careful to hear a matter and deliberate its merits before passing judgment.
- Elymas works to prevent Governor Paulus from receiving the truth (1 Thes 2:16) and is an evil influence on him as Jezebel had been on King Ahab (1 Kings 21:7). Jannes and Jambres had similarly confronted Moses (Exod 7:11, 2 Tim 3:8). Alexander will likewise withstand Paul (2 Tim 4:14-15).

[9] Then Saul, (who also is called Paul,) filled with the Holy Ghost, set his eyes on him,

Saul (his Hebrew name) is hereafter referred to as Paul (his Roman name), as his ministry will focus on Gentiles (Rom 11:13) when his fellow Jews reject the gospel (Acts 13:46).

The Roman governor Sergius Paulus becomes a believer when Paul and Barnabas preach the gospel at Paphos on Cyprus (Acts 13:6-12).
Kochneva Tetyana / Shutterstock.com

[10] And said, O full of all subtilty and all mischief, thou child of the devil, thou enemy of all righteousness, wilt thou not cease to pervert the right ways of the Lord?

[11] And now, behold, the hand of the Lord is upon thee, and thou shalt be blind, not seeing the sun for a season. And immediately there fell on him a mist and a darkness; and he went about seeking some to lead him by the hand.

[12] Then the deputy, when he saw what was done, believed, being astonished at the doctrine of the Lord.

- Paul reprimands the sorcerer Elymas, as did Peter the sorcerer Simon in Samaria (Acts 8:20). The apostle tells Elymas, named son of Jesus ("Bar-jesus"), that he is more appropriately called "son of the devil" (John 8:44) because he, like the devil, is full of subtlety (Gen 3:1) and mischief (Psalm 36:4). Both Paul and Jesus reserve this strongest language (Matt 23:33) for false teachers who prevent others from receiving the truth (Matt 23:13, 1 Thes 2:15-16).
- A veil (2 Cor 3:14) of darkness falls over Elymas, who, like Israel (Rom 11:7-8, 25), has been blinded (2 Cor 4:4) for a season (2 Chron 15:3). The Lord performs a miracle of judgment through Paul as He did through Old Testament prophets (Exod 7:20, 1 Kings 13:4-5, 2 Kings 1:10-12). Paul's striking Elymas with physical blindness illustrates the man's spiritual blindness, as with the similar miracle performed by Elisha (2 Kings 6:16-20).
- Sergius Paulus now embraces the gospel (Prov 25:5).

Language
- "Subtilty" means craftiness and deceit.
- *Hebraism* (a Hebrew manner of expression) - "child of the devil" is more vivid than "devilish person."

[13] Now when Paul and his company loosed from Paphos, they came to Perga in Pamphylia: and John departing from them returned to Jerusalem.

John Mark may depart because of hardships (2 Cor 11:23-28), a longing for home (Acts 12:12), or being uncomfortable with the evangelism of Gentiles without requiring conversion to Judaism (Acts 15:1-2). Paul will show his displeasure when planning his next mission and refuse Mark's company (Acts 15:37-39).

[14] But when they departed from Perga, they came to Antioch in Pisidia, and went into the synagogue on the sabbath day, and sat down.

They now visit Antioch in Pisidia and afterward will visit Iconium (Acts 13:51), Lystra (Acts 14:8), and Derbe (Acts 14:20). These cities are all in the Roman province of Galatia (Acts 18:23), to whom Paul will later write the Epistle to the Galatians.

[15] And after the reading of the law and the prophets the rulers of the synagogue sent unto them, saying, Ye men and brethren, if ye have any word of exhortation for the people, say on.

The Lord Jesus read from Isaiah (Luke 4:16-17) per this Sabbath tradition of reading from the law and the prophets. Paul now has an opportunity to preach a sermon (to give a "word of exhortation"). An example of a "word of exhortation" is the Epistle to the Hebrews, which is a letter containing a sermon (Heb 13:22).

[16] Then Paul stood up, and beckoning with his hand said, Men of Israel, and ye that fear God, give audience.

Paul speaks to Jews and God-fearing Gentiles (Acts 10:2, 13:26) who worship in the synagogue. His sermon is like Stephen's in that he addresses his fellow Israelites, gives an overview of their history (Acts 7:2-50, 13:17-22), preaches Christ and His resurrection (Acts 7:56, 13:23-39), and ends with a stern warning against rejection (Acts 7:51-53, 13:40-41).

[17] The God of this people of Israel chose our fathers, and exalted the people when they dwelt as strangers in the land of Egypt, and with an high arm brought he them out of it.

- Paul summarizes the book of Exodus.
- A "high hand" is a salute of victory (Exod 14:8).

[18] And about the time of forty years suffered he their manners in the wilderness.

Paul summarizes the book of Numbers.

[19] And when he had destroyed seven nations in the land of Chanaan, he divided their land to them by lot.

- Paul summarizes the book of Joshua.
- Moses had prophesied Israel's miraculous victories. "When the Lord thy God shall bring thee into the land whither thou goest to possess it, and hath cast out many nations before thee, the Hittites, and the Girgashites, and the Amorites, and the Canaanites, and the Perizzites, and the Hivites, and the Jebusites, seven nations greater and mightier than thou" (Deut 7:1).
- After Joshua conquered Canaan, the Lord determined the tribes' land inheritance by lot (Josh 23:4), a seemingly random procedure directed by God (Prov 16:33, compare with Acts 1:26).

Language
"Canaan" (Josh 14:1) translated from Hebrew is equivalent to "Chanaan" translated from Greek.

[20] And after that he gave unto them judges about the space of four hundred and fifty years, until Samuel the prophet.

- Paul summarizes the book of Judges.
- "After that" indicates that the era of the judges followed the conquest of Canaan (first the book of Joshua, then the book of Judges). The 450-year timeline starts with Moses, the first judge.
- "He gave unto them judges," starting with Moses (Exod 18:13), who was accused of acting as one (Exod 2:14) when at age 40 (Acts 7:23) he first tried to deliver (Judg 2:16) the oppressed Israelites (Exod 2:11-12, Acts 7:24-25). He was rejected from that time (Acts 7:27) until he presented himself again 40 years later at age 80 (Exod 7:7, Acts 7:30, 35).
- "Until Samuel the prophet" became Israel's final judge (1 Sam 7:15)

when he gave the people King Saul (Acts 13:21, 1 Sam 11:15).
- "About ... 450 years." There had been 480 years from the Exodus to
  the building of the temple and 476 years from the Exodus to the
  start of Solomon's reign (1 Kings 6:1). David and Saul each reigned
  forty years (2 Sam 5:4, Acts 13:21), so there were 436 years from the
  Exodus to David and 396 years from the Exodus to Saul. Moses had
  presented himself as a judge 40 years before the Exodus (Acts 7:30),
  which is 436 years before Saul. So from the time that Moses first
  presented himself as a judge until Samuel established Saul as king
  is 436 years or "about 450 years."
  480 Exodus to temple
  476 Exodus to Solomon
  436 Exodus to David
  396 Exodus to Saul
  436 Moses' first appearance to Saul

**[21] And afterward they desired a king: and God gave unto them Saul the
son of Cis, a man of the tribe of Benjamin, by the space of forty years.**

Paul summarizes the book of 1st Samuel. The Lord answered the people's
request for a king "like all the nations" (1 Sam 8:5) by giving them Saul of
Benjamin (1 Sam 9:21), a flawed man (1 Sam 15:26) "like all the nations."

Language
"Kish" (Saul's father, 1 Sam 14:51) translated from Hebrew is equivalent to
"Cis" translated from Greek.

**[22] And when he had removed him, he raised up unto them David to be
their king; to whom also he gave testimony, and said, I have found David
the son of Jesse, a man after mine own heart, which shall fulfil all my will.**

- King Saul was "removed" in two steps. First, Saul was rejected from
  being king (1 Sam 16:1), and David was anointed king by Samuel
  (1 Sam 16:13). Next, Saul died in battle (1 Sam 31:4-5), and David
  ascended to the throne (2 Sam 5:3).
- "I have found David the son of Jesse" (quoting Psalm 89:20), "a man
  after mine own heart" (quoting 1 Sam 13:14), "which shall fulfil all
  my will" (quoting Isa 44:28).

- Solomon chose wisdom (2 Chron 1:10), yet despite his glorious kingdom (1 Kings 10:7, Ecc 2:9) and magnificent writings (Proverbs, Ecclesiastes, Song of Solomon), he is remembered for bringing idolatry to Israel (2 Kings 23:13, Neh 13:26).
- David chose fellowship with God, yet despite his serious moral failings (2 Sam 12:9) and scandalous family strife (2 Sam 13:14, 28-29, 15:6, 18:33), God commemorates him in scripture as a man after His own heart (1 Sam 13:14, Psalm 89:20). David chose the good part (Luke 10:42) when he desired fellowship with God, as should every believer (1 Cor 1:9, 1 John 1:3).

[23] Of this man's seed hath God according to his promise raised unto Israel a Saviour, Jesus:

- The Lord Jesus Christ is both fully man (Rom 1:3) and fully God (Rom 1:4, 1 Tim 3:16). Jesus is God from all eternity (John 1:1, 8:58). He received His humanity from Mary as the "seed of the woman" (Gen 3:15) through the line of David (2 Sam 7:12–16, Isa 11:1, Luke 3:31, 2 Tim 2:8).
- Paul proclaims that Jesus was raised up as a Savior to Israel, and will next declare that "God raised him from the dead" (Acts 13:30).

[24] When John had first preached before his coming the baptism of repentance to all the people of Israel.

John the Baptist never left the land of Israel. Still, his calling of Israel to repentance (Mark 1:4, Acts 19:4) is known to the Jews of Asia Minor (Acts 19:1-3), who view him as a prophet (Mark 11:32) and should have understood his ministry as the fulfillment of prophecy (Isa 40:3, Mal 3:1, Matt 3:1-3).

[25] And as John fulfilled his course, he said, Whom think ye that I am? I am not he. But, behold, there cometh one after me, whose shoes of his feet I am not worthy to loose.

- John the Baptist denied being the Messiah, Elijah, or the prophet like Moses (John 1:19-21). He identified Jesus the Messiah as the One he is unworthy to serve (John 1:26-27).

- Paul uses King David (Acts 13:22-23) and John the Baptist as links to Jesus.

[26] Men and brethren, children of the stock of Abraham, and whosoever among you feareth God, to you is the word of this salvation sent.

Paul brings the good news of salvation first to the Jews (Rom 1:16) and God-fearing Gentiles present in the synagogue (Acts 13:16,26) and subsequently to all Gentiles at Antioch (Acts 13:42, 44).

[27] For they that dwell at Jerusalem, and their rulers, because they knew him not, nor yet the voices of the prophets which are read every sabbath day, they have fulfilled them in condemning him.

The rulers at Jerusalem do not believe from the heart the scriptures (John 5:46) that they read every Sabbath (Acts 13:14-15), and so in ignorantly rejecting Christ (Acts 3:17, 1 Cor 2:8), they fulfill these very scriptures (Isa 53, Psalm 22, 69).

239

[28] And though they found no cause of death in him, yet desired they Pilate that he should be slain.

Christ was proclaimed innocent by Pilate (Luke 23:14), Pilate's wife (Matt 27:19), Herod (Luke 23:15), Judas (Matt 27:4), the thief (Luke 23:41), and the centurion (Mark 15:39). Nevertheless the people of Jerusalem asked Pilate to put Jesus to death (Matt 27:20, Luke 23:23, John 19:7).

[29] And when they had fulfilled all that was written of him, they took him down from the tree, and laid him in a sepulchre.

The rulers at Jerusalem (first "they") fulfilled prophecy in crucifying Christ (Luke 24:25-27). Joseph of Arimathaea and Nicodemus (second "they") buried Jesus (John 19:38-42).

Language
Omission (words left out to emphasize those remaining) – Joseph of Arimathaea and Nicodemus are unnamed to underscore the act (which affirms that Jesus was dead and buried) rather than the persons involved.

[30] But God raised him from the dead:

The resurrection of Jesus (Eph 1:20) is the disciples' favorite preaching topic (Acts 4:33).

[31] And he was seen many days of them which came up with him from Galilee to Jerusalem, who are his witnesses unto the people.

- Jesus was raised in Galilee (Matt 21:11) and some of his apostles are from that region, including Peter, Andrew, and Philip (John 1:44, Mark 1:28-29), James and John (Mark 1:19), and Nathaniel (John 21:2). Female disciples also "followed him from Galilee" (Luke 23:49).
- Christ was seen alive after His resurrection by many witnesses over forty days (Acts 1:3), including the apostles (Acts 1:22, 2:32), disciples (John 21:1-2), and a group of over five hundred at one time (1 Cor 15:6).

[32] And we declare unto you glad tidings, how that the promise which was made unto the fathers,

[33] God hath fulfilled the same unto us their children, in that he hath raised up Jesus again; as it is also written in the second psalm, Thou art my Son, this day have I begotten thee.

- Paul places himself ("we") among those who have witnessed the resurrected Christ (1 Cor 15:8). Jesus fulfills the promise (John 9:35-37) that the Messiah would be the Son of God (Psalm 2:7, 2 Sam 7:14, Zech 12:10).
- "Thou art my Son" (Psalm 2:7) means that Jesus Christ is the Son of God (Dan 3:25) from all eternity (John 1:1, Isa 9:6). "This day have I begotten thee" means that He entered the world (1 Peter 1:20) through the incarnation (Gal 4:4). "Raised up Jesus again" (Mark 8:31) means that He was alive, then dead, and then "raised to life again" (Heb 11:35) as the "first begotten of the dead" (Rev 1:5) never to die again (Rom 6:9). The resurrection openly confirms that Jesus is the Son of God (Rom 1:4).

[34] And as concerning that he raised him up from the dead, now no more to return to corruption, he said on this wise, I will give you the sure mercies of David.

- Quoting Isa 55:3 and 2 Sam 7:15. Peter also preached from 2 Sam 7 (Acts 2:29-30).
- Resurrected individuals such as the widow of Nain's son (Luke 7:11-16), Jairus' daughter (Luke 8:41-42, 49-56), Lazarus (John 11:1-46), and Dorcas (Acts 9:36-41) eventually die and their bodies decay ("corrupt") in the grave. The Lord Jesus was resurrected never to die again ("firstborn from the dead," Col 1:18); His body "now no more to return to corruption." His is an example of the glorified body that saints one day will receive ("firstfruits of them that slept," 1 Cor 15:20).
- God promised King David a descendant who would reign eternally over David's kingdom (2 Sam 7:12-16). This promise (called a "mercy," 2 Sam 7:15, Psalm 89:28) will find fulfillment in the Messiah (Matt 22:42 and Isa 55:3), who will have to overcome death to reign forever. Paul argues in the following three verses (Acts 13:35-37) that Jesus defeated death (Rom 6:9, Rev 1:18) by fulfilling God's promise of resurrection (Psalm 16:10). Jesus will fulfill God's kingdom promise to David when He returns to reign over the earth (Rev 20:6, 22:16).

Language
Incongruity (a noun is replaced by one remotely related to it) – the "sure *mercies* of David" means "God's faithful *promises* to David."

[35] Wherefore he saith also in another psalm, Thou shalt not suffer thine Holy One to see corruption.

[36] For David, after he had served his own generation by the will of God, fell on sleep, and was laid unto his fathers, and saw corruption:

[37] But he, whom God raised again, saw no corruption.

- Paul is preaching from Psalm 16:10, as did Peter (Acts 2:31-32).

- The Lord Jesus was raised from the dead and is the One whom David foresaw fulfilling God's promise (Psalm 16:10, 1 Thes 1:10). The fact that He will now never die and His body will never corrupt (decay) in the grave proves that He is God the Son ("the uncorruptible God" as opposed to "corruptible man," Rom 1:23).

[38] Be it known unto you therefore, men and brethren, that through this man is preached unto you the forgiveness of sins:

Forgiveness of sins is through Jesus Christ, of whom God the Father has confirmed His approval by raising Him from the dead (Rom 1:4).

[39] And by him all that believe are justified from all things, from which ye could not be justified by the law of Moses.

- Paul's listeners are no doubt thinking about the sins for which the law has no remedy, such as adultery (Lev 20:10), murder (Num 35:31), or other willful transgressions (Num 15:30-31). The wording of his sermon invites those Jews who may feel comfortable in their law-based relationship with God (Luke 18:20-21) to consider sin in their life that stands unforgiven. Yet even for those sins for which the law designates rituals, the prescribed ceremony provides only a temporary means for dealing with sins (Heb 10:1-4) and cannot permanently take them away (Exod 34:7). God did not design the law to bring justification (Gal 3:11) but to reveal man's sinful nature (Rom 3:20) and complete lack of ability to save himself (Rom 3:23).
- Justified means "declared righteous." The death and resurrection of Jesus Christ provide the means by which God can justly forgive sins (Eph 1:7). Justification goes far beyond mere pardon; through it, God applies the righteousness of Jesus Christ (Rom 3:22) to the believer's account (Rom 3:24). Henceforth God no longer sees sin in the believer but instead sees Christ's righteousness (Rom 3:21-22). Divine wrath for sin on the individual is wholly averted (Rom 5:9), his sins are forever purged (Heb 1:3), and he enjoys peace with God (Rom 5:1).
- Paul thus teaches that Christ justifies (Rom 4:25) the believer from all charges of sin, unlike Moses' law, which cannot justify from any (Rom 3:28, Gal 2:16).

[40] Beware therefore, lest that come upon you, which is spoken of in the prophets;

[41] Behold, ye despisers, and wonder, and perish: for I work a work in your days, a work which ye shall in no wise believe, though a man declare it unto you.

Paul quotes Habakkuk to recall how Jerusalem was destroyed when the people ignored God's warnings (Hab 1:5). With this, the apostle warns his listeners of eternal destruction should they overlook the gospel message (Matt 10:28).

<u>Language</u>
Hendiadys (two words for one idea) – "despisers shall perish," i.e., shall perish wonderfully (astonishingly).

[42] And when the Jews were gone out of the synagogue, the Gentiles besought that these words might be preached to them the next sabbath.

Paul preached first in the synagogue primarily to reach Jews with the gospel message (Acts 13:15). The Gentiles might well have been offended at their apparent neglect, but instead, they hunger for the truth (Matt 5:6). Like the Gentile woman who humbly asked Jesus for help stating that the "dogs eat of the crumbs which fall from their masters' table" (Matt 15:27), so too these Gentiles ask Paul for preaching and arrive *en masse* the next Sabbath (Acts 13:44).

[43] Now when the congregation was broken up, many of the Jews and religious proselytes followed Paul and Barnabas: who, speaking to them, persuaded them to continue in the grace of God.

The new believers are encouraged to live their lives in the grace that God gives to every believer for daily living (2 Cor 12:9, 2 Tim 2:1, James 4:6).

[44] And the next sabbath day came almost the whole city together to hear the word of God.

[45] But when the Jews saw the multitudes, they were filled with envy, and spake against those things which were spoken by Paul, contradicting and blaspheming.

- The synagogue leaders are filled with envy (Rom 1:29), but the disciples are filled with the Holy Ghost (Acts 13:52).
- On the previous Sabbath Paul presented himself as a devout Jew (Acts 13:14–15) who addressed God-fearing Gentiles within the context of Judaism and so was tolerated when he preached the gospel (Acts 13:23–39). Paul now reaches out directly to a large group of Gentiles, and the synagogue leaders are offended at the implication that salvation is available to Gentiles outside the confines of Judaism (Acts 15:1, 22:21–22).
- The unbelieving Jews resent the success of Paul and Barnabas (as they had of Jesus, Matt 27:18, and as they will of Paul and Silas, Acts 17:4-5) and spitefully resist their preaching (Acts 7:51). The contradicting and blaspheming are done by twisting Paul's words and vilifying his character (Acts 21:21).

[46] Then Paul and Barnabas waxed bold, and said, It was necessary that the word of God should first have been spoken to you: but seeing ye put it from you, and judge yourselves unworthy of everlasting life, lo, we turn to the Gentiles.

- Paul seeks to provoke his fellow Jews to consider the gospel (Rom 11:14) when he uses sarcasm ("judge yourselves unworthy of everlasting life") and taunts them by stating that the gospel went first to them (Acts 3:26) but will now go to their rivals, the Gentiles (Acts 22:21-22). Despite these harsh words and his future emphasis on Gentile ministry (2 Tim 1:11), Paul will still seek to reach Jewish people with the gospel by first preaching in synagogues whenever possible (Acts 17:1-2).
- The Jewish leadership rejects the gospel here in Asia Minor as they had in Jerusalem (Acts 7:54-60) and will in Europe (Acts 18:6) and Rome (Acts 28:28). Instead, the gospel message will bear fruit among the Gentiles as God calls "out of them a people for his name" (Acts 15:14).

[47] For so hath the Lord commanded us, saying, I have set thee to be a light of the Gentiles, that thou shouldest be for salvation unto the ends of the earth.

Isaiah prophesied that the Messiah would bring spiritual light to the Gentiles (Isa 49:6). Simeon identified the young Jesus as the One who would fulfill Isaiah's prophesy (Luke 2:32), and now Paul identifies Jesus as the One who is fulfilling Isaiah's prophesy (also Acts 26:23). The apostle also desires to be a light (Matt 5:16) by preaching the gospel to Gentiles (Eph 3:8).

[48] And when the Gentiles heard this, they were glad, and glorified the word of the Lord: and as many as were ordained to eternal life believed.

- Christ draws all men unto Him (John 12:32). Those who choose

Multitudes believe the gospel when Paul and Barnabas preach in Antioch of Pisidia (Acts 13:14-48).

Izabela Miszczak / Shutterstock.com

to believe the gospel (Rom 1:16) are said to have been appointed (ordained) to eternal life.
- Jews believe that surely they are ordained to eternal life (Gal 3:8), and Luke informs his readers that now Gentiles who believe the gospel are ordained to eternal life, too!

[49] And the word of the Lord was published throughout all the region.

"Published" means "proclaimed." The length of the missionaries' visit is unstated, but it was long enough to bring the gospel to the city of Antioch and to the region around it.

[50] But the Jews stirred up the devout and honourable women, and the chief men of the city, and raised persecution against Paul and Barnabas, and expelled them out of their coasts.

[51] But they shook off the dust of their feet against them, and came unto Iconium.

- The religious leaders at Antioch persecute Paul, as will those in Thessalonica (Acts 17:5, 13). The missionaries are expelled from Antioch's borders ("coasts") and head to Iconium.
- Among Jews, "shaking off the dust" indicates disapproval (Neh 5:13, Luke 9:5), and Paul does this to underscore their rejection of the gospel. Paul does not do this in a Gentile context because the symbolism is lost there (e.g., Acts 17:33).

[52] And the disciples were filled with joy, and with the Holy Ghost.

Although Paul and Silas are now expelled from Antioch, they will stop there again on their way back home (Acts 14:21). They are joyful (John 15:11) because they are filled with the Holy Spirit (Rom 15:13) and because of the souls in Antioch who have been saved (Luke 15:7).

Persuasive Speech

Paul's Spirit-filled sermon shows a mastery of persuasive speech (rhetoric).

Introduction *(exordium)* – "Men of Israel, and ye that fear God, give audience." Acts 13:16b

Narrative *(narratio)* – Paul reviews Israel's history to remind his audience how God delivered the people from Egypt and brought them into the promised land. He promised King David a descendant whom John the Baptist identified as Jesus the Messiah. Acts 13:17-25

Thesis *(propositio)* – this message of salvation through Jesus Christ is offered to you, the people of Israel. Acts 13:26

Arguments *(probatio)* – Jesus was rejected by the leadership at Jerusalem and was unjustly slain, but God raised him from the dead. He was seen alive by many witnesses. He is the Messiah promised in scripture. Acts 13:27-37

Final appeal *(peroratio)* – Jesus Christ provides justification for sins in a way the law of Moses never could. To reject Him is to suffer eternal loss. Acts 13:38-41

Teaching Question

<u>Question</u>: What three socio-political factors enable the rapid spread of the gospel in the first century AD?

<u>Answer</u>:

1. Pax Romana – this unique 200-year period of world peace inaugurated by Caesar Augustus[226] allows Christian missionaries to readily cross (former) international borders and spread the gospel "to the uttermost part of the earth" (Acts 1:8).

2. Roman road system – "The Roman road system made possible Roman conquest and administration and later provided highways ... for the diffusion of Christianity... Their numerous feeder roads extending far into the Roman provinces led to the proverb 'All roads lead to Rome.'"[227]

3. Worldwide network of synagogues – the apostle Paul enters synagogues whenever possible, both for his love for the Jewish people

---

[226] "Pax Romana." *Encyclopedia Britannica Online*, accessed 30 Mar 2020
[227] "Roman road system." *Encyclopedia Britannica Online*, accessed 30 Mar 2020

and because people there know the Old Testament well and can readily understand the gospel message of Jesus the Messiah. Synagogues are specified in Jerusalem (Acts 6:9), Damascus (Acts 9:2), Asia Minor (Acts 13:14, 14:1, 18:19), Macedonia (Acts 17:1), and Greece (Acts 18:4).

Challenge Questions

1. What does it mean "they ministered to the Lord" (Acts 13:2)?
2. In what way are believers to "continue in the grace of God" (Acts 13:43)?

Acts Chapter 14

[1] And it came to pass in Iconium, that they went both together into the synagogue of the Jews, and so spake, that a great multitude both of the Jews and also of the Greeks believed.

Both Jews and Gentiles believe gospel in Iconium, as they had in Antioch (Acts 13:42-44).

[2] But the unbelieving Jews stirred up the Gentiles, and made their minds evil affected against the brethren.

Paul and Barnabas experience opposition and eventually persecution (Acts 14:5) in Iconium as they had in Antioch (Acts 13:45, 50).

[3] Long time therefore abode they speaking boldly in the Lord, which gave testimony unto the word of his grace, and granted signs and wonders to be done by their hands.

- Paul and Barnabas are able to continue their ministry, despite initial opposition (Acts 14:2).
- Paul will later write back to the Galatian believers, reminding them how "the Spirit, . . . worketh miracles among you" (Gal 3:5). He will also tell the council at Jerusalem about the "miracles and wonders God had wrought among the Gentiles by them" (Acts 15:12).

[4] But the multitude of the city was divided: and part held with the Jews, and part with the apostles.

God's truth can cause division (Matt 10:34, John 7:43).

[5] And when there was an assault made both of the Gentiles, and also of the Jews with their rulers, to use them despitefully, and to stone them,

[6] They were ware of it, and fled unto Lystra and Derbe, cities of Lycaonia,

and unto the region that lieth round about:

- Paul and Barnabas follow the instructions of Christ, who said, "But when they persecute you in this city, flee ye into another" (Matt 10:23a). The missionaries therefore leave the region of Pisidia and enter into Lycaonia.
- Paul escapes stoning here, but those from Iconium intent on murder will catch up to Paul in Lystra (Acts 14:19).

[7] And there they preached the gospel.

This is the first mention of the gospel in connection with Paul (1 Cor 15:1-4). The apostle has traveled far from home to preach and will later explain why. "For I am not ashamed of the gospel of Christ: for it is the power of God unto salvation to every one that believeth" (Rom 1:16a).

[8] And there sat a certain man at Lystra, impotent in his feet, being a cripple from his mother's womb, who never had walked:

As with the "man lame from his mother's womb" in Jerusalem (Acts 3:2), the man here has a disability originating from birth rather than from a recent injury that might heal spontaneously.

[9] The same heard Paul speak: who stedfastly beholding him, and perceiving that he had faith to be healed,

Paul heals a man who has faith, but persons lacking faith have also received miraculous healing (Mark 6:5-6).

[10] Said with a loud voice, Stand upright on thy feet. And he leaped and walked.

Paul heals a lame man, as did Peter (Acts 3:1-8) and the Lord Jesus (Mark 2:10-12).

[11] And when the people saw what Paul had done, they lifted up their voices, saying in the speech of Lycaonia, The gods are come down to us in the likeness of men.

[12] And they called Barnabas, Jupiter; and Paul, Mercurius, because he was the chief speaker.

- The people of Lystra show their belief that "gods" had previously come down to earth as men (Gen 6:1-4) and their expectation that they will do so again.
- The Lystrans know the legend of Philemon and Baucis, who lived "upon the hills of Phrygia" and were visited by two gods appearing as men. "Jupiter went there, disguised as a mortal, and Mercury ... setting aside his wings, went with his father."[228]
- Barnabas they name after the supreme Roman god Jupiter (Acts 19:35), who foreshadows the coming world leader (the "beast," Rev 13:1-6) who will have power over all nations of the earth (Rev 13:7) and be worshiped by all that dwell on the earth (Rev 13:8). Paul they name Mercurius (Mercury), who foreshadows the coming false prophet who will speak with the power of Satan (Rev 13:11) and lead everyone on earth to worship the beast (Rev 13:12-17).

251

Language
- The Roman god "Jupiter" is equivalent to the Greek god "Zeus."
- The Roman god "Mercurius" is equivalent to the Greek god "Hermes."

[13] Then the priest of Jupiter, which was before their city, brought oxen and garlands unto the gates, and would have done sacrifice with the people.

They attempt to sacrifice to Barnabas and Paul as gods (1 Kings 18:25-26, Prov 21:27).

[14] Which when the apostles, Barnabas and Paul, heard of, they rent their clothes, and ran in among the people, crying out,

- Barnabas and Paul only now perceive the purpose of the proceedings because they speak the universal language of Greek (Acts 21:37) and do not understand the local language of Lycaonia (Acts

---

[228] Ovid, *The Metamorphoses*, 8.632-633 and 8.643-645

14:11). They tear their clothes to signify their horror (Job 2:12) that the people have misunderstood their message (Gal 4:11) and would worship them as gods.

- Barnabas and Paul are both called apostles ("sent ones"), but each is considered one in a different sense. The Lord Jesus had personally chosen the original twelve apostles (Luke 6:13) and likewise chose Paul to be an apostle (Gal 1:1, 17, 1 Cor 9:1, 1 Tim 1:1). The original twelve apostles minister primarily to Jews and Paul primarily to Gentiles (Gal 2:8-9, 2 Tim 1:11). Barnabas and others (Rom 16:7) are called apostles when they do the work of an apostle, such as when Barnabas preaches the gospel and performs miracles (Acts 14:1, 3, 2 Cor 12:12).

[15] And saying, Sirs, why do ye these things? We also are men of like passions with you, and preach unto you that ye should turn from these vanities unto the living God, which made heaven, and earth, and the sea, and all things that are therein:

They quote Psalm 146:6 and preach that the one, true, living God has created everything and that it is vain to use His creation to fabricate lifeless idols (1 Cor 12:2). Likewise it is futile to make an idol of mere men, such as Barnabas and Paul (1 Cor 4:6).

Language
Metonymy (a noun is replaced by one related to it) – "vanities" is substituted for "idols."

[16] Who in times past suffered all nations to walk in their own ways.

- Humans inherited the knowledge of God from Adam but also inherited Adam's fallen nature and went astray (Rom 5:12). They refused to acknowledge and worship the Creator (Rom 1:21) even while all of nature proclaimed God's greatness (Acts 14:17, Rom 1:20). Therefore God called Abraham (Gen 12:1-3) and focused on the nation of Israel (Psalm 135:4) as the people to whom He would bring His truth (Rom 3:1-2). The rest of humanity (Gentiles) God gave up to idolatry (Rom 1:24-25) while patiently withholding immediate judgment, giving them time to repent (Ezek 18:23, 32).

- Now, with the coming of the Lord Jesus Christ, everyone must repent and turn to Him (Acts 17:29-31) because "the day of salvation" is **now** (2 Cor 6:2).

[17] Nevertheless he left not himself without witness, in that he did good, and gave us rain from heaven, and fruitful seasons, filling our hearts with food and gladness.

Although God gave up humanity to idolatry for rejecting Him, He never completely abandoned them. He still gave them evidence of His Being (Psalm 19:1-6) so they might seek Him out (Deut 4:29, Jer 29:13). The heaven in bringing forth rain (Psalm 68:9, Jer 14:22) and the earth in bringing forth food (Psalm 104:15, 27) give witness to the goodness of God (James 1:17).

[18] And with these sayings scarce restrained they the people, that they had not done sacrifice unto them.

Paul and Barnabas defuse the awkward tension and come to an understanding with the people of Lystra.

[19] And there came thither certain Jews from Antioch and Iconium, who persuaded the people, and, having stoned Paul, drew him out of the city, supposing he had been dead.

- Paul's enemies from Antioch (Acts 13:50) and Iconium (Acts 14:5) convince the people of Lystra to perform an execution by stoning (as with Stephen, Acts 7:59-60). Their fickle opinion of Paul first as a god and subsequently as someone worthy of death is the reverse order of events at Melita (Acts 28:4-6). They drag Paul out of the city where he is left for dead but do not consider that the same Lord who has the power to make the lame walk (Acts 14:10) can also raise the dead (Matt 9:24-25).
- Paul will later write about being stoned (2 Cor 11:25) and describe an out-of-body experience of being caught up to heaven (2 Cor 12:2-4). Paul's seeing the glories of heaven would help explain his subsequent disregard for his safety (2 Cor 11:23-27).

[20] Howbeit, as the disciples stood round about him, he rose up, and came into the city: and the next day he departed with Barnabas to Derbe.

- Paul's quick recovery shows the miraculous nature of his healing. His returning to the city that just stoned him shows the same zeal (Titus 2:14) and incautiousness that he will display when subjecting himself to angry mobs at Jerusalem (Acts 21:31) despite warnings (Acts 21:4, 11). Although boldness can be fruitful (Acts 16:16-34), escape from harm is often the wisest choice (Acts 17:10, 14) and can be used by God to spread the gospel (Acts 8:4).
- Timotheus may have been present at the stoning (2 Tim 3:10-11) and converted, becoming Paul's son in the faith (1 Cor 4:17). He will accompany Paul when the latter returns here on his second missionary journey (Acts 16:1-3). Timothy's Jewish mother Eunice (Acts 16:1) and grandmother Lois might also become believers now (Acts 16:1, 2 Tim 1:5).
- Gaius is also from Derbe. He will accompany Paul from Macedonia into Asia Minor on the third missionary journey (Acts 20:4).

[21] And when they had preached the gospel to that city, and had taught many, they returned again to Lystra, and to Iconium, and Antioch,

Paul and Barnabas could head back to their sending church at Antioch in Syria over the land route through Paul's hometown of Tarsus. That route is the shortest and safest because it avoids the cities that persecuted them. However, the missionaries choose to trek the extra miles and accept the risk of danger to strengthen the new believers.

[22] Confirming the souls of the disciples, and exhorting them to continue in the faith, and that we must through much tribulation enter into the kingdom of God.

- The New Testament pattern is to preach the gospel to win souls (Acts 14:1), teach new believers (Acts 14:22), and establish churches (Acts 14:23).
- Paul works tirelessly to bring people the gospel and to confirm that new converts are growing in the faith by teaching them (Acts 28:31) and encouraging them to mature in their walk with the Lord (Eph

4:13-15, Col 1:10, 1 Peter 5:10). Believers face trials and tribulations but have God's grace to support them (Eph 4:7) and Christ's example to follow (1 Peter 2:21); in the end, they will receive His glorious blessings (Rom 8:17-18, 1 Peter 1:7).

- The kingdom of God is present wherever God the Son rules as king. His kingdom is now spiritual as the Lord Jesus rules in the hearts of believers (Luke 17:21, Rom 14:17) who enter through the spiritual new birth (John 3:3). His kingdom will one day be present physically when He returns to rule on the earth (John 18:36, 2 Tim 4:1).

[23] And when they had ordained them elders in every church, and had prayed with fasting, they commended them to the Lord, on whom they believed.

Each church is led (1 Tim 5:17) by a group of elders (Acts 11:30, 20:17,

Paul is stoned and left for dead outside Lystra. He miraculously revives then immediately returns to the city and preaches the gospel (Acts 14:6-21).

Northern Imagery / Shutterstock.com

21:18, Titus 1:5). Paul ordains elders when he revisits churches to see who has grown spiritually (Eph 4:15, 2 Peter 3:18).

[24] And after they had passed throughout Pisidia, they came to Pamphylia.

[25] And when they had preached the word in Perga, they went down into Attalia:

When Paul and Barnabas sailed from Cyprus to the province of Pamphylia, they entered Perga only as a brief waypoint en route to Antioch in Pisidia (Acts 13:13-14). Now on the way home they pause here to preach the gospel.

[26] And thence sailed to Antioch, from whence they had been recommended to the grace of God for the work which they fulfilled.

Earlier Paul and Barnabas only passed through Perga (Acts 13:13), but now on their way home they stop here and preach the gospel (Acts 14:25).

[27] And when they were come, and had gathered the church together, they rehearsed all that God had done with them, and how he had opened the door of faith unto the Gentiles.

[28] And there they abode long time with the disciples.

The church of Antioch sent Paul and Barnabas (Acts 13:1-3) and now rejoices when the missionaries report ("rehearse") that a door is open (1 Cor 16:9) to bring the gospel to the Gentiles of Asia Minor. The apostles at Jerusalem had likewise rejoiced when they heard the gospel had gone to the Gentiles as a nation (Acts 11:18).

Challenge Questions

1. Which persons in the modern world do men exalt almost to the level of false gods (Acts 14:11)?
2. What does it mean to "continue in the faith" and "through much tribulation enter into the kingdom of God" (Acts 14:22)?

Acts Chapter 15

[1] And certain men which came down from Judæa taught the brethren, and said, Except ye be circumcised after the manner of Moses, ye cannot be saved.

On Pentecost, the Lord gave the Holy Ghost to Jews who believed on Israel's Messiah (Acts 2:1-5). All believers were either Jews by birth or circumcised proselytes (Acts 2:10). The "Judaizers" who have come from Jerusalem (Acts 15:24) to Antioch (Acts 14:26) teach that Gentiles, to be saved, must undergo circumcision (Exod 12:48-49) and thereby commit to follow the entire law of Moses (Acts 15:5, Deut 27:26, Matt 19:17). These Jewish believers do not oppose Paul's preaching of Christ as do unbelieving Jews (1 Thes 2:14-16). Instead, they add law-keeping to his gospel, something they claim that he omits to better appeal to his Gentile audience (Gal 1:10).

[2] When therefore Paul and Barnabas had no small dissension and disputation with them, they determined that Paul and Barnabas, and certain other of them, should go up to Jerusalem unto the apostles and elders about this question.

- Paul continues to practice the basic tenets of Judaism: he goes to synagogue on the Sabbath (Acts 13:14, 18:4), observes the feast days of Israel (Acts 18:21), participates in certain vows (Acts 18:18) and rituals (Acts 21:26), and will state "I am a Pharisee" (present tense, Acts 23:6). Although he will be accused of many wrongdoings (Acts 24:1–6), Paul will never be charged with personally violating Moses' law. He lives this way not to win favor with God but to follow his conscience (Acts 23:1) and show respect for tradition as he evangelizes other Jews (1 Cor 9:19–23). Although he practices circumcision of Jews (Acts 16:3) he forbids ritual circumcision of Gentiles (Gal 2:3) because doing so places them under obligation to keep the entire law (Gal 5:3, 6:12-13) and undermines the principle that salvation is a free gift (Rom 5:15-18) without works of the law

(Gal 2:16).
- The apostles and elders previously expressed support for Paul's evangelism of Gentiles (Gal 2:7-9). The council will now address the issue of directly converting Gentiles without teaching them to observe Jewish rituals (Gal 4:9-11). The Apostle Paul recognizes the authority of the Jerusalem apostles (Gal 2:9a) but will certainly dissent (Gal 2:5, 11) if the truth of the gospel is not upheld (Gal 1:6-9).
- Paul likely writes the Epistle to the Galatians now.

[3] And being brought on their way by the church, they passed through Phenice and Samaria, declaring the conversion of the Gentiles: and they caused great joy unto all the brethren.

- The cities of Phoenicia ("Phenice") include Tyre and Sidon.
- That Paul and Barnabas are joyfully accepted in Samaria shows that believers, because they are united with Christ (Col 3:11), have abandoned the old man-made prohibitions regarding Jews and Samaritans (John 4:9).
- Paul and Barnabas describe how Gentiles had been saved by faith in Christ alone without first converting to Judaism at Antioch in Syria (Acts 11:26), Antioch in Pisidia (Acts 13:48), Iconium (Acts 14:1), Lystra, and Derbe (Acts 14:6-7).

259

[4] And when they were come to Jerusalem, they were received of the church, and of the apostles and elders, and they declared all things that God had done with them.

They no doubt review their ministry at Antioch in Syria (Acts 11:25-26), their charitable visit to Jerusalem (Acts 11:27-30), and their missionary journey to Cyprus and Galatia (Acts 13:1-14:26).

[5] But there rose up certain of the sect of the Pharisees which believed, saying, That it was needful to circumcise them, and to command them to keep the law of Moses.

These Pharisees teach that Gentile believers must place themselves under the covenant of Abraham through circumcision (Gen 17:9-14) to become saved (Acts 15:1) and must subsequently keep the law of Moses, as do Jews (Gal 5:3).

[6] And the apostles and elders came together for to consider of this matter.

They meet to determine if Gentiles must first become Jews to follow Jesus the Messiah. To do so they consider two questions: Must works such as circumcision be performed to be saved (Acts 15:1)? Must works such as keeping the law of Moses be performed to stay saved (Acts 15:5)?

[7] And when there had been much disputing, Peter rose up, and said unto them, Men and brethren, ye know how that a good while ago God made choice among us, that the Gentiles by my mouth should hear the word of the gospel, and believe.

The Gentiles at Caesarea had been saved when they simply heard the message of the gospel and believed by faith (Acts 10:36-44).

[8] And God, which knoweth the hearts, bare them witness, giving them the Holy Ghost, even as he did unto us;

God saw their hearts' belief (John 1:12) and showed His approval by giving them the Holy Ghost (Acts 10:44). They were granted salvation without works such as circumcision. Water baptism was performed only after their salvation and filling with the Holy Ghost (Acts 10:45-48).

[9] And put no difference between us and them, purifying their hearts by faith.

- Peter no doubt remembers the lesson about believing Gentiles given through the vision of the clean and unclean animals (Acts 10:9-16) and the summarizing message, "What God hath cleansed, that call not thou common" (Acts 10:15). His words also show agreement with Paul's reproof at Antioch (Gal 2:11-16).
- God grants salvation to those who place their faith in the Lord Jesus, whether Jew or Gentile (Gal 5:6, 6:15). Jews in the temple have Old Testament rituals of purifying (Num 8:7) to which Gentiles have no access (Eph 2:11-12). However, now in the New Testament,

God has graciously granted Gentiles purification by faith in Christ Jesus (Eph 2:13).

[10] Now therefore why tempt ye God, to put a yoke upon the neck of the disciples, which neither our fathers nor we were able to bear?

- How does requiring Gentiles to keep the law "tempt God"? It questions His righteousness in giving the Holy Ghost to Cornelius (Acts 10:44) without first requiring him to convert to Judaism.
- The law is a heavy yoke or burden (Matt 23:4, Gal 5:1) in contrast to the grace of God available through Jesus Christ (Matt 11:30).

[11] But we believe that through the grace of the Lord Jesus Christ we shall be saved, even as they.

Peter's statement that salvation is by grace through faith (Acts 15:9), without works, fully agrees with the Apostle Paul's teaching (Eph 2:8-9). His wording that Jews are saved as are Gentiles, rather than by Gentiles becoming Jews, emphasizes the irrelevance of following Old Testament rites to obtain personal salvation.

261

[12] Then all the multitude kept silence, and gave audience to Barnabas and Paul, declaring what miracles and wonders God had wrought among the Gentiles by them.

Their listeners know how God had shown His approval of the apostles' ministry to the Jews in Jerusalem by granting miracles and wonders (Acts 3:6, 5:5, 10, 12, 19, 12:7-11). Barnabas and Paul now describe how God showed the same approval of their ministry to the Gentiles by granting miracles (Acts 14:3) such as the blinding of Elymas (Acts 13:11), the healing of the lame man (Acts 14:8-10), and the miraculous revival of Paul (Acts 14:19-20).

[13] And after they had held their peace, James answered, saying, Men and brethren, hearken unto me:

James, the half-brother of Jesus (Gal 1:19), is a leader in the church at Jerusalem (Acts 12:17, Acts 21:18). He is the author of the epistle of James and is known for precisely following the law (Acts 21:23-24, Gal 2:12-13, James 2:10). Like his other brothers, James initially had not believed on his half-brother Jesus as the Messiah (John 7:5). However, the Savior appeared to him after His resurrection (1 Cor 15:7), and James became a believer and promptly joined with the disciples in Jerusalem (Acts 1:14). The Apostle Paul met James at his first (Gal 1:19) and second (Gal 2:9) post-conversion visits to Jerusalem; Paul meets him now again at his third visit and will meet him at his fourth (Acts 21:18). James' decision here (re-affirmed in Acts 21:25) is in complete harmony with Paul's teaching that salvation is a free gift from God (Rom 3:24) without works (Rom 4:5-6).

[14] Simeon hath declared how God at the first did visit the Gentiles, to take out of them a people for his name.

- James uses Peter's Hebrew name "Simeon" when addressing this Jewish audience.

- The Gentiles were never a people of God (Eph 2:12), but now He has made a way for them through Jesus Christ. Here James alludes to Hosea 2:23, a verse that Paul will also apply to Gentile believers when writing, "I will call them my people, which were not my people" (Rom 9:25). Peter will likewise write that Gentiles "in time past were not a people, but are now the people of God: which had not obtained mercy, but now have obtained mercy" (1 Peter 2:10).
- The whole world will not turn to Christ during the Church Age (Luke 13:23-24), so God is calling people *out* of the world system (John 10:16, 1 Peter 2:9) to follow the Savior (Matt 16:24, 1 Cor 11:1). The pattern of salvation is that which God demonstrated to Simon Peter in Caesarea (Acts 15:7-11).

[15] And to this agree the words of the prophets; as it is written,

James now quotes scripture (Amos 9:11-12) to show that God's future kingdom will not be made exclusively of Jews (native-born Jews and converted Gentiles). Instead, His kingdom will consist of restored Israel (centered in the rebuilt "tabernacle of David") and Gentiles who receive God's blessings through Israel without losing their national identities (Isa 2:2-4, Zech 8:22-23). So the practice of bringing salvation to the Gentiles now through the Church is consistent with God bringing salvation to the Gentiles in the future kingdom age through Israel. James will conclude that it therefore would be wrong to withstand God's direction (compare Peter's words in Acts 11:17) of bringing the gospel directly to Gentiles.

[16] After this I will return, and will build again the tabernacle of David, which is fallen down; and I will build again the ruins thereof, and I will set it up:

Ever since God's promise to Abraham, Gentiles could not lay hold on God's promises (Eph 2:11-12) without converting to Judaism. Now that Gentiles are placed on equal footing before God with Jews by following Jesus the Messiah, James' listeners wonder what the future holds for Israel. He explains that the Lord is now building His Church (Matt 16:18) by calling out Gentiles (as well as Jews) to salvation until their fullness is accomplished (Rom 11:25). "After this" (the tribulation, Amos 9:8-10) the Lord Jesus Christ (of the "tabernacle" or "house" of David, Luke 1:69) will return and restore the nation of Israel as He establishes His kingdom on earth (Amos 9:11, Matt 25:31, Heb 8:10).

263

[17] That the residue of men might seek after the Lord, and all the Gentiles, upon whom my name is called, saith the Lord, who doeth all these things.

Those remaining Gentiles who survive the judgments of the great tribulation (Matt 24:21-22, Rev 9:15) will worship Christ in the Millennial Kingdom (Psalm 86:9, Isa 11:10, Amos 9:12).

[18] Known unto God are all his works from the beginning of the world.

James knows that some Jews in his audience may be disturbed by God's new way of dealing with Gentiles. So he explains that this "new" plan is not new to God. From the very beginning (Gen 1:1) God foresaw (Isa 45:21, 46:10) the future kingdom of Jesus Christ and those blessed to enter it (Matt 25:34).

[19] Wherefore my sentence is, that we trouble not them, which from among the Gentiles are turned to God:

- Some members "of the sect of the Pharisees which believed" (Acts 15:5) have taught the Gentiles (Gal 6:12-13) that "except ye be circumcised after the manner of Moses, ye cannot be saved" (Acts 15:1). James declares that it is wrong to trouble the Gentiles with such an unnecessary requirement because they have already turned to God by faith.
- Therefore the judgment (Deut 17:9) of the Holy Ghost (Acts 15:28) working through the apostles and elders (Acts 15:6) including Peter (Acts 15:7-11), Barnabas and Paul (Acts 15:12), and James (Acts 15:13) is that salvation is by grace (Acts 15:11) through faith (Acts 15:9) without works (Gal 2:16) required to be saved (Acts 15:1) or to stay saved (Acts 15:5).

[20] But that we write unto them, that they abstain from pollutions of idols, and from fornication, and from things strangled, and from blood.

[21] For Moses of old time hath in every city them that preach him, being read in the synagogues every sabbath day.

- Jewish believers have been taught the law of Moses for many generations and are offended by pagan practices. They believe that everyone, Jew or Gentile, is responsible for keeping the covenant that God made with Noah after the flood (Genesis 9:1-17), which they interpret as containing seven distinct commandments. "The descendants of Noah, i.e., all of humanity, were commanded to observe seven mitzvot [commandments]: The mitzva of establishing courts of judgment; and the prohibition against ... cursing, the name of God; and the prohibition of idol worship; and the prohibition against forbidden sexual relations; and the prohibition of bloodshed; and the prohibition of robbery; and the prohibition against eating a limb from a living animal."[229]
- Concerning the commandments given to Noah, Jews feel that idol worship, adultery, and murder[230] are so evil that one would do better

---

[229] *Babylonian Talmud*, Sanhedrin 56a

[230] To "abstain ... from blood" (Acts 15:20) can refer to eating raw, bloody meat (Gen 9:3-4, Lev 17:10-14) or can refer to murder (Gen 9:5-6, Deut 19:10).

to die than commit such sin. "With regard to all other transgressions in the Torah, if a person is told: 'Transgress this prohibition and you will not be killed, he may transgress that prohibition and not be killed ... except for those [sins] of idol worship, forbidden sexual relations, and bloodshed. Concerning those prohibitions, one must allow himself to be killed rather than transgress them."[231]

- James instructs Gentile Christians on how to maintain a righteous testimony before Jews, and he does so by pointing them to Noah, **not** to Moses' law. By avoiding sexual immorality (Rom 1:24) and foods associated with pagan idol worship (1 Cor 8:7-13, Rev 2:14, 20), they will establish a clear testimony as followers of Christ. Paul will later explain that although a Christian is not required to follow the dietary regulations of the law (1 Tim 4:4), he should not use this liberty in a way that offends the conscience of other believers (Rom 14:1-23, 1 Cor 10:25-33).

[22] Then pleased it the apostles and elders, with the whole church, to send chosen men of their own company to Antioch with Paul and Barnabas; namely, Judas surnamed Barsabas, and Silas, chief men among the brethren:

- Silas is a prophet and a preacher (Acts 15:32), a Roman citizen (Acts 16:37-38), and a scribe ("Silvanus," 1 Thes 1:1, 2 Thes 1:1, 1 Peter 5:12). He will accompany Paul on his second missionary journey (Acts 15:40, 2 Cor 1:19).
- Simon Peter is not mentioned further in the book of Acts. He will eventually travel to Babylon, where he will be joined by Silas (Silvanus, 1 Peter 5:12), who will scribe the apostle's first epistle, and John Mark (Marcus, 1 Peter 5:13), who will write the Gospel of Mark based on Peter's testimony. Peter will also write a second epistle preserved as scripture.

[23] And they wrote letters by them after this manner; The apostles and elders and brethren send greeting unto the brethren which are of the Gentiles in Antioch and Syria and Cilicia:

---

[231] *Babylonian Talmud*, Sanhedrin 74a

Antioch is the capital of the provinces of Syria and Cilicia. Paul may have brought the gospel to these regions on his prior journey home to Tarsus (Acts 9:30, Gal 1:21) and again on his first trip to Antioch (Acts 11:25-26).

[24] Forasmuch as we have heard, that certain which went out from us have troubled you with words, subverting your souls, saying, Ye must be circumcised, and keep the law: to whom we gave no such commandment:

- The church at Jerusalem had sent men to Antioch (Gal 2:12a) but had not sent these "false brethren" (Gal 2:4) or endorsed their subversive teaching (2 Tim 2:14).
- Paul will later write that a true follower of God is not one who is physically circumcised, but one whose heart is right with God (Rom 2:28-29, Rev 2:9).

[25] It seemed good unto us, being assembled with one accord, to send chosen men unto you with our beloved Barnabas and Paul,

The apostles and elders provided leadership at the meeting (Acts 15:6), and the church body showed great unity as they assembled "in one accord" (Acts 1:14, 2:1, 2:46, 4:24) and supported the decision (Acts 15:22).

[26] Men that have hazarded their lives for the name of our Lord Jesus Christ.

Paul and Barnabas suffered persecution while evangelizing Galatia (Acts 13:50). Paul was even stoned and left for dead (Acts 14:5, 19). The apostle will later remind Timothy of "persecutions [and] afflictions, which came unto me at Antioch, at Iconium, at Lystra" (2 Tim 3:11).

[27] We have sent therefore Judas and Silas, who shall also tell you the same things by mouth.

Judas and Silas will accompany Paul and Barnabas back to the church at Antioch to act as two witnesses (Deut 17:6, 19:15) of the council's decision.

[28] For it seemed good to the Holy Ghost, and to us, to lay upon you no

greater burden than these necessary things;

- James and the believers in Jerusalem are "filled with the Holy Ghost" (Acts 4:31), and their decision reflects His will.
- To insist that Gentiles converting to Christianity become circumcised and keep the law of Moses (as some have insisted, Acts 15:1, 5) would be to lay a burden upon them (here and Matt 23:4) or "trouble" them (Acts 15:19) by placing upon them a spiritual "yoke" (Acts 15:10).

[29] That ye abstain from meats offered to idols, and from blood, and from things strangled, and from fornication: from which if ye keep yourselves, ye shall do well. Fare ye well.

From Acts 15:19-20. In this letter from the apostles and elders in Jerusalem (Acts 15:4, 6), James writes not "ye shall be saved" by following these instructions but "ye shall do well" in maintaining a Christian testimony.

[30] So when they were dismissed, they came to Antioch: and when they had gathered the multitude together, they delivered the epistle:

[31] Which when they had read, they rejoiced for the consolation.

The wise advice received from the apostles and elders at Jerusalem (Acts 15:2) is well-accepted by the church at Antioch, and they rejoice that division is avoided.

[32] And Judas and Silas, being prophets also themselves, exhorted the brethren with many words, and confirmed them.

Judas and Silas (Acts 15:22) use their spiritual gifts to preach to and teach believers.

[33] And after they had tarried there a space, they were let go in peace from the brethren unto the apostles.

[34] Notwithstanding it pleased Silas to abide there still.

Judas Barsabas returns to Jerusalem, but Silas stays with Paul and Barnabas at Antioch.

[35] Paul also and Barnabas continued in Antioch, teaching and preaching the word of the Lord, with many others also.

Paul and Barnabas are among the many teachers and prophets in the church at Antioch (Acts 13:1).

[36] And some days after Paul said unto Barnabas, Let us go again and visit our brethren in every city where we have preached the word of the Lord, and see how they do.

Paul and Barnabas previously established churches in the province of Galatia in Asia Minor (Acts 13:1-14:26).

[37] And Barnabas determined to take with them John, whose surname was Mark.

John Mark is "sister's son to Barnabas" (Col 4:10).

[38] But Paul thought not good to take him with them, who departed from them from Pamphylia, and went not with them to the work.

John Mark traveled with Paul and Barnabas from Antioch in Syria through Cyprus and as far as Pamphylia in Asia Minor. He then returned home for unstated reasons, and Paul still feels offended (Prov 18:19).

[39] And the contention was so sharp between them, that they departed asunder one from the other: and so Barnabas took Mark, and sailed unto Cyprus;

- Barnabas is from Cyprus (Acts 4:36) and previously evangelized the island with Paul and John Mark (Acts 13:4). Their strong disagreement appears confined to this one issue, as Paul will still write approvingly of Barnabas (1 Cor 9:6).
- John Mark will join Peter and Silas in Babylon ("Silvanus" and "Marcus," 1 Peter 5:12-13), where he will write the Gospel of Mark. John

Mark will fully earn back Paul's favor (Col 4:10, 2 Tim 4:11, Philem 24).

[40] And Paul chose Silas, and departed, being recommended by the brethren unto the grace of God.

Paul begins his second missionary journey (ending at Acts 18:22). His initial plan is to deliver the encouraging declaration of the Jerusalem council (Acts 15:23-29) to Gentile believers (Acts 16:4). Therefore, it is fitting that he takes Silas, a leader in the Jerusalem church (Acts 15:22) who speaks with authority on the Gentile matter (Acts 15:27).

[41] And he went through Syria and Cilicia, confirming the churches.

Paul and Silas take the land route from Antioch, through Syria, and into Cilicia (Paul's home province, Acts 21:39), as Paul had previously done shortly after his conversion (Acts 9:30, Gal 1:21). These churches doubtless include some of Paul's converts who have grown in the Lord and now 269 minister to others. When Paul sees them, he rejoices as the Apostle John, "I have no greater joy than to hear that my children walk in truth" (3 John 4).

Challenge Questions

1. Why does Paul appear to play such a minor role in the Jerusalem church meeting?
2. What does James mean when he says that "the tabernacle of David [has] fallen down" (Acts 15:16)?
3. Was Paul right to exclude John Mark from his company?

Acts Chapter 16

[1] Then came he to Derbe and Lystra: and, behold, a certain disciple was there, named Timotheus, the son of a certain woman, which was a Jewess, and believed; but his father was a Greek:

- Paul previously planted churches in Lystra and Derbe (Acts 14:6) and now returns to strengthen the believers (Acts 15:36). The apostle parted company with Barnabas and the young John Mark (Acts 15:37-39) and now travels with Silas and will recruit the young Timothy.
- Timothy becomes a lifelong disciple and co-worker of Paul (1 Tim 1:2, Rom 16:21). He has a spiritual gift imparted by the Apostle Paul (1 Tim 4:14, 2 Tim 1:6) and will labor as a minister (1 Tim 4:6), a preacher (2 Cor 1:19, 2 Tim 4:2), and an evangelist (2 Tim 4:5). Although his father is a Gentile (Acts 16:3), Timothy learned the scriptures as a child (2 Tim 3:15) from his Jewish mother Eunice and his grandmother Lois (both now believers, 2 Tim 1:5). He may have been present at Paul's prior stoning at Lystra (Acts 14:19-20, 2 Tim 3:10-11).
- Timothy will now follow Paul through Asia Minor and into Macedonia and Achaia (Acts 17:14-15, 18:5). Later he will assist Paul during the apostle's extended stay at Ephesus (Acts 19:22) and then travel with him again into Macedonia and Achaia (Acts 20:4) and possibly on to Jerusalem. He will act as Paul's trusted messenger on two missions to Macedonian churches (1 Thes 3:2, Acts 18:5, 19:22) and one assignment to Corinth (1 Cor 4:17, 16:10). Paul will show deep affection for him in his two letters to Timothy (e.g., "my dearly beloved son," 2 Tim 1:2), in his commendation to the Philippian brethren (Phil 2:19-23), and by his inclusion of Timothy's name in church letter salutations (2 Cor 1:1, Phil 1:1, Col 1:1, 1 Thes 1:1, 2 Thes 1:1, Philem 1:1).
- Timothy will be with Paul at his first imprisonment in Rome (Phil 1:1, Col 1:1, Philem 1:1) and, at some point, also imprisoned and released himself (Heb 13:23). After Paul's release from prison (after

Acts 28), Timothy will again travel with him until the apostle asks him to minister at Ephesus (1 Tim 1:3, 4:6). When Paul suffers his final imprisonment in Rome, he will call Timothy to his side when almost everyone else has forsaken him (2 Tim 4:9-11).

[2] Which was well reported of by the brethren that were at Lystra and Iconium.

Timothy has shown himself to be of good character, even though he is young (1 Tim 4:12, 2 Tim 2:22).

[3] Him would Paul have to go forth with him; and took and circumcised him because of the Jews which were in those quarters: for they knew all that his father was a Greek.

- "Greeks" can refer to the peoples of the Aegean peninsula, to "civilized" nations that have adopted Greek language and culture (Acts 16:1, Rom 1:14), or to Gentiles in contrast to Jews (Acts 20:21, Rom 1:16).
- Paul previously refused to give in to pressure from the circumcision party (Acts 15:1) to circumcise Titus (Gal 2:3-5) since he is a Gentile and doing so would give credence to their false doctrine that keeping the law of Moses is necessary for salvation (Acts 15:5).
- Timothy is considered a Jew because of his Jewish mother (Ezra 10:3). She would not have circumcised Timothy because "it is the duty of the father to have his child circumcised."[232] Because the community knows that his Gentile father would never have circumcised him, Paul has Timothy circumcised to maintain a good testimony before those Jews with whom they expect to come in contact during their ministry (1 Cor 9:19-23). Paul does not hesitate because here the act of circumcision is simply a matter of showing respect for custom and has nothing to do with personal salvation (Gal 5:6, 6:15).

[4] And as they went through the cities, they delivered them the decrees for to keep, that were ordained of the apostles and elders which were at

---

[232] Emil Hirsch et al. "Circumcision." *Jewish Encyclopedia*, 1906

Jerusalem.

Paul, Silas, and Timothy convey the instructions from the apostles and elders in Jerusalem, which state that it is wrong to teach Gentiles that "ye must be circumcised, and keep the law" (Acts 15:23-29).

[5] And so were the churches established in the faith, and increased in number daily.

- The issue of circumcising Gentiles no longer stands in the way of the Holy Spirit's work in Galatia, and the disciples are free to bring the gospel directly to Gentiles.
- Luke gives the fifth of seven summary statements in the book of Acts now that the gospel has spread into Asia Minor.

[6] Now when they had gone throughout Phrygia and the region of Galatia, and were forbidden of the Holy Ghost to preach the word in Asia,

- Paul had previously established churches in the province of Galatia at Antioch in Pisidia (Acts 13:14), Iconium (Acts 14:1), Lystra, and Derbe (Acts 14:6). Phrygia overlaps western Galatia and eastern Asia; some of its inhabitants heard the gospel preached in Jerusalem on Pentecost (Acts 2:10).
- Paul and his companions do not simply go where they feel best but proceed as the Holy Ghost leads them (John 16:13, Acts 16:9). Although forbidden to evangelize the province of Asia now, Paul on his return (Acts 18:19) will have a ministry there so mightily blessed of God that Luke will write that "all they which dwelt in Asia heard the word of the Lord Jesus, both Jews and Greeks" (Acts 19:10). They will now be led farther west and into Europe (Acts 16:11-12) to fulfill Christ's commission to be witnesses "unto the uttermost part of the earth" (Acts 1:8).

[7] After they were come to Mysia, they assayed to go into Bithynia: but the Spirit suffered them not.

- Paul travels through (but does not evangelize) the province of Asia to reach the territory of Mysia. He intended to travel to Bithynia, but

Paul's Second Missionary Journey

Acts 15-18

Base map (land, water, roads) from Ancient World Mapping Center "A-la-carte"
Modifications (borders, routes) by Gregory Cotton
Creative Commons Attribution 4.0 International License (CC BY 4.0)

God the Spirit has other plans.
- The gospel will later reach the people of Bithynia, and Simon Peter will write to believers there (1 Peter 1:1).

[8] And they passing by Mysia came down to Troas.

Paul will later return to Troas, where he will preach the gospel (2 Cor 2:12) and, on a future visit, will resurrect Eutychus (Acts 20:9-10).

[9] And a vision appeared to Paul in the night; There stood a man of Macedonia, and prayed him, saying, Come over into Macedonia, and help us.

- God communicates indirectly through circumstances (e.g., Paul will bring the gospel to Malta when he is shipwrecked there, Acts 28:1) and through advice from other believers (e.g., Paul came to Antioch because Barnabas brought him there, Acts 11:25-26). He also communicates directly through His written word (Isa 34:16). God also gives His word through believers (via preaching and prophecy, Acts 15:32), or sometimes through an unbeliever (2 Chron 35:20-22) or even an animal (Num 22:28, 2 Peter 2:16). He may give a message directly from the Holy Spirit (Acts 13:2) or the angel of the Lord (Acts 8:26). In the Old Testament, God spoke audibly to men such as Noah (Gen 6:13), Abraham (Gen 22:1, 11), and Moses (Exod 33:11). God also speaks directly through visions and dreams (Num 12:6, Dan 1:17).
- God may give a vision in a forthright manner, such as when the heavens were opened at Jesus' baptism (Matt 3:16-17) or when the women saw a vision of angels at the empty tomb (Luke 24:23). God may also give a vision with the recipient in a trance (Acts 22:17-21), during which the individual appears awake though transfixed to observers (Num 24:4) who are unable to see (Acts 9:7) or hear (John 12:28-29) God's directed message. Moses (Exod 33:18-23), Isaiah (Isa 6), and Ezekiel (Ezek 1) all had visions of God's glory. Other memorable visions include Daniel's visions of the last days (Dan 7-12), the transfiguration (Matt 17:1-9), tongues like fire at Pentecost (Acts 2:2-3), Stephan's vision of Jesus at God's right hand (Acts 7:55-56), Paul's vision of Jesus on the road to Damascus (Acts 9:3-6,

26:19) and his vision of paradise (2 Cor 12:1-4), Simon Peter's vision of the sheet let down from heaven (Acts 11:5-10), and John's Revelation.

- During sleep, God may give a direct revelation through a dream or a "vision of the night" (Job 33:15). Biblical examples include Abimelech's warning (Gen 20:6-7), Jacob's ladder (Gen 28:12), Joseph's dreams of his future rule (Gen 37:5-10), the dreams of Pharaoh's butler and baker (Gen 40:5-19), Eliphaz's night vision of a spirit (Job 4:13-21), Nebuchadnezzar's dream of the statue (Dan 2:1, 31-35), the wise men's warning (Matt 2:12), the premonition of Pilate's wife (Matt 27:19), and Paul's night vision of this man of Macedonia.

[10] And after he had seen the vision, immediately we endeavoured to go into Macedonia, assuredly gathering that the Lord had called us for to preach the gospel unto them.

Luke writes, "we," indicating that he is now joining Paul, Silas, and Timothy. The course of western civilization is forever changed as they bring the gospel to Europe (Acts 17:6).

[11] Therefore loosing from Troas, we came with a straight course to Samothracia, and the next day to Neapolis;

They sail on the Aegean Sea from Troas in Asia Minor to Neapolis in Europe via the island of Samothrace.

[12] And from thence to Philippi, which is the chief city of that part of Macedonia, and a colony: and we were in that city abiding certain days.

- Julius Caesar crossed the Rubicon River with his army in 49 BC after conquering the Gauls. Long-standing enmity between him and the Senate culminated when he entered Rome and declared himself dictator. Five years of civil war followed, leaving a victorious Julius Caesar, popular with the Roman people but despised by the Senate, whose power he had usurped. On 15 March (the Ides of March), 44 BC, he was assassinated by a faction led by Senators Cassius and

Brutus.[233] These two Senators fled Rome and raised an army to fight against forces led by Mark Anthony and Caesar's nephew and heir, Octavian, who was later given the title "Caesar Augustus" and ordered a taxation which brought Joseph and his pregnant wife Mary to Bethlehem in Judea (Luke 2:1-5). Mark Anthony and Octavian defeated Cassius and Brutus at the Battle of Philippi in 42 BC, ending the civil war.[234]

- Julius Caesar had initiated a policy of establishing colonies outside of the Italian peninsula to accelerate the spread of Roman law and culture.[235] A colony is "a Roman settlement in conquered territory... The colonists could exercise full political rights in Rome and elect their own magistrates, who had limited judicial and financial power."[236] Therefore the colony of Philippi is considered the most prestigious ("chief") city of the province despite Thessalonica's designation as the capital. Here at Philippi the magistrates are expected to carefully uphold justice in the case of Roman citizens such as Paul and Silas.

- Veterans of the Battle of Philippi were among those who established this Roman colony. The Philippians are very proud of their civil status (Phil 2:21), whereas Paul will choose not to avail himself of his rights as a Roman citizen if he feels doing so will undermine the message of the gospel (Acts 16:22,37). Paul will later remind the Philippians to live their lives not merely as citizens of earth but as citizens of heaven (Phil 3:20).

[13] And on the sabbath we went out of the city by a river side, where prayer was wont to be made; and we sat down, and spake unto the women which resorted thither.

The Jewish population of Philippi is apparently too small to support a synagogue like those in Thessalonica (Acts 17:1) and Berea (Acts 17:10), so sabbath prayer is customarily made ("wont to be made") at the riverside.

---

[233] "Julius Caesar." *Encyclopedia Britannica Online*, accessed 4 Nov 2019

[234] "Battle of Philippi." *Encyclopedia Britannica Online*, accessed 4 Nov 2019

[235] "Civitas." *Encyclopedia Britannica Online*, accessed 4 Nov 2019

[236] "Colony, Ancient Roman Settlement." *Encyclopedia Britannica Online*, accessed 7 Sept 2019

[14] And a certain woman named Lydia, a seller of purple, of the city of Thyatira, which worshipped God, heard us: whose heart the Lord opened, that she attended unto the things which were spoken of Paul.

- Lydia is noted to be a devout worshipper of God (Psalm 86:9) when she first hears the gospel message. She believes from the heart (Acts 8:37) and becomes the first Christian (Gal 3:28) in Europe. She is wealthy due to her sales of purple textile, which is an expensive luxury (Prov 31:22, Luke 16:19).
- Lydia is ironically from Thyatira in Asia, where Paul was forbidden to preach (Acts 16:6). A church will eventually be established in Thyatira and will receive one of the letters to the seven churches (Rev 2:18-29).

[15] And when she was baptized, and her household, she besought us, saying, If ye have judged me to be faithful to the Lord, come into my house, and abide there. And she constrained us.

The members of Lydia's household have certainly believed before being baptized, as had the Ethiopian treasurer (Acts 8:36-38) and as will the local jailer and his family (Acts 16:33-34). She convinces them of her moral integrity and compels them to partake of her hospitality (Rom 12:13, 1 Peter 4:9).

[16] And it came to pass, as we went to prayer, a certain damsel possessed with a spirit of divination met us, which brought her masters much gain by soothsaying:

These men direct their servant girl to make prophecies of the future using an evil spirit, but scripture forbids such practice (Lev 20:6, 27). The Lord had punished King Saul with death in part for his use of such witchcraft (1 Sam 28:7-8, 1 Chron 10:13-14). The girl's masters use spiritism for economic gains (Micah 3:11), as did Simon the sorcerer (Acts 8:9,18-19) and Elymas (Acts 13:8) and as will Demetrius the silversmith (Acts 19:24). Balaam greedily took a financial reward (Jude 11) to curse Israel (Neh 13:2) with his divination (Num 22:7) and suffers eternal punishment (Jude 13) for his unrighteous (2 Peter 2:15) doctrine (Rev 2:14).

Language
"Divination" and "soothsaying" refer to foretelling future events by supernatural means.

[17] The same followed Paul and us, and cried, saying, These men are the servants of the most high God, which shew unto us the way of salvation.

Evil spirits know (James 2:19) and may proclaim the truth (Luke 4:34), but the corrupt speech of the wicked does not glorify God (Prov 7:5, Phil 1:15).

[18] And this did she many days. But Paul, being grieved, turned and said to the spirit, I command thee in the name of Jesus Christ to come out of her. And he came out the same hour.

Paul, like Jesus (Mark 1:23-25), does not accept the testimony of an evil spirit lest people should think his work done in the power of the Holy Ghost (Acts 16:6) is done in the power of the devil (Matt 12:24). He casts out the unclean spirit (Mark 16:17, Eph 6:12) as did Jesus (Luke 4:35-36), the other apostles (Matt 10:1, Acts 5:16), and Philip (Acts 8:6-7). Paul and Silas will suffer for their good deed (2 Tim 2:9, 1 Peter 3:17).

[19] And when her masters saw that the hope of their gains was gone, they caught Paul and Silas, and drew them into the marketplace unto the rulers,

Her masters are not the first to be offended by miraculous healing (Mark 3:4-6, Luke 13:14), which in this case removes the source of their unjust gains (Job 27:8, Prov 28:8, Ezek 22:13). The merchants of Ephesus will likewise take offense when their incomes are threatened (Acts 19:27).

[20] And brought them to the magistrates, saying, These men, being Jews, do exceedingly trouble our city,

- "These Jews attacked our religion!" However, the religious accusation is merely cover for their real frustration, that "the hope of their gains was gone" (Acts 16:19). Demetrius the silversmith will also use a religious pretext to protest his loss of income (Acts 19:24-27).

Furthermore, Paul did not start this conflict; he was peacefully on his way to prayer when disturbed by the evil spirit (Acts 16:16-17).

- Previously when the Lord Jesus was criticized for performing miraculous healing, He retorted, "And ought not this woman ... whom Satan hath bound ... be loosed from this bond?" (Luke 13:16).
- The city is not troubled by Paul, but by those (1 Kings 18:17-18) who have exploited a woman possessed by an evil spirit who is now delivered (Luke 8:2, Acts 10:38). The plaintiffs do not reject Paul; they reject God's grace (1 Sam 8:7, Titus 2:11).

[21] And teach customs, which are not lawful for us to receive, neither to observe, being Romans.

- Here at Philippi Paul is accused of promoting Jewish practices that are unlawful for Romans. Ironically, at Jerusalem he will be accused

Paul and Silas bring the gospel to Philippi, where Lydia becomes the first convert to Christianity in Europe (Acts 16:12-15).

stoyanh / Shutterstock.com

of promoting Gentile practices unlawful for Jews (Acts 21:21).
- Paul is a law-abiding Roman citizen (Acts 16:37, Rom 13:1-7), and the charges of bringing unlawful customs are false (Acts 28:17), as they were with Stephen (Acts 6:13-14). Fraudulent charges will also be brought against Paul at Corinth (Acts 18:13) and Jerusalem (Acts 24:5-6).
- Paul apparently does not wear a toga or other article of clothing that would signal his rank as a Roman citizen.[237] Instead he chooses garments that show that he is a devout Jew (Acts 23:6).
- When Paul willingly suffers punishment for doing right, he demonstrates that the cause of Christ is more important than his safety (Phil 1:29, 1 Peter 4:16). To appeal to his Roman citizenship here would negate that message, although he will later make such an appeal under different circumstances (Acts 22:25).

[22] And the multitude rose up together against them: and the magistrates rent off their clothes, and commanded to beat them.

- Under the Porcian laws of Rome, a citizen cannot be flogged or executed without a formal trial (during which the accused may defend himself, Acts 25:16) and without a chance to conduct a legal appeal before his fellow citizens.[238]
- The magistrates are negligent when they fail to first determine the citizenship (Acts 16:37-38) of Paul and Silas. Instead, they proceed to administer unlawful punishment.

[23] And when they had laid many stripes upon them, they cast them into prison, charging the jailor to keep them safely:

Paul and Silas are unjustly beaten (2 Cor 6:5) and jailed without trial.

[24] Who, having received such a charge, thrust them into the inner prison, and made their feet fast in the stocks.

---

[237] "Dress, ancient Rome." *Encyclopedia Britannica Online*, accessed 10 Nov 2019
[238] "The Transformation of Rome and Italy During the Middle Republic." *Encyclopedia Britannica Online*, accessed 18 Sept 2019

They are restrained in prison as had been Joseph (Psalm 105:17-18). God is likewise with them (Acts 7:9).

[25] And at midnight Paul and Silas prayed, and sang praises unto God: and the prisoners heard them.

Paul and Silas sing (Job 35:10, Psalm 42:8, 119:62), "rejoicing that they were counted worthy to suffer shame for his name" (Acts 5:41, also Luke 6:22-23).

[26] And suddenly there was a great earthquake, so that the foundations of the prison were shaken: and immediately all the doors were opened, and every one's bands were loosed.

- The Lord now sends an earthquake when He opens the prison doors, as He did when opening Jesus' tomb (Matt 28:2). This earthquake follows the prayers of Paul and Silas as one followed the prayer of the disciples (Acts 4:31).
- Paul and Silas are miraculously freed from prison, as Peter was twice before (Acts 5:19, 12:7-11). This earthquake is not a natural event, for their shackles come off, none of the prisoners leave, the building is not reported to suffer damage, and nobody is harmed.

281

[27] And the keeper of the prison awaking out of his sleep, and seeing the prison doors open, he drew out his sword, and would have killed himself, supposing that the prisoners had been fled.

- The Philippian jailer knows Roman policy will require his life for losing so many prisoners (Acts 12:19, 27:42) and chooses suicide over the humiliation of a public execution (1 Sam 31:4).
- Consistent with Luke's factual account is one fictional story from this era, which tells of a Roman soldier who, when he lost a condemned prisoner, "declared that he would not wait for a court-martial but would punish his own neglect with a thrust of his sword."[239]
- Roman policy is indeed harsh. "The custody and care of imprisoned persons devolves upon the jailer, who must not think that [the

---

[239] Petronius, *Satyricon*, 112

escapee] will be responsible, if a prisoner should in any way escape, for we desire that he himself shall suffer the same penalty to which the prisoner who escaped is shown to have been liable."[240]

[28] But Paul cried with a loud voice, saying, Do thyself no harm: for we are all here.

Paul shows concern for his captor's life (Matt 5:44, Luke 9:56). He will also show concern for the lives of others on his perilous sea voyage to Rome as a prisoner (Acts 27).

[29] Then he called for a light, and sprang in, and came trembling, and fell down before Paul and Silas,

[30] And brought them out, and said, Sirs, what must I do to be saved?

- The jailer may have heard the damsel cry, "These men are the servants of the most high God, which shew unto us the way of salvation" (Acts 16:17).
- He asks the most important question an individual can ask. He asks sincerely, unlike Pilate's cynical, "What is truth?" (John 18:38).

[31] And they said, Believe on the Lord Jesus Christ, and thou shalt be saved, and thy house.

- They answer with the name of the only One who can save a man's soul: the Lord Jesus Christ. They do not suggest a religious symbol or relic, for no object can bring salvation, as did the people when they falsely hoped of the ark of the covenant that "it may save us" (1 Sam 4:3,10). They do not recommend science (1 Tim 6:20), philosophy (Col 2:8), empty prayers (Mark 12:40), vain repentance (Matt 27:4), a prophet or a priest (Jer 23:11), or any religious ceremony (Heb 10:1). Instead, they offer the "only name under heaven given among men whereby we must be saved" (Acts 4:12).
- Paul and Silas inform him that salvation is likewise available to the members of his household (Acts 11:14).

---

[240] *The Code of Justinian*, 9.4.4

[32] And they spake unto him the word of the Lord, and to all that were in his house.

[33] And he took them the same hour of the night, and washed their stripes; and was baptized, he and all his, straightway.

- The jailer cleanses their linear wounds created by flogging ("stripes") to prevent infection.
- The jailer and his household experience conversion in the same manner as the Ethiopian treasurer (Acts 8:35-37) and Cornelius (Acts 10:43-48), which is the pattern of New Testament salvation. They heard the word of God (Acts 16:32), believed (Acts 16:34), and received salvation by simple faith in Jesus Christ (Rom 10:9-10). Only now after they are saved do they receive baptism.

[34] And when he had brought them into his house, he set meat before them, and rejoiced, believing in God with all his house.

The Ethiopian treasurer, after he was saved, "went on his way rejoicing" (Acts 8:39). Likewise Philip and his household now rejoice at their salvation (Psalm 70:4, Isa 25:9, Hab 3:18).

[35] And when it was day, the magistrates sent the serjeants, saying, Let those men go.

[36] And the keeper of the prison told this saying to Paul, The magistrates have sent to let you go: now therefore depart, and go in peace.

[37] But Paul said unto them, They have beaten us openly uncondemned, being Romans, and have cast us into prison; and now do they thrust us out privily? nay verily; but let them come themselves and fetch us out.

[38] And the serjeants told these words unto the magistrates: and they feared, when they heard that they were Romans.

- Paul and Silas were punished though "uncondemned," meaning they had not received a formal trial that led to a guilty verdict. Cicero wrote, "Does a Roman citizen have a right to a trial before receiving punishment?" "Certainly, for otherwise a defendant cannot [justly] be condemned, however guilty he may be."[241] Governor Festus will give similar words in Acts 25:16.

- Gaius Verres, former governor of Sicily, was prosecuted "when he destroyed Roman citizens by execution, by torture, by the cross."[242] When writing his legal opinion against Verres, Cicero asked rhetorically, "Have all our rights fallen so far, that in a province of the Roman people, – in a town of our confederate allies, – a Roman citizen should be bound in the forum, and beaten with rods … ?"[243] Rather than face a looming guilty verdict, Gaius Verres chose to go into exile, and years later was finally executed.[244]

- The Philippian officials doubtless know of the disgraced Gaius Verres and are afraid when they realize their neglect in upholding the law. Roman commander Claudius Lysias will likewise be fearful when he finds himself in violation of the law in his treatment of Paul (Acts 22:29).

- Paul and Silas had meekly submitted to Christ's example (Mark 15:5, 1 Peter 2:21) when they were "shamefully" (1 Thes 2:2) denied their right to trial as Roman citizens (Acts 22:25). Understandably, Paul is indignant now that the magistrates ask them to leave in disgrace as if guilty of wrongdoing.

Language
"Serjeants" means "sergeants" and refers to police officers.

[39] And they came and besought them, and brought them out, and desired them to depart out of the city.

The embarrassed magistrates release Paul and ask him to leave immediately before he can cause them any more trouble, but he is now vindicated and free to proceed as the Lord directs.

---

[241] Marcus Tullius Cicero, *Against Verres*, 2.1.9
[242] Ibid., 2.1.4
[243] Ibid., 2.5.63
[244] "Gaius Verres." *Encyclopedia Britannica Online*, accessed 5 Nov 2019

[40] And they went out of the prison, and entered into the house of Lydia: and when they had seen the brethren, they comforted them, and departed.

Paul returns to Lydia's house to encourage the brethren with news of his release and the salvation testimony of the jailer's household (Acts 16:34). He departs from Philippi but will often think joyfully of their days of fellowship (Phil 1:3-8). Paul leaves Luke behind but will return (Acts 20:1-2) and reunite with him as they resume their travels together on Paul's third missionary journey (Luke will again write "we" in Acts 20:6).

Teaching Questions

Question: Is Lydia a Jew or a Gentile? Also consider "Justus, one that worshipped God, whose house joined hard to the synagogue" (Acts 18:7).
Gentile: By describing her as a woman who "worshipped God," Luke is indicating that she is a Gentile like Cornelius of Caesarea (Acts 10:1-2) and Justus of Corinth (Acts 18:7) who worship the God of Israel as Gentiles. If she were a Jew, she would worship in the synagogue on the Sabbath, not by the riverside.

Jew: King David "worshipped God" (2 Sam 15:32), so the phrase is not specific to Gentiles. There may be an unnamed synagogue by the river because such a location would provide a source of water for Jewish baptism. Besides, a few verses earlier, Luke goes out of his way to show that Timothy's father is a Gentile (Acts 16:3) in contrast to Lydia, who Luke describes as worshipping on the Sabbath as any Jewish person would.
Gentile: If Lydia is a Jew worshipping in a synagogue by the river, why does Luke describe a group of women and not make mention of any men? Why does he not describe a synagogue building? Why would Luke add the phrase "worshipped God" except to draw attention to the fact that despite being a non-Jew, she worships the God of Israel? Regarding Justus, Paul says, "I will go unto the Gentiles" (Acts 18:6), and in the next verse, Luke says Paul "entered into a certain man's house named Justus, one that worshipped God" (Acts 18:7). So if Luke tells us that Paul announced that he would go to the Gentiles and the following verse shows Luke lodging with Justus, then it would seem that Luke intends us to believe Justus is a Gentile who worships the God of Israel, as does Lydia.

Jew: We do not know why Luke mentions only women in this scene. He does not explain any unique circumstances which may have existed for Jews in the Roman colony of Philippi, such as whether or not they were persecuted and exiled from Philippi as they were from Rome by Emperor Claudius (Acts 18:2). A group of devout women who worship at a place of prayer on the Sabbath would naturally be thought of as Jews unless the description specifically indicated otherwise. In the same way a devout man (Justus) who lives next door to a synagogue, worships God, and readily gives lodging to a Pharisee such as Paul would almost certainly be a Jew.

Challenge Questions

1. Was it right for Paul to direct Timothy to be circumcised (Acts 16:3)?
2. What does Lydia mean when she says, "If ye have judged me to be faithful to the Lord ..." (Acts 16:15)?
3. Many people teach that Acts 16:31-33 implies that Paul baptized infants. What is your conclusion?

Acts Chapter 17

[1] Now when they had passed through Amphipolis and Apollonia, they came to Thessalonica, where was a synagogue of the Jews:

[2] And Paul, as his manner was, went in unto them, and three sabbath days reasoned with them out of the scriptures,

Paul preaches first in local synagogues whenever possible (Acts 13:5, 13:14, 14:1). Here at Thessalonica he preaches in the synagogue for three Sabbaths, then outside the synagogue for many weeks (1 Thes 2:9, Phil 4:16).

[3] Opening and alleging, that Christ must needs have suffered, and risen again from the dead; and that this Jesus, whom I preach unto you, is Christ.

287

- The Jews expect a Messiah that will immediately usher in a physical kingdom. So Paul explains ("opens") and proves ("alleges") from the scriptures (Luke 24:45) that the Messiah would have to first suffer for sins (Psalm 22:6-21, Isa 53:5, Luke 24:26) and be resurrected from the dead (Psalm 16:10, Isa 53:10) before reigning as King (Psalm 99:1-5). He preaches that the Lord Jesus has fulfilled these prophecies of suffering and resurrection and is therefore the promised Messiah (Christ). One day the Savior will return to earth and reign as King (Rev 19:11-13).
- Paul preaches confidently despite opposition. He will later write how "we were bold in our God to speak unto you the gospel of God with much contention" (1 Thes 2:2).

Language
Enthymeme (an element of reasoning is not stated) –
Major premise: the Messiah (Christ) must suffer and die to fulfill Old Testament prophecy.
Minor premise (unstated): Jesus suffered and died.

Conclusion: Jesus is the Messiah.

[4] And some of them believed, and consorted with Paul and Silas; and of the devout Greeks a great multitude, and of the chief women not a few.

- Those who believe (1 Thes 2:13) and join with Paul and Silas (1 Thes 1:6) include Jews (fewer than there will be at Berea, Acts 17:11) and devout Gentiles who fear God (Acts 10:2, 13:16), such as Jason (Acts 17:5), Aristarchus (Acts 27:2), and Secundus (Acts 20:4). Furthermore, pagan Gentiles have "turned to God from idols to serve the living and true God" (1 Thes 1:9).
- Paul will later write back to the church, joyfully explaining that "when ye received the word of God which ye heard of us, ye received it not as the word of men, but as it is in truth, the word of God, which effectually worketh also in you that believe" (1 Thes 2:13).
- Paul's helpers in the ministry include Silas and Timothy ("Silvanus, and Timotheus," 1 Thes 1:1).
- While at Thessalonica, Paul works making tents (Acts 18:3) to avoid being a financial burden to the local believers (1 Thes 2:9, 2 Thes 3:7-8). He also twice receives a gift of material support from the church at Philippi (Phil 4:15-16).

[5] But the Jews which believed not, moved with envy, took unto them certain lewd fellows of the baser sort, and gathered a company, and set all the city on an uproar, and assaulted the house of Jason, and sought to bring them out to the people.

- The unbelieving Jews stir up the people here at Thessalonica (and will again at Berea, Acts 17:13), as did those at Antioch in Pisidia (Acts 13:45, 50). The rabble-rousers ("lewd fellows") lead an angry mob to the house of Jason, where Paul and Silas apparently had been lodging.
- Paul will later describe these unbelieving Jews as "forbidding us to speak to the Gentiles that they might be saved" (1 Thes 2:16). They resent the success of the missionaries and are offended that they directly reach out to Gentiles (Acts 22:21–22) without bringing them into the confines of Judaism.

[6] And when they found them not, they drew Jason and certain brethren unto the rulers of the city, crying, These that have turned the world upside down are come hither also;

Their enemies lavish them with unintentional praise when saying they have "turned the world upside down"! Paul's ministry will become so widespread that his accusers will say he influences "all men every where" (Acts 21:28).

[7] Whom Jason hath received: and these all do contrary to the decrees of Cæsar, saying that there is another king, one Jesus.

They accuse Paul and Silas of treason, as they had accused Jesus (John 19:12). The charge of treason is false because the missionaries preach

Paul and his fellow missionaries preach in Thessalonica, where the gospel bears fruit "of the devout Greeks a great multitude, and of the chief women not a few" (Acts 17:1-4).

that Jesus is presently ruling over a spiritual rather than a physical kingdom (John 18:36, Rom 14:17). The Roman governor of Judea had previously determined that this doctrine does not violate Roman law (John 18:37-38). Paul teaches obedience to civil law (Rom 13:1-7), and allegations to the contrary here are as baseless as they were at Philippi (Acts 16:21).

[8] And they troubled the people and the rulers of the city, when they heard these things.

The unbelieving Jews (Acts 17:5) instigate trouble here, as did the unbelieving Gentiles at Philippi (Acts 16:19-20).

[9] And when they had taken security of Jason, and of the other, they let them go.

The city rulers cannot find the missionaries, so they compel Jason and his companion to give a financial guarantee that there will be no further public disturbances.

[10] And the brethren immediately sent away Paul and Silas by night unto Berea: who coming thither went into the synagogue of the Jews.

The brethren are concerned for Paul's safety and ask him to leave town (1 Thes 2:17) until the crisis abates, as they did at Damascus (Acts 9:24-25) and Jerusalem (Acts 9:29-30).

[11] These were more noble than those in Thessalonica, in that they received the word with all readiness of mind, and searched the scriptures daily, whether those things were so.

Paul preaches in the synagogue of Berea as he had at Thessalonica that the Lord Jesus is the Messiah (Acts 17:3). The difference here is that instead of reacting with envy (Acts 17:5), they seek the truth of God's word by studying the scriptures (Psalm 119:130, John 5:39, 2 Tim 2:15). The Bereans, like Paul, can rightly say, "I believe God" (Acts 27:25) because they believe His word.

[12] Therefore many of them believed; also of honourable women which

were Greeks, and of men, not a few.

The believers include Sopater (Acts 20:4) and many of Berea's leading men and women, as at Thessalonica (Acts 17:4).

[13] But when the Jews of Thessalonica had knowledge that the word of God was preached of Paul at Berea, they came thither also, and stirred up the people.

The unbelieving Jews again want to incite mob violence (Acts 17:5).

[14] And then immediately the brethren sent away Paul to go as it were to the sea: but Silas and Timotheus abode there still.

The brethren escort Paul out of town and away from danger, as at Thessalonica (Acts 17:10). They feign a sea voyage and slip away overland.

[15] And they that conducted Paul brought him unto Athens: and receiving a commandment unto Silas and Timotheus for to come to him with all speed, they departed.

- Paul leaves Macedonia and enters the Roman province of Achaia. His first stop is at Athens then afterward he will travel to Corinth (Acts 18:1). He greatly desires to return to the believers in Thessalonica now, "but Satan hindered us" (1 Thes 2:17-18).
- The apostle now recalls Silas and Timothy from Berea. Once they arrive, Paul will send them both to churches in Macedonia (Acts 18:5). He will be left alone here at Athens while Timothy goes to Thessalonica (1 Thes 3:1-2), and Silas likely goes to Philippi (Phil 4:15). When the three later meet in Corinth (Acts 18:5), Timothy will report the persecution of Thessalonian believers (1 Thes 2:14, 3:4) but will also bring encouraging news of their faithfulness (1 Thes 3:6-7).

[16] Now while Paul waited for them at Athens, his spirit was stirred in him, when he saw the city wholly given to idolatry.

- Athens is famous for its pagan temples and thousands of idols to false gods. Its people are representative of Gentiles who have rejected God's truth and have been given up by Him to idolatry (Rom 1:23-24, Rev 21:8, 22:15). Petronius of Athens quipped that "truly our neighborhood is so well stocked with deities to hand, you will easier meet with a god [idol] than a man."[245]

- Paul *knows* that idolatry is wrong ("Thou shalt not make unto thee any graven image," Exod 20:4). As a Jew, he also *feels* offended by idolatry ("for I the Lord thy God am a jealous God," Exod 20:5).

[17] Therefore disputed he in the synagogue with the Jews, and with the devout persons, and in the market daily with them that met with him.

Paul works to convince Jews, other religious persons, and the public at large that Jesus is the Messiah (Acts 17:3). Here he might convert "Epaenetus, who is the firstfruits of Achaia unto Christ" (Rom 16:5).

[18] Then certain philosophers of the Epicureans, and of the Stoicks, encountered him. And some said, What will this babbler say? other some, He seemeth to be a setter forth of strange gods: because he preached unto them Jesus, and the resurrection.

The **Epicureans** teach that man finds happiness not by fulfilling his desires but by eliminating pain and fear. The founder of the movement, Epicurus, wrote, "Pleasure is our first and kindred good. It is the starting-point of every choice and of every aversion ... When we say, then, that pleasure is the end and aim, we do not mean the pleasures of the prodigal [excess] or the pleasures of sensuality ... By pleasure we mean the absence of pain in the body and of trouble in the soul."[246]

The **Stoics** teach that man is good and can forge his own path through perseverance. One day Marcus Aurelius (then the Emperor of Rome) will promote the Stoic perspective in his writings, the *Meditations*:
Man is basically good: "Look within. A fountain of good will bubble up if you just keep digging."
Man can forge his own path through perseverance: "Not to feel exasperated, or defeated, or despondent because your days aren't packed with wise

---

[245] Petronius, *The Satyricon*, 3:17
[246] Epicurus, *Letter to Menoeceus*

and moral actions. But to get back up when you fail, to celebrate behaving like a human – however imperfectly – and fully embrace the pursuit that you've embarked on."

<u>Man will have peace when he focuses only on what he can control</u>: "You have power over your mind – not outside events. Realize this, and you will find strength."

<u>Man has no access to absolute truth</u>: "Everything we hear is an opinion, not a fact. Everything we see is a perspective, not the truth."

The Epicureans promote a philosophy of pleasure (1 Cor 15:32) and the Stoics a philosophy of pride (Psalm 10:4). Their teachings may superficially sound wise (1 Cor 3:19-20) but are deficient because they fail to see man's need for Christ (Col 2:8). Paul's teaching on the resurrected Savior certainly seems strange to those who do not believe in a resurrection (Acts 17:32) and readily agree that none of their revered Greek philosophers ever rose from the dead.

"Now while Paul waited for them at Athens, his spirit was stirred in him, when he saw the city wholly given to idolatry" (Acts 17:16).

Tomas Marek / Shutterstock.com

[19] And they took him, and brought him unto Areopagus, saying, May we know what this new doctrine, whereof thou speakest, is?

[20] For thou bringest certain strange things to our ears: we would know therefore what these things mean.

- "Areopagus" means "Ares' rocky hill" or "Mars' hill" (Acts 17:22), which is located just outside the Acropolis of Athens. "Areopagus" also refers to the Council of the Areopagus that meets on Mars' Hill, as evidenced by an inscription at Athens: "... it shall not be permitted for the councillors of the Council of the Areopagos, if the People or the democracy at Athens have been overthrown, to go up to the Areopagos or to sit in session or to deliberate about anything ..."[247]
- The Areopagus had been the seat of government several hundred years ago when Athens was a Greek city-state. In Hellenistic times the Areopagus was the high court over cases of murder. Now in the Roman era, it has authority over essential aspects of city administration, local education, and matters of religion.[248] Therefore the council members scrutinize Paul because they are responsible for examining the claims of anyone vouching for a new god.

Language
The Roman god "Mars" is equivalent to the Greek god "Ares," so Mar's Hill is called "Areopagus."

[21] (For all the Athenians and strangers which were there spent their time in nothing else, but either to tell, or to hear some new thing.)

- The gospel had been a completely new idea to the Bereans when Paul preached in their synagogue, but they had an open mind to the truth, and many became believers (Acts 17:10-12). The people of Athens live in a university-type setting where they claim to be open to new ideas. Yet when Paul brings the gospel to the people of Athens, their minds are closed to the truth, and most will only scoff and mock when told of Christ's resurrection and their future judgment

---

[247] *Inscriptiones Graecae* II3 1 320
[248] "Areopagus." *Encyclopedia Britannica Online*, accessed 27 Sept 2019

(Acts 17:31-32).
- Perhaps the philosophers of Athens believe Paul will make a weak speech and be an easy target of ridicule. Yet the apostle is more than up to the task. First, he is "filled with the Holy Ghost" (Acts 13:9), who will guide his speech (Luke 12:11-12). Second, Paul has not only a deep knowledge of the Old Testament ("brought up in [Jerusalem] at the feet of Gamaliel," Acts 22:3), but he has a superior Greco-Roman education (his family is from Tarsus). "The people at Tarsus have devoted themselves so eagerly, not only to philosophy, but also to the whole round of education in general, that they have surpassed Athens, Alexandria, or any other place that can be named where there have been schools and lectures of philosophers."[249]

[22] Then Paul stood in the midst of Mars' hill, and said, Ye men of Athens, I perceive that in all things ye are too superstitious.

The Athenians take pride in their city and its commitment to pagan worship. Paul tells them that worshipping these Greco-Roman gods is irrational ("superstitious"). After all, the Epicureans do not believe in a deity who is involved in human affairs (they believe the gods are indifferent), and the Stoics do not think that any distinct individual is god (they are pantheists and believe all the universe is god). Paul will explain that the one true God is the Creator of all (Acts 17:24) and holds everyone accountable for their living (Acts 17:30).

[23] For as I passed by, and beheld your devotions, I found an altar with this inscription, TO THE UNKNOWN GOD. Whom therefore ye ignorantly worship, him declare I unto you.

- The "superstitious" (Acts 17:22) Athenians have an anonymous idol just in case their thousands of shrines leave out somebody important.
- Deep inside, humans have an innate longing for the one, true God, a void that can be filled only by Him. At Athens they are surrounded by idols ("devotions") but do not know God. By using the term "unknown," the Athenians acknowledge that they do not know (are

---

[249] Strabo, *Geography*, 14.5.13

ignorant of) Him (Exod 5:2, Matt 7:23).
- Paul is accused of being "a setter forth of strange gods" (Acts 17:18). He is not on trial as he stands before the court of the Areopagus. Instead, his spiritual ideas are being scrutinized by these men whose business it is to investigate claims of new gods. Paul brilliantly explains that he is not introducing a new deity but merely proclaiming the One whose existence they already acknowledge, as evidenced by the inscription on their altar.

[24] God that made the world and all things therein, seeing that he is Lord of heaven and earth, dwelleth not in temples made with hands;

- Magnificent temples surround Paul as he stands on Mar's Hill, but they are of no value to God, as He does not live in any temple (Acts 7:48). God made the entire world so it is absurd to confine Him to a building.
- Although the Athenians believe in a pantheon of gods, they do not believe in a supreme Creator. Yet Paul understands that God holds everyone responsible for knowing that He has created the world (Rom 1:20). He preaches like Stephen did (Acts 7:50), that all should rightfully attribute everything in the world to Him.
- Paul is not the only one to point out the contradiction between Athenian philosophy and idolatry. Plutarch will write, "It is a doctrine of Zeno's not to build temples of the gods, because a temple not worth much is also not sacred and no work of builders or mechanics is worth much. The Stoics, while applauding this as correct, attend the mysteries in temples, go up to the Acropolis, do reverence to statues, and place wreaths upon the shrines, though these are works of builders and mechanics. Yet they think that the Epicureans are confuted by the fact that they sacrifice to the gods, whereas they are themselves worse confuted by sacrificing at altars and temples which they hold do not exist and should not be built."[250]
- Not only is Paul not introducing a new deity to Athens, but he also is not seeking to build a new shrine because the One, true God does not live in one.

---

[250] Plutarch, *Moralia*, Stoic Self-Contradictions, 1034

[25] Neither is worshipped with men's hands, as though he needed any thing, seeing he giveth to all life, and breath, and all things;

God has given life to all creatures (John 1:1-4, Col 1:16-17) and does not benefit from sacrificial offerings made by humans (Heb 10:6).

[26] And hath made of one blood all nations of men for to dwell on all the face of the earth, and hath determined the times before appointed, and the bounds of their habitation;

- When the people of Athens gaze upon their majestic temples, they feel proud of their prominent place in the world of pagan religion. "If we care to compare our national characteristics with those of foreign peoples, we shall find that ... in the sense of religion, that is, in reverence for the gods, we are far superior."[251] So Paul cautions his audience against a feeling of superiority because all bloodlines can be traced back to humanity's common ancestor, Adam, who was

[251] Marcus Tullius Cicero, *On the Nature of the Gods*, 2.3.8

Paul stands on Mar's Hill as he preaches before Athen's council, the Areopagus (Acts 17:19-31).

Aerial-motion / Shutterstock.com

made in the image of God and was told to fill the earth (Gen 1:28). Yet Adam fell (Gen 3:6-7), so his descendants are made in Adam's fallen image (Gen 5:3). One becomes a son of God only through adoption by Jesus Christ (Gal 4:5, Eph 1:5).

- Likewise all bloodlines can be traced back to Noah, which Paul implies here when he quotes Deut 32:8, which refers to Noah's descendants in Genesis 10, the "Table of Nations." Noah's family repopulated the earth (Gen 9:1) with seventy families (paralleling Jacob's seventy sons and grandchildren, Deut 32:8 and Gen 46:27) that grew into distinct nations (each had its own borders or "boundaries"). God prepared humanity as seventy groups of people, each with an opportunity to seek fellowship with Him. Although some individuals stayed faithful to God, none of the nations wholly followed Him and instead united in rebellion against God at the tower of Babel (Gen 11:1-9).

- Since God has dominion over the entire earth, it is absurd to confine Him to a building (Acts 17:24). The truth is the opposite, that God assigns living places for humanity ("the bounds of their habitation").

- God plans and accomplishes His will ("hath determined") in the affairs of humanity (Dan 2:21), unlike the gods of the Athenians, whom they believe to be generally uninvolved in human affairs. Nations may boast of their dominion, but God distributes power according to His will (Rom 13:1).

<u>Language</u>
Redundancy (words beyond those needed to convey the message) – "the face of" is an Old Testament expression (Gen 11:8) that is not grammatically necessary but is added to emphasize how God accomplishes His will among humans "on all the face of the earth."

[27] That they should seek the Lord, if haply they might feel after him, and find him, though he be not far from every one of us:

God wants mankind to seek a relationship with Him (Jer 29:13, Heb 11:6) through His Son (1 John 1:3). Yet, although God is omnipresent, humanity's search for Him is that of a blind man stumbling around in the dark who can never quite find what he is looking for. Individuals can fellowship with God only through the Lord Jesus Christ, who is seeking the lost to come unto God by Him (Matt 18:11-14, Heb 7:25).

[28] For in him we live, and move, and have our being; as certain also of your own poets have said, For we are also his offspring.

- The phrase "for in him we live, and move, and have our being" apparently originates from the Greek poet Epimenides.[252] The phrase "for we are also his offspring" apparently originates from Aratus of Cilicia (Paul's home province).[253]
- The Epicureans believe that God is (or "the gods" are) indifferent to the affairs of humans. "Epicurus speaking thus ... for the nature of gods ... far removed and withdrawn from our concerns; since, exempt from every pain, exempt from all dangers, strong in its own resources, not wanting anything of us, it is neither gained by favours nor moved by anger."[254]
- The Stoics are pantheists and believe all the universe is God. "Chrysippus ... declares that the world itself is God ... such as water, earth, and air, then the sun, the moon, the stars, the universal existence in which all things are contained ..."[255]
- Since Paul's listeners do not believe in a deity who has created and actively sustains the universe (as is true of God the Son, Col 1:17, Heb 1:3), the Apostle brilliantly quotes their own poets whose words suggest this very idea.
- By quoting Greek poets, Paul does not mean to say that these pagan teachers accurately explain the nature of God or that he agrees with them. Instead, he simply wishes to tell his listeners that if they are devoted to their philosophy, they will consider the One, true God of the universe who created everything and everyone and now seeks to reconcile humanity to Himself through His Son Jesus Christ, the resurrected Savior.

299

---

[252] J. Rendel Harris, "The Cretans Always Liars," *The Expositor,* Vol. 2 (Warwick Square, London: Hodder and Stoughton, Oct 1906), p. 309-311

[253] Paul turns this pagan poem on its head by rejecting "Zeus" and pointing to the God of the Bible. "From Zeus let us begin; Him do we mortals never leave unnamed ... Always we all have need of Zeus. For we are also his offspring." A.W. Mair and G.R. Mair, translators. Loeb Classical Library 129, Hymns and Epigrams. Aratus: *Phaenomena*, 1921, p. 207

[254] Lactantius, *On the Anger of God*, chap. 8

[255] Marcus Tullius Cicero, *On the Nature of the Gods*, 1.14.36

[29] Forasmuch then as we are the offspring of God, we ought not to think that the Godhead is like unto gold, or silver, or stone, graven by art and man's device.

- Humans are not God's *natural* "offspring" (Paul uses this term to connect to the Greek poet above) because "God is not a man" (Num 23:19). Rather, humans are God's *created* "offspring" because He made them (Acts 17:25). Therefore it is incorrect to imagine God as an object made by humans.
- An individual will create an idol to have a "god" of his liking (Rom 1:23) that will justify his way of living. However, since humans made by God are so much more complex (Psalm 8:5, 139:14) than any idol, God must be far greater than humans.

[30] And the times of this ignorance God winked at; but now commandeth all men every where to repent:

- In the Old Testament, Jews understood God through the law of Moses, and He accordingly held the nation of Israel accountable to that knowledge.
- Before the resurrection of Christ, the Gentiles ("nations of men," Acts 17:26) were unaware ("ignorant") of the law of Moses. Rather than bringing immediate judgment upon them, He tolerated ("winked at") their pagan idolatry (Acts 14:16) and instead held them accountable to the light given to them (Rom 2:12).
- Since the resurrection, the message of the gospel is that everyone must repent of their ignorance of God. Each individual must change his mind (repent) about who God is and come to Him through Jesus Christ. The gospel must be proclaimed throughout the entire world because the day of judgment is coming (Acts 17:31), and there is no hope for anyone outside of Christ (John 3:36, Acts 4:12).

[31] Because he hath appointed a day, in the which he will judge the world in righteousness by that man whom he hath ordained; whereof he hath given assurance unto all men, in that he hath raised him from the dead.

- Stoic philosophy ignores the future day of judgment: "Mark how fleeting and paltry is the estate of man – yesterday in embryo, to-morrow a mummy or ashes. So for the hairsbreadth of time assigned to thee, live rationally, and part with life cheerfully, as drops the ripe olive, extolling the season that bore it and the tree that matured it."[256]
- Mankind establishes his own standard of right and wrong through false religion (Acts 17:16) or self-serving philosophy (Acts 17:18). God the Father has shown His approval of Jesus Christ by raising Him from the dead (Rom 1:4) and placing Him at His right hand (Eph 1:20) where He may now pardon sinners who repent (Heb 7:25) and will one day judge everyone (John 5:22, Rom 2:16) accord-ing to God's standard of right and wrong (Psalm 9:8, 98:9).
- Paul speaks using sophisticated terms familiar to his Athenian listeners. Yet, his conclusion is the simple message of Galilee: "The time is fulfilled, and the kingdom of God is at hand: repent ye, and believe the gospel" (Mark 1:15).

301

[32] And when they heard of the resurrection of the dead, some mocked: and others said, We will hear thee again of this matter.

- Paul's Greek listeners reject the idea of resurrection. An ancient play concerning the myth behind the Areopagus explains: "But after the dust has absorbed a dead man's blood, there is no resurrection."[257] Felix (Acts 24:21-22, 25) and Festus (Acts 26:23-24) also reject the idea of resurrection and will interrupt Paul when he preaches it.
- The Epicureans see no need for a resurrection: "Death, therefore, the most awful of evils, is nothing to us, seeing that, when we are, death is not come, and, when death is come, we are not. It is nothing, then, either to the living or to the dead, for with the living it is not and the dead exist no longer."[258]
- They count the gospel as a foolish thing (1 Cor 1:18) when they mock (2 Chron 36:16, Jude 18) and make empty promises to hear Paul again later (Prov 13:13, Acts 24:25).

---

[256] Marcus Aurelius, *Meditations*
[257] Aeschylus, *Eumenides*, 647–8
[258] Epicurus, *Letter to Menoeceus*

- The Sadducees, whose religious order administers the Jerusalem temple (Acts 4:1-2, 5:17), also believe there is no resurrection (Matt 22:23, Acts 23:8). To teach of a resurrection is to dispraise their glorious temple (1 Chron 22:5, Mark 13:1) as a temporary, inadequate, and inferior shadow of the greater temple of heaven (Heb 8:5, 10:1, Rev 11:19), which will give way to the One greater than the temple (Matt 12:6, Rev 21:22). So too these prideful Greeks cannot accept that "man in all his glory" (Psalm 8:5, Prov 20:29) is only a fallen being (Psalm 39:5, Rom 5:12) whose glory will fade away (1 Peter 1:24) and be replaced at the first resurrection (of those who are saved) by a far more glorious body (Rom 8:18-23, 1 Cor 15:51-53).

[33] So Paul departed from among them.

Paul can do little with the proud (Isa 13:11), idolatrous (Ezek 14:6), novelty-seeking (2 Tim 3:7), scornful (Isa 29:20) philosophers (Col 2:8) of Athens who perceive no need of a Savior. The Lord Jesus explained that it is hard for those who trust in riches to be saved (Mark 10:24), and Paul shows that it is hard for those who trust their intellect to be saved (1 Cor 1:26).

[34] Howbeit certain men clave unto him, and believed: among the which was Dionysius the Areopagite, and a woman named Damaris, and others with them.

- The Lord could have performed a great work in the acclaimed city of Athens that would have shaken the Greek world, but instead will choose the disreputable city of Corinth (Acts 18:8) from which to bring glory to His name (1 Cor 1:27-29).
- Nevertheless, among those saved is Dionysius, a member of the Areopagus; Damaris, a woman prominent enough to be mentioned by name; and other unnamed believers.

Persuasive Speech

Paul's Spirit-filled sermon shows a mastery of persuasive speech (rhetoric).
Introduction *(exordium)* – "Ye men of Athens, I perceive that in all things ye are too superstitious." Acts 17:22
Narrative *(narratio)* – Paul tells how he found an altar "to the unknown god." Acts 17:23a
Thesis *(propositio)* – the Athenians (by their own admission) do not know God. Acts 17:23b
Arguments *(probatio)* – God is not like an idol made by humans and does not live in temples made by humans. He made people of all nationalities and placed them in their respective environments to seek Him. Acts 17:24-29
Final appeal *(peroratio)* – the Athenians must repent of their ignorance of God and turn to the resurrected Savior. Acts 17:30-31

Challenge Questions

1. What is the difference between the Epicureans and the Stoics?
2. Why does Paul point out the altar of the "unknown god"?
3. What point does Paul make in quoting Greek poets?

Acts Chapter 18

[1] After these things Paul departed from Athens, and came to Corinth;

Corinth is widely known as a city wholly given to sexual immorality[259] (Rom 1:24). Paul will have reason to instruct members of the local church regarding righteous living (1 Cor 5:1, 9-11, 6:9, 13, 18, 7:2, 10:8, 2 Cor 12:21).

[2] And found a certain Jew named Aquila, born in Pontus, lately come from Italy, with his wife Priscilla; (because that Claudius had commanded all Jews to depart from Rome:) and came unto them.

Priscilla and Aquila are originally from the province of Pontus (north of Galatia in eastern Asia Minor) but had been living in Rome until now. They may have received the gospel from travelers returning to Pontus (Acts 2:9) or Rome (Acts 2:10) after Pentecost. In Corinth they labor with Paul and lodge him (Acts 18:3). They will follow Paul to Ephesus (Acts 18:18-19), where they will hold church meetings in their house (1 Cor 16:19) and disciple Apollos, whose subsequent ministry will bear fruit back in Corinth (1 Cor 3:5-7). Priscilla and Aquila will eventually move back to Rome, where they will start another house church and be commended by Paul as helpers in his ministry (Rom 16:3-5). They will finally be found again at Ephesus, working alongside Timothy (1 Tim 1:3). Paul's love for them is evident when he reserves his last greeting at the end of his final letter before his death for this faithful couple (2 Tim 4:19).

[3] And because he was of the same craft, he abode with them, and wrought: for by their occupation they were tentmakers.

Paul works (1 Cor 4:12), as at Thessalonica (1 Thes 2:9, 2 Thes 3:7-8), to

---

[259] "On account of the multitude of harlots at Corinth, who are dedicated to Venus, and attracted by the festivities of the place, strangers resorted thither in great numbers. Merchants and soldiers were quite ruined, so that hence the proverb originated, 'every man cannot go to Corinth'" (Strabo, *Geography*, 12.3.36).

avoid being a financial burden to local believers (2 Cor 12:13-14). He also receives financial support from the church at Philippi (2 Cor 11:9, Phil 4:15) and Thessalonica (1 Thes 3:6).

[4] And he reasoned in the synagogue every sabbath, and persuaded the Jews and the Greeks.

Paul again begins his ministry by preaching in the local synagogue (Acts 13:5, 14, 14:1, 17:1, 10, 17) to Jews and devout Gentiles.

[5] And when Silas and Timotheus were come from Macedonia, Paul was pressed in the spirit, and testified to the Jews that Jesus was Christ.

Previously Paul recalled Silas and Timothy from Berea to join him at Athens (Acts 17:14-15). From Athens he sent them back to other churches in Macedonia (1 Thes 3:1-2). Silas and Timothy now meet up again with Paul here in Corinth (2 Cor 1:19). The two arrive with a love gift from the faithful brethren at Thessalonica (1 Thes 3:6). The apostle is greatly encouraged by the "good tidings of [their] faith and charity," which compels him all the more to proclaim Jesus as the Messiah (1 Cor 9:16) like he did at Thessalonica (Acts 17:3).

[6] And when they opposed themselves, and blasphemed, he shook his raiment, and said unto them, Your blood be upon your own heads; I am clean: from henceforth I will go unto the Gentiles.

- The Jewish leadership rejects the gospel here in Europe as they did in Jerusalem (Acts 7:54-60) and Asia Minor (Acts 13:46) and will in Rome (Acts 28:28). In so doing they oppose the salvation of their own souls (2 Tim 2:25), and Paul states that he has done everything possible to warn them of judgment to come (Ezek 3:17-19, Acts 20:26).
- Paul symbolically shakes off "the very dust of your city" (Luke 10:10-11). He says, "I will go unto the Gentiles" for the sake of his fellow Jews "to provoke them to jealousy" (Rom 11:11b). Despite his grave pronouncement, Paul will still seek to reach Jewish people in synagogues (Acts 18:19, 19:8).

[7] And he departed thence, and entered into a certain man's house, named Justus, one that worshipped God, whose house joined hard to the synagogue.

Paul has a falling-out with the synagogue leadership then boldly moves in next door to continue his ministry to fellow Jews.

[8] And Crispus, the chief ruler of the synagogue, believed on the Lord with all his house; and many of the Corinthians hearing believed, and were baptized.

- Baptism in the early Church is performed promptly after salvation (Acts 2:41, 8:36, 10:47, 16:33).
- Paul baptizes only a few of his converts here to avoid future schism (1 Cor 1:11-17). Those baptized by Paul include Crispus and Stephanas (1 Cor 16:15) as well as Gaius, with whom Paul will lodge during his next visit to Corinth (Rom 16:23).
- Other believers associated with Corinth include Sosthenes (1 Cor 1:1, Acts 18:17), Chloe (1 Cor 1:11), Fortunatus and Achaicus (1 Cor 16:17), Phoebe (Rom 16:1), Lucius, Jason, and Sosipater (Rom 16:21), Tertius (Rom 16:22), Erastus and Quartus (Rom 16:23).

[9] Then spake the Lord to Paul in the night by a vision, Be not afraid, but speak, and hold not thy peace:

- The words of Christ alleviate Paul's uncertainties and fears (1 Cor 2:3). He had wisely left other cities in the past when the opposition was too strong (Acts 14:6, 17:10, 14), but now he receives assurance that he may preach the gospel in Corinth as long as necessary.
- Paul will receive two other visions, one in Jerusalem (Acts 23:11) and one on a ship in a storm (Acts 27:23-24). Visions elsewhere in the book of Acts include those received by Ananias (Acts 9:10), Cornelius (Acts 10:3), and Peter (Acts 11:5). Visions will be common in the kingdom age (Acts 2:17).

[10] For I am with thee, and no man shall set on thee to hurt thee: for I have much people in this city.

The Lord has many believers here in Corinth (Acts 18:8) and will continue to add many more to His church (1 Cor 3:6-9).

[11] And he continued there a year and six months, teaching the word of God among them.

- The apostle teaches "the word of truth, by the power of God" (2 Cor 6:7) as he is driven by the words of the Savior (Acts 18:9-10). Paul's ministry here includes "the working of miracles" (1 Cor 12:10), and he will later remind the Corinthian believers that "truly the signs of an apostle were wrought among you in all patience, in signs, and wonders, and mighty deeds" (2 Cor 12:12).
- Paul is thankful for the souls saved under his preaching in Corinth (1 Cor 4:15) and pleased to have "come as far as to you also in preaching the gospel of Christ" (2 Cor 10:14). He will later write to Roman believers about how God has blessed his ministry here (Rom 1:13, written from Corinth). Although Luke's narrative focuses on Corinth, Paul's ministry bears fruit in the entire province of Achaia (2 Cor 1:1), as evidenced by his acknowledgment of the generosity of the churches in this region (2 Cor 9:2, 11:10) and implied by his wintering in Nicopolis (Titus 3:12).
- Paul writes the two epistles to the Thessalonians during this time. In his salutations he includes Silas and Timothy, who also preach the gospel at Corinth (2 Cor 1:19).

[12] And when Gallio was the deputy of Achaia, the Jews made insurrection with one accord against Paul, and brought him to the judgment seat,

Junius Gallio is the older brother of the well-known philosopher Seneca, the tutor of the soon-to-be-emperor Nero.[260] Gallio will show himself to be a governor of sound judgment, like Sergius Paulus, the deputy of Cyprus (Acts 13:7).

<u>Language</u>
"Macedonia" refers to northern Greece and "Achaia" to southern Greece.

---

[260] "Junius Gallio." Encyclopedia Britannica Online, accessed 28 Oct 2019

[13] Saying, This fellow persuadeth men to worship God contrary to the law.

Unbelieving Jews in Thessalonica had accused Paul of violating Roman law by presenting Jesus as King (Acts 17:7). Gallio examines the charges before him and understands this as a dispute over religious law ("your law," Acts 18:15).

[14] And when Paul was now about to open his mouth, Gallio said unto the Jews, If it were a matter of wrong or wicked lewdness, O ye Jews, reason would that I should bear with you:

Gallio sees this argument as nothing more than a quarrel between two sects of Judaism (Acts 28:22) and notes the lack of legitimate criminal charges. Governor Pilate made similar comments (John 18:31) when he perceived that charges were brought against Jesus because of envy (Mark 15:10).

[15] But if it be a question of words and names, and of your law, look ye to it; for I will be no judge of such matters.

Rome considers Judaism a legitimate religion with its own laws to judge its members (John 18:31a). Gallio has determined that preaching about the Jewish Messiah falls within the scope of Judaism. The governor's ruling means that Paul is free to preach the gospel throughout the Roman empire.

[16] And he drave them from the judgment seat.

Gallio dismisses the case for lack of merit. Pontius Pilate attempted the same at Jesus' trial (John 18:38) but found himself under much greater pressure than Gallio (John 19:12) and lacked the moral courage to take responsibility for his decision (Matt 27:24).

[17] Then all the Greeks took Sosthenes, the chief ruler of the synagogue, and beat him before the judgment seat. And Gallio cared for none of those things.

- Sosthenes is beaten by spectators apparently for bringing frivolous charges. He will later become a believer (1 Cor 1:1), as has the former synagogue ruler Crispus (Acts 18:8).
- Gallio, the governor of Achaia, does not care to judge religious matters and apparently does not care that the crowd beats the plaintiff.
- Paul remains unharmed as the Lord promised (Acts 18:10). He will later write back to the Corinthian believers instructing them to address contentious matters between church members within the church rather than a courtroom (1 Cor 6:1-8).

Current Events

- Emperor Claudius dies under suspicious circumstances. He is believed to have been poisoned by his fourth wife so that her son Nero (rather than Claudius' older son Britannicus) would become

Paul spends 18 months in Corinth preaching the word of God during his second missionary journey (Acts 18:11).

Tatiana Popova / Shutterstock.com

the next emperor.[261]
- Nero is proclaimed Caesar and grants Herod Agrippa II (Acts 25:13) rule over Galilee.[262]

[18] And Paul after this tarried there yet a good while, and then took his leave of the brethren, and sailed thence into Syria, and with him Priscilla and Aquila; having shorn his head in Cenchrea: for he had a vow.

- Paul still maintains his Jewishness (Acts 21:39) and faithfully follows the law (Acts 21:20-26) in any way that does not diminish "the truth of the gospel" (Gal 2:5). He took an unspecified vow (e.g., Num 6:1-21), which may look something like the following: Paul made a vow in Cenchrea, which he began by shaving his head. He will not cut his hair again (Num 6:5) until he reaches the Jerusalem temple (Acts 18:22) where he will again shave his head and offer the cuttings as an offering along with a ram and unleavened bread (Num 6:18-20).
- The apostle now travels from Cenchrea (Rom 16:1) to Antioch in Syria (Acts 18:22) with a stop at Ephesus (Acts 18:19). He is accompanied by Priscilla and Aquila, Silas, Timothy (Acts 19:22), and Gaius and Aristarchus (Acts 19:29).

[19] And he came to Ephesus, and left them there: but he himself entered into the synagogue, and reasoned with the Jews.

- Priscilla and Aquila do not travel with Paul to Jerusalem but stay behind here at Ephesus, where they will start a church in their house (1 Cor 16:19) and teach the word of God (Acts 18:26).
- Earlier in his journey Paul was "forbidden of the Holy Ghost to preach the word in Asia" (Acts 16:6b). However, now he is free to preach the gospel at Ephesus in the province of Asia.

310

[261] Cassius Dio, *Roman History*, 61.34
[262] Josephus, *Antiquities*, 20.8.1-4

[20] When they desired him to tarry longer time with them, he consented not;

The Jews of this synagogue are open to the gospel, in contrast to those at Corinth (Acts 18:6, 12-13). They are undoubtedly impressed by Paul's commitment to the law as he completes his vow (Acts 18:18) and prepares to keep this feast (Acts 18:21) at Jerusalem. The apostle readily uses his devotion to Judaism to bring the gospel to Jews here (1 Cor 9:20) as he had used his Greek education (he quoted Greek poets, Acts 17:28) to reach lost Gentiles at Athens (1 Cor 9:21).

[21] But bade them farewell, saying, I must by all means keep this feast that cometh in Jerusalem: but I will return again unto you, if God will. And he sailed from Ephesus.

Paul purposes to keep one of the three feasts that were formerly (Col 2:16) required of all Jewish males (Deut 16:16). He will return to Ephesus, Lord willing (1 Cor 4:19, James 4:15), for a two-year ministry (Acts 19:10).

[22] And when he had landed at Cæsarea, and gone up, and saluted the church, he went down to Antioch.

- The phrase "go up to Jerusalem" (Acts 15:2, 21:4,12) is commonly used because Jerusalem is considered physically and spiritually higher than any other city (1 Kings 11:36, Psalm 137:5). Therefore when Paul leaves the coastal town of Caesarea, it is implied that the city to which he goes "up" is Jerusalem. This visit is Paul's fourth to Jerusalem since conversion (Acts 9:28, 12:25, 15:2).
- Silas met Paul in Jerusalem before their missionary journey (Acts 15:22) and likely parts with him here. Silas will later join Simon Peter and John Mark in Babylon (Silvanus and Marcus, 1 Peter 5:12-13).
- Paul returns to Antioch in Syria, where he had initiated his first and second missionary journeys (Acts 13:1; Acts 15:30,40) and will now begin his third.

[23] And after he had spent some time there, he departed, and went over all the country of Galatia and Phrygia in order, strengthening all the disciples.

- Paul begins his third missionary journey, which will end when he returns to Jerusalem (Acts 21:17). He travels back through Asia Minor, as before (Acts 16:6), visiting the churches he previously founded. Paul will bring a charitable contribution to poor believers in Jerusalem at the end of his journey (Acts 24:17). He now asks the churches of Galatia to take a collection for this purpose every Sunday (1 Cor 16:1-2).
- Paul's traveling companions include Timothy and Erastus (Acts 19:22), Gaius and Aristarchus (Acts 19:29), and Titus (2 Cor. 8:23).

[24] And a certain Jew named Apollos, born at Alexandria, an eloquent man, and mighty in the scriptures, came to Ephesus.

- Apollos is from Alexandria, Egypt, founded by Alexander the Great during his war against the Persian Empire. Before Alexander was born, Daniel prophesied of him, a warrior who would come from "the realm of Grecia. And a mighty king shall stand up, that shall rule with great dominion, and do according to his will" (Dan 11:2b-3). Now in Apollos' day Alexandria has a famous library, and the city is known to be a major center of Greek knowledge.[263] Alexandria's port facilitates large shipments of grain leaving Egypt for Rome, and Alexandria's lighthouse will be called one of the seven wonders of the ancient world.[264] The Apostle Paul will sail on two different ships originating from there (Acts 27:6, 28:11).
- Apollos is a Jew with extensive knowledge of the Old Testament ("mighty in the scriptures"). He is highly trained in Greek rhetoric ("an eloquent man"), meaning he is an effective public speaker both when teaching and debating. His educational background is similar to that of the Apostle Paul, who has deep knowledge of the Old Testament ("brought up in [Jerusalem] at the feet of Gamaliel," Acts 22:3) and was from a city reputed for its Greco-Roman education ("born in Tarsus, a city in Cilicia," Acts 22:3).

---

[263] "Alexandria Egypt." *Encyclopedia Britannica Online*, accessed 9 Nov 2019
[264] "Seven Wonders of the World." *Encyclopedia Britannica Online*, accessed 9 Nov 2019

[25] This man was instructed in the way of the Lord; and being fervent in the spirit, he spake and taught diligently the things of the Lord, knowing only the baptism of John.

Apollos knows the "way of the Lord" (Judg 2:22, Prov 10:29) according to the Old Testament scriptures and the preaching of John the Baptist (Isa 40:3, Matt 3:3). Apollos may have heard of the ministry of Jesus (Acts 10:37-38, 26:26b) but does not know in a spiritual sense (1 John 5:20) the Christ of whom John had spoken.

Language
- "Fervent in spirit" means "very zealous."
- *Synecdoche* (the whole is given for the part, or the part is given for the whole) – "the baptism of John" refers to his entire ministry (Luke 20:4).

[26] And he began to speak boldly in the synagogue: whom when Aquila and Priscilla had heard, they took him unto them, and expounded unto him the way of God more perfectly.

- Apollos preaches as John the Baptist did, that Israel has sinned in practicing idolatry, ignoring God's law, and rejecting His prophets (2 Chron 36:14-16). He rebukes those who proudly perform ritual sacrifices in the temple but fail to obey (1 Sam 15:22) God's directive to humbly practice justice and mercy (Prov 21:3, Mic 6:8). He proclaims that each member of Israel must repent individually (Matt 3:8) so the nation as a whole will be prepared for the Messiah to come and establish His kingdom (Matt 3:2).
- Aquila and Priscilla remind Apollos how John the Baptist had identified the Lord Jesus (Acts 19:4) as the Lamb of God (John 1:29-34, Isa 53:7) and foretold the coming of the Holy Ghost (Luke 3:16). They show how the Savior fulfilled scripture when He laid down His life and rose from the dead (Acts 8:32-35). They describe the coming of the Holy Ghost at Pentecost (Acts 2:1-4). They teach Apollos the doctrine of justification by grace through faith (Acts 13:38-39, 15:7-9). They show how God has brought salvation to the Gentiles (Acts 11:18) and does not require them to first convert to Judaism (Acts 15:11).

[27] And when he was disposed to pass into Achaia, the brethren wrote, exhorting the disciples to receive him: who, when he was come, helped them much which had believed through grace:

- Apollos is given a letter of commendation (Rom 16:1, 2 Cor 3:1) and is sent to the church of Corinth in the province of Achaia, where he both helps believers and wins souls (Acts 18:28, 1 Cor 3:5). Through no fault of his, he will become a subject of contention (1 Cor 1:10-12) and choose to travel back to Ephesus (1 Cor 16:8,12), no doubt so that the factions may dissipate.
- From Ephesus Paul will write favorably of Apollos' ministry at Corinth (1 Cor 3:6) but will note Apollos' reluctance to return there again (1 Cor 16:12). Apollos will later minister faithfully with Titus (Titus 3:13).

[28] For he mightily convinced the Jews, and that publickly, shewing by the scriptures that Jesus was Christ.

Paul and Apollos both know scripture well (Acts 18:4-5 and here), and both preach that Jesus is the Messiah. Yet the two differ in their style of public speaking, which might look somewhat like the following:
- Although Paul can speak in a sophisticated manner (Acts 17:22-31), he typically chooses words that persons of all educational levels can understand (2 Cor 3:12, 10:1). His presentation style has brought him criticism (2 Cor 10:10, 11:6), but he explains that he speaks plainly so the Holy Spirit may have free course to work in his listeners' hearts (1 Cor 2:4-5). Some respond negatively to Paul's preaching, such as the men of Athens (indifference, Acts 17:32), Felix (fearful neglect, Acts 24:25), Festus (frustration, Acts 26:24), and Eutychus (sleep, Acts 20:9). Many respond positively with faith unto salvation (Acts 13:43-44).
- Apollos speaks eloquently, giving dramatic metaphors and anecdotes to hold the attention of his audience and relying on his powerful rhetoric to overwhelm his opponent. Some respond positively to Apollos' preaching (Acts 18:28, 1 Cor 3:6) whereas others will react in an overly enthusiastic manner that creates factions (1 Cor 1:12, 3:4) unintended by Apollos (1 Cor 16:12).

Teaching Questions

Question: Did Emperor Claudius expel the Jews from Rome at the first sign of conflict?
Answer: No, he first tried to maintain order through other means. "As for the Jews, who had again increased so greatly that by reason of their multitude it would have been hard without raising a tumult to bar them from the city, he did not drive them out, but ordered them, while continuing their traditional mode of life, not to hold meetings."[265]
Question: So why did Emperor Claudius eventually expel the Jews from Rome (Acts 18:2)?
Answer: "Since the Jews constantly made disturbances at the instigation of Chrestus, he expelled them from Rome."[266]
Question: Who is Chrestus?
Answer: Chrestus is either:
- The name of a Jewish provocateur.
- A mangled reference to "Christus" or "Christ," referring ultimately to Jewish followers of Jesus Christ. The historian Tacitus mentions Christians and writes that "Christus, the founder of the name, had undergone the death penalty in the reign of Tiberius, by sentence of the procurator Pontius Pilatus ..."[267]

315

Question: The Roman Governor Gallio has ruled that contentions about Paul's preaching of Jesus are issues between fellow Jews. Why is his legal decision important?
Answer: Julius Caesar had declared that Jews are allowed to follow their religion. "Julius Gaius, praetor and consul of the Romans ... Jews who passed through there, have told us ... that by decree you forbid them to follow their ancestral customs and ways of worship. I do not want such decrees made against our friends and allies, forbidding them to live by their own customs and send contributions for common suppers and holy festivals, which they are not forbidden to do even in Rome itself... While forbidding other religious assemblies I permit this people to assemble

---

[265] Cassius Dio, *Roman History*, 60.6.6
[266] Suetonius, *The Life of Claudius*, 25.4
[267] Tacitus, *Annals*, 15.44.28

and celebrate according to their ancestral customs and laws. If you have made any decree against these our friends and allies, abrogate them because of their virtue and goodwill towards us."[268]

Locales throughout the empire, such as Ephesus, have affirmed this policy of tolerance. "The decree of the Ephesians ... 'Since the Jews living in this city have asked Marcus Junius Pompeius, son of Brutus, the proconsul, that they might be allowed to observe their Sabbaths and to act in all things according to their ancestral customs, without impediment from anyone, the praetor has granted their petition. It was decreed by the senate and people, that in this affair about the Romans none of them be hindered from keeping the sabbath day, or fined for doing so, but they be allowed to do all things according to their own laws.'"[269]

Therefore Gallio's decision that belief in the Jewish Messiah Jesus falls under the purview of Judaism means that believers in Christ are to be afforded the same legal protections as Jews.

Challenge Questions

1. What does it mean that "Paul was pressed in the spirit" (Acts 18:5)?
2. Why in Cenchrea did Paul believe it necessary to make a vow (Acts 18:18)?

---

[268] Josephus, *Antiquities*, 14.10.8
[269] Ibid., 14.10.25

Acts Chapter 19

[1] And it came to pass, that, while Apollos was at Corinth, Paul having passed through the upper coasts came to Ephesus: and finding certain disciples,

- Paul had met Priscilla and Aquila at Corinth, where he lodged with them and worked alongside them, making tents (Acts 18:2-3). On his way to Antioch in Syria, Paul took them to Ephesus (Acts 18:18-19), where they have started a church in their house (1 Cor 16:19). The couple also met and instructed Apollos, who has been sent to minister at Corinth (Acts 18:27).
- Paul left Antioch in Syria and traveled through the provinces of Cilicia and Galatia (Acts 18:23). He now travels through the province of Asia into Ephesus, along the road Luke says runs through the "upper coasts." He again reunites with Priscilla and Aquila, who will whole-heartedly assist his ministry even to the point of risking their lives for him (Rom 16:3-4).

[2] He said unto them, Have ye received the Holy Ghost since ye believed? And they said unto him, We have not so much as heard whether there be any Holy Ghost.

- These disciples of John the Baptist are like Apollos when he first arrived at Ephesus (Acts 18:24-25) in that they have incomplete knowledge of the ministry of Jesus Christ. Paul knows John taught them of a coming Messiah who would send the Holy Ghost (Matt 3:11) but is uncertain if they have believed on the Christ (Acts 16:31) of whom John had spoken (John 1:29).
- Paul knows that the Holy Ghost indwells all true believers (Rom 8:9, 1 John 3:24, Jude 19) and asks if they received the Holy Ghost when (the Old English meaning of the conjunction "since") they believed. They inform him that they are not aware of the Holy Ghost having been given (John 7:39), and by this Paul understands they have not received God's Spirit because although they may know *about* God's

Son, they do not actually *know* Him (1 John 4:13).

[3] And he said unto them, Unto what then were ye baptized? And they said, Unto John's baptism.

Paul understands they have been physically baptized by John the Baptist, but not spiritually baptized by the Holy Ghost (Luke 3:16).

[4] Then said Paul, John verily baptized with the baptism of repentance, saying unto the people, that they should believe on him which should come after him, that is, on Christ Jesus.

- The purpose of John's ministry (Mark 1:4, Acts 13:24) was truly ("verily") to prepare the people of Israel spiritually for Jesus the Messiah (Isa 40:3, Matt 3:3).
- Repentance is a change of heart and mind, which leads to a change of action. John's followers showed their repentance by being baptized in water and then living their lives in a praiseworthy manner (Luke 3:8).

318

[5] When they heard this, they were baptized in the name of the Lord Jesus.

These disciples of John the Baptist now believe on Jesus Christ and undergo water baptism in His name (Acts 8:12).

[6] And when Paul had laid his hands upon them, the Holy Ghost came on them; and they spake with tongues, and prophesied.

- The Jews (Acts 2:1-5) and the Gentiles (Acts 10:44-45) received the Holy Ghost without the laying on of hands. Yet, in this occurrence, John's disciples receive the Holy Ghost through the actions of the Apostle Paul to confirm that Jesus is the Messiah of whom John had spoken (John 1:29) and that this is the Holy Ghost of whom John had spoken (Matt 3:11).
- Paul imparting the Holy Ghost here as the Apostle Peter did to the Samaritans (Acts 8:17) confirms Paul's apostolic authority (Eph 1:1).
- The gift of tongues is the supernatural ability to speak in a lan-

Bithynia &
Pontus
Galatia
Cappadocia

Mysia
Asia
Phrygia
Pisidia
Lycaonia
Cilicia

Antioch
Iconium
Lystra
Derbe
Tarsus
Antioch

Ephesus
Trogyllium
Miletus
Assos
Troas
Samothrace

Mitylene
Chios
Samos
Coos
Rhodes
Patara
Perga
Lycia & Pamphylia

Thrace
Neapolis
Amphipolis
Apollonia
Thessalonica
Berea

Macedonia
Achaia
Athens
Corinth
Cenchrea

Crete

Cyrene

Cyprus
Paphos

Mediterranean Sea

Syria
Damascus
Tyre
Ptolemais
Caesarea
Jerusalem
Judea
Arabia

Egypt
Alexandria

Paul's Third Missionary Journey

Acts 18-21

Base map (land, water, roads) from Ancient World Mapping Center "A-la-carte"
Modifications (borders, routes) by Gregory Cetton
Creative Commons Attribution 4.0 International License (CC BY 4.0)

guage one has not learned (Acts 2:4–12). This gift is demonstrated three times in the book of Acts, each as a sign to Israel (1 Cor 1:22, 14:22): to confirm to Jews that the Holy Ghost has been given (Acts 2:1-4), to confirm to Jews that God has brought salvation to the Gentiles (Acts 10:44-46), and to confirm to Jews that Paul preaches the same Savior as John the Baptist.

- Prophecy examples include Agabus foretelling the future (Acts 11:28, 21:10-11) and Judas and Silas forth-telling through words of exhortation (Acts 15:32, 1 Cor 14:3).

[7] And all the men were about twelve.

The number "twelve" here underscores the Jewish nationality of the disciples of John the Baptist, as twelve is the number of the tribes of Israel (Gen 49:28) and the number of Jesus' chosen Jewish apostles (Luke 6:13).

[8] And he went into the synagogue, and spake boldly for the space of three months, disputing and persuading the things concerning the kingdom of God.

Paul preaches the kingdom of God, which is now entered spiritually through faith (John 3:3) and which will one day be present physically on earth at Christ's return (2 Tim 4:1). Paul no doubt warns the Jews of the synagogue that if they reject the King, they will have no part in His kingdom (Matt 21:43, Luke 13:28).

[9] But when divers were hardened, and believed not, but spake evil of that way before the multitude, he departed from them, and separated the disciples, disputing daily in the school of one Tyrannus.

- The disciples preach Jesus Christ as the only way (Matt 7:14, John 14:6) of salvation (Acts 16:17) and call this belief the "way" (Acts 9:2, 19:23, 22:4, 24:14,22).
- Since Paul is no longer welcome to teach in the synagogue, he secures the use of a classroom for his ministry. Paul's students learn the scripture and learn how to debate. "A traditional learning interaction is filled with energy and dialogue, debate and discussion . . . Conversations are lively, loud and filled with gesticulations and

frustrations. Jewish debate takes place in a *Beit Midrash*, a study hall. Unlike our contemporary libraries where silence resounds, Jewish schools are ... packed with books, people, noise and tumult."[270]
- At Ephesus Paul teaches in public settings and private homes (Acts 20:20).

[10] And this continued by the space of two years; so that all they which dwelt in Asia heard the word of the Lord Jesus, both Jews and Greeks.

- The ministry of 24 or more months in the school of Tyrannus (Acts 19:9-10) plus 3 months in the synagogue (Acts 19:8) rounds up to "three years" time (Acts 20:31) during which Paul provides his own financial support (Acts 20:33-34), probably by making tents (Acts 18:3).
- Every individual in the province of Asia open to the truth has heard the gospel message, both Jew and Gentile. Demetrius the silver-smith will confirm Luke's words, saying, "almost throughout all Asia, this Paul hath persuaded and turned away much people, saying that they be no gods, which are made with hands" (Acts 19:26). Later Paul will write that the gospel has gone out "to every creature which is under heaven" (Col 1:5-6, 23), signifying that every member of humanity is now responsible for the message of the gospel and must choose Jesus Christ or stand condemned for rejecting Him (John 3:18).
- Paul encounters great hardships at Ephesus (1 Cor 15:32, 2 Cor 1:8-10) yet has a great door of opportunity open (1 Cor 16:9). Through it, he helps establish the seven churches in the province of Asia to whom the Lord Jesus will write seven letters (Rev 1:11). An example of Paul's influence is how Epaphras, Philemon, and Archippus of Colosse (a city Paul had not visited, Col 2:1) apparently meet the apostle at Ephesus, are converted, and bring the gospel back to Colosse, Laodicea, and Hierapolis (Col 4:12-13, 17, Philem 1-2).
- While here at Ephesus, Paul makes a second visit to Corinth unrecorded by Luke but evidenced by the apostle describing his upcoming visit (Acts 20:2) as his third (2 Cor 12:14, 13:1).

---

[270] Micah D. Halpern, "The Art of Debate: Jewish Style." *Asia Society*, asiasociety.org/new-york/art-debate-jewish-style, accessed 27 Aug 2019

Language

Hyperbole (facts are exaggerated to describe feelings) – "so many people have heard the gospel through Paul's preaching that it feels like everyone has!"

[11] And God wrought special miracles by the hands of Paul:

Paul works "mighty signs and wonders, by the power of the Spirit of God" (Rom 15:19).

[12] So that from his body were brought unto the sick handkerchiefs or aprons, and the diseases departed from them, and the evil spirits went out of them.

- God the Father placed His seal of approval on the Son in giving Him the power to heal physical illness and cast out evil spirits (Acts 10:38). God has likewise shown His approval of Paul's apostolic ministry (2 Cor 12:12) by providing an outpouring of the Holy Ghost so overflowing that those with direct or even indirect contact receive healing, as was the case with Simon Peter (Acts 5:15) and the Lord Jesus (Mark 6:56, Luke 7:7-11, 8:43-44).
- Although Paul is grateful to be used of God to cleanse people of evil spirits, he knows to "rejoice not, that the spirits are subject unto you; but rather rejoice, because your names are written in heaven" (Luke 10:20).

[13] Then certain of the vagabond Jews, exorcists, took upon them to call over them which had evil spirits the name of the Lord Jesus, saying, We adjure you by Jesus whom Paul preacheth.

[14] And there were seven sons of one Sceva, a Jew, and chief of the priests, which did so.

- Sceva presents himself as "chief of the priests," but the legitimate priests serve at Jerusalem, as did Zacharias (Luke 1:5) and Simeon (Luke 2:25).
- The Lord Jesus "cast out devils by the spirit of God" (Matt 12:28) and

gave the same power to his disciples (Matt 10:1), including Paul. Sceva and his sons travel about (they are "vagabond"), performing dark rituals, no doubt for financial gain. They have apparently seen Paul casting out evil spirits (Acts 19:12) in Jesus' name (Mark 16:17) and hope to do the same (Matt 7:22). They formally command ("adjure") the spirits using Jesus' name as a magical word.
- Simon the sorcerer also attempted to appropriate the apostles' spiritual power for financial gain (Acts 8:18-20).

[15] And the evil spirit answered and said, Jesus I know, and Paul I know; but who are ye?

The powers of darkness acknowledge the Lord Jesus (Mark 1:24). They take special note of Paul (as at Philippi, Acts 16:17) as they did Simon Peter (Luke 22:31) and Job (Job 1:8-9).

323

Paul spends nearly three years at Ephesus preaching the gospel (Acts 20:31).
Nejdet Duzen / Shutterstock.com

[16] And the man in whom the evil spirit was leaped on them, and overcame them, and prevailed against them, so that they fled out of that house naked and wounded.

Individuals who lack saving faith cannot cast out evil spirits (Luke 9:40-41) and only make matters worse (Luke 11:26). Now the possessed man has supernatural strength (Mark 5:1-4).

Language
Irony (unexpected outcome or event) – Sceva is cast out, not the evil spirits as he intended.

[17] And this was known to all the Jews and Greeks also dwelling at Ephesus; and fear fell on them all, and the name of the Lord Jesus was magnified.

They learn that God gives power over evil forces not through magical words but through the power of the Holy Ghost (Acts 1:8) to those who know God's Son (Mark 16:17). The fear of God falls on those under the ministry of Paul as previously with Jesus (Luke 7:16) and Peter (Acts 5:11). God is glorified through the exorcists' downfall, as He was through Pharaoh's (Rom 9:17).

[18] And many that believed came, and confessed, and shewed their deeds.

Many people confess their sins and verbally show (explain) what they have done. They repent when they see the judgment of Sceva the exorcist, as did Sergius Paulus when he saw the judgment of Elymas the sorcerer (Acts 13:12). Paul will later write the Ephesian believers with instructions on spiritual warfare (Eph 6:10-20).

[19] Many of them also which used curious arts brought their books together, and burned them before all men: and they counted the price of them, and found it fifty thousand pieces of silver.

- These expensive books of sorcery ("curious arts") illustrate how the love of money (1 Tim 6:10) motivates individuals to pervert their spiritual practices (Rom 1:21-23), as seen with Simon the sorcerer (Acts 8:19-20), the handlers of the spirit-possessed girl (Acts 16:18-19), and Demetrius the silversmith (Acts 19:24-25).

- The new believers here demonstrate true repentance (unlike Rev 9:21) when they voluntarily destroy their sorcery books and count their financial loss as spiritual gain (Phil 3:7-8).

[20] So mightily grew the word of God and prevailed.

- The church experienced extraordinary growth after God's judgment of Herod Agrippa I (Acts 12:24) and does so now after the judgment of Sceva.
- Luke gives the sixth of seven summary statements in the book of Acts now that the gospel has spread into Europe.

[21] After these things were ended, Paul purposed in the spirit, when he had passed through Macedonia and Achaia, to go to Jerusalem, saying, After I have been there, I must also see Rome.

- Paul has completed his goal of planting churches throughout the eastern part of the Roman Empire (Rom 15:23) from his base in Antioch of Syria (Acts 13:1-3). He now desires to travel to Rome and establish a base to evangelize the western part of the Roman empire (Rom 15:24).
- The apostle plans to travel first to Macedonia (Acts 20:1), Achaia (Acts 20:2), and then Jerusalem (Acts 21:15), where he will bring the charitable gift he has been asking churches to collect (1 Cor 16:1-4, 2 Cor 9:1-8, Rom 15:25-27). He originally hoped to visit Corinth in Achaia first, then Macedonia, then Corinth again (2 Cor 1:16-17), but he ultimately decided to visit Macedonia first (1 Cor 16:5).
- Paul has a sense of foreboding about the trip (Rom 15:30-31). Doubtless, he feels that his presence in Jerusalem is necessary both to help the poor saints and to demonstrate unity between Jewish and Gentile believers (Rom 15:27). His charitable gift will be accepted (Acts 24:17), and he will make his intended journey to Rome (Rom 1:15, 15:23), although as a prisoner (Acts 27:1).

[22] So he sent into Macedonia two of them that ministered unto him, Timotheus and Erastus; but he himself stayed in Asia for a season.

- Timothy and Erastus go to Macedonia now and to Corinth later (1 Cor 4:17, 16:10, 2 Tim 4:20). Paul remains at Ephesus for now. After Pentecost he plans to leave for Macedonia and go to Corinth, where he will winter for three months (1 Cor 16:5-8, Acts 20:2-3).
- From Corinth Paul receives word from members of the household of Cloe (1 Cor 1:11); a gift brought by Stephanas, Fortunatus, and Achaicus (1 Cor 16:17); and at least one letter (1 Cor 7:1) asking many questions (1 Cor 7:1, 25, 8:4, 12:1, 16:1). Paul responds by writing the epistle of 1 Corinthians (1 Cor 16:8), in which he answers their questions and reminds them of Apollos, who was at Corinth and is now at Ephesus (1 Cor 16:12, Acts 19:1). Paul would like Apollos to return to Corinth, but the man is reluctant to do so, no doubt because of the previous dissension within the Corinthian church (1 Cor 1:10-12).

[23] And the same time there arose no small stir about that way.

The "way" is a reference to Christianity (Acts 19:9).

[24] For a certain man named Demetrius, a silversmith, which made silver shrines for Diana, brought no small gain unto the craftsmen;

Demetrius will speak to the craftsmen of religious devotion, but his real motives are financial (1 Tim 6:10), as were those of the exorcists of Philippi (Acts 16:19).

[25] Whom he called together with the workmen of like occupation, and said, Sirs, ye know that by this craft we have our wealth.

Demetrius readily admits the financial self-interests of these idol-makers who oppose God (Deut 27:15, Hosea 13:2).

[26] Moreover ye see and hear, that not alone at Ephesus, but almost throughout all Asia, this Paul hath persuaded and turned away much people, saying that they be no gods, which are made with hands:

Demetrius unintentionally praises Paul's thriving ministry (as had Paul's enemies at Thessalonica, Acts 17:6) and confirms Luke's similar appraisal (Acts 19:10). Demetrius is correct in saying that Paul persuades many (Acts 19:8) that nothing made by human hands is God (Acts 17:29).

[27] So that not only this our craft is in danger to be set at nought; but also that the temple of the great goddess Diana should be despised, and her magnificence should be destroyed, whom all Asia and the world worshippeth.

- The temple of Diana at Ephesus has been famous for hundreds of years. Around 400 BC, Xenophon wrote of "the great temple at Ephesus" with its Diana statue "made ... of gold."[271]
- Demetrius has seen the burning of sorcery books (Acts 19:19) and worries about the future of Diana worship. His suspicions will be proven correct when Christianity spreads throughout the world and the goddess Diana is abandoned.
- These craftsmen of Ephesus profit from the worldwide religion of the goddess Diana as the merchants of "Mystery Babylon" (Rev 17:5) will one day profit (Rev 18:3) from the worldwide religion of "the great whore" (Rev 17:1-2) until the day all ungodly craftsmen cease their work (Rev 18:22).

<u>Language</u>
Dramatic Irony (the character is unaware of the inconsistency) – Demetrius says he defends Diana out of religious devotion, but Luke's readers know that religion is only a pretext for financial interests (Acts 19:25).

[28] And when they heard these sayings, they were full of wrath, and cried out, saying, Great is Diana of the Ephesians.

Demetrius stirs up the people against Paul (Acts 13:50, 14:2, 17:13).

[29] And the whole city was filled with confusion: and having caught Gaius and Aristarchus, men of Macedonia, Paul's companions in travel,

---

271 Xenophon, *Anabasis*, 5.3

they rushed with one accord into the theatre.

- Four men named Gaius appear in scripture: Gaius of Macedonia (referred to in this verse), Gaius of Derbe (Acts 20:4), Gaius of Corinth (he lodges Paul, Rom 16:23, 1 Cor 1:14), and "wellbeloved" Gaius (3 John 1).
- Aristarchus of Thessalonica (Acts 20:4) will travel with Paul to Macedonia, Jerusalem, and Rome, where he will be with Paul while the apostle is under house arrest (Acts 27:2, Col 4:10, Philem 24).

[30] And when Paul would have entered in unto the people, the disciples suffered him not.

Paul hopes to calm this crowd by words of persuasion as he had at Lystra (Acts 14:14-18). However, the brethren see the danger of this situation and keep him out of harm's way as they had at Damascus (Acts 9:24-25) and Jerusalem (Acts 9:29-30).

[31] And certain of the chief of Asia, which were his friends, sent unto him, desiring him that he would not adventure himself into the theatre.

Among Paul's friends are civil officials who advise him not to risk ("adventure") entry into the outdoor amphitheater (arena).

[32] Some therefore cried one thing, and some another: for the assembly was confused; and the more part knew not wherefore they were come together.

Ironically, the angry mob does not know why they should be angry. A wicked mob had also assembled against Lot, who was providentially delivered (Gen 19:4-11).

[33] And they drew Alexander out of the multitude, the Jews putting him forward. And Alexander beckoned with the hand, and would have made his defence unto the people.

If this Alexander is the coppersmith of whom Paul will later warn Timothy (2 Tim 4:14-15), then he is a copper craftsman (underselling the silversmiths) who is put forward by the unbelieving Jews (Acts 19:9) to speak against Paul.

[34] But when they knew that he was a Jew, all with one voice about the space of two hours cried out, Great is Diana of the Ephesians.

- The multitude knows Jews oppose idols like Diana (Lev 26:1), so Alexander's presence enrages them even more.
- Diana's temple is so magnificent that it will be described as one of the seven wonders of the ancient world.[272] So "Great is Diana of the Ephesians" really means "Great are we Ephesians!"
- They use "vain repetitions" (Matt 6:7, 1 Kings 18:26) to pridefully boast of what they have created (Dan 4:30).

---

[272] "Seven Wonders of the World." *Encyclopedia Britannica Online*, accessed 9 Nov 2019

Demetrius and the silversmiths start a riot in the amphitheater at Ephesus when sales of their pagan shrines diminish because so many people have become Christians (Acts 19:24-41).

Ryzhkov Oleksandr / Shutterstock.com

- The Jews of Ephesus are undoubtedly angry that Paul, a fellow Jew, has (from their faulty perspective) precipitated this riot and are humiliated that their Jewish spokesman Alexander has been soundly rejected. They will vengefully take out their frustration on Paul when they find him at the temple in Jerusalem (Acts 21:27-28).

Language
The Roman goddess "Diana" is equivalent to the Greek goddess "Artemis."

[35] And when the townclerk had appeased the people, he said, Ye men of Ephesus, what man is there that knoweth not how that the city of the Ephesians is a worshipper of the great goddess Diana, and of the image which fell down from Jupiter?

- The Ephesian official calms the crowd by first reminding them that Paul's teaching that "they be no gods, which are made with hands" (Acts 19:26) should not disturb them because the image of their goddess was not made with human hands (it "fell down from Jupiter").
- "All Asia and the world worshipeth" (Acts 19:27) this image, which is said to be not of Ephesian origin, but divine origin from Jupiter. This idolatry foreshadows when all the world will worship the image of the beast that is given life by the god-like false prophet (Rev 13:14-15) who, in type was also likened unto the god Jupiter by the Lyconians (Acts 14:11-12).

[36] Seeing then that these things cannot be spoken against, ye ought to be quiet, and to do nothing rashly.

The town clerk gives wise and prudent advice, as did Sergius Paulus (Acts 13:7).

[37] For ye have brought hither these men, which are neither robbers of churches, nor yet blasphemers of your goddess.

- "Church" can refer to any assembly of people, such as that of Israel (Acts 7:38), Christians (Acts 9:31), or even pagan silversmiths (present verse). The town clerk explains that although the silversmiths may have lost income, Paul and company did nothing to defraud them.

- The words of the town clerk reveal that Paul and his companions have not denounced any icon by name but instead have "persuaded and turned away much people" from idol worship with the simple message that "they be no gods, which are made with hands" (Acts 19:26).

[38] Wherefore if Demetrius, and the craftsmen which are with him, have a matter against any man, the law is open, and there are deputies: let them implead one another.

Demetrius has not pleaded against ("impleaded" or prosecuted) Paul in a court of law (as in Acts 18:12) because the apostle has broken no law. Paul is "guilty" only of persuading people to forsake idols, which has led to a decrease in the sales of shrines.

The temple of Diana falls to ruins as Christianity spreads across the globe.
NiglayNik / Shutterstock.com

[39] But if ye enquire any thing concerning other matters, it shall be determined in a lawful assembly.

Matters not appropriate for a court hearing should be addressed by a lawfully convened citizens' assembly,[273] not by a disorderly mob.

[40] For we are in danger to be called in question for this day's uproar, there being no cause whereby we may give an account of this concourse.

Demetrius has accused Paul of wrongdoing, but the town clerk warns the mob that it is their unruly assembly ("concourse") that violates Roman law for which the governor may impose severe punishment (Luke 13:1, Rom 13:1-4).

[41] And when he had thus spoken, he dismissed the assembly.

The people realize the rashness of their actions (Acts 19:36) and are persuaded to depart.

Persuasive Speech

Demetrius the silversmith (Acts 19:24-27) attacks Paul using persuasive speech (rhetoric).
Introduction *(exordium)* – speaking about money grabs everyone's attention. Acts 19:25
Narrative *(narratio)* – Paul has persuaded many throughout the region to give up idol worship. Acts 19:26
Thesis *(propositio)* – the silversmiths' income and Diana's glory are at risk because of Paul. Acts 19:27
Arguments *(probatio)* – absent! The angry crowd is already stirred into a frenzy. Acts 19:28.

---

273 "Ecclesia." *Encyclopedia Britannica Online*, accessed 3 May 2020

The town clerk (Acts 19:35-41) defends Paul using persuasive speech (rhetoric).
Introduction *(exordium)* – after the crowd chants for two hours, he says, "Come on guys, the world already knows that we love Diana!" Acts 19:35
Thesis *(propositio)* – "Be quiet, and to do nothing rashly." Acts 19:36
Arguments *(probatio)* – Paul and his colleagues did not rob the silver-smiths or attack Diana. Demetrius and his colleagues should air their grievances lawfully in court or a citizens' assembly, not unlawfully in the amphitheater. Acts 19:37-39
Final appeal *(peroratio)* – the greatest danger is not Paul but the Roman government that could come down on our heads for rioting. Acts 19:40

Challenge Questions

1. How are these disciples of John the Baptist (Acts 19:1-7) like or unlike Apollos when he first met Aquila and Priscilla (Acts 18:24-28)?
2. What does Luke mean when he writes that "all they which dwelt in Asia heard the word of the Lord Jesus" (Acts 19:10)?

Acts Chapter 20

[1] And after the uproar was ceased, Paul called unto him the disciples, and embraced them, and departed for to go into Macedonia.

- Paul had earlier made a second visit from Ephesus to Corinth (unrecorded by Luke) to address challenges to his apostolic authority (2 Cor 11:4, 12:11-12), but the visit was unsuccessful (2 Cor 2:1, 12:14-15, 13:1-2). On return to Ephesus he wrote a "tearful" letter (2 Cor 2:3-4, 7:12; the letter is not preserved in the Bible) which he sent to Corinth by the hand of Titus (2 Cor 12:18), but now worries they may have been overly offended by his harsh letter (2 Cor 7:8-9). Paul plans to settle the matter in person (1 Cor 16:5, 2 Cor 1:15-16) by making a third visit (2 Cor 12:14, 13:1).
- So Paul leaves Ephesus for Troas, where he finds a door open to preach the gospel. Despite this ministry opportunity, Paul has "no rest" because he is anxious to hear from Titus how the Corinthians have taken his most recent letter, but Titus never arrives. Therefore, Paul leaves Troas for Macedonia in search of Titus (2 Cor 2:12-13).
- In Macedonia Paul does find Titus and learns that the Corinthian church has not only taken his letter well (2 Cor 7:5-16) but has also disciplined the offenders (2 Cor 2:5-11), although some opposition persists (2 Cor 10-13). Paul now writes the epistle of 2 Corinthians and sends Titus and other brethren to deliver the letter and prepare a charitable collection for the poor saints in Jerusalem (2 Cor 8:16-24).

[2] And when he had gone over those parts, and had given them much exhortation, he came into Greece,

- As Paul travels through Macedonia, he undoubtedly visits the churches he previously founded in Philippi (Acts 16:12-15), Thessalonica (Acts 17:1-4), and Berea (Acts 17:10-12). He might also now bring the gospel to Illyricum, as evidenced by a soon-to-be-written

statement (Rom 15:19) and the fact that Titus will later be found at Dalmatia, which is within the province of Illyricum (2 Tim 4:10).
- Paul next travels to Corinth in Achaia (Greece), apparently accompanied by some brethren from Macedonia (2 Cor 9:4).

[3] And there abode three months. And when the Jews laid wait for him, as he was about to sail into Syria, he purposed to return through Macedonia.

Paul resides with Gaius (Rom 16:23) while wintering in Corinth (1 Cor 16:6). He writes the Epistle to the Romans and tells how he plans to visit them after he delivers to Jerusalem the charitable collection he is now gathering (Acts 19:21, Rom 15:25-27, 1 Cor 16:1-3). He is about to sail from the port of Cenchrea (Acts 18:18) on a ship bound for Tyre in Syria (Acts 21:3) when he learns of a plot against him (they "laid wait for him") and instead returns to Philippi in Macedonia (Acts 20:6). Paul leaves Philippi now, but while imprisoned in Rome he will write the Epistle to the Philippians.

[4] And there accompanied him into Asia Sopater of Berea; and of the Thessalonians, Aristarchus and Secundus; and Gaius of Derbe, and Timotheus; and of Asia, Tychicus and Trophimus.

- As Paul has worked to raise a charitable collection for poor saints at Jerusalem (Acts 24:17), churches have provided delegates (2 Cor 8:16-24) at Paul's request (1 Cor 16:3-4) to aid him with this project and to ensure financial integrity (Rom 12:17). They accompany him into the province of Asia and doubtless to Jerusalem.
- Sopater may be the Sosipater who was with Paul at Corinth (Rom 16:21). Aristarchus of Thessalonica nearly lost his life in the riot at Ephesus (Acts 19:29); he will travel with Paul to Jerusalem and then to Rome, where he will be with Paul while the apostle is under house arrest (Acts 27:2, Col 4:10, Philem 24). Secundus, along with Sopater and Aristarchus, represents the province of Macedonia.
- Timothy had been sent to Macedonia (Acts 19:22), then Corinth (1 Cor 4:17), and has rejoined Paul. Four men named Gaius appear in scripture: Gaius of Derbe (referred to in this verse), who with Timotheus represents the province of Galatia; Gaius of Macedonia (Acts 19:29); Gaius of Corinth (he lodges Paul, Rom 16:23, 1 Cor 1:14); and

"wellbeloved" Gaius (3 John 1).

- Tychicus is a faithful messenger of Paul (2 Tim 4:12, Titus 3:12) and will deliver at least two epistles (Eph 6:21-22, Col 4:7-8). Trophimus of Ephesus is a Gentile who will travel with Paul to Jerusalem; he will unwittingly be the pretext for a riot against Paul in the temple (Acts 21:29). Tychicus and Trophimus represent the province of Asia.

[5] These going before tarried for us at Troas.

The seven delegates leave Philippi (Acts 20:6), and sail via the port of Neapolis (Acts 16:11) to Troas (in the province of Asia, Acts 20:4) where Paul had recently found an open door to preach the gospel (2 Cor 2:12).

[6] And we sailed away from Philippi after the days of unleavened bread, and came unto them to Troas in five days; where we abode seven days.

Paul and Luke previously met in Troas, then parted at Philippi ("we" section, Acts 16:10-17) and now reunite. They journey now to Troas and will travel together to Jerusalem ("we" through Acts 21:18) and eventually to Rome ("we" section, Acts 27:1-28:16). They leave Philippi after observing Passover with the week-long Feast of Unleavened Bread (Exod 12:14-15) and hope to arrive at Jerusalem in time to celebrate the Feast of Pentecost (Acts 20:16), which is fifty days after Passover (Lev 23:15-17).

[7] And upon the first day of the week, when the disciples came together to break bread, Paul preached unto them, ready to depart on the morrow; and continued his speech until midnight.

The all-night meeting here in Troas shows that believers meet on Sunday (John 20:19, 26, 1 Cor 16:2).

[8] And there were many lights in the upper chamber, where they were gathered together.

The lights' warm air ascends to the upper levels making it easy to sleep (unlike cold air, Gen 31:40).

[9] And there sat in a window a certain young man named Eutychus, being

fallen into a deep sleep: and as Paul was long preaching, he sunk down with sleep, and fell down from the third loft, and was taken up dead.

- Precipitous sleep leads to a three-story fall, and the youth suffers fatal internal injuries.
- Jesus' disciples also fell asleep at inopportune times (Luke 9:32, 22:45-46).

[10] And Paul went down, and fell on him, and embracing him said, Trouble not yourselves; for his life is in him.

Paul "fell on him" as did Elijah (1 Kings 17:21) and Elisha (2 Kings 4:34). Paul resurrects a fellow believer, as did the Apostle Peter (he resurrected Dorcas, Acts 9:40). Paul gives reassuring words as did the Lord Jesus

Paul spends seven days in Troas during his third missionary journey. He resurrects Eutychus when the young man dies from a fall that occurs when he drifts into sleep "as Paul was long preaching" (Acts 20:6-12).

Nejdet Duzen / Shutterstock.com

(Luke 8:52). The notable similarities between these accounts show that the same God who brought resurrection life through Elijah, Elisha, Peter, and the Savior now works in like manner through the Apostle Paul (2 Cor 1:9b).

[11] When he therefore was come up again, and had broken bread, and eaten, and talked a long while, even till break of day, so he departed.

Paul does not let the drama of a death and resurrection end the meeting but pauses to break bread[274] and then preaches all night until dawn the next day.

[12] And they brought the young man alive, and were not a little comforted.

Language
Understatement (emphasize a fact by diminishing it) – "were not a little comforted" indicates that they were greatly relieved.

[13] And we went before to ship, and sailed unto Assos, there intending to take in Paul: for so had he appointed, minding himself to go afoot.

[14] And when he met with us at Assos, we took him in, and came to Mitylene.

The apostle now leaves Troas but will return one day again and loan his cloak to Carpus (2 Tim 4:13). Paul may desire solitude to plan and pray (as did the Lord Jesus, Matt 14:23) when he leaves his eight friends to walk from Troas to Assos, where he then boards ship. Paul shows his all-encompassing zeal for the ministry when he chooses this long hike of 31 miles (50 km) after being up all through the night before ("in watchings," 2 Cor 6:5).

[15] And we sailed thence, and came the next day over against Chios; and the next day we arrived at Samos, and tarried at Trogyllium; and the next day we came to Miletus.

---

[274] See comments on Acts 2:42.

[16] For Paul had determined to sail by Ephesus, because he would not spend the time in Asia: for he hasted, if it were possible for him, to be at Jerusalem the day of Pentecost.

[17] And from Miletus he sent to Ephesus, and called the elders of the church.

- Pentecost (Feast of Weeks, Deut 16:10) is fifty days after Passover (Lev 23:15-17). Paul left Philippi after observing Passover with the week-long Feast of Unleavened Bread (Exod 12:14-15), spent five days traveling to Troas, where he stayed for seven days (Acts 20:6), then spent four days traveling to Miletus (Acts 20:13-15). So Paul has only twenty-seven days left to reach Jerusalem by Pentecost.
- Paul knows that if he stops at Ephesus (in the province of Asia), he will be tempted to spend more time there, and the delay may cause him to miss the Jerusalem feast. So instead Paul arranges a meeting

Paul chooses the solitude of a walk from Troas to Assos, where he rejoins Luke and his companions on their ship (Acts 20:13-14).

muratart / Shutterstock.com

at Miletus with the church leadership, who can bring his message and salutations back to Ephesus.

[18] And when they were come to him, he said unto them, Ye know, from the first day that I came into Asia, after what manner I have been with you at all seasons,

- Paul was forbidden to preach in the province of Asia (Acts 16:6) at the start of his second missionary journey when the Holy Ghost instead led him to Macedonia (Acts 16:9). His first contact with Ephesus occurred on his way back when he preached in their synagogue (Acts 18:19).
- Paul conducts his ministry openly for all to see (2 Cor 4:2, 8:21, 2 Tim 3:10). People may speak good or ill of him (Rom 3:8, 2 Cor 6:8), but in the end, he cares only about God's assessment (1 Cor 4:1-5).

[19] Serving the Lord with all humility of mind, and with many tears, and temptations, which befell me by the lying in wait of the Jews:

- Paul recognizes that all the good he experiences in life is a gift from God (1 Cor 4:7, James 1:17), so he chooses to be humble (Col 3:12). In so doing, he pleases God (Isa 57:15, 1 Peter 5:5-6).
- Paul had been under constant threat to life during his stay at Ephesus (1 Cor 15:31-32, 2 Cor 1:8-10).

[20] And how I kept back nothing that was profitable unto you, but have shewed you, and have taught you publickly, and from house to house,

Paul has kept back nothing that would benefit them spiritually. He has taught in public places, such as synagogues and schools (Acts 19:8-9) and private homes (Acts 16:32).

[21] Testifying both to the Jews, and also to the Greeks, repentance toward God, and faith toward our Lord Jesus Christ.

- Repentance is a change of heart and mind, which leads to a change of action. For example, the people of Nineveh repented of their sin, and God repented of the judgment pronounced upon them (Jonah

3:10). Paul preaches repentance (Rom 2:4), that everyone should turn away from following his sinful self and trust in Jesus Christ; each is to demonstrate this change of mind by a change of life (Matt 3:8, Acts 26:20). God also calls Christians who have wandered from the way of righteous living to repent of their sins and restore fellowship with Him (2 Cor 7:9-10, Rev 3:3,19).
- The deity of Jesus Christ is affirmed when the Savior's words of "faith in God" (Mark 11:22) are replaced by "faith toward our Lord Jesus Christ."

[22] And now, behold, I go bound in the spirit unto Jerusalem, not knowing the things that shall befall me there:

[23] Save that the Holy Ghost witnesseth in every city, saying that bonds and afflictions abide me.

- Paul asks believers to pray for him on his charitable mission to Jerusalem to deliver a gift for poor believers (Acts 24:17, Rom 15:30-32, 1 Cor 16:1-4). The prophecies of "bonds and afflictions" will come true, and he will be arrested (Acts 21:33) and taken to Rome as a prisoner (Acts 27:1). As a result, he will lose over four years of freedom (Acts 24:27, 28:30). Nevertheless, God will use this for good (Rom 8:28), and Paul will have the opportunity to spread the gospel even during his imprisonment (Phil 1:12-13).
- Luke in his gospel shows the Lord Jesus wholeheartedly submitting to the will of God (Luke 22:42) despite three predictions of upcoming suffering in Jerusalem (Luke 9:22, 44, 18:31-34) related to conflict with the religious leaders (Luke 22:2) that would result in Him being turned over to the Gentiles (Luke 23:1). So too Luke shows Paul wholeheartedly submitting to the will of God (Acts 21:13-14) despite three predictions of upcoming suffering in Jerusalem (Acts 20:23, 21:4,11) related to conflict with the religious leaders (Acts 24:1) that will result in him being turned over to the Gentiles (Acts 21:33).

[24] But none of these things move me, neither count I my life dear unto myself, so that I might finish my course with joy, and the ministry, which I have received of the Lord Jesus, to testify the gospel of the grace of God.

- Paul understands the danger he faces in going to Jerusalem. He explains that he lives his life without regard to his safety, as directed by Christ (Luke 9:24) and exemplified by Stephen (Acts 7). Indeed, his friends have often been the ones to keep him out of harm's way (Acts 9:25, 30, 17:10, 14, 19:30), and in Jerusalem it will be Roman soldiers who remove him from mortal danger (Acts 21:31-32).
- Paul had received his ministerial commission directly from the Lord Jesus (Acts 9:15) and will remain faithful to the end (2 Tim 4:7-8). When he testifies the "gospel of the grace of God," he preaches that the death, burial, and resurrection of Jesus Christ (1 Cor 15:1-4) provides the means of salvation which is available as a gift to lost sinners who deserve only the judgment of hell (Rom 5:8).

[25] And now, behold, I know that ye all, among whom I have gone preaching the kingdom of God, shall see my face no more.

When Paul preaches the gospel of the grace of God, he invites people to enter the kingdom of God through the spiritual new birth (John 3:3) because God's kingdom is now spiritual until Christ the King returns to rule on earth (John 18:36). This "preaching the kingdom of God" now should not be confused with the future preaching of the "gospel of the kingdom" (Matt 24:14). The former will be preached until the Savior returns in the air to remove all believers from the earth ("caught up together with them in the clouds," 1 Thes 4:17). The latter will subsequently be preached during the great tribulation (Matt 24:21) until Jesus Christ returns physically to establish His kingdom on the earth (2 Tim 4:1).

[26] Wherefore I take you to record this day, that I am pure from the blood of all men.

Paul has a clear conscience (Ezek 3:17-19, Acts 18:6) because he has done everything conceivable to bring the gospel to as many people as he possibly can (Acts 19:10).

[27] For I have not shunned to declare unto you all the counsel of God.

Paul teaches doctrines that are easy to hear, such as eternal salvation (2 Tim 2:10), God's enduring love for the believer (Rom 8:38-39), and rewards for good works given in heaven (1 Cor 3:14). He also teaches doctrines that are difficult to hear, such as God's eternal judgment of the lost (2 Thes 1:8-9), the importance of financial giving (2 Cor 9:7), and the loss of potential rewards unfruitful believers may face in heaven (1 Cor 3:15).

Language
Enthymeme (an element of reasoning is not stated) –
Major premise (unstated): one who fails to warn sinners of God's impending judgment is held guilty ("his blood will I require at thine hand," Ezek 33:8-9).

Paul meets the Ephesian elders at Miletus, where he gives a farewell message and exhorts them to "feed the church of God, which he hath purchased with his own blood" (Acts 20:15-38).

BearFotos / Shutterstock.com

Minor premise: Paul has *not* failed "to declare unto you all the counsel of God."
Conclusion: Paul is guiltless of "the blood of all men."

[28] Take heed therefore unto yourselves, and to all the flock, over the which the Holy Ghost hath made you overseers, to feed the church of God, which he hath purchased with his own blood.

- These overseers are also called elders (Acts 20:17). Equivalent terms include bishops (1 Tim 3:1) and presbyters (1 Tim 4:14). They are to shepherd (pastor, Eph 4:11) the flock (1 Peter 5:2), unlike neglectful shepherds (Ezek 34:1-10) or the "idol shepherd" (Zech 11:16-17).
- The head Bishop and Shepherd of the church is the Lord Jesus Christ (Heb 13:20, 1 Peter 2:25), whose deity Paul proclaims when he states that God the Son became human flesh (1 Tim 3:16) and paid the purchase price of mankind's redemption with "his own blood" (here and 1 Peter 1:18-19), which He shed on the cross of Calvary (Col 1:20).

344

[29] For I know this, that after my departing shall grievous wolves enter in among you, not sparing the flock.

- The Lord Jesus warned to "beware of false prophets, which come to you in sheep's clothing, but inwardly they are ravening wolves" (Matt 7:15).
- Ezekiel warned of those who "are like wolves ravening the prey, to shed blood, and to destroy souls, to get dishonest gain" (Ezek 22:27b).

[30] Also of your own selves shall men arise, speaking perverse things, to draw away disciples after them.

- Satan will seek to undermine God's church from without and from within. Paul will write back to Ephesus (1 Tim 1:3), warning Timothy of "perverse disputings of men of corrupt minds, and destitute of the truth" (1 Tim 6:5a).
- False teachers associated with Ephesus will include Hymeneus and Alexander (1 Tim 1:3,20), Phygellus & Hermogenes (2 Tim 1:15),

Philetus (2 Tim 2:17), Diotrephes (3 John 9), and the Nicolaitans (Rev 2:6).
- The church at Ephesus will heed Paul's warnings. The Lord Jesus will conclude that "thou hast tried them which say they are apostles, and are not, and hast found them liars." (Rev 2:2b).

[31] Therefore watch, and remember, that by the space of three years I ceased not to warn every one night and day with tears.

The three years of Paul's ministry at Ephesus include his brief initial visit (Acts 18:19-20) and subsequent stays of three months (Acts 19:8) and two years (Acts 19:10).

[32] And now, brethren, I commend you to God, and to the word of his grace, which is able to build you up, and to give you an inheritance among all them which are sanctified.

- Paul does not leave behind an apostolic successor but instead instructs the brethren to follow God through His written word of scripture (2 Tim 3:14-17). The word of God helps the believer grow spiritually (1 Peter 2:2) and is thus likened unto food (Job 23:12, Jer 15:16) that will "build you up": apples (Prov 25:11), bread (Luke 4:4), honey (Psalm 119:103), meat and milk (1 Cor 3:2, Heb 5:12), and water (Eph 5:26).
- When Paul speaks of the inheritance believers will one day receive (1 Peter 1:4) as a gift from God (Gal 3:18,29), he repeats the words that Jesus told him on the road to Damascus. The event was record-ed in Acts 9:3-8 and the words in Acts 26:18b as "inheritance among them which are sanctified by faith that is in me."

[33] I have coveted no man's silver, or gold, or apparel.

Paul's words (also 2 Cor 7:2, 11:7-9) against covetousness (Exod 20:17, Prov 21:26) echo those of the prophet Samuel (1 Sam 12:3).

[34] Yea, ye yourselves know, that these hands have ministered unto my necessities, and to them that were with me.

Paul earns his financial support by making tents (Acts 18:3, 1 Cor 4:12, 2 Thes 3:8). With his business proceeds he purchases for himself little more than necessities such as food and clothing (1 Tim 6:8) and then charitably helps others ("them that were with me") that lack these.

[35] I have shewed you all things, how that so labouring ye ought to support the weak, and to remember the words of the Lord Jesus, how he said, It is more blessed to give than to receive.

This otherwise unrecorded (John 21:25) quotation of the Lord Jesus reminds the reader of the sermon on the mount (Matt 5:42) and the sermon on the plain (Luke 6:38). Paul may have heard this saying from Simon Peter (Gal 1:18) or one of the other apostles (Acts 15:2). Paul follows this principle of giving (Acts 20:34) and teaches others to do so as well (1 Cor 16:1-4, 2 Cor 8:1-9:15).

[36] And when he had thus spoken, he kneeled down, and prayed with them all.

Paul comes before God with humility of mind (Acts 20:19) when he kneels to pray as did Solomon (1 Kings 8:54), Daniel (Dan 6:10), Peter (Acts 9:40), and the Lord Jesus (Luke 22:41).

[37] And they all wept sore, and fell on Paul's neck, and kissed him,

The Ephesian brethren love Paul, who has endured great hardships to bring them the gospel (2 Cor 1:8). They remember the fatherly way he urged them to do right, comforted them in sorrow, and charged each individual to live a life pleasing to God (1 Thes 2:11-12). Paul likewise loves the Ephesian brethren and will remember them daily in his prayers (Eph 1:16).

[38] Sorrowing most of all for the words which he spake, that they should see his face no more. And they accompanied him unto the ship.

- Paul has given a farewell address, as did Jacob (Gen 49), Moses (Deuteronomy), Joshua (Josh 23-24), Samuel (1 Sam 12), and Jesus Christ (Luke 22:14-38).

- In the future Paul will send both Timothy (1 Tim 1:3) and Tychicus (2 Tim 4:12) to Ephesus. While imprisoned in Rome, Paul will write the Epistle to the Ephesians. The apostle will also send two letters to Ephesus addressed to Timothy (1 Tim 1:3, 2 Tim 1:18).
- Due to the dangers awaiting him in Jerusalem, Paul anticipates not seeing these Ephesian believers (Acts 20:17) again. However, they might meet again after his release from prison in Rome when he returns to neighboring Troas and Miletum (2 Tim 4:13,20) and possibly to Ephesus (1 Tim 1:3, 3:14, 4:13).

Persuasive Speech

Paul's Spirit-filled sermon shows a mastery of persuasive speech (rhetoric).
Introduction *(exordium)* – not recorded
Narrative *(narratio)* – Paul endured great hardships to bring the gospel to the people of Ephesus. Acts 20:18-21

Thesis *(propositio)* – joy comes not from focusing on oneself, but from living a life led by the Holy Spirit. Acts 20:22-24
Arguments *(probatio)* – Paul departs Ephesus only after giving the gospel to everybody he possibly could. The elders are to shepherd the believers under the guidance of the Holy Spirit. The church will face opposition from evildoers both within and without. Acts 20:25-30
Final appeal *(peroratio)* – Paul's way of ministering selflessly to others should not be unique to him as an apostle but is an example that all believers should follow. Acts 20:31-35.

Following the speech, Paul and the Ephesian elders express their affection *(pathos)* for one another. Acts 20:36-38

Challenge Questions

1. Why does Luke present an extensive list of Paul's traveling companions (Acts 20:4)?
2. Why does Paul choose to walk rather than sail from Troas to Assos (Acts 20:13)?

Acts Chapter 21

[1] And it came to pass, that after we were gotten from them, and had launched, we came with a straight course unto Coos, and the day following unto Rhodes, and from thence unto Patara:

- Paul and his companions leave the Ephesian believers at the port of Miletus and set sail with a favorable tailwind ("straight course") on their journey to Jerusalem.
- When sailing into the port of Rhodes, Paul sees the Colossus, one of the seven wonders of the ancient world.[275]

[2] And finding a ship sailing over unto Phenicia, we went aboard, and set forth.

348

[3] Now when we had discovered Cyprus, we left it on the left hand, and sailed into Syria, and landed at Tyre: for there the ship was to unlade her burden.

"We left it on the left hand" is how Luke, the eyewitness describes their eastbound voyage around the south of Cyprus. The ship from Patara then unloads its cargo at Tyre in the region of Syria-Phoenicia ("Syrophenicia," Mark 7:26). Disciples fleeing persecution in Jerusalem had previously evangelized Phoenecia ("Phenice," Acts 11:19), and Paul met with believers here before (Acts 15:3).

[4] And finding disciples, we tarried there seven days: who said to Paul through the Spirit, that he should not go up to Jerusalem.

Paul was previously warned of the danger of going to Jerusalem (Acts 20:23) and will be warned again (Acts 21:11). He sees these prophecies not as a Divine prohibition but as a forewarning of what he must endure while fulfilling God's will in his life (Acts 19:21).

---

[275] "Seven Wonders of the World." Encyclopedia Britannica Online, accessed 9 Nov 2019

[5] And when we had accomplished those days, we departed and went our way; and they all brought us on our way, with wives and children, till we were out of the city: and we kneeled down on the shore, and prayed.

At the end of the week, the local believers of Tyre accompany Paul back to the beach, where they pray together (as at Miletus, Acts 20:36) and depart.

[6] And when we had taken our leave one of another, we took ship; and they returned home again.

[7] And when we had finished our course from Tyre, we came to Ptolemais, and saluted the brethren, and abode with them one day.

[8] And the next day we that were of Paul's company departed, and came unto Cæsarea: and we entered into the house of Philip the evangelist, which was one of the seven; and abode with him.

- Paul's party sails from Tyre to Ptolemais (formerly Accho, Judg 1:31) and then to Caesarea.
- Philip is one of the seven original deacons of Jerusalem (Acts 6:5). He is called an evangelist (Eph 4:11, 2 Tim 4:5) because he brought the gospel to the people of Samaria (Acts 8:5) and coastal Judea (Acts 8:40) and to the Ethiopian treasurer (Acts 8:27).
- When Philip's fellow deacon Stephen (Acts 6:5) was stoned, Saul (then unconverted) "was standing by, and consenting unto his death, and kept the raiment of them that slew him" (Acts 22:20, 7:58, 8:1a). The subsequent persecution brought by Saul drove believers such as Philip out of Jerusalem to evangelize Samaria and beyond (Acts 8:1b). Philip's hospitality (rather than hostility) toward Saul (now Paul) shows the work of God in the heart of Paul (who was saved, Acts 9:6) and of Philip (who has forgiven Paul).

[9] And the same man had four daughters, virgins, which did prophesy.

Other female prophets (1 Cor 11:5) include Miriam (Exod 15:20), Deborah (Judg 4:4), Huldah (2 Kings 22:14), Noadiah (Neh 6:14), Isaiah's wife (Isa 8:3), Anna (Luke 2:36), and the false prophetess Jezebel (Rev 2:20).

[10] And as we tarried there many days, there came down from Judæa a certain prophet, named Agabus.

Agabus had predicted the famine that affected believers in Judea to whom Barnabas and Saul were then sent with a charitable gift (Acts 11:28-30).

[11] And when he was come unto us, he took Paul's girdle, and bound his own hands and feet, and said, Thus saith the Holy Ghost, So shall the Jews at Jerusalem bind the man that owneth this girdle, and shall deliver him into the hands of the Gentiles.

- Agabus uses a dramatic illustration as did Old Testament prophets (Hosea 1:2, Jer 27:2, Isa 20:2, Ezek 4) to tell how Paul will be "delivered prisoner from Jerusalem into the hands of the Romans" (Acts 28:17).

- An Old Testament prophet would begin his message with a phrase such as "thus saith the LORD God" (Isa 52:4, Jer 7:20). Agabus affirms the deity of the Holy Ghost when substituting His name for "LORD God."

[12] And when we heard these things, both we, and they of that place, besought him not to go up to Jerusalem.

Paul's traveling companions (including Luke) and the local believers (no doubt Philip and his four daughters, Acts 21:8-9) are concerned for his welfare and ask him to change his plans.

[13] Then Paul answered, What mean ye to weep and to break mine heart? for I am ready not to be bound only, but also to die at Jerusalem for the name of the Lord Jesus.

During the riot at Ephesus, Paul allowed other believers to prevent him from entering the theater (Acts 19:30), but here will not allow them to prevent him from entering Jerusalem.

[14] And when he would not be persuaded, we ceased, saying, The will of

the Lord be done.

It is God's will that Paul preach to "the Gentiles, and kings, and the children of Israel" (Acts 9:15). Although the apostle has received warnings from God's prophets (Acts 20:23, 21:4,11) and directly from the Savior (Acts 22:18), he strongly feels that he accomplishes God's will (Rom 8:28, 12:2) by going to Jerusalem (Acts 19:21). Paul will later arrive safely at Rome (Acts 23:11, 28:16) and via this journey will preach to Gentiles (Acts 24:25, 28:31), kings (King Agrippa, Acts 26:2; Caesar Nero, Acts 25:12, 27:24), and the children of Israel (Acts 22:1, 23:1, 28:17).

[15] And after those days we took up our carriages, and went up to Jerusalem.

"... we took up what we carried ..."

[16] There went with us also certain of the disciples of Cæsarea, and brought with them one Mnason of Cyprus, an old disciple, with whom we should lodge.

Mnason, a long-time believer ("old disciple"), may have been one of the original converts of Pentecost (Acts 2:9-11) and an evangelist from Cyprus to Antioch (Acts 11:20). He has a house large enough to lodge Paul, Luke, and apparently seven others (Acts 20:4).

[17] And when we were come to Jerusalem, the brethren received us gladly.

- Paul's third missionary journey (which started in Acts 18:23) ends now upon his arrival in Jerusalem, his fifth and final visit here since his conversion (Acts 9:28, 12:25, 15:2, 18:22).
- Paul and his companions present the charitable gift (Acts 24:17) they have been collecting for poor saints (Rom 15:26, 1 Cor 16:1-4, 2 Cor 8:1-15). Paul has been criticized for his Gentile ministry (Gal 1:10) by both unbelieving (Acts 14:2) and believing Jews (Acts 15:1-2). The church at Jerusalem had previously sided with Paul (Acts 15:23-29) but is now under pressure to avoid association with Gentiles while bringing the gospel to devout Jews (Gal 2:12). So

Paul has been worrying that the church will not want to risk Jewish offense in accepting his charitable gift collected from both Jews and Gentiles (Rom 15:30-31) by him, the "minister ... to the Gentiles" (Rom 15:16). He is doubtless relieved and joyful now that the Jerusalem saints have warmly received him and (apparently, Acts 24:17) his charitable gift.

[18] And the day following Paul went in with us unto James; and all the elders were present.

- Luke has been with Paul ("us") since they reunited at Philippi (Acts 20:6). The narrative will now focus on Paul until Luke indicates his presence again at the time of Paul's voyage to Rome ("we," Acts 27:1). Luke will be with Paul during his first imprisonment at Rome (Col 4:14) and remain loyal to Paul when almost everyone else has forsaken him (2 Tim 4:9-11).
- James, the half-brother of Jesus (Gal 1:19), is a leader in the Jerusalem church.[276] He previously asked Paul to "remember the poor" (Gal 2:10) and is doubtless encouraged by the charitable gift brought by Paul (Acts 24:17).
- The twelve apostles (Acts 6:2) are not mentioned and have apparently left Jerusalem to fulfill Christ's commission to spread the gospel (Acts 1:8).

[19] And when he had saluted them, he declared particularly what things God had wrought among the Gentiles by his ministry.

Since Paul last visited Jerusalem (Acts 18:22), he revisited Galatia (Acts 18:23), Macedonia (Acts 20:1), and Achaia (Greece, Acts 20:2), had a fruitful ministry at Ephesus (Acts 19:10) and has brought the gospel to new areas such as Illyricum (Rom 15:19). Although Paul deeply wishes to evangelize Jews (Rom 10:1), most of his converts have been Gentiles (Rom 11:13).

[20] And when they heard it, they glorified the Lord, and said unto him, Thou seest, brother, how many thousands of Jews there are which believe; and they are all zealous of the law:

---

[276] See biographical comments at Acts 15:13.

- Years ago when Paul visited Jerusalem, the apostles had encouraged Paul to evangelize the Gentile world (Gal 2:9). James and the elders now rejoice when they hear how so many Gentiles have turned to the God of Israel.
- The faithful in Israel do not lose their Jewish nationality when they believe on Jesus the Messiah. They know that the law is "holy, and just, and good" (Rom 7:12) even when it shows each one his inability to meet God's standard (Gal 3:24) rather than justifying him (Acts 13:39). They honor the Sabbath day (Acts 16:13, 18:4), circumcise their children (Acts 16:3), and participate in vows (Acts 18:18) and ceremonies such as ritual cleansing (Acts 21:26) that show respect for tradition. Any sacrifices they might offer are made not as a means of dealing with sin (Heb 10:1-4), but as a memorial of Christ's work (Heb 10:12). They do not teach Gentiles that they must be circumcised (Gal 5:2-4) or follow the law of Moses (Acts 21:25). They live in a way that points their countrymen to the Savior (1 Cor 9:20) and hence there are now "many thousands of Jews ... which believe."

[21] And they are informed of thee, that thou teachest all the Jews which are among the Gentiles to forsake Moses, saying that they ought not to circumcise their children, neither to walk after the customs.

[22] What is it therefore? the multitude must needs come together: for they will hear that thou art come.

- Here in Jerusalem Paul is accused of promoting Gentile practices that are unlawful for Jews (Acts 21:21). Ironically, in Philippi Paul was accused of promoting Jewish practices unlawful for Romans (Acts 16:20).
- Paul blamelessly keeps the law (Phil 3:6) because a Jewish believer keeping the law does not detract from the message of the gospel (contrast a Gentile believer, Gal 2:3-5). In doing so he maintains a testimony to other Jews (1 Cor 9:20), whom he does not teach to forsake the law but instead teaches to understand that the law cannot save them (Gal 2:16). Paul may choose to observe feast days (Acts 20:6,16) and the Sabbath (Acts 13:14, 17:2), although he

teaches that such observance is not required (Rom 14:5, Gal 4:9-11, Col 2:14-16). He does not condone circumcision of Gentiles as a religious rite (Acts 15:1-2) but allows circumcision of Jews as a show of respect for tradition (Acts 16:3).

- However, Paul has not spent much time in Jerusalem in recent years. James and the elders understand his faithfulness both to the gospel and to Israel, but most citizens of Jerusalem do not. Jews who believe on Jesus the Messiah rejoice that Paul reaches out to Gentiles (Acts 21:19-20a; unlike unbelieving Jews, Acts 22:21-22). Yet anyone in Jerusalem (saved or lost) is offended by someone teaching Jews to forsake the teachings of scripture. James therefore asks how they might respond to these false rumors since the people will expect an answer.

[23] Do therefore this that we say to thee: We have four men which have a vow on them;

Four Jewish believers have already begun the process of taking a vow.

[24] Them take, and purify thyself with them, and be at charges with them, that they may shave their heads: and all may know that those things, whereof they were informed concerning thee, are nothing; but that thou thyself also walkest orderly, and keepest the law.

Paul is asked to take an unspecified vow (which may or may not be a Nazarite vow, Num 6:1-21) with these four men for seven days, perform the temple ceremony of purification (Acts 21:26-27), and cover any related financial charges. Paul teaches that God grants righteousness based on the work of Jesus Christ without works of the law (Rom 3:20-22), but a vow is a voluntary commitment (Deut 23:21-22) and not necessary for moral acceptance with God. Therefore this ritual will demonstrate Paul's commitment to Jewish tradition without compromising his principles.

[25] As touching the Gentiles which believe, we have written and concluded that they observe no such thing, save only that they keep themselves from things offered to idols, and from blood, and from strangled, and from fornication.

James and the elders recite their prior agreement (Acts 15:19-20) to reassure Paul that they still approve of him bringing the gospel directly to Gentiles (Gal 2:9) without requiring conversion to Judaism (Gal 5:1-4). Although as Jews they honor the law, Gentile believers do not need to keep the law of Moses but are to follow these stated principles to maintain a righteous testimony before Jews (Acts 15:21). Paul is likewise participating in this vow (Acts 21:24) not to earn favor with God but to maintain a righteous testimony before Jews.

[26] Then Paul took the men, and the next day purifying himself with them entered into the temple, to signify the accomplishment of the days of purification, until that an offering should be offered for every one of them.

- Ritual purifying is not performed to absolve sin, but to complete formal ceremonies, such as those for cleansing priests (Num 8:5-7), cleansing after touching a dead body (Num 19:11-13), and cleansing after childbirth (Lev 12).
- Paul knows that believing Jews may live an honorable life before God if they continue to follow the law of Moses or if they choose not to (1 Cor 7:19, Gal 5:6, 6:15). However, Paul chooses to devoutly follow the law for two reasons. First, he was born a Jew and raised in Jerusalem under the teachings of a respected rabbi (Acts 22:3, Phil 3:5). He genuinely values his Jewish heritage (Rom 3:1-2, 9:4-5) and can honestly tell the spiritual leaders of Israel that "I have lived [as a Jew] in all good conscience before God until this day" (Acts 23:1). Second, Paul greatly desires to bring the gospel to his people (Rom 9:1-3, 1 Cor 9:20) and knows they will respect only a messenger who is "a devout man according to the law" of Moses (Acts 22:12).
- The apostle now participates in this purification ceremony (Acts 24:18) and behaves quietly (Acts 24:12; he would prefer a lively debate as in Acts 15:2, 17:17, 19:8-9) to show respect for tradition, as recommended by James (Acts 21:24).
- Although Paul now carries out this religious ritual with Jewish believers, he would never ask Gentile believers to do so (Gal 5:11, 6:12).

[27] And when the seven days were almost ended, the Jews which were of Asia, when they saw him in the temple, stirred up all the people, and laid hands on him,

- Jews from all over the world have come for the Feast of Pentecost (Acts 20:16). Some from the province of Asia had earlier recognized Trophimus and Paul (Acts 21:29) from their days at Ephesus (Acts 19:8-10, 2 Cor 1:8-9). They are angry with Paul in general for converting Gentiles without requiring circumcision (Gal 6:12-13). They are angry with him in particular for taking converts to Christianity out of their Ephesian synagogue (Acts 19:8-9) and for (from their perspective) bringing (monotheistic) Jews into further conflict with (polytheistic) pagans in the riot at Ephesus (Acts 19:26, 33-34).
- Paul's enemies from Ephesus now use this opportunity to stir up the people against him as they did against Stephen (Acts 6:12). When they violently seize Paul they dishonor the temple, which is supposed to be a place of refuge (1 Kings 1:50, 2:28).

[28] Crying out, Men of Israel, help: This is the man, that teacheth all men every where against the people, and the law, and this place: and further brought Greeks also into the temple, and hath polluted this holy place.

[29] (For they had seen before with him in the city Trophimus an Ephesian, whom they supposed that Paul had brought into the temple.)

- Paul's enemies unintentionally compliment him when they proclaim his far-reaching sphere of influence ("teacheth all men every where") as did his enemies in Thessalonica (Acts 17:6) and Demetrius the silversmith (Acts 19:26). They show that they value human opinion above God (Matt 16:23) when they primarily accuse Paul of speaking against "the people" (Luke 23:14) and only secondarily against God's holy law.
- Trophimus is one of the church delegates who has accompanied Paul (Acts 20:4) to Jerusalem with the charitable gift for poor believers (Acts 24:17). The "Jews which were of Asia" (Acts 21:27) know he is a Gentile and use him as a pretext for the riot.
- The apostle is falsely accused of speaking against the law of Moses (as was Stephen, Acts 6:13) and of defiling the temple (as were

Acts Chapter 21

Stephen and Jesus, Mark 14:58). The charge is serious as the Roman General Titus will later explain. "Have not you ... by our permission, put up this partition-wall before your sanctuary? Have not you been allowed to put up the pillars ... and on it to engrave in Greek, and in your own letters, this prohibition, that no foreigner should go beyond that wall? Have not we given you leave to kill such as go beyond it, though he were a Roman?"[277]

- Paul has been in the temple for nearly seven days publicly showing that he honors the law, so the charges of disrespecting the law and dishonoring the temple are clearly false. He has performed a vow of purity (Acts 21:26) at his own expense (Acts 21:24) and, ironically, Paul's accusers dishonor the law by preventing him from completing the temple ritual ("the seven days were almost ended," Acts 21:27).

[30] And all the city was moved, and the people ran together: and they took Paul, and drew him out of the temple: and forthwith the doors were shut.

- Previously the "righteous [man] ... Zacharias son of Barachias [was slain] between the temple and the altar" (Matt 23:35). The people now want to avoid shedding blood inside the temple, although ironically, they have no qualms about murdering Paul. Therefore the mob drags Paul out of the temple's inner court, and then its doors are shut to preserve its sanctity (unlike Matt 23:35).
- There have been five previous uproars associated with Paul: at Lystra (Acts 14:19), Philippi (Acts 16:19), Thessalonica (Acts 17:5), Berea (Acts 17:13), and Ephesus (Acts 19:29). This riot now at Jerusalem is the sixth uproar associated with Paul, and again it is evident that he has committed no wrongdoing and is not the cause (Acts 24:18).

[31] And as they went about to kill him, tidings came unto the chief captain of the band, that all Jerusalem was in an uproar.

Chief captain Claudius Lysias (Acts 23:26, 24:7) commands the Roman legionary cohort at Jerusalem and is responsible for maintaining order. He observes the riot from the Fortress Antonia, the military garrison built by

---

[277] Josephus, *Jewish War*, 6.2.4

Herod the Great in honor of Mark Anthony.[278]

"The Antonia tower was situated at the corner of two porticoes of the temple court, the west and the north. It was built on a rock fifty feet high, on the edge of a great precipice and was the work of king Herod, where he showed his innate genius. Firstly the rock itself was covered from the ground up with smooth stone, both for ornament and that anyone trying either to get up or to go down could not get a foothold. Next, before coming to the tower itself, was a wall three feet high, within which was built the whole of the Antonia tower to a height of forty feet. The inner area was like a palace in size and form, divided into various rooms and other uses, like courts and baths and a broad area for troops, so that with all conveniences it seemed a city, but by its magnificence resembled a palace. Since the entire structure was that of a tower, it contained four other distinct towers at its four corners, three of which were fifty feet high but the one on the southeast corner was seventy feet high, commanding a view of the whole temple. On the corner where it joined to the two porticoes of the temple, it had passages to them both, through which the sentries went in and out. A Roman legion was always based there, and armed men stood round the porticoes during the festivals to keep watch on the people and prevent any revolt. For the temple guarded the city, and the Antonia tower the temple, and within the tower were the guardians of all three."[279]

[32] Who immediately took soldiers and centurions, and ran down unto them: and when they saw the chief captain and the soldiers, they left beating of Paul.

Captain Lysias quickly descends with soldiers and officers from their elevated position on the Fortress Antonia.

[33] Then the chief captain came near, and took him, and commanded him to be bound with two chains; and demanded who he was, and what he had done.

---

[278] "Herod King of Judea." *Encyclopedia Britannica Online*, accessed 26 Jan 2020
[279] Josephus, *Jewish War*, 5.5.8

Captain Lysias arrests Paul for his protection (thereby answering Paul's prayer for safety, Rom 15:31). He orders him chained (as predicted by Agabus, Acts 21:11) between two soldiers (as was Peter, Acts 12:6), but neglects to determine his Roman citizenship before restraining him (Acts 22:29).

[34] And some cried one thing, some another, among the multitude: and when he could not know the certainty for the tumult, he commanded him to be carried into the castle.

Paul is to be taken to the Fortress Antonia.

[35] And when he came upon the stairs, so it was, that he was borne of the soldiers for the violence of the people.

Paul's enemies from Ephesus start a riot at the Jerusalem temple. But "when they saw the chief captain and the soldiers, they left beating of Paul" (Acts 21:32).   Meunierd / Shutterstock.com

The crowd is still a threat to Paul, so the soldiers carry him up the stairs.

[36] For the multitude of the people followed after, crying, Away with him.

Paul preaches salvation through Jesus Christ (Acts 13:38), and the people of Jerusalem now reject Paul as they had rejected the Savior (Luke 23:18).

[37] And as Paul was to be led into the castle, he said unto the chief captain, May I speak unto thee? Who said, Canst thou speak Greek?

Most local Jews speak Hebrew (Acts 21:40) and Aramaic (Mark 15:34), but Paul was born outside Israel (Acts 21:39) and also knows the universal language of Greek. The Roman captain presumably speaks Greek and Latin (Luke 23:38) and is impressed to hear Paul speak his native Greek tongue.

[38] Art not thou that Egyptian, which before these days madest an uproar, and leddest out into the wilderness four thousand men that were murderers?

Captain Lysias is accustomed to dealing with revolutionaries like Barabbas, who committed sedition and murder (Luke 23:18-19). Lysias worries that a notorious Egyptian renegade has returned. "There came out of Egypt about this time to Jerusalem one that said he was a prophet, and advised the multitude of the common people to go along with him to the Mount of Olives ... He said further, that he would show them from hence how, at his command, the walls of Jerusalem would fall down; and he promised them that he would procure them an entrance into the city through those walls, when they were fallen down. Now when Felix was informed of these things, he ordered his soldiers to take their weapons, and came against them with a great number of horsemen and footmen from Jerusalem, and attacked the Egyptian and the people that were with him. He also slew four hundred of them, and took two hundred alive. But the Egyptian himself escaped out of the fight, but did not appear any more."[280]

[39] But Paul said, I am a man which am a Jew of Tarsus, a city in Cilicia, a citizen of no mean city: and, I beseech thee, suffer me to speak unto the

---

[280] Josephus, *Antiquities*, 20.8.5

people.

Paul reveals his citizenship of the respected city of Tarsus to impress the chief captain and obtain permission to speak but does not tell of his Roman citizenship (Acts 22:25). Although revealing his citizenship might help his standing before the military officer, it would not promote his desire to appear to his people as a devout Jew (Acts 22:3).

<u>Language</u>
Understatement (emphasize a fact by diminishing it) – "no mean city" means "a very prominent city."

[40] And when he had given him licence, Paul stood on the stairs, and beckoned with the hand unto the people. And when there was made a great silence, he spake unto them in the Hebrew tongue, saying,

Paul speaks from the stairs of the Fortress Antonia in the "Hebrew tongue."[281]

Challenge Question

Luke's narrative in some places seems to indicate that it is God's will for Paul to travel to Jerusalem (Acts 19:21, 20:22), and in other places seems to indicate that it is not (Acts 20:23, 21:4,11, 22:18). How do you reconcile the two?

---

[281] See comments on Acts 22:2.

Acts Chapter 22

[1] Men, brethren, and fathers, hear ye my defence which I make now unto you.

Paul makes a brief introduction, like Stephen (Acts 7:2).

[2] (And when they heard that he spake in the Hebrew tongue to them, they kept the more silence: and he saith,)

- Jews in Israel know how to speak Aramaic (Mark 5:41), having learned it during the Babylonian captivity. "In the period following the return from the Babylonian Exile, Aramaic, a cognate of [related to] Hebrew, functioned as the ... language in official life and gained a foothold as a vernacular [everyday spoken language]."[282] However, faithful Jews also speak Hebrew (John 5:2, Acts 26:14, Rev 9:11, 16:16, 19:3), because Aramaic "did not, despite claims made by some scholars, displace the everyday Hebrew of the people."[283]
- Faithful Jews also write Hebrew (Luke 23:38), their everyday spoken language, as evidenced by contemporary religious texts, written in a verbal dialect. "The language of the Mishna, far from being a scholar's dialect, seems to reflect popular speech, as did the Koine (common) Greek of the New Testament."[284]
- Paul was born outside Israel (Acts 22:3), where he would be more likely to learn Greek than Hebrew. "Displacement of Hebrew – both in its literary form in Scriptures and in its popular usage – occurred [among those living outside Israel], however, as illustrated by the translation of Scriptures into Greek in some communities and into Aramaic in others."[285] Paul was also raised in Jerusalem, where he would have learned Hebrew. Therefore he gains credibility by speaking in Hebrew, which his audience knows is the original

---

[282] Judaism, the sacred language." *Encyclopedia Britannica Online*, accessed 10 Nov 2019
[283] Ibid.
[284] Ibid.
[285] Ibid.

language of the Israelites and Old Testament scripture.

[3] I am verily a man which am a Jew, born in Tarsus, a city in Cilicia, yet brought up in this city at the feet of Gamaliel, and taught according to the perfect manner of the law of the fathers, and was zealous toward God, as ye all are this day.

- Paul had been born in Tarsus and brought to Jerusalem as a youth to study (Acts 26:4-5) under Gamaliel, the Pharisee who subsequently advised the council against persecuting the apostles (Acts 5:34-39).
- The unsaved Saul had "a zeal of God, but not according to knowledge" (Rom 10:2). His misdirected drive was no doubt influenced by fierce men such as Phinehas (Num 25:7-11), Elijah (1 Kings 18:40, 19:10), and Jehu (2 Kings 10:16-17, 23-25).

Language
Hebraism (a Hebrew manner of expression) – "at the feet of Gamaliel" corresponds with "he went up with ten thousand men at his feet" (Judg 4:10). One could simply say "under the authority of" but "at his feet" pictures respectfully bowing in submission (Esther 8:3, Mark 5:22, Luke 10:39).

[4] And I persecuted this way unto the death, binding and delivering into prisons both men and women.

Paul describes how he was every bit as zealous as his listeners, willing even to murder for his cause (Acts 9:1-2). The "way" is a reference to Christianity (Acts 19:9).

[5] As also the high priest doth bear me witness, and all the estate of the elders: from whom also I received letters unto the brethren, and went to Damascus, to bring them which were there bound unto Jerusalem, for to be punished.

Ananias (Acts 23:2) has succeeded high priests Annas and Caiaphas (Luke 3:2, Acts 4:6). The "estate of the elders" is the high council of Jewish elders who previously tried Jesus (Luke 22:66), the apostles (Acts 4:5), and Stephen (Acts 6:12).

Language

Conciliation (words given to obtain goodwill before delivering a weighty message) – Paul connects himself to the high priest to prepare his devout Jewish audience (Acts 22:3-5) for a difficult message about his calling to preach to Gentiles (Acts 22:6-21).

[6] And it came to pass, that, as I made my journey, and was come nigh unto Damascus about noon, suddenly there shone from heaven a great light round about me.

[7] And I fell unto the ground, and heard a voice saying unto me, Saul, Saul, why persecutest thou me?

[8] And I answered, Who art thou, Lord? And he said unto me, I am Jesus of Nazareth, whom thou persecutest.

Acts 9:3-5. Paul shows that he was wholly opposed to "the way" when Jesus the Messiah sought him out (Luke 19:10). Paul now recognizes Him as Lord (1 Cor 12:3). The apostle proclaims Christ's resurrection when he tells how he saw the Savior alive.

[9] And they that were with me saw indeed the light, and were afraid; but they heard not the voice of him that spake to me.

His companions heard the voice from heaven (Acts 9:7, 26:14) but did not understand the meaning of the words that were spoken (John 12:28-29, Dan 10:7).

[10] And I said, What shall I do, Lord? And the Lord said unto me, Arise, and go into Damascus; and there it shall be told thee of all things which are appointed for thee to do.

Acts 9:6

[11] And when I could not see for the glory of that light, being led by the hand of them that were with me, I came into Damascus.

Paul was blinded (Acts 9:8-9) but would be miraculously healed. His companions "saw indeed the light" (Acts 22:9) yet were not blinded because they did not see "the glory of that light," Jesus Christ (Acts 9:5, 1 Cor 15:8).

[12] And one Ananias, a devout man according to the law, having a good report of all the Jews which dwelt there,

Paul assures his listeners that Ananias, who had received God's message (Acts 9:10-16), was also a religiously devout man.

[13] Came unto me, and stood, and said unto me, Brother Saul, receive thy sight. And the same hour I looked up upon him.

Acts 9:17-18

[14] And he said, The God of our fathers hath chosen thee, that thou shouldest know his will, and see that Just One, and shouldest hear the voice of his mouth.

Paul uses the Jewish title "God of our fathers" (Deut 26:7) to describe the One who chose him (Acts 9:15) to visibly see Jesus Christ (Acts 26:16, 1 Cor 9:1, 15:8). Ananias calls the Lord Jesus the "Just One" as did Pilate (Matt 27:24) and his wife (Matt 27:19), Simon Peter (Acts 3:14), and Stephen (Acts 7:52).

[15] For thou shalt be his witness unto all men of what thou hast seen and heard.

Paul had been commissioned to testify to both Jews and Gentiles (Acts 9:15), but for now he avoids the inflammatory word "Gentile" (Acts 22:21-22) by saying "all men."

[16] And now why tarriest thou? arise, and be baptized, and wash away thy sins, calling on the name of the Lord.

- Paul was not baptized to obtain salvation, as he had already been spiritually "born again" (1 Cor 15:8, John 3:3) three days prior (Acts 9:6-9). Instead, he was baptized like all New Testament believers to identify with the death, burial, and resurrection of Jesus Christ (Rom 6:4-11).

- In the New Testament, **salvation** is described as washing (1 Cor 6:11), *not* by literal water, but by "the washing of water by the word" (Eph 5:26); by "washing of regeneration" (Titus 3:5); or "washed us from our sins in his own blood" (Rev 1:5).
- In the Old Testament, **ritual purification** is performed by washing in actual water. Sometimes the hands are washed (Exod 30:19, Deut 21:6), and sometimes the entire body is washed (Num 19:19) as a form of baptism.
- Ananias, a "devout man according to the law," knows the Old Testament well (the New Testament has not yet been written). He knows that God desires to spiritually cleanse those who turn to Him (Ezek 36:25-27). His exuberant statement reflects his knowledge of Old Testament ceremonial and figurative cleansing. Luke quotes Ananias to show this devout Jewish believer's approval of Paul's conversion, not to explain New Testament baptism.

[17] And it came to pass, that, when I was come again to Jerusalem, even while I prayed in the temple, I was in a trance;

- Paul's account now moves forward at least three years post-conversion, either to his first (Acts 9:26-30, Gal 1:17-18) or second visit to Jerusalem (Acts 12:25).
- A "trance" is a state between waking and sleeping in which the individual appears awake though transfixed to observers.

[18] And saw him saying unto me, Make haste, and get thee quickly out of Jerusalem: for they will not receive thy testimony concerning me.

More recently Paul has received additional prophetic warnings about the rejection he would encounter here in Jerusalem (Acts 20:23, 21:4,11) yet has pressed on because he feels "bound in the spirit" (Acts 20:22) to complete his mission.

[19] And I said, Lord, they know that I imprisoned and beat in every synagogue them that believed on thee:

Like Abraham (Gen 18:23-32), Paul had tried to negotiate with the Lord. He argued that his testimony would be accepted because the Jews knew of his extreme religious zeal (Acts 26:10) and would want to hear him speak of the Savior who caused such a radical transformation of his life (Phil 3:5-10).

[20] And when the blood of thy martyr Stephen was shed, I also was standing by, and consenting unto his death, and kept the raiment of them that slew him.

Acts 7:58

[21] And he said unto me, Depart: for I will send thee far hence unto the Gentiles.

Paul had been reluctant to leave Jerusalem because of his sincere desire to bring the gospel to his fellow Israelites, so the Lord's command to depart (Acts 22:18) had to be repeated. Paul would fulfill his original commission to preach to Gentiles (Acts 9:15) and plant churches across much of the known world (Acts 21:28).

[22] And they gave him audience unto this word, and then lifted up their voices, and said, Away with such a fellow from the earth: for it is not fit that he should live.

These Jews take great pride in their religion (Rom 2:17-20) and believe they are better in the eyes of God than Gentiles, who do not have the law (Eph 2:11-12, 1 Thes 4:5). They therefore become enraged by Paul's use of the word "Gentile" because he seeks to bring Gentiles to God through Jesus Christ without converting them to Judaism (Matt 23:15), thereby implying that Jews and Gentiles are on equal footing before God (Rom 3:9, 10:12). The furious crowd at Jerusalem calls for death for Paul, as they previously did for Jesus (Luke 23:18,21).

[23] And as they cried out, and cast off their clothes, and threw dust into the air,

- Casting off or tearing clothing shows revulsion against speech that is offensive, such as blasphemy (Matt 26:65, Acts 14:14). Placing dust on one's head shows mourning (2 Sam 13:19, Job 2:12).

- The people of Jerusalem reject God's messenger and the gospel he preaches. They forget the words of the prophet Joel, who told the people to "rend your heart, and not your garments, and turn unto the Lord your God" (Joel 2:13).

[24] The chief captain commanded him to be brought into the castle, and bade that he should be examined by scourging; that he might know wherefore they cried so against him.

Chief captain Claudius Lysias (Acts 23:26, 24:7) is frustrated, so he orders (he "bade") this brutal interrogation because he does not understand Paul's speech in the Hebrew language (Acts 22:2) or the cause of the mob's unruly display of emotion.

Language

Irony (unexpected outcome or event) – Paul is rescued from a beating by civilians (Acts 21:32) only to be nearly beaten by soldiers (compare Amos 5:19).

[25] And as they bound him with thongs, Paul said unto the centurion that stood by, Is it lawful for you to scourge a man that is a Roman, and uncondemned?

"It is a crime to bind a Roman citizen; to scourge him is a wickedness."[286] Paul had unflinchingly taken punishment in public when his testimony as a Christian was at stake (Acts 16:19-22). Since there is no such point to be made here behind closed doors, he appeals to his Roman citizenship. His goal is to obtain another opportunity to present the gospel to the people of Jerusalem (Acts 22:30).

[26] When the centurion heard that, he went and told the chief captain, saying, Take heed what thou doest: for this man is a Roman.

Captain Lysias has unlawfully ordered Paul to be bound with chains (Acts

---

[286] Marcus Tullius Cicero, *Against Verres*, 2.5.66

21:33) and beaten, but the centurion does not carry out the latter order when he learns Paul is a Roman citizen.

[27] Then the chief captain came, and said unto him, Tell me, art thou a Roman? He said, Yea.

[28] And the chief captain answered, With a great sum obtained I this freedom. And Paul said, But I was free born.

- The chief captain is Claudius Lysias (Acts 23:26, 24:7). He may have purchased his citizenship from the late emperor Claudius, whose policy of granting new citizenship was criticized. "A great many other persons unworthy of citizenship were also deprived of it, whereas he granted citizenship to others quite indiscriminately, sometimes to individuals and sometimes to whole groups. For inasmuch as Romans had the advantage over foreigners in practically all respects, many sought the franchise by personal application to the emperor ..."[287] If the chief captain did obtain his citizenship from the late emperor, then from his birth name "Lysias" he would have added the name "Claudius" in honor of the ruler who granted him citizenship.[288] Paul's parents were Roman citizens, so he received the same privilege by birth.
- Paul is the picture of a man released from the bondage of sin (Acts 22:30, Rom 6:22, 8:2) and spiritually reborn (John 3:3, 1 Peter 1:23) as a free gift of God (Rom 3:24, 6:23) before whom he now stands uncondemned (Acts 22:25, John 5:24). In contrast, Captain Lysias is the picture of a man who works as a debtor to purchase God's favor (Rom 4:4, Eph 2:8-9).

[29] Then straightway they departed from him which should have examined him: and the chief captain also was afraid, after he knew that he was a Roman, and because he had bound him.

- The interrogators ("examiners") leave because they, along with

---

[287] Cassius Dio, *Roman History*, 60.17.5
[288] Some of the newly-made citizens were criticized for "not adopting Claudius' name." Ibid., 60.17.7

Captain Lysias, fear the possibility of being accused of mistreating a Roman citizen. They may well know of Gaius Verres, the former governor of Sicily, who was prosecuted for ignoring the rights of those declaring their Roman citizenship. "The necks of Roman citizens were broken in a most infamous manner in the prison; so that very expression and form of entreaty, 'I am a Roman citizen,' which has often brought to many, in the most distant countries, succour and assistance, even among the barbarians, only brought to these men a more bitter death and a more immediate execution."[289]

- The Philippian magistrates were also afraid when they perceived their unlawful mistreatment of Paul (Acts 16:37-38).

[30] On the morrow, because he would have known the certainty wherefore he was accused of the Jews, he loosed him from his bands, and commanded the chief priests and all their council to appear, and brought Paul down, and set him before them.

370

Captain Lysias still does not understand the accusations against Paul and hopes the Jewish council will clarify them for him, but he will quickly be disappointed (Acts 23:10).

Persuasive Speech

Paul's Spirit-filled sermon shows a mastery of persuasive speech (rhetoric). **Introduction** (*exordium*) – "Men, brethren, and fathers, hear ye my defence which I make now unto you" spoken in the Hebrew language. Acts 22:1-2
Narrative (*narratio*) – Paul was a devout, zealous Jew who turned to Jesus the Messiah during a divine meeting on the road to Damascus. At the Jerusalem temple, while in prayer, the Lord directed him to preach to the Gentiles. Acts 22:3-21
Thesis (*propositio*), **arguments** (*probatio*), and **final appeal** (*peroratio*) – absent because the audience interrupts Paul's speech at the word "Gentiles." Acts 22:22

---

[289] Marcus Tullius Cicero, *Against Verres*, 2.5.57

Teaching Question

Question: How does Paul prove his claim of Roman citizenship (Acts 22:27)?
Answer: In Paul's case it is uncertain, but some citizens possess official documents. The emperor Nero was pleased with the "dances by some Greek youths, handing each of them certificates of Roman citizenship at the close of his performance."[290] In any case, Captain Lysias takes Paul's claim seriously because the penalty for misrepresenting Roman citizenship is very severe. Emperor Claudius "forbade men of foreign birth to use the Roman names ... [and] those who usurped the privileges of Roman citizenship he executed ..."[291]

Challenge Questions

1. Why does Paul say "Gentiles" (Acts 22:21) when he knows the word is so inflammatory?
2. Why does Paul declare his Roman citizenship only before being interrogated (Acts 22:25) and not when he is first arrested (Acts 21:33)?

---

[290] Suetonius, *The Life of Nero*, 12.1
[291] Suetonius, *The Life of Claudius*, 25.3

Acts Chapter 23

[1] And Paul, earnestly beholding the council, said, Men and brethren, I have lived in all good conscience before God until this day.

Conscience is the inner voice of right and wrong given to everyone by God (Rom 2:14-15). The conscience, when ignored, will eventually cease to function (1 Tim 4:2, Titus 1:15) and lead to moral ruin (1 Tim 1:19). When an individual has wronged someone, conscience makes it difficult for him to look the offended person in the eye (Luke 22:60-62). Paul exercises his conscience (Acts 24:16) by following its directives (Acts 2:37) and living without unconfessed sin (1 John 1:9) so that he may spiritually look God in the eye without hesitation.

[2] And the high priest Ananias commanded them that stood by him to smite him on the mouth.

- The hatred and contempt of these religious leaders comes from their envy of Paul, who has removed so many people from their religious authority (Acts 13:45, 17:4-5) and into his "sect" (Acts 28:22). Ananias thus views Paul as guilty of sedition (Acts 24:5) and makes no false pretenses of being an impartial judge when he gives this spiteful order.
- "But as for the high priest, Ananias he … was a great hoarder up of money … he also had servants who were very wicked … and went to the thrashing-floors, and took away the [food] tithes that belonged to the priests by violence, and did not refrain from beating such as would not give these tithes to them … priests, that of old were [supposed] to be supported with those tithes, died for want of food."[292] When the nation eventually rebels against Rome, the Israelite revolutionaries will treat Ananias as an enemy and it will be reported that "on the next day the high priest [Ananias] was caught where he had concealed himself in an aqueduct; he was

---

[292] Josephus, *Antiquities*, 20.9.2

slain, together with Hezekiah his brother."[293]

[3] Then said Paul unto him, God shall smite thee, thou whited wall: for sittest thou to judge me after the law, and commandest me to be smitten contrary to the law?

- Worse than the sharp sting across Paul's face is his painful realization that he will not receive a fair hearing. In the heat of the moment, he lashes out with words that he feels represent righteous indignation (Deut 28:28).
- A "whited wall" looks beautiful on the outside but is corrupt on the inside (like the wall of a tomb, Matt 23:27).

[4] And they that stood by said, Revilest thou God's high priest?

- They are not disturbed by the high priest's injustice and failure to follow proper legal procedure (Lev 19:15). Appealing to Ananias' position to justify his wrongdoing serves only to underscore his abuse of the high priest's office.
- Paul knows that since the resurrection, "God's high priest" is the Lord Jesus Christ (Heb 3:1), who will one day judge everyone righteously (Acts 17:31).

[5] Then said Paul, I wist not, brethren, that he was the high priest: for it is written, Thou shalt not speak evil of the ruler of thy people.

Paul realizes his emotional outburst did not follow the teaching (Matt 5:39) or example of Christ, who had respectfully objected under similar circumstances (John 18:22-23) and never lashed out at those who personally wronged Him (1 Peter 2:23). Paul cites scripture (Exod 22:28) as he apologizes.

[6] But when Paul perceived that the one part were Sadducees, and the other Pharisees, he cried out in the council, Men and brethren, I am a Pharisee, the son of a Pharisee: of the hope and resurrection of the dead I am called in question.

---

[293] Josephus, *The Jewish War*, 2.17.9

- Paul intended to make a defense based on his moral integrity (Acts 23:1) and meticulous adherence to the law (Acts 23:3). He doubtless intended to give his conversion testimony to the council as he had to the multitude the previous day (Acts 22:1-21). However, initial events have proven true the words of the Lord Jesus that "they will not receive thy testimony concerning me" (Acts 22:18), so Paul must change course.
- From an evangelistic perspective, Paul chooses to talk about resurrection because he knows that his audience must first be open to this doctrine to seriously consider the resurrection of Jesus Christ (1 Cor 15:13-14).
- From a legal perspective, Paul does not want to be judged by the Jewish Sanhedrin (Acts 25:9-10) and wants Captain Lysias to understand that he (Paul) is caught in a religious dispute and has not violated Roman law; in this, he succeeds (Acts 23:29).

374

Language
Hendiadys (two words for one idea) – "hope and resurrection of the dead," i.e., not some undefined hope, but a resurrection hope.

[7] And when he had so said, there arose a dissension between the Pharisees and the Sadducees: and the multitude was divided.

[8] For the Sadducees say that there is no resurrection, neither angel, nor spirit: but the Pharisees confess both.

- The Pharisees believe in a future resurrection. "The Pharisees ... believe that souls have an immortal rigor in them ... [and may be rewarded with] power to revive and live again."[294]
- "The doctrine of the Sadducees is ... that souls die with the bodies."[295] They do not believe in life after death, a condition sometimes envisioned as being in the form of an angel (Acts 12:15) or spirit (Luke 24:36-37). The Sadducees did not learn from Christ's lesson on the resurrection (Matt 22:23-32) or from the testimony (Matt

---

[294] Josephus, *Antiquities*, 18.1.3
[295] Ibid., 18.1.4

28:11-15) of the soldiers they assigned to guard His tomb (Matt 27:62-66). The resurrection is a stumbling block for the Sadducees as it is for the people of Athens (Acts 17:32).

- The doctrinal conflict between the Pharisees and Sadducees is long-standing. "The Pharisees have delivered to the people a great many observances [they received] from their fathers, which are not written in the laws of Moses; and for that reason it is that the Sadducees reject them, and say that we are to esteem those observances to be obligatory which are in the written word, but are not to observe what are derived from the tradition of our forefathers. And concerning these things it is that great disputes and differences have arisen among them."[296]

[9] And there arose a great cry: and the scribes that were of the Pharisees' part arose, and strove, saying, We find no evil in this man: but if a spirit or an angel hath spoken to him, let us not fight against God.

The Pharisees' rivalry with the Sadducees (Matt 22:34) is greater than their hatred of Paul. They go so far as to declare Paul guiltless to use his conversion testimony of being spoken to by "a spirit or an angel" (Acts 22:6-10, 17-21) as support for their doctrine of the supernatural.

[10] And when there arose a great dissension, the chief captain, fearing lest Paul should have been pulled in pieces of them, commanded the soldiers to go down, and to take him by force from among them, and to bring him into the castle.

Chief captain Claudius Lysias (Acts 23:26, 24:7) is responsible for protecting Roman citizens such as Paul (Acts 22:27) and orders him to be brought back to the military fortress.

[11] And the night following the Lord stood by him, and said, Be of good cheer, Paul: for as thou hast testified of me in Jerusalem, so must thou bear witness also at Rome.

Paul had hoped to bring the gospel to Jews in Jerusalem and is

---

[296] Ibid., 13.10.6

undoubtedly discouraged by their hard-heartedness (Prov 28:14, Rom 2:5). He had also planned to travel onward to Rome (Acts 19:21, Rom 15:24) but cannot proceed now because he is a prisoner. So the Lord Jesus comes to him with encouragement as He did at Corinth (Acts 18:9-10) and as He will do on Paul's voyage to Rome (Acts 27:23-24).

[12] And when it was day, certain of the Jews banded together, and bound themselves under a curse, saying that they would neither eat nor drink till they had killed Paul.

These men ignore the lesson of scripture (Matt 22:29) when taking this foolish vow. King Saul had placed his men under a similar curse (1 Sam 14:24), which brought disaster. By the end of the day, King Saul's men ate raw, bloody meat (1 Sam 14:32, forbidden in Deut 12:23), the Lord withheld His direction from Saul (1 Sam 14:37), his son Jonathan nearly lost his life (1 Sam 14:44), the king lost face in front of his men by breaking his oath (1 Sam 14:45), and the Israelite army lost the initiative it had against the Philistines (1 Sam 14:46).

[13] And they were more than forty which had made this conspiracy.

The number "forty" in scripture often signifies a time of probation, such as the forty years of wilderness wanderings (Num 32:13). Israel is given forty years to repent from the time of Jesus Christ beginning His ministry until the destruction of the temple by the Romans (Matt 24:1-2). Israel's blindness to the gospel (Rom 11:25) is underscored here when "forty" is the number (Acts 23:21) of men plotting to kill Paul.

[14] And they came to the chief priests and elders, and said, We have bound ourselves under a great curse, that we will eat nothing until we have slain Paul.

The chief priests and elders have a proven track record of murder (Matt 23:37, Acts 7:52, 22:4, 1 Thes 2:15). They fulfill Christ's words "that whosoever killeth you will think that he doeth God service" (John 16:2).

[15] Now therefore ye with the council signify to the chief captain that he bring him down unto you to morrow, as though ye would enquire some-

thing more perfectly concerning him: and we, or ever he come near, are ready to kill him.

The forty men are so hateful of Paul that they are willing to risk their lives and face death either in battle against Roman soldiers (Matt 26:52) or in a public execution (Prov 26:26) by crucifixion.

[16] And when Paul's sister's son heard of their lying in wait, he went and entered into the castle, and told Paul.

Paul was born in Tarsus but raised here in Jerusalem (Acts 22:3), where he still has good relations with family.

[17] Then Paul called one of the centurions unto him, and said, Bring this young man unto the chief captain: for he hath a certain thing to tell him.

[18] So he took him, and brought him to the chief captain, and said, Paul the prisoner called me unto him, and prayed me to bring this young man unto thee, who hath something to say unto thee.

[19] Then the chief captain took him by the hand, and went with him aside privately, and asked him, What is that thou hast to tell me?

[20] And he said, The Jews have agreed to desire thee that thou wouldest bring down Paul to morrow into the council, as though they would enquire somewhat of him more perfectly.

[21] But do not thou yield unto them: for there lie in wait for him of them more than forty men, which have bound themselves with an oath, that they will neither eat nor drink till they have killed him: and now are they ready, looking for a promise from thee.

[22] So the chief captain then let the young man depart, and charged him, See thou tell no man that thou hast shewed these things to me.

Captain Lysias does not doubt the report, knowing the violent character of the high priest Ananias (Acts 23:2) and the zealousness of Jerusalem's Jews (Acts 21:30-32, 23:10).

[23] And he called unto him two centurions, saying, Make ready two hundred soldiers to go to Cæsarea, and horsemen threescore and ten, and spearmen two hundred, at the third hour of the night;

Captain Lysias dispatches 472 men to leave with Paul for Caesarea, the Roman capital of the region, under cover of darkness (Acts 9:25, 17:10) at 9 PM.

[24] And provide them beasts, that they may set Paul on, and bring him safe unto Felix the governor.

Paul will have a mount of his own to ride.

[25] And he wrote a letter after this manner:

[26] Claudius Lysias unto the most excellent governor Felix sendeth greeting.

Captain Lysias addresses Felix as "most excellent" (like Theophilus, Luke 1:3) because of his position as governor.

[27] This man was taken of the Jews, and should have been killed of them: then came I with an army, and rescued him, having understood that he was a Roman.

Captain Lysias embellishes the story, for he had rescued Paul incidentally when he found him the subject of the temple riot, which he moved in to suppress (Acts 21:31-32). He unlawfully ordered Paul to be bound with chains (Acts 21:33) and almost had him tortured (Acts 22:24) until he finally learned of Paul's Roman citizenship (Acts 22:27).

[28] And when I would have known the cause wherefore they accused him, I brought him forth into their council:

Acts 22:30

[29] Whom I perceived to be accused of questions of their law, but to have

nothing laid to his charge worthy of death or of bonds.

Captain Lysias confirms the Pharisees' judgment that Paul is not guilty of any criminal acts (Acts 23:9).

[30] And when it was told me how that the Jews laid wait for the man, I sent straightway to thee, and gave commandment to his accusers also to say before thee what they had against him. Farewell.

Acts 23:20-21

[31] Then the soldiers, as it was commanded them, took Paul, and brought him by night to Antipatris.

"Herod [the Great] erected another city ... where a river encompassed the city itself, and a grove of the best trees for magnitude was round about it: this he named Antipatris, from his father Antipater."[297]

|379

[32] On the morrow they left the horsemen to go with him, and returned to the castle:

The foot soldiers return to Jerusalem, and the mounted soldiers escort Paul to Caesarea.

[33] Who, when they came to Cæsarea, and delivered the epistle to the governor, presented Paul also before him.

[34] And when the governor had read the letter, he asked of what province he was. And when he understood that he was of Cilicia;

[35] I will hear thee, said he, when thine accusers are also come. And he commanded him to be kept in Herod's judgment hall.

Governor Felix agrees to hear Paul's case since he is not from a nearby province to which he could be otherwise sent (Luke 23:7). Herod the Great (Matt 2:1) built Caesarea, and the judgment hall is named in his honor.

---

[297] Josephus, *Antiquities*, 16.5.2

Teaching Question

<u>Question</u>: How is it that the high priest sentences Paul to be struck on the mouth (Acts 23:2) without first allowing Paul to present his defense? <u>Answer</u>: A court of law will hear testimony before determining a verdict and possible sentence. Yet Paul is sentenced to be struck on the mouth before he can give his defense. This disgraceful behavior of the high priest toward the apostle is satirized as follows:

"'Let the jury consider their verdict,' the King said, for about the twentieth time that day.

'No, no!' said the Queen. 'Sentence first--verdict afterwards.'

'Stuff and nonsense!' said Alice loudly. 'The idea of having the sentence first!'

'Hold your tongue!' said the Queen, turning purple.

'I won't!' said Alice.

'Off with her head!' the Queen shouted at the top of her voice."

– from *Alice's Adventures in Wonderland* by Lewis Carroll

Challenge Questions

1. Was it wrong for Paul to protest his treatment by the high priest?
2. Why did Paul derail the legal proceeding by introducing a contentious subject?
3. How can Paul claim to be both a Pharisee and a Christian at the same time?

Acts Chapter 24

[1] And after five days Ananias the high priest descended with the elders, and with a certain orator named Tertullus, who informed the governor against Paul.

The high priest, unlike Paul, has financial resources that give him access to an advocate such as Tertullus (James 2:6), who now brings charges against Paul before Governor Felix.

[2] And when he was called forth, Tertullus began to accuse him, saying, Seeing that by thee we enjoy great quietness, and that very worthy deeds are done unto this nation by thy providence,

[3] We accept it always, and in all places, most noble Felix, with all thankfulness.

- Felix and his brother Pallas are freedmen. They were slaves when raised in the royal household and have now been freed by Emperor Claudius, who assigns them government jobs because of their expected loyalty, not because of their competence. "Claudius entrusted the province of Judaea to ... his own freedmen, one of whom, Antonius Felix, indulging in every kind of barbarity and lust, exercised the power of a king in the spirit of a slave."[298] "Of his freedmen he .. . was equally fond of Felix, giving him the command of cohorts and of troops of horse, as well as of the province of Judaea ... But most of all he was devoted to his secretary Narcissus and his treasurer Pallas, and ... he permitted them to amass such wealth by plunder, that when he once complained of the low state of his funds, the witty answer was made that he would have enough and to spare, if he were taken into partnership by his two freedmen."[299]
- Since Pallas is wealthy and holds high government office, his broth-

---

[298] Tacitus, *Histories*, 5.9
[299] Suetonius, *The Life of Claudius*, 28.1

er Felix "had for some time been governor of Judaea, and thought that he could do any evil act with impunity, backed up as he was by such power." Felix governs Judea and Samaria while his rival Cumanus governs Galilee. In their hatred for one another "they plundered each other, letting loose bands of robbers, forming ambushes, and occasionally fighting battles, and carrying the spoil and booty to the two procurators, who at first rejoiced at all this, but, as the mischief grew, they interposed with an armed force, which was cut to pieces." The two governors hired men to fight but then executed those who went so far as to kill Roman soldiers. Eventually Felix and Cumanus are brought to trial for their crimes. However, Quadratus, governor of Syria, appoints his friend Felix as judge in his own trial, "and so Cumanus was condemned for the crimes which the two had committed," and Felix got off scot-free.[300]

- Any semblance of peace ("great quietness") brought about by the actions of Felix comes not from his desire for the public good but from his strategy of killing anyone who might compete with his criminal enterprise. "But as to the number of the robbers whom he caused to be crucified, and of those who were caught among them, and whom he brought to punishment, they were a multitude not to be enumerated."[301]

- Here Tertullus falsely portrays (Prov 26:28) the Roman governor as a man who keeps the peace while framing Paul as a criminal who disrupts the peace (Acts 24:5-6). Yet those in the room who know Felix will hear Tertullus' flattering words as being very inconsistent with the facts. Ironically, Paul's accusers are the ones guilty of disrupting the peace (Acts 21:27-31, 23:10).

- Tertullus praises Felix for "worthy deeds," but the governor's actions will prove unworthy when he neglects justice for bribes (Acts 24:26) and political favors (Acts 24:27).

[4] Notwithstanding, that I be not further tedious unto thee, I pray thee that thou wouldest hear us of thy clemency a few words.

"Without further delay, I kindly ask you to hear my brief address."

---

[300] Tacitus, *Annals*, 12.53-54
[301] Josephus, *Jewish War*, 2.13.2

[5] For we have found this man a pestilent fellow, and a mover of sedition among all the Jews throughout the world, and a ringleader of the sect of the Nazarenes:

- The first charge is that Paul is a public nuisance (a pest) who causes sedition by leading an unlawful sect. The Lord Jesus was similarly charged with stirring "up the people, teaching throughout all Jewry" (Luke 23:5). The charge of sedition (Luke 23:19) carries the death penalty.
- Tertullus shows his contempt for Paul when he refuses to name him ("this man"). Yet he unintentionally compliments Paul when describing his influence as extending "among all the Jews throughout the world." Paul received similar undesigned praise at Thessalonica (Acts 17:6) and Ephesus (Acts 19:26).
- Although Paul has considerable influence among *Gentile* believers throughout the eastern half of the Roman Empire, Tertullus maliciously exaggerates Paul's influence among *Jews* within Israel (Acts 21:21) and outside of Israel (Acts 13:46, 18:6, 28:28).

[6] Who also hath gone about to profane the temple: whom we took, and would have judged according to our law.

The second charge is that Paul sought to profane the temple. Tertullus implies that the temple authorities had arrested Paul to bring him to trial, but the truth is that a mob intent on beating him to death had attacked him (Acts 21:31-32). The charge of profaning the temple (Acts 21:28b-29) also carries the death penalty.

[7] But the chief captain Lysias came upon us, and with great violence took him away out of our hands,

Tertullus praised Governor Felix as a man of peace (Acts 24:2) yet ironically criticizes his soldiers of assaulting temple worshipers. The truth is that the mob stopped rioting at the sight of Captain Lysias with his soldiers, so bloodshed was not required (Acts 21:32).

[8] Commanding his accusers to come unto thee: by examining of whom thyself mayest take knowledge of all these things, whereof we accuse him.

When Captain Lysias was informed of the assassination plot against Paul (Acts 23:19-21), he correctly transferred him to Caesarea for lawful trial before the Roman governor (Acts 23:30). However, Tertullus falsely implies that Lysias found fault in Paul when the captain wrote that Paul has "nothing laid to his charge worthy of death or of bonds" (Acts 23:29).

[9] And the Jews also assented, saying that these things were so.

The high priest Ananias and the elders are present with Tertullus, but the Jews from the province of Asia, who initially accused Paul (Acts 21:27-29), are not (Acts 24:18-19).

[10] Then Paul, after that the governor had beckoned unto him to speak, answered, Forasmuch as I know that thou hast been of many years a judge unto this nation, I do the more cheerfully answer for myself:

Paul hopes that Governor Felix's years of experience in Judea and the influence of his Jewish wife Drusilla (Acts 24:24) will help him better understand the issues in this case. However, a more principled judge, such as Gallio (Acts 18:12-16), would have already ordered dismissal for lack of criminal charges since Tertullus' accusations are of a religious nature.

[11] Because that thou mayest understand, that there are yet but twelve days since I went up to Jerusalem for to worship.

Paul now answers the first charge, that he is a public nuisance who causes sedition by leading an unlawful sect. He offers two points of consideration.
- First, the apostle can hardly be deemed a public nuisance like the notorious Egyptian revolutionary (Acts 21:38) or the disastrous Theudas and Judas (Acts 5:36-37) because he arrived at Jerusalem only a short time ago. Twelve days ago (the day after meeting with James and the elders, Acts 21:18,26), Paul went up to the temple to worship for an intended seven days. About six days in, the riot broke

out (Acts 21:27); one day later he appeared before the Jerusalem council (Acts 22:30), and now five days later (Acts 24:1), he appears before Felix.

- Second, Paul came to the Jerusalem temple to worship. He apparently came for the Feast of Pentecost (Acts 20:16), which Felix knows from experience (he has been for "many years a judge unto this nation," Acts 24:10) is attended by numerous worshippers from all over the world. Therefore Paul's presence should be presumed ordinary and harmless, as with other temple worshippers.

[12] And they neither found me in the temple disputing with any man, neither raising up the people, neither in the synagogues, nor in the city:

Paul cannot be considered a revolutionary who causes sedition when he has not been seen publicly debating in Jerusalem (unlike at Ephesus, Acts 19:9), let alone causing subversion. Instead, he had come to Jerusalem for charity and worship (Acts 24:17).

[13] Neither can they prove the things whereof they now accuse me.

Tertullus has provided no evidence supporting his claims. The case against Paul should be immediately dismissed for lack of evidence.

[14] But this I confess unto thee, that after the way which they call heresy, so worship I the God of my fathers, believing all things which are written in the law and in the prophets:

Paul cannot be smeared as a sect leader since he worships the same God and believes the same scriptures as all Jews. What Paul confesses to is not a crime, and his accusers can testify to the truth of his statement. His teaching of Jesus as the Messiah (a belief called "the way," Acts 9:2) is in harmony with the Old Testament.

[15] And have hope toward God, which they themselves also allow, that there shall be a resurrection of the dead, both of the just and unjust.

Even the Pharisees believe in a general resurrection of the dead as revealed in the Old Testament (Job 19:25-27, Dan 12:2, John 11:24). The

New Testament describes a first resurrection (Rev 20:4-6) at the rapture (1 Cor 15:51-54, 1 Thes 4:13-18) of those made spiritually just by the work of Christ (Rom 3:24) and a second resurrection of lost sinners for the final judgment (Rev 20:11-15).

[16] And herein do I exercise myself, to have always a conscience void of offence toward God, and toward men.

Paul can freely affirm his clear conscience here before Governor Felix but was not allowed to before the High Priest Ananias (Acts 23:1-2).

[17] Now after many years I came to bring alms to my nation, and offerings.

- Paul had left Jerusalem after his initial post-conversion visit due to conflict over the gospel (Acts 9:28–30). Therefore he has avoided preaching during subsequent visits until this temple riot made it necessary for him to make a public defense.
- Paul had raised support for a charitable collection in Galatia, Macedonia, and Achaia (1 Cor 16:1-4, 2 Cor 8-9, Rom 15:26). He also committed to paying the cost of temple vow offerings for himself and four others (Acts 21:24,26).

[18] Whereupon certain Jews from Asia found me purified in the temple, neither with multitude, nor with tumult.

Paul now answers the second charge of profaning the temple. He argues that he had been found ceremonially purified (Acts 21:26) and not effecting sacrilege as had been falsely rumored (Acts 21:29).

[19] Who ought to have been here before thee, and object, if they had ought against me.

If Paul's rivals from Asia (Acts 19:8-9) had a legitimate accusation against him, they would be present in-person to face him before this court as required by Roman law (Acts 25:16). Their absence reflects their fear of discovery of their guilt in starting the temple riot (Acts 21:27-28). The case against Paul should be immediately dismissed for lack of witnesses.

[20] Or else let these same here say, if they have found any evil doing in me, while I stood before the council,

The council at Jerusalem did not convict Paul of any crimes, and some of its members judged him not guilty (Acts 23:9).

[21] Except it be for this one voice, that I cried standing among them, Touching the resurrection of the dead I am called in question by you this day.

The only issue the council discussed was the resurrection (Acts 23:6-8), which is of a religious and not a criminal nature. The case against Paul should be immediately dismissed for lack of criminal charges.

[22] And when Felix heard these things, having more perfect knowledge of that way, he deferred them, and said, When Lysias the chief captain shall come down, I will know the uttermost of your matter.

- Governor Felix knows more (he has "more perfect knowledge") about Christianity than Paul's accusers assume that he does. Within his territory of Judea, there are "many thousands ... which believe" (Acts 21:20). There are believers right here at Caesarea (Acts 21:8-9,16) and even some among his own soldiers (Acts 10:1,24,44). He therefore knows that Christians are not the ones causing sedition against Rome, as Tertullus falsely claims (Acts 24:5). He certainly understands that the charges against Paul are religious rather than criminal.
- The governor previously stated that he needed to interview only Paul's accusers (Acts 23:35). He already received Lysias' written report and agrees with his assessment that Paul is not guilty (Acts 23:29). The governor should immediately dismiss the case for lack of legitimate criminal charges (Acts 24:21), lack of evidence (Acts 24:13), and lack of witnesses (Acts 24:19). However, Felix sees Paul as a valuable prisoner whose potential release he can hold over the heads of the Jewish national leadership as a threat, and whose continued imprisonment will be accounted to him as a political favor.

[23] And he commanded a centurion to keep Paul, and to let him have liberty, and that he should forbid none of his acquaintance to minister or come unto him.

- Although Paul is chained (Acts 26:29), he can freely receive visitors while under house arrest for the next two years (Acts 24:27). His favorable treatment by Felix implies the governor believes he is not guilty.
- Paul is undoubtedly disappointed, as he came to Jerusalem willing to die for the sake of the gospel (Acts 21:13). However, he had not understood the warning of "bonds and afflictions" (Acts 20:23) to mean that he might be detained for years at a time with no foreseeable date of release.

[24] And after certain days, when Felix came with his wife Drusilla, which was a Jewess, he sent for Paul, and heard him concerning the faith in Christ.

Drusilla is the daughter of the late Herod Agrippa I (Acts 12) and great-granddaughter of Herod the Great (Matt 2:16). Her siblings are Herod Agrippa II and Bernice (Acts 25:13), who will also hear Paul preach (Acts 25:23). Felix convinced Drusilla to leave her first husband to marry him.

[25] And as he reasoned of righteousness, temperance, and judgment to come, Felix trembled, and answered, Go thy way for this time; when I have a convenient season, I will call for thee.

- Felix hears his prisoner (Paul) preach as Herod Antipas heard his prisoner (John the Baptist) preach (Mark 6:20).
- Paul preaches these topics because he knows the Holy Spirit convicts of the sinfulness (intemperance) of humanity, the righteousness of God, and the judgment to come (John 16:8). People always seem to find a convenient time for their own affairs (Mark 6:21), but when Felix is spiritually convicted, he misses the opportunity for salvation (2 Cor 6:2) by deferring to a day which never comes (Acts 17:32).

[26] He hoped also that money should have been given him of Paul, that he might loose him: wherefore he sent for him the oftener, and communed with him.

- The governor's instincts of greed outweigh his sense of justice (Exod 23:8, Prov 17:23), and Felix cannot bring himself to release Paul without financial compensation.
- Felix continues to hear Paul, but apparently his wife, Drusilla, does not. She and Felix will have a son also named Agrippa, but he and Drusilla will die in the eruption of Mount Vesuvius.[302]

[27] But after two years Porcius Festus came into Felix' room: and Felix, willing to shew the Jews a pleasure, left Paul bound.

- Felix continues to flaunt his disregard for justice on numerous occasions. When "he also caught Eleazar, the son of Dineas, who had gotten together a company of robbers; and this he did by treachery; for he gave him assurance that he should suffer no harm, and thereby persuaded him to come to him; but when he came, he bound him, and sent him to Rome."[303]
- Furthermore "Felix also bore an ill-will to Jonathan, the high priest, because he frequently gave him admonitions about governing the Jewish affairs better than he did ... Wherefore Felix persuaded one of Jonathan's most faithful friends, a citizen of Jerusalem, whose name was Doras, to bring the [assassins] upon Jonathan, in order to kill him; and this he did by promising to give him a great deal of money for so doing." The men Felix hires to murder the high priest Jonathan are emboldened by their success and continue to act as hired assassins and will play an important role in commencing the disastrous Jewish rebellion against Rome.[304]
- When there previously arose a serious disturbance between Jews and Gentiles in Caesarea, the former governors arrested the individuals responsible and punished the guilty. When hostilities flare again under Felix's tenure, he instead goes to the Jewish section of

389

---

[302] Josephus, *Antiquities*, 20.7.2
[303] Ibid., 20.8.5
[304] Ibid., 20.8.5

town and "he armed his soldiers, and sent them out upon them, and slew many of them, and took more of them alive, and permitted his soldiers to plunder some of the houses of the citizens, which were full of riches."[305]
- Felix is now recalled to Rome to answer accusations by Jewish authorities regarding his deplorable conduct at Caesarea; he weakly attempts to show them a favor by prolonging Paul's detention. Felix journeys back to Rome but still manages to escape justice. It will be recorded that "the principal of the Jewish inhabitants of Caesarea went up to Rome to accuse Felix; and he had certainly been brought to punishment unless Nero had yielded to the importunate solicitations of his brother Pallas."[306]
- Festus succeeds Felix as governor and inherits the case of Paul, who has been kept prisoner as a political favor.

Persuasive Speech

Tertullus (Acts 24:2-8) attacks Paul using persuasive speech (rhetoric).
Introduction *(exordium)* – Tertullus flatters Felix as a man of effective actions, thereby encouraging him to move against the threats allegedly imposed by Paul. Acts 24:2-4
Narrative *(narratio)* and **thesis** *(propositio)* – twisted "facts" are given. Acts 24:5-8a
Arguments *(probatio)* – absent; Tertullus fails to present any proof supporting his charges!
Final appeal *(peroratio)* – Felix is assured that by questioning Paul, he will come to the same conclusion as Tertullus. Acts 24:8b

---

305 Ibid., 20.8.7
306 Ibid., 20.8.9

Paul's Spirit-filled sermon (Acts 24:10-21) shows a mastery of persuasive speech (rhetoric).

Introduction *(exordium)* – "Forasmuch as I know that thou hast been of many years a judge unto this nation, I do the more cheerfully answer for myself." Acts 24:10

Narrative *(narratio)* – Paul's time in Jerusalem has been too brief for him to cause serious trouble. Acts 24:11

Arguments *(probatio)* – the evidence shows that Paul behaved devoutly in the temple. Acts 24:12-13

Refutation *(refutatio)* – Paul freely admits to following the resurrected Messiah, who was promised in the Old Testament. His enemies are angry over these religious differences, not over matters of secular law. None of Paul's accusers have appeared today proving otherwise. Acts 24:14-20

Final appeal *(peroratio)* – Paul's only "crime" is preaching the resurrection, which is not a crime at all. Acts 24:21

Challenge Question

Why do the high priest and elders feel they need to hire a professional speaker?

Acts Chapter 25

[1] Now when Festus was come into the province, after three days he ascended from Cæsarea to Jerusalem.

The new governor leaves the political capital to visit the religious capital of Judea.

[2] Then the high priest and the chief of the Jews informed him against Paul, and besought him,

The Jewish leadership pressed charges against Paul before Governor Felix (Acts 24:1), who deferred judgment (Acts 24:22) and has kept Paul imprisoned these last two years as a political favor to them (Acts 24:27).

[3] And desired favour against him, that he would send for him to Jerusalem, laying wait in the way to kill him.

They previously plotted to murder Paul using similar false pretenses (Acts 23:15).

[4] But Festus answered, that Paul should be kept at Cæsarea, and that he himself would depart shortly thither.

Governor Festus saves Paul from assassination, either unwittingly or with knowledge of the prior attempt reported by Captain Lysias (Acts 23:30).

[5] Let them therefore, said he, which among you are able, go down with me, and accuse this man, if there be any wickedness in him.

[6] And when he had tarried among them more than ten days, he went down unto Cæsarea; and the next day sitting on the judgment seat commanded Paul to be brought.

[7] And when he was come, the Jews which came down from Jerusalem

stood round about, and laid many and grievous complaints against Paul, which they could not prove.

Paul was correct when he noted the lack of evidence against him, stating, "Neither can they prove the things whereof they now accuse me" (Acts 24:13).

[8] While he answered for himself, Neither against the law of the Jews, neither against the temple, nor yet against Cæsar, have I offended any thing at all.

Paul observes the religious law of Israel (Phil 3:5–6), most important to the Pharisees (Matt 12:2); respects the Jewish temple (Acts 24:18), most important to the Sadducees (Acts 4:1); and abides by the secular laws of the State (Rom 13:1–7), represented by Caesar.

[9] But Festus, willing to do the Jews a pleasure, answered Paul, and said, Wilt thou go up to Jerusalem, and there be judged of these things before me?

Further hearings are unnecessary, for Paul's innocence has been proclaimed by the judgment of the Pharisees (Acts 23:9), the report of Captain Lysias (Acts 23:29), the hearings before Felix (Acts 24:13), and the lack of damning evidence presented today (Acts 25:7). But Festus, like his predecessor Felix (Acts 24:27), is more interested in exchanging political favors than administering justice.

[10] Then said Paul, I stand at Cæsar's judgment seat, where I ought to be judged: to the Jews have I done no wrong, as thou very well knowest.

- Paul bluntly points out that Festus knows he is innocent of any wrongdoing against the Jewish people (Acts 25:25). Paul will later explain that the Roman governor would have let him go but failed to do so in the face of objections from Jerusalem's religious leaders (Acts 28:18-19).
- Paul is asked to stand before a Jewish court in Jerusalem but knows he will not receive a fair hearing there (Acts 23:1–2). He certainly remembers the plot on his life there (Acts 23:12) and may or may

not know of the present threat if he leaves Caesarea for Jerusalem (Acts 25:3). So with no hope of acquittal in Israel, Paul exercises his right as a Roman citizen (Acts 22:27) to seek judgment from Caesar at Rome (the city in which the Lord Jesus had told him he would bear witness, Acts 23:11).

[11] For if I be an offender, or have committed any thing worthy of death, I refuse not to die: but if there be none of these things whereof these accuse me, no man may deliver me unto them. I appeal unto Cæsar.

Paul has, on many occasions, submitted to undeserved corporal punishment (2 Cor 11:24–25) but is not willing to accede to the requested sentence of capital punishment (Acts 25:24) when innocent.

[12] Then Festus, when he had conferred with the council, answered, Hast thou appealed unto Cæsar? unto Cæsar shalt thou go.

Festus gladly grants Paul his request for appeal because it gives the governor a way to save face before the Jewish leadership, a group he does not want to needlessly offend by releasing Paul.

[13] And after certain days king Agrippa and Bernice came unto Cæsarea to salute Festus.

- Herod Agrippa II is the son of the late (Acts 12:20-23) Herod Agrippa I (who slew James the apostle and almost executed Simon Peter, Acts 12:1-3) and great-grandson of Herod the Great (who murdered the young children of Bethlehem, Matt 2:16). His two sisters are Bernice (accompanying him) and Drusilla (wife of the former Governor Felix, Acts 24:24). Agrippa visits Festus to establish a rapport with the new governor (Luke 23:12).
- Bernice is the sister of Herod Agrippa II and great-granddaughter of Herod the Great. When her first husband Marcus Alexander died, she at age 16 was given in marriage to her uncle Herod of Chalcis, by whom she had two sons.[307] After her second husband died, Bernice lived for quite some time with her brother, Agrippa II. To dispel ru-

---

[307] Josephus, *Antiquities*, 19.5.1, 19.9.1, and 20.5.2

mors of incest between her and her brother (a perpetual bachelor), she married Poleme, king of Cilicia, but left him before long[308] and returned to the company of her brother with whom she now travels to Caesarea. When future governor Florus persecutes innocent Jews at Jerusalem, she will risk her life to intercede on their behalf, unsuccessfully.[309]

- Later when Rome sends the military to suppress rebellion in Jerusalem, Bernice will charm the commander (and future emperor) Vespasian[310] and become a lover to his son Titus.[311] The latter will assume command of the army when Vespasian becomes emperor. When Titus conquers Jerusalem, he will return to Rome, and Bernice will reunite with him (before his father dies and he becomes emperor). "Berenice was at the very height of her power and consequently came to Rome along with her brother Agrippa. The latter was given the rank of praetor while she dwelt in the palace, cohabiting with Titus. She expected to marry him and was already behaving in every respect as if she were his wife; but when he perceived that the Romans were displeased with the situation, he sent her away."[312]

[14] And when they had been there many days, Festus declared Paul's cause unto the king, saying, There is a certain man left in bonds by Felix:

Acts 24:27

[15] About whom, when I was at Jerusalem, the chief priests and the elders of the Jews informed me, desiring to have judgment against him.

[16] To whom I answered, It is not the manner of the Romans to deliver any man to die, before that he which is accused have the accusers face to face, and have licence to answer for himself concerning the crime laid against him.

[17] Therefore, when they were come hither, without any delay on the

---

[308] Ibid., 20.7.3
[309] Josephus, *Jewish War*, 2.15.1
[310] Tacitus, *Histories*, 2.81
[311] Ibid., 2.2
[312] Cassius Dio, *Roman History*, 65.15.3-4

morrow I sat on the judgment seat, and commanded the man to be brought forth.

Acts 25:2-5

[18] Against whom when the accusers stood up, they brought none accusation of such things as I supposed:

Acts 25:6-7. Festus expected Paul's relentless accusers to charge him with capital crimes (ones "worthy of death," Acts 25:25).

[19] But had certain questions against him of their own superstition, and of one Jesus, which was dead, whom Paul affirmed to be alive.

Acts 25:8. Festus rejects the Lord Jesus when he rejects His resurrection (1 Cor 15:17), as have other Gentiles (Acts 17:32) as well as Jews (Acts 4:1–2).

[20] And because I doubted of such manner of questions, I asked him whether he would go to Jerusalem, and there be judged of these matters.

[21] But when Paul had appealed to be reserved unto the hearing of Augustus, I commanded him to be kept till I might send him to Cæsar.

Acts 25:9-12. As emperor of Rome, Nero holds the titles "Caesar" (in honor of Julius Caesar) and "Augustus" (a title first given to Caesar Augustus, Luke 2:1).

[22] Then Agrippa said unto Festus, I would also hear the man myself. To morrow, said he, thou shalt hear him.

Herod Agrippa II desires to meet Paul out of curiosity as his granduncle Herod Antipas had been to meet Jesus (Luke 9:9, 23:8).

[23] And on the morrow, when Agrippa was come, and Bernice, with great pomp, and was entered into the place of hearing, with the chief captains, and principal men of the city, at Festus' commandment Paul was brought forth.

- Luke shows evidence of his eyewitness account when he recalls the self-promoting entrance ("great pomp") of King Agrippa and Bernice.
- Agrippa's father made a pompous display that did not glorify God (Acts 12:21) and suffered death for it (Acts 12:23, Isa 14:11).

[24] And Festus said, King Agrippa, and all men which are here present with us, ye see this man, about whom all the multitude of the Jews have dealt with me, both at Jerusalem, and also here, crying that he ought not to live any longer.

- The mob at the temple cried of Paul, "Away with such a fellow from the earth: for it is not fit that he should live" (Acts 22:22).
- Festus blames the Jews for his lack of courage to grant justice to Paul as Pontius Pilate blamed them for his lack of courage to grant justice to Christ (Matt 27:24).

[25] But when I found that he had committed nothing worthy of death, and that he himself hath appealed to Augustus, I have determined to send him.

Former Governor Felix believed Paul to be innocent but did not wish to anger the Jewish leadership by releasing him, so he deferred Paul's case to his successor Festus (Acts 24:27). Now Festus likewise believes Paul to be innocent but does not wish to anger them either, so he conveniently defers Paul's case to Caesar.

[26] Of whom I have no certain thing to write unto my lord. Wherefore I have brought him forth before you, and specially before thee, O king Agrippa, that, after examination had, I might have somewhat to write.

The governor must provide Caesar ("my lord") with a list of charges alleged against Paul but has little to write since he knows that Paul is not guilty of any capital crime (Acts 25:25). Festus tries to cover his judiciary incompetence by deflecting blame to his prisoner ("Paul's request for an appeal has sure put me in an awkward spot!"). He now hopes that Agrippa's knowledge of Judaism (Acts 26:3) will help him better understand the issues of this case.

[27] For it seemeth to me unreasonable to send a prisoner, and not withal to signify the crimes laid against him.

Festus unwittingly describes **himself** as being unreasonable in sending a prisoner accused merely of religious dissent, an issue which Caesar (undoubtedly like Gallio, Acts 18:14–15) will not care to address.

Challenge Question

Does Paul make the right decision in appealing to Caesar (Acts 25:12)?

Acts Chapter 26

[1] Then Agrippa said unto Paul, Thou art permitted to speak for thyself. Then Paul stretched forth the hand, and answered for himself:

[2] I think myself happy, king Agrippa, because I shall answer for myself this day before thee touching all the things whereof I am accused of the Jews:

Paul directly addresses Herod Agrippa II, who is visiting Governor Festus today (Acts 25:13). His audience also includes Festus (Acts 26:24), Bernice (Acts 26:30), and prominent community members and military officers (Acts 25:23).

[3] Especially because I know thee to be expert in all customs and questions which are among the Jews: wherefore I beseech thee to hear me patiently.

- Herod Agrippa is like Paul in that he is both a Jew (as are his sisters Bernice and Drusilla, Acts 24:24) and a Roman citizen. He therefore is not ignorant of Judaism, like Paul's Roman captors (Acts 25:19), nor anti-Gentile, like Paul's Jewish accusers (Acts 22:21-22). So Paul is genuinely happy to give his testimony to one who is both knowledgeable and open-minded (unlike Acts 23:1-2).
- Paul's sermon before King Agrippa fulfills prophecy (Matt 10:18, Acts 9:15).
- Although Paul politely asks to be heard patiently, his speech will be rudely interrupted by Festus (Acts 26:24).

Language
Conciliation (words given to obtain goodwill before delivering a weighty message) – Paul finds common ground with King Agrippa (Acts 26:2-3) before presenting matters of eternal significance (Acts 26:4-23).

[4] My manner of life from my youth, which was at the first among mine

own nation at Jerusalem, know all the Jews;

Paul was born in Tarsus but raised in Jerusalem (Acts 22:3).

[5] Which knew me from the beginning, if they would testify, that after the most straitest sect of our religion I lived a Pharisee.

Acts 23:6, Phil 3:5–6. The Pharisees are strict ("strait") in their devotion to the law (Matt 12:2).

[6] And now I stand and am judged for the hope of the promise made of God unto our fathers:

The "hope of Israel" (Jer 14:8, Acts 28:20) is Jesus the Messiah (Joel 3:16, Titus 2:13), who was crucified, resurrected, and glorified (Acts 2:22–36).

[7] Unto which promise our twelve tribes, instantly serving God day and night, hope to come. For which hope's sake, king Agrippa, I am accused of the Jews.

Devout Jews scattered throughout the world (James 1:1) faithfully worship God, earnestly ("instantly") hoping for the coming Messiah (Luke 2:29-32, 37-38). It is sadly ironic that those who look for the Messiah would attack Paul, whose only "crime" is in pointing the way to the Messiah.

[8] Why should it be thought a thing incredible with you, that God should raise the dead?

Paul has been preaching Jesus as the risen Messiah but usually receives doubtful responses from his Jewish audiences. He points out that the twelve tribes of Israel who faithfully serve God believe in the promise of the Messiah and undoubtedly believe in the scriptures that speak of resurrection (1 Sam 2:6, Job 14:14, 19:25-27, Isa 25:8, 26:19, Dan 12:2). Therefore the idea of a risen Messiah (whom Paul will identify as Jesus in Acts 26:15) should not be difficult to accept.

[9] I verily thought with myself, that I ought to do many things contrary to the name of Jesus of Nazareth.

[10] Which thing I also did in Jerusalem: and many of the saints did I shut up in prison, having received authority from the chief priests; and when they were put to death, I gave my voice against them.

Acts 8:1a, 9:1-2

[11] And I punished them oft in every synagogue, and compelled them to blaspheme; and being exceedingly mad against them, I persecuted them even unto strange cities.

The unconverted Saul was completely opposed to the gospel, and only a divine encounter with Jesus Christ could change his heart.

[12] Whereupon as I went to Damascus with authority and commission from the chief priests,

Acts 22:4-5

[13] At midday, O king, I saw in the way a light from heaven, above the brightness of the sun, shining round about me and them which journeyed with me.

Acts 9:3, 22:6. Scripture describes the Lord's glory as the light of the sun (Psalm 84:11, Ezek 1:26–28, Matt 17:2, Rev 1:16, 21:23) and Christ's return to earth as the sun shining forth (Gen 19:23–24, Psalm 50:1–3, 80:1).

[14] And when we were all fallen to the earth, I heard a voice speaking unto me, and saying in the Hebrew tongue, Saul, Saul, why persecutest thou me? it is hard for thee to kick against the pricks.

[15] And I said, Who art thou, Lord? And he said, I am Jesus whom thou persecutest.

Acts 9:4-5, 22:7-8. Paul proclaims Christ's resurrection when he tells how he saw the Savior alive, as in Acts 22:8.

[16] But rise, and stand upon thy feet: for I have appeared unto thee for this purpose, to make thee a minister and a witness both of these things which thou hast seen, and of those things in the which I will appear unto thee;

Ezek 2:1, Acts 22:10

[17] Delivering thee from the people, and from the Gentiles, unto whom now I send thee,

Paul had been commissioned to preach to the people of Israel and the Gentiles (Acts 9:15). He initially avoided saying "Gentile" when speaking to Jews at the temple (Acts 22:15) then triggered a riot when he eventually used the word (Acts 22:21-22). Now that Paul is before King Agrippa, who harbors no bias against non-Jews, he can safely use the word "Gentile" again.

[18] To open their eyes, and to turn them from darkness to light, and from the power of Satan unto God, that they may receive forgiveness of sins, and inheritance among them which are sanctified by faith that is in me.

- This verse, spoken by the resurrected Savior (now quoted by Paul), presents a concise summary of the benefits of the gospel ("the gospel in a nutshell").
- Paul was to reconcile lost sinners to God (2 Cor 5:20) by opening their eyes spiritually (2 Cor 4:4) and turning them from Satan's darkness (John 3:19, 2 Tim 2:26) to God's light (John 8:12, 12:46). Those who repent receive forgiveness of sins (Eph 1:7) and an eternal inheritance (Col 3:24, 1 Peter 1:4) as a free gift (Rom 5:15-16) received through faith in Jesus Christ (1 Cor 6:11).

[19] Whereupon, O king Agrippa, I was not disobedient unto the heavenly vision:

- Although Paul speaks before a wide audience (Acts 25:23), he directly addresses King Agrippa because he is presenting the gospel in a way this Jewish ruler would understand.
- Paul obeyed his divine vision as Cornelius (Acts 10:30-33) and Peter

(Acts 11:12) obeyed theirs.
- Paul's calling mirrors those of Ezekiel (Ezek 2:1-3), Jeremiah (Jer 1:7-8), Isaiah (Isa 42:6-7), the Lord Jesus (Luke 4:17-21), and every believer (Matt 5:16, Eph 5:8).

<u>Language</u>
Understatement (emphasize a fact by diminishing it) – "not disobedient unto the heavenly vision" means Paul's complete submission to Christ's instructions has guided his entire life.

[20] But shewed first unto them of Damascus, and at Jerusalem, and throughout all the coasts of Judæa, and then to the Gentiles, that they should repent and turn to God, and do works meet for repentance.

Paul preached the gospel in Damascus (Acts 9:20), in Jerusalem (Acts 9:28–29), while traveling through Judea (Acts 9:30), and to Gentiles throughout the eastern part of the Roman Empire (Rom 15:19). He does not merely convert Gentiles to a new religion (contrast Matt 23:15), but teaches them to repent (a change of heart and mind which leads to a change of action), receive salvation, and subsequently live lives that bear fruit (Luke 3:8, Acts 20:21).

[21] For these causes the Jews caught me in the temple, and went about to kill me.

"So with Gentiles forsaking their pagan ways, turning to the God of Israel, and showing a genuine change in their behavior, was there any reason to attack me in the temple?!?" (Acts 21:31).

[22] Having therefore obtained help of God, I continue unto this day, witnessing both to small and great, saying none other things than those which the prophets and Moses did say should come:

By God's grace, Paul preaches the gospel to everyone who will hear it. Accusing him of leading an unorthodox sect (Acts 24:5) is unreasonable because the Savior he proclaims as Messiah is the One spoken of in the Old Testament scriptures (Luke 24:27,44, John 5:39).

[23] That Christ should suffer, and that he should be the first that should rise from the dead, and should shew light unto the people, and to the Gentiles.

- Like Stephen (Acts 7:48-53), Paul has fearlessly moved beyond a personal legal defense and now preaches the gospel to his audience, as instructed by the Savior (Luke 21:12-13).
- The Lord Jesus exemplifies the believer's resurrection ("firstfruits of them that slept," 1 Cor 15:20) as the first to be raised never to die again ("firstborn from the dead," Col 1:18). The preaching of the gospel, that "Christ died for our sins" and "rose again" from the dead (1 Cor 15:1–4), gives spiritual light to the people of Israel and the Gentiles (Isa 49:6).
- The three trigger words that stumble Paul's listeners are "cross" (the idea that the Messiah would be crucified, 1 Cor 1:23), "resurrection" (Acts 17:32, 23:6-9, 26:8), and "Gentiles" (Acts 22:21-22). If he were to eliminate these three words, Paul would have attentive audiences and no riots. Yet he never compromises and now preaches all three concepts before King Agrippa.

[24] And as he thus spake for himself, Festus said with a loud voice, Paul, thou art beside thyself; much learning doth make thee mad.

The gospel message is foolish (John 10:20, 1 Cor 1:18) to Festus, who rejects the risen Savior (Acts 25:19). Like most men, he finds it entirely impractical to concern himself with abstract issues such as sin and salvation (Mark 4:19).

[25] But he said, I am not mad, most noble Festus; but speak forth the words of truth and soberness.

Paul affirms that he is no fool but preaches words that are true (James 1:18) and rational (2 Cor 5:13).

[26] For the king knoweth of these things, before whom also I speak freely: for I am persuaded that none of these things are hidden from him; for this thing was not done in a corner.

King Agrippa is a Jew and should know the scriptural prophecies of the Messiah (the scribes knew, Matt 2:4–6) and be informed of the public ministry of Jesus, which is widely known in Israel (Cornelius knew, Acts 10:37–38). The disciples have not kept the message of Christ's death, burial, and resurrection a secret!

Language
Understatement (emphasize a fact by diminishing it) – "not done in a corner" prompts the reader to recall how the disciples loudly and publicly proclaimed that Jesus Christ is alive and "we all are witnesses"! (Acts 2:32).

[27] King Agrippa, believest thou the prophets? I know that thou believest.

Paul confronts Agrippa with the challenge that if he really believes the Old Testament prophets as he professes to do, he will also believe in the Christ of whom the prophets spoke (John 5:46).

405

Language
Correction (a phrase is immediately clarified with additional material) – Paul asks if King Agrippa believes then clarifies that a devout Jew such as he certainly believes.

[28] Then Agrippa said unto Paul, Almost thou persuadest me to be a Christian.

Herod Agrippa II comes from a long line of Christ-rejecting despots. He is the great-grandson of Herod the Great (who attempted to kill the young Jesus, Matt 2:16), great-nephew of Herod Antipas (who tried Jesus and mocked Him, Luke 23:11), and son of Herod Agrippa I (who slew James the apostle and almost murdered Simon Peter, Acts 12:1-3). Here, in a marvelous display of grace (Titus 2:11), God allows Agrippa to hear the gospel; but by saying "almost," he forever misses the opportunity for salvation, as did Felix (Acts 24:25).

[29] And Paul said, I would to God, that not only thou, but also all that hear me this day, were both almost, and altogether such as I am, except these bonds.

Paul wishes for all men to be saved (1 Tim 2:4, Titus 2:11) and live a life wholly committed to Jesus Christ (2 Tim 3:10–11). Paul does not wish for anyone to be treated unjustly.

[30] And when he had thus spoken, the king rose up, and the governor, and Bernice, and they that sat with them:

[31] And when they were gone aside, they talked between themselves, saying, This man doeth nothing worthy of death or of bonds.

They agree that Paul is not guilty, as did the Pharisees (Acts 23:9), Captain Lysias (Acts 23:29), Felix (Acts 24:13), and Festus (Acts 25:25). But although they acknowledge Paul's blamelessness, they, like Pontius Pilate and Herod Antipas (Luke 23:13–15), lack the moral courage to free an innocent man in the face of political pressure (Acts 25:24).

[32] Then said Agrippa unto Festus, This man might have been set at liberty, if he had not appealed unto Cæsar.

- Paul was brought before the Roman authorities to answer for crimes alleged by the Jewish religious leaders (Acts 24:5–6). He receives a moral victory with this judgment of guiltlessness from Agrippa. The king's candid remark that an innocent man such as Paul should be freed is an indictment of former Governor Felix and current Governor Festus, who have kept Paul as a prisoner for their political benefit (Acts 24:27, 25:9).
- Luke shows that Paul's innocence is established today before an impressive group of officials: the Roman governor Festus, King Agrippa, Princess Bernice, and "the chief captains, and principal men of the city" (Acts 25:23).

Current Events

Governor Festus will die after a short term in office. Caesar Nero will appoint Albinus as the new governor. At the same time Annas (Ananus junior) will become the new high priest, a son of the former high priest Annas (Ananus senior), who tried both Jesus (John 18:13) and Peter with the apostles (Acts 4:6). "But this younger Ananus, who ... took the high priesthood, was a bold man in his temper, and very insolent; he was also of the sect of the Sadducees, who are very rigid in judging offenders, above all the rest of the Jews ... When, therefore, Ananus was of this disposition, he thought he had now a proper opportunity [to take advantage of the situation]. Festus was now dead, and [the new governor] Albinus was but upon the road; so he assembled the sanhedrin of judges, and brought before them the brother of Jesus, who was called Christ, whose

When Paul at Caesarea is brought before Governor Festus and King Agrippa (Acts 25:22-23), he preaches "that Christ should suffer, and that he should be the first that should rise from the dead, and should shew light unto the people, and to the Gentiles" (Acts 26:23).

GOR Photo / Shutterstock.com

name was James, and some others; and when he had formed an accusation against them as breakers of the law, he delivered them to be stoned: but as for those who seemed the most equitable of the citizens ... they disliked what was done; they also sent to the king [Agrippa II], desiring him to send to Ananus that he should act so no more, for that what he had already done was not to be justified; nay, some of them went also to meet Albinus, as he was upon his journey from Alexandria, and informed him that it was not lawful for Ananus to assemble a sanhedrin without his consent. Whereupon Albinus complied with what they said, and wrote in anger to Ananus, and threatened that he would bring him to punishment for what he had done; on which king Agrippa took the high priesthood from him, when he had ruled but three months."[313]

King Agrippa II will desperately try to dissuade the Jewish people from revolting against Rome.[314] When he fails to prevent war, he will affirm his support for the Empire and provide troops to fight against Jerusalem.[315] Afterward he will travel to Rome and be rewarded by Emperor Vespasian with the rank of praetor.[316]

Persuasive Speech

Paul's Spirit-filled sermon shows a mastery of persuasive speech (rhetoric).
Introduction *(exordium)* – Paul is genuinely pleased to speak to someone like himself, a Roman citizen who is also a Jew. Acts 26:2-3
Narrative *(narratio)* – Paul describes his conversion and the events leading up to today's hearing. Acts 26:4-21
Thesis *(propositio)* – God called Paul to preach to both Jews and Gentiles about Jesus the Messiah, a message consistent with the Old Testament. Acts 26:22-23
Arguments *(probatio)* – absent; his speech is interrupted before he can directly link Jesus to Old Testament prophecy (as in Acts 13:33-37). Acts 26:24

---

[313] Josephus, *Antiquities*, 20.9.1
[314] Josephus, *Jewish War*, 2.16.2-5
[315] Ibid., 2.18.9
[316] Cassius Dio, *Roman History*, 66.15.3

Refutation *(refutatio)* – the truth of Paul's words is corroborated by the facts, which are public knowledge. Acts 26:25-26
Final appeal *(peroratio)* – all who believe God's word will follow Paul's example and believe in Jesus Christ. Acts 26:27, 29

Teaching Question

"And now I stand and am judged for the hope of the promise made of God unto our fathers ... saying none other things than those which the prophets and Moses did say should come" (Acts 26:6, 22b).
Question: Why does Paul emphasize to his Roman audience that his teachings are part of an ancient belief system?
Answer: A new religion garners suspicion (Acts 17:18-20), whereas an ancient belief system (one of "antiquity") commands respect. Josephus argues that "... our Jewish nation is of very great antiquity ... [whereas] almost all which concerns the Greeks happened not long ago."[317] The Roman historian Tacitus disapproves of Jewish customs yet allows them some deference because "... these rites are maintained by their antiquity."[318] The Jewish nation has indeed received official favor on this basis. "[By decree of] the senate and people of Rome, they may assemble, according to their ancient legal custom ... as did their ancestors, their prayers and sacrifices to God ... and to act according to their own laws."[319]

409

Challenge Questions

What is it about Paul's speech that Agrippa finds persuasive? What considerations keep him from turning to Jesus Christ?

---

[317] Josephus, *Against Apion*, 1.1-2
[318] Tacitus, *Histories*, 5.5
[319] Josephus, *Antiquities*, 14.10.24

Acts Chapter 27

[1] And when it was determined that we should sail into Italy, they delivered Paul and certain other prisoners unto one named Julius, a centurion of Augustus' band.

- Paul sails to Italy for his legal appeal to Caesar Nero and is accompanied by Luke (he writes "we should sail").
- Centurion Julius's military unit is named "Augustus," as Cornelius' is called the "Italian" (Acts 10:1).

[2] And entering into a ship of Adramyttium, we launched, meaning to sail by the coasts of Asia; one Aristarchus, a Macedonian of Thessalonica, being with us.

- They start on a ship apparently returning to its home port in Adramyttium in the Roman province of Asia. Later they will transfer to a first (Acts 27:6) and a second ship from Alexandria, Egypt (Acts 28:11).
- Despite his harrowing ordeal with the angry mob at Ephesus (Acts 19:29), the faithful Aristarchus continued at Paul's side to Jerusalem (Acts 20:4) and will remain loyal during the apostle's imprisonment in Rome (Col 4:10, Phil 24).

[3] And the next day we touched at Sidon. And Julius courteously entreated Paul, and gave him liberty to go unto his friends to refresh himself.

- The Phoenician city of Sidon (Zidon) should have been conquered by the Israelites (Josh 13:6), but they failed to do so (Judg 1:31). The city subsequently brought idolatry to Israel through the wives of King Solomon (1 Kings 11:1) and the wife of King Ahab, Jezebel (1 Kings 16:31). The prophets condemned Sidon (Jer 47:4, Ezek 32:30), and later its inhabitants came to hear Jesus (Luke 6:17), who exceptionally healed the daughter of a Gentile woman (Mark 7:24-30). Sidon was evangelized after the martyrdom of Stephen (Acts 11:19), and its representatives observed the death of Herod Agrippa I (Acts 12:20-23). Believers in this once-hopelessly pagan city now show hospitality to Paul.

- Luke does not explain why Centurion Julius treats Paul so considerately. He may have been one of the military officers present when Paul preached in Caesarea (Acts 25:23).

[4] And when we had launched from thence, we sailed under Cyprus, because the winds were contrary.

They sail north around Cyprus rather than sailing directly west.

[5] And when we had sailed over the sea of Cilicia and Pamphylia, we came to Myra, a city of Lycia.

Paul sails from Caesarea in Israel toward Rome to conduct his legal appeal to Caesar (Acts 27:1).

Rostislav Ageev / Shutterstock.com

[6] And there the centurion found a ship of Alexandria sailing into Italy; and he put us therein.

They board a ship from Alexandria, Egypt, with a cargo of wheat (Acts 27:38) bound for Italy.

[7] And when we had sailed slowly many days, and scarce were come over against Cnidus, the wind not suffering us, we sailed under Crete, over against Salmone;

After nearing Cnidus, they can no longer sail directly west due to the prevailing winds and instead travel southwest to the southern coast of Crete.

[8] And, hardly passing it, came unto a place which is called The fair havens; nigh whereunto was the city of Lasea.

[9] Now when much time was spent, and when sailing was now dangerous, because the fast was now already past, Paul admonished them,

Sailing is now dangerous with winter coming (Acts 28:11) after "the fast" or day of Atonement (Lev 16:29–30) observed each Fall.

[10] And said unto them, Sirs, I perceive that this voyage will be with hurt and much damage, not only of the lading and ship, but also of our lives.

Paul is a survivor of three prior shipwrecks (2 Cor 11:25) and accurately predicts the loss of cargo ("lading" is a load of cargo, Acts 27:38) and ship (Acts 27:41), but God will intervene and prevent loss of life (Acts 27:22-24).

[11] Nevertheless the centurion believed the master and the owner of the ship, more than those things which were spoken by Paul.

Under normal circumstances, a shipowner would be hesitant to sail while winter is approaching because he could lose his vessel, cargo, and hope of a profit. However, the demand for grain in Rome is so high that he is willing to take extraordinary risks. The former emperor Claudius "resorted to every possible means to bring grain to Rome, even in the winter season.

To the merchants he held out the certainty of profit by assuming the expense of any loss that they might suffer from storms."[320]

[12] And because the haven was not commodious to winter in, the more part advised to depart thence also, if by any means they might attain to Phenice, and there to winter; which is an haven of Crete, and lieth toward the south west and north west

The Fair Havens is not a suitable winter port, so they decide to sail to the port of Phenice, which faces southwest to northwest.

[13] And when the south wind blew softly, supposing that they had obtained their purpose, loosing thence, they sailed close by Crete

---

[320] Suetonius, *The Life of Claudius*, 18.3

Paul's ship en route to Rome stops at the bay of Fair Havens on Crete before leaving and encountering a deadly storm (Acts 27:8-15).

Georgios Tsichlis / Shutterstock.com

They initially sail westward along the southern coast of Crete with a favorable south wind. Although Paul now leaves Crete, he will later return with Titus to support local churches (Titus 1:5).

[14] But not long after there arose against it a tempestuous wind, called Euroclydon

Paul and company experience a severe storm (compare Jonah 1:4) named "Euroclydon," meaning "northeast wind" or "nor'easter."

[15] And when the ship was caught, and could not bear up into the wind, we let her drive

The ship cannot tack west against the severe northeast wind and is thus driven southwest toward Clauda.

[16] And running under a certain island which is called Clauda, we had much work to come by the boat:

[17] Which when they had taken up, they used helps, undergirding the ship; and, fearing lest they should fall into the quicksands, strake sail, and so were driven.

- Their ship is towing a small boat, which they now take up into their ship due to the storm.
- Next, they tie cables around the ship's hull ("undergirding") to strengthen it. They fear they might beach the ship into sandbanks ("quicksands") due to the fierce storm and so take down the sail (they strike or "strake" sail) and let the storm drive the vessel.
- "The Syrtis[321] is an arm of the Mediterranean ... [with] shoals, cross-currents, and long sand-bars extending a great distance out [which] make the sea utterly impassable or troublesome."[322] "It sometimes happens, on the ebbing and flowing of the tide, that vessels are carried upon the shallows, settle down, and are seldom

---

[321] The dangerous "quicksands" of Syrtis are in the gulf of Sidra along the coast of modern-day Libya. "Gulf of Sidra." *Encyclopedia Britannica Online*, accessed 8 Nov 2021
[322] Dio Chrysostom, *Discourses*, 5:8-9

Paul's Voyage to Rome
Acts 27-28

Base map (land, water, roads) from Ancient World Mapping Center "A-la-carte"
Modifications (borders, routes) by Gregory Cetton
Creative Commons Attribution 4.0 International License (CC BY 4.0)

Black Sea

Bithynia & Pontus

Cappadocia

Galatia

Asia

Adramyttium

Tarsus

Cilicia

Sea of Cilicia

Cyprus

Sidon

Caesarea

Judea

Jerusalem

Lycia & Pamphylia

Sea of Pamphylia

Myra

Cnidus

Salmone

Crete

Fair Havens & Lasea

Clauda

Phenice

Aegean Sea

Macedonia

Achaia

Ionian Sea (Adria)

Mediterranean Sea

Alexandria

Egypt

Cyrene

"Quicksands" of Syrtis

Adriatic Sea

Italy

Rhegium

Sicily

Syracuse

Malta (Melita)

Puteoli

The Three Taverns
Appii Forum

Rome

recovered. Sailors therefore, in coasting, keep at a distance (from the shore), and are on their guard, lest they should be caught by a wind unprepared, and driven into these gulfs."[323]

[18] And we being exceedingly tossed with a tempest, the next day they lightened the ship;

The ship takes on water in the storm and throwing out excess items lightens it.

[19] And the third day we cast out with our own hands the tackling of the ship.

Throwing out the ship's rigging further lightens it.

[20] And when neither sun nor stars in many days appeared, and no small tempest lay on us, all hope that we should be saved was then taken away.

"Many days" will be clarified as fourteen days of darkened skies from the continuous storm (Acts 27:27).

[21] But after long abstinence Paul stood forth in the midst of them, and said, Sirs, ye should have hearkened unto me, and not have loosed from Crete, and to have gained this harm and loss.

After a two-week abstinence from food (Acts 27:33), Paul points out their failure to heed his prior prophetic warning (Acts 27:10). He says this not in pride but to admonish them to follow his advice this time.

[22] And now I exhort you to be of good cheer: for there shall be no loss of any man's life among you, but of the ship.

Paul accurately predicts the loss of the ship (Acts 27:41) and no loss of life (Acts 27:44).

---

[323] Strabo, *Geography*, 17.3.20

[23] For there stood by me this night the angel of God, whose I am, and whom I serve,

The Son of God (Gal 4:14, Exod 3:2, Zech 12:8) gives Paul a message of comfort (as in Acts 23:11), and Paul believes Him (believes God, Acts 27:25).

[24] Saying, Fear not, Paul; thou must be brought before Cæsar: and, lo, God hath given thee all them that sail with thee.

God spares the passengers' lives for Paul's sake (as He was willing to do for Abraham, Gen 18:23-32), who now inspires the crew as a leader despite his status as a prisoner.

Paul sails to Rome in a transport ship. During a storm, the sails can be lowered and the two rudders removed from the water and secured inside the ship (Acts 27:40).

Massimo Todaro / Shutterstock.com

[25] Wherefore, sirs, be of good cheer: for I believe God, that it shall be even as it was told me.

Paul believes God, who cannot lie (Num 23:19, Titus 1:2). Faith in God's word leads to salvation (James 1:21) as it did for those believers of Thessalonica (1 Thes 2:13) and Rome (Rom 1:8)

[26] Howbeit we must be cast upon a certain island.

Paul accurately predicts that the ship will arrive at an island (Malta or "Melita," Acts 28:1) rather than the Italian peninsula.

[27] But when the fourteenth night was come, as we were driven up and down in Adria, about midnight the shipmen deemed that they drew near to some country;

The "Sea of Adria" (ancient term) lies south of the Adriatic Ocean between Greece and Sicily and is equivalent to the "Ionian Sea" (modern term).[324]

[28] And sounded, and found it twenty fathoms: and when they had gone a little further, they sounded again, and found it fifteen fathoms.

A line is placed in the water to check depth. A sailor's outstretched arms measure the length of rope, with each fathom of cable being 5-6 feet. As they sail closer to land they measure the depth, first at 100-120 feet (35 m) then at 75-90 feet (25 m).

[29] Then fearing lest we should have fallen upon rocks, they cast four anchors out of the stern, and wished for the day.

The present darkness makes navigation dangerous, so they cast four anchors out of the back of the ship to stay in place until daybreak.

[30] And as the shipmen were about to flee out of the ship, when they had let down the boat into the sea, under colour as though they would have cast anchors out of the foreship,

---

[324] "The Ionian Gulf forms part of what we now call the Adriatic." Strabo, *Geography*, 2.5.20

The sailors try to escape in the boat (Acts 27:16) they lowered in front of the ship (the "foreship") under the guise of placing more anchors.

[31] Paul said to the centurion and to the soldiers, Except these abide in the ship, ye cannot be saved.

The sailors will be needed to work the ship when they get underway again in the morning.

[32] Then the soldiers cut off the ropes of the boat, and let her fall off.

Centurion Julius previously disregarded Paul's warnings. However, now that the apostle's words have come true (Acts 27:21), the officer defers to him and orders his soldiers to keep the sailors on board.

[33] And while the day was coming on, Paul besought them all to take meat, saying, This day is the fourteenth day that ye have tarried and continued fasting, having taken nothing.

The troubled sailors (Jonah 1:5, Mark 4:38, Psalm 107:23-30) have been fasting for two weeks.

[34] Wherefore I pray you to take some meat: for this is for your health: for there shall not an hair fall from the head of any of you.

[35] And when he had thus spoken, he took bread, and gave thanks to God in presence of them all: and when he had broken it, he began to eat.

[36] Then were they all of good cheer, and they also took some meat.

- "Meat" can refer to any food, including bread (Acts 27:35) made from wheat (Acts 27:38). See Acts 2:42 for comments on breaking bread.
- Paul shows greater leadership than "the centurion ... [and] the master and the owner of the ship ..." (Acts 27:11) when he rallies everyone on board.

<u>Language</u>
Proverb (a widely-used saying) – "there shall not an hair fall from the head of any of you" compares with "there shall not one hair of his head fall to the ground" (1 Sam 14:45).

[37] And we were in all in the ship two hundred threescore and sixteen souls.

Paul travels in a grain ship large enough to hold 276 passengers, but some vessels carry many more. "Accordingly I came to Rome ... by sea; for as our ship ... we that were in it, being about six hundred in number ..."[325]

[38] And when they had eaten enough, they lightened the ship, and cast out the wheat into the sea.

The cargo is lost as predicted by Paul (Acts 27:10).

[39] And when it was day, they knew not the land: but they discovered a certain creek with a shore, into the which they were minded, if it were possible, to thrust in the ship.

They do not recognize the shoreline but determine the best place to beach the ship.

[40] And when they had taken up the anchors, they committed themselves unto the sea, and loosed the rudder bands, and hoised up the mainsail to the wind, and made toward shore.

After taking up the anchors, they lower the two rudders back into place (which had been secured during the storm by bands) and raise the sail ("hoised up the mainsail") to travel to shore.

[41] And falling into a place where two seas met, they ran the ship aground; and the forepart stuck fast, and remained unmoveable, but the hinder part was broken with the violence of the waves.

---

[325] Josephus, *The Life of Flavius Josephus*, 3

The front of the ship is stuck into the ground, and the rear is broken apart by waves. Paul had predicted the ship's destruction (Acts 27:22).

[42] And the soldiers' counsel was to kill the prisoners, lest any of them should swim out, and escape.

A Roman soldier pays with his life for losing a prisoner who escapes (Acts 12:19, 16:27). This strict policy has also been applied in Israel (1 Kings 20:39-40).

[43] But the centurion, willing to save Paul, kept them from their purpose; and commanded that they which could swim should cast themselves first into the sea, and get to land:

Paul suffers shipwreck at the island of Malta, but miraculously he and the passengers "escaped all safe to land" (Acts 27:44).

ZGPhotography / Shutterstock.com

[44] And the rest, some on boards, and some on broken pieces of the ship. And so it came to pass, that they escaped all safe to land.

- Centurion Julius shows how much he trusts Paul when he takes on great personal risk by giving this order, which might result in some prisoners escaping custody under ordinary circumstances.
- As had been predicted by Paul (Acts 27:22), no lives are lost.

Devotional
Life is like a sea voyage. The physical vessel is the human body (2 Tim 2:20-21), which will not survive the journey (2 Cor 4:16). The spiritual vessel is the Lord Jesus Christ (anticipated by Noah's ark, Gen 6:14), who will save those in Him (Heb 11:7). A new physical vessel awaits those who make the spiritual journey in Christ (1 Cor 15:53, 2 Cor 5:1).

Challenge Question

How does Paul's experience in the storm compare to Jonah's?

Acts Chapter 28

[1] And when they were escaped, then they knew that the island was called Melita.

"Melita" is the island of Malta.

[2] And the barbarous people shewed us no little kindness: for they kindled a fire, and received us every one, because of the present rain, and because of the cold.

- Paul and his fellow travelers exit the ocean wearing minimal clothing that is now soaking wet. They welcome a warm fire on this cold and rainy day.
- Although the locals do not understand the travelers' language (the meaning of "barbarian," 1 Cor 14:11), they charitably (Prov 19:17) provide them warmth, shelter (Acts 28:7), and supplies (Acts 28:10).

[3] And when Paul had gathered a bundle of sticks, and laid them on the fire, there came a viper out of the heat, and fastened on his hand.

Paul, throughout this voyage, has helped and encouraged others (Acts 27:10, 22, 31, 34). He is now found "working with his hands" (Eph 4:28, also Acts 20:34) in service of those needing warmth.

[4] And when the barbarians saw the venomous beast hang on his hand, they said among themselves, No doubt this man is a murderer, whom, though he hath escaped the sea, yet vengeance suffereth not to live.

Gentiles ignorant of Moses' law show the workings of conscience when they imply that the sin of murder deserves death (Rom 2:14, Gen 9:6, Num 35:31).

Language
Personification (an object or idea is described as a person) – "vengeance"

(justice) will not allow a murderer to live.

[5] And he shook off the beast into the fire, and felt no harm.

- The words of Christ are fulfilled (Mark 16:17-18, Luke 10:19, Acts 23:11) when Paul suffers no harm from the poisonous serpent and when he subsequently performs healings (Acts 28:8-9).
- Moses also had divine power over serpents (Exod 7:8-12) and miraculously healed Israelites bitten by them (Num 21:6-9).

[6] Howbeit they looked when he should have swollen, or fallen down dead suddenly: but after they had looked a great while, and saw no harm come to him, they changed their minds, and said that he was a god.

Their fickle opinion of Paul first as a man worthy of death and subsequently as a god is in reverse order of the events at Lystra (Acts 14:11-19).

[7] In the same quarters were possessions of the chief man of the island, whose name was Publius; who received us, and lodged us three days courteously.

Paul and his companions are shown great hospitality by Publius, Malta's "chief man" (governor or leading citizen).

[8] And it came to pass, that the father of Publius lay sick of a fever and of a bloody flux: to whom Paul entered in, and prayed, and laid his hands on him, and healed him.

Publius' father is miraculously healed of his infectious diarrhea.

[9] So when this was done, others also, which had diseases in the island, came, and were healed:

Paul undoubtedly brings the gospel (1 Cor 9:16) to those healed as Peter had at Lydda (Acts 9:32-35) and Joppa (Acts 9:36-42).

[10] Who also honoured us with many honours; and when we departed, they laded us with such things as were necessary.

The local people show their appreciation for Paul and his companions by providing supplies for their journey.

[11] And after three months we departed in a ship of Alexandria, which had wintered in the isle, whose sign was Castor and Pollux.

- The grain ship (Acts 27:38) they previously boarded in Myra was also from Alexandria and headed for Italy (Acts 27:6) but suffered a shipwreck on the beach of Malta (Acts 27:41). Alexandria, Egypt sends a continuous supply of grain to Rome[326] so Centurion Julius quickly finds a similar ship.
- Castor and Pollux are the mythological twin sons of Zeus (equiva-

---

[326] Africa supplies "fruits of the earth, which maintain the multitude of the Romans for eight months in the year" (Josephus, *Jewish War*, 16.4).

Paul spends three months on the island of Malta before setting sail again to Rome (Acts 28:1-11).

Karina Movsesyan / Shutterstock.com

lent to "Jupiter," Acts 14:11-13, 19:35) of the constellation Gemini who bring "good luck" to sailors.[327] Luke shows evidence of his eye-witness account when he records this colorful detail from the ship's emblem.

[12] And landing at Syracuse, we tarried there three days.

[13] And from thence we fetched a compass, and came to Rhegium: and after one day the south wind blew, and we came the next day to Puteoli:

They sail on a circuitous route ("fetched a compass") from Syracuse (in Sicily) to Rhegium (in Italy). A south wind readily brings them northward from Rhegium to Puteoli.

---

[327] "Dioscuri." *Encyclopedia Britannica Online*, accessed 12 Nov 2019

Paul lands at Puteoli and spends seven days with believers there before heading on foot toward Rome (Acts 28:13-14).

auralaura / Shutterstock.com

[14] Where we found brethren, and were desired to tarry with them seven days: and so we went toward Rome.

Three years earlier, when in Corinth, Paul wrote to believers in Rome that he anticipated meeting them one day (Rom 15:22-29).

[15] And from thence, when the brethren heard of us, they came to meet us as far as Appii forum, and The three taverns: whom when Paul saw, he thanked God, and took courage.

Paul reaches Appii Forum and The Three Taverns through the Via Appia (the Appian Way), "the first of the great Roman roads."[328]

[16] And when we came to Rome, the centurion delivered the prisoners to

---

[328] "Roman road system." *Encyclopedia Britannica Online*, accessed 30 Mar 2020

Paul meets fellow believers while traveling toward Rome on the via Appia, the Appian Way (Acts 28:14-15).

matremors / Shutterstock.com

the captain of the guard: but Paul was suffered to dwell by himself with a soldier that kept him.

Paul arrives safely in Rome, as was promised (Acts 23:11, 27:24), where he can live in a private residence (Acts 28:30) under house arrest. Previously he desired to visit Rome (Acts 19:21) although not as a prisoner, which he became when arrested in Jerusalem (Acts 21:33) and subsequently sent here for his legal appeal to Caesar (Acts 25:11).

[17] And it came to pass, that after three days Paul called the chief of the Jews together: and when they were come together, he said unto them, Men and brethren, though I have committed nothing against the people, or customs of our fathers, yet was I delivered prisoner from Jerusalem into the hands of the Romans.

The late Emperor Claudius' command for all Jews to depart from Rome (Acts 18:2) is no longer in force under Emperor Nero, and many Jews have returned. Paul now meets with the local Jewish leadership in Rome. He tells them of his arrest in Jerusalem but graciously avoids mentioning those in Jerusalem who started a riot in the temple and tried to kill him, which prompted the Romans to arrest him for his own protection (Acts 21:27-35).

[18] Who, when they had examined me, would have let me go, because there was no cause of death in me.

[19] But when the Jews spake against it, I was constrained to appeal unto Cæsar; not that I had ought to accuse my nation of.

Paul was found not guilty by Governor Festus (Acts 25:25) and by King Agrippa (Acts 26:31-32), yet Governor Felix kept him imprisoned for two years as a political favor to Paul's accusers (Acts 24:27). Therefore Paul's only recourse was to appeal to Caesar (Acts 25:11).

[20] For this cause therefore have I called for you, to see you, and to speak with you: because that for the hope of Israel I am bound with this chain.

- Paul is under house arrest and cannot go to the local synagogue as

has been his usual manner (Acts 9:20, 13:14, 14:1, 17:10, 18:4, 18:19, 19:8). Instead, he invites the leaders to meet at his lodging (Acts 28:23). He became a prisoner when he went to Jerusalem despite warnings of danger (Acts 20:22-23, 21:4, 11-12) because of his love for the people of Israel (Rom 9:1-5).
- The "hope of Israel" (Jer 14:8, Acts 26:6) is Jesus the Messiah (Joel 3:16, Titus 2:13).

[21] And they said unto him, We neither received letters out of Judæa concerning thee, neither any of the brethren that came shewed or spake any harm of thee.

[22] But we desire to hear of thee what thou thinkest: for as concerning this sect, we know that every where it is spoken against.

They have heard ill of Christianity, but not of Paul, so they will consider his views since he has presented himself as a devout Jew.

[23] And when they had appointed him a day, there came many to him into his lodging; to whom he expounded and testified the kingdom of God, persuading them concerning Jesus, both out of the law of Moses, and out of the prophets, from morning till evening.

- They study scripture all day, "from morning till evening," living out the words of Job, who wrote, "I have esteemed the words of his mouth more than my necessary food" (Job 23:12).
- Paul speaks of God's spiritual kingdom (Rom 14:17), which one may enter because of the work of Christ (2 Peter 1:11).
- Jesus' death, burial, and resurrection had been prophesied directly in scripture (Gen 3:15, Psalm 22, Isa 53, Luke 24:25-27, 44-47) and indirectly through types such as Noah's ark, the serpent of brass, and the sacrificial system.

[24] And some believed the things which were spoken, and some believed not.

Humans freely choose whether or not to believe God's word (Exod 9:20-21, Matt 28:17).

[25] And when they agreed not among themselves, they departed, after that Paul had spoken one word, Well spake the Holy Ghost by Esaias the prophet unto our fathers,

[26] Saying, Go unto this people, and say, Hearing ye shall hear, and shall not understand; and seeing ye shall see, and not perceive:

[27] For the heart of this people is waxed gross, and their ears are dull of hearing, and their eyes have they closed; lest they should see with their eyes, and hear with their ears, and understand with their heart, and should be converted, and I should heal them.

- Paul bluntly challenges his listener's willingness to hear the truth by quoting Isa 6:9-10. Christ had quoted these words of Isaiah (John 12:40), as did Paul three years ago in his epistle to the Romans (Rom 11:8).
- When in the next verse the apostle speaks of God showing favor to Gentiles, they will depart offended, as also happened when Paul preached at the temple (Acts 22:21-22) and when the Lord Jesus had spoken at the synagogue in Nazareth (Luke 4:16-30).

[28] Be it known therefore unto you, that the salvation of God is sent unto the Gentiles, and that they will hear it.

- The Jewish leadership had rejected the gospel in Jerusalem (Acts 7:54-60), in Asia Minor (Acts 13:46), in Europe (Acts 18:6), and now here in Rome, symbolizing worldwide rejection.
- The gospel is now carried by the Gentiles (Matt 21:43) until their fullness is complete (Luke 21:24), and Israel's spiritual blindness is lifted (Rom 11:25-27, 2 Cor 3:14).

[29] And when he had said these words, the Jews departed, and had great reasoning among themselves.

Debate is unfruitful when it leads one to justify their sin of unbelief (Rom 1:29).

[30] And Paul dwelt two whole years in his own hired house, and received all that came in unto him,

Paul carries on his ministry while under house arrest (Acts 28:31), and his gospel message reaches even Caesar's household (Phil 1:12-13, 4:22). While in Rome Paul writes epistles to the Ephesians, Philippians, Colossians, and Philemon. The brethren who assist him include Aristarchus (Acts 27:2, Col 4:10, Philem 24), Demas (Col 4:14, Philem 24), Epaphras (Col 1:7, 4:12, Philem 23), Epaphroditus (Phil 2:25, 4:18), John Mark (Col 4:10, Philem 24), Justus (Col 4:11), Luke (Col 4:14, Philem 24), Onesimus (Col 4:9, Philem 10), Tychicus (Eph 6:21, Col 4:7), and Timothy (Phil 1:1, 2:19, Col 1:1, Philem 1).

[31] Preaching the kingdom of God, and teaching those things which concern the Lord Jesus Christ, with all confidence, no man forbidding him.

- Luke's account started with 120 Jewish believers in Jerusalem and now ends with the gospel confidently preached in the heart of the Roman Empire.
- "No man forbidding him" describes Paul's unhindered ministry in Rome and also implies that no one can prevent the gospel from going "unto the uttermost part of the earth" (Acts 1:8).
- Luke gives the seventh of seven summary statements in the book of Acts now that the gospel has spread throughout the eastern half of the Roman Empire, and Paul has arrived in Rome. The apostle hopes to be released and bring the gospel to the western half of the Roman Empire (Rom 15:18-24).

Teaching Questions

Question: Paul will soon appear before Caesar Nero the **first time** for judgment. What sort of reputation has the emperor earned?
Answer: When Paul first appears before him, Nero is young, and his rule is moderated by the guidance of Seneca (the brother of Gallio, Acts 18:12). "Seneca and Burrus, who were at once the most sensible and the most influential of the men at Nero's court (the former was his teacher and the

latter was prefect of Praetorian Guard) ... took the rule entirely into their own hands and administered affairs in the very best and fairest manner they could, with the result that they won the approval of everybody alike. As for Nero, he was not fond of business in any case, and was glad to live in idleness ... His two advisers, then, after coming to a common understanding, made many changes in existing regulations, abolished some altogether, and enacted many new laws, meanwhile allowing Nero to indulge himself, in the expectation that [he would have satisfied] his desires without any great injury to the public interests at large."[329]

Question: Luke's account ends here, where his narrative catches up to current events. What happens next?
Answer: Further events in Paul's life are uncertain, but it appears that after his two years of house arrest (Acts 28:30), he will appear before Caesar Nero (Acts 27:24) and be released from prison (Phil 1:26, Philem 22). He will write 1 and 2 Timothy, Titus, and possibly Hebrews. He will visit places such as Colosse (Philem 22), Corinth (2 Tim 4:20), Crete (Titus 1:5), Ephesus (1 Tim 1:3, 3:14), Macedonia (1 Tim 1:3), Miletum (2 Tim 4:20), Nicopolis (Titus 3:12), Troas (2 Tim 4:13), and possibly Spain (Rom 15:24). He will be arrested and imprisoned in Rome (2 Tim 1:16-17) a second time under harsher conditions (2 Tim 2:9) and most of his friends will desert him (2 Tim 4:9-11).

Question: Paul will eventually appear before Caesar Nero a **second time** for judgment. What sort of reputation will the emperor have earned by then?
Answer: "Consequently he began to indulge in each of these [immoral] pursuits in a more open and precipitate fashion. And in case his guardians ever said anything to him by way of advice or his mother by way of admonition, he would appear [embarrassed] while they were present, and would promise to reform; but as soon as they were gone, he would again become the slave of his desire and yield to those who were leading him in the other direction, since they were dragging him downhill."[330]

---

[329] Cassius Dio, *Roman History*, 61.3.3 and 61.4.1-2
[330] Ibid., 61.4.4

"Finally he lost all shame, dashed to the ground and trampled underfoot all their [Seneca and Burrus'] precepts … he practiced his vices at home and … even indulged them publicly. Thus he brought great disgrace upon the whole Roman race and committed many outrages against the Romans themselves. Innumerable acts of violence and outrage, of robbery and murder, were committed by the emperor … great sums of money naturally were spent, great sums unjustly procured, and great sums seized by force."[331] Nero "would accordingly have put numerous persons out of the way immediately, had not Seneca said to him: 'No matter how many you may slay, you cannot kill your successor.'"[332]

<u>Question</u>: When Paul is finally condemned to death (2 Tim 4:6-8), can he be executed by crucifixion?
<u>Answer</u>: No, it is unlawful to crucify a Roman citizen. Cicero asked rhetorically, "Did you dare to drag anyone, to the cross who said that he was a Roman citizen?"[333] Gaius Verres, former governor of Sicily, was prosecuted for this very act. His unlawful order to crucify a Roman citizen was described as "[murder] by the most miserable and most painful punishment appropriate to slaves alone."[334]

433

Challenge Question

Why does Luke seem to end *Acts* so abruptly without telling the reader what happens to Paul?

---

[331] Ibid., 61.5.1-3
[332] Ibid., 62.18.3
[333] Marcus Tullius Cicero, *Against Verres*, 2.5.63
[334] Ibid., 2.5.66

Appendix A

Constructing Maps for the Book of Acts

Simplified maps are found in the back of many Bibles. Typically one will find maps of Paul's three missionary journeys and his voyage to Rome. The color maps in this book are different because they include actual roads from the Roman era.

Luke describes Paul's travels using both Roman political regions (provinces) and old national regions (countries prior to Roman rule).

Old national regions: Lycaonia, Mysia, Phrygia, and Pisidia.

Roman provinces: Achaia, Asia, Bithynia & Pontus, Cappadocia, Cilicia, Galatia, Judea, Lycia, Macedonia, Pamphylia, and Syria.

Mapping these areas using ancient sources is challenging because few ancient maps have survived to the present day. Ancient authors, such as Strabo and Pliny the Elder, described various areas, but they were not always certain. "A proverbial saying is applied to the Phrygians and Mysians, 'The boundaries of the Mysi and Phryges are apart from one another,' but it is difficult to define them respectively" (Strabo, *Geography*, 12.4.4).

How to construct a map for *Acts*:
1. Data from the *Barrington Atlas of the Greek and Roman World* is available online at the Antiquity À-la-carte application (http://awmc.unc.edu/awmc/applications/alacarte/).
Maps are released under the Creative Commons Attribution 4.0 International License (CC BY 4.0) (http://creativecommons.org/licenses/by/4.0/). Obtain a base layer map with land and sea outlines, lakes and waterways, and roads.
2. Color-shade Roman provinces.

3. Draw national boundaries that existed before Roman rule. You may skip those not found in *Acts*, such as Caria, Isauria, Lydia, and Paphlagonia.
4. Draw travel routes based on the biblical text. Some routes are highly certain, such as Philippi to Thessalonica. Others are less certain, such as Antioch in Pisidia back to Pamphylia; Paul may have traveled the main road (the *via Sebaste*) or evangelized "throughout Pisidia" on back roads.

The most effective way to determine ancient boundaries is to take a given city and search for regional references, using ancient literature whenever possible. Certain key cities are used to build map borders. These can be seen on the map in this book titled "Pre-Map Paul's Missionary Journeys."

Old national regions

Lycaonia
Inhabited by the Galatian peoples
"The Galatians ... migrated into Phrygia, and spread themselves as far as Lycaonia" (Strabo, *Geography*, 12.1.1).

Coropassus (Koropassos) and Garsaura (Gareathyra)
"Here the Taurus approaches this country, separating Cappadocia and Lycaonia from Cilicia Tracheia. It is the boundary of the Lycaonians and Cappadocians, between Coropassus [Koropassos], a village of the Lyc-aonians, and Gareathyra [Garsaura], a small town of the Cappadocians" (Strabo, *Geography*, 12.6.1).

Isaura (old and new)
"To Lycaonia belongs Isaurica, near the Taurus, in which are the Isaura, two villages of the same name, one of which is surnamed Palæa, or the Old, the other [the New]; the latter is well fortified" (Strabo, *Geography*, 12.6.2).

Lystra and Derbe
"They were ware of it, and fled unto Lystra and Derbe, cities of Lycaonia, and unto the region that lieth round about:" (Acts 14:6).

Derbe and Lyranda (Laranda)
"Derbe, the royal seat of the tyrant Antipater, surnamed Derbætes, is on

the side of the Isaurian territory close upon Cappadocia. Laranda also belonged to Antipater" (Strabo, *Geography*, 12.6.3).

Thebasa

"In Lycaonia itself the most noted places are Thebasa on Taurus, and Hyde, on the confines of Galatia and Cappadocia" (Pliny, *Natural History*, 5.25).

Mysia

Mount Olympus

"Prusa, situated below the Mysian Olympus, on the borders of the Phrygians and the Mysians, is a well-governed city; it was founded by Cyrus" (Strabo, *Geography*, 12.4.3).

Aegean Sea, Elaitic Gulf, Propontis Sea, and Rhyndakos River

"... as settled under Augustus, [Mysia] occupied the whole of the north-western corner of the peninsula, between the Hellespont on the north-west; the Propontis on the north; the River Rhyndacus and Mount Olympus on the east, which divided it from Bythynia and Phrygia ... the southern side of the Elaïtic Gulf on the south, where it bordered with the Aegean Sea on the west" (William Smith, *A New Classical Dictionary of Greek and Roman Biography, Mythology, and Geography* (New York: Harper and Brothers, 1851), p. 534).

Mount Ida

"There are two mountains situated above the Propontis, the Mysian Olympus and Ida. At the foot of Olympus is Bithynia, and, contiguous to the mountain, between Ida and the sea, is Troy" (Strabo, *Geography*, 12.8.8).

Pergamum

"Mysia extends in the inland parts from Olympene [Mt Olympus] to Pergamene [Pergamum] ... The country to the north of Pergamum is principally occupied by Mysians" (Strabo, *Geography*, 12.8.12).

Thyatira

"... the city Thyateira, a colony of the Macedonians, which some authors say is the last city belonging to the Mysians." (Strabo, *Geography*, 13.4.4).

Pre-Map Paul's Missionary Journeys

Acts 13-28

Base map (land, water, roads) from Ancient World Mapping Center "À-la-carte"
Modifications (borders, routes) by Gregory Cetton
Creative Commons Attribution 4.0 International License (CC BY 4.0)

Hadrianeia
"Hadrianeia [is] in Mysia" (Christian Marek, *In the Land of a Thousand gods: A History of Asia Minor in the Ancient World* (Princeton University Press, 2016), chap. 9, Kindle edition).

Phrygia
"Phrygia, a country of Asia Minor, which was of very different existent at different periods. According to the division of the provinces under the Roman empire, Phrygia formed the province of Asia, and was bounded on the west by Mysia, Lydia, and Caria, on the south by Lycia and Pisidia, on the east by Lycaonia (which is often reckoned as a part of Phrygia) and Galatia (which formerly belonged to Phrygia), and on the north by Bithynia" (William Smith, *New Classical Dictionary*, p. 661).

Mount Olympus
"... Mysian Olympus, on the borders of the Phrygians and the Mysians ..." (Strabo, *Geography*, 12.4.3).

Halys River
"Next after Phrygia it comes to the river Halys, where there is both a defile which must be passed before the river can be crossed and a great fortress to guard it. After the passage into Cappadocia ..." (Herodotus, *Histories*, 5.52).

Lake Tatta (Lake Tuz)
"Next to Galatia towards the south is the lake Tatta, lying parallel to that part of the Greater Cappadocia which is near the Morimeni. It belongs to the Greater Phrygia" (Strabo, *Geography*, 12.5.4).

Ancyra (Ankara)
"[Phrygia contains] three nations, one of them dwelling near to the city of Ancyra" (Strabo, *Geography*, 4.1.13).

Ancyra and Midaion (Midaium)
"On [Mysia's] northern side ... the more celebrated towns there, besides those already mentioned, are Ancyra ... and Midaium." (Pliny, *Natural History*, 5.41).

Iconium

"Hence he advanced, three days' march, a distance of twenty parasangs, to **Iconium, the last town of Phrygia**; where he halted three days. He then went forward through Lycaonia, five days' march" (Xenophon, *Anabasis*, 1.2.19). This statement confirms Luke's description in Acts 14:6.

Cibyra

"... Cibyra being a town of Phrygia ..." (Pliny, *Natural History*, 5.29).

Dorylaion

"It rises near Dorylæum, a city of Phrygia" (Pliny, *Natural History*, 5.31).

Aizanoi (Azani), Dorylaion, and Kotiaeion (Cotiaeium)

"To Phrygian Epictetus belong the Azani, and the cities Nacoleia, Cotiaeium, Midiaeium, Dorylæum, and Cadi" (Strabo, *Geography*, 12.8.12).

Apamea (Apameia) and Laodicea

"Next are Apameia Cibotus, and Laodiceia, the largest cities in Phrygia" (Strabo, *Geography*, 12.8.13).

439

Karoura (Carura) and Philomelion (Philomelium)

"Carura, the first town in Phrygia ... through Philomelium" (Strabo, *Geography*, 14.2.29).

Pisidia

Amblada, Selge, Sinda, and Termessos

"Artemidorus says that Selge ... Amblada ... Sinda ... Termessus are cities of the Pisidians. Of these some are entirely among the mountains, others extend on each side even as far as the country at the foot of the mountains, and reach to Pamphylia and Milyas, and border on Phrygians, Lydians, and Carians" (Strabo, *Geography*, 12.7.2).

Antioch (Antiochia)

"But when they departed from Perga, they came to Antioch in Pisidia, and went into the synagogue on the sabbath day, and sat down" (Acts 13:14).

"The Pisidæ, formerly called the Solymi, occupy the higher parts of the mountains. In their country there is the colony of Cæsarea, also called

Antiochia" (Pliny, *Natural History*, 5.24).

Roman provinces

Asia
The province of Asia includes several former nations.
"This Asia comprises, first, the nations on the east, Paphlagonians, Phrygians, and Lycaonians; then Bithynians, Mysians, and the Epictetus; besides these, Troas, and Hellespontia" (Strabo, *Geography*, 12.1.3).

Ephesus
"But to Ephesus, that other great luminary of Asia ..." (Pliny, *Natural History*, 5.31).

Pergamum
"Pergamum, by far the most famous city in Asia" (Pliny, *Natural History*, 5.33).

Apamea
"Eratosthenes tells us that in Asia there have perished the nations of .. . the Capretæ, settled on the spot where Apamea stands" (Pliny, *Natural History*, 5.33).

Rhyndakos (Rhyndacus) River
"We then come to ... Mount Olympus, known as the 'Mysian Olympus,' and the city of Olympena. There are also the rivers Horisius and Rhyndacus, formerly called the Lycus; this last river rises in Lake Artynias, near Miletopolis, and receives the Macestos, and many other streams, dividing in its course Asia from Bithynia" (Pliny, *Natural History*, 5.40).

Philomelion (Philomelium)
"... belongs to the jurisdiction of the province of Asia, to which also resort the people of Philomelium ..." (Pliny, *Natural History*, 5.25).

Ephesus, Laodicea, Pergamum (Pergamos), and Thyatira
"Saying, I am Alpha and Omega, the first and the last: and, What thou

seest, write in a book, and send it unto the seven churches which are in Asia; unto Ephesus, and unto Smyrna, and unto Pergamos, and unto Thyatira, and unto Sardis, and unto Philadelphia, and unto Laodicea" (Revelation 1:11).

Aizanoi (Azani), Dorylaion (Dorylæum), Kotiaeion (Cotiaeium), and Midaion (Midiaeium)
"To Phrygian Epictetus [which is in Asia] belong the Azani, and the cities Nacoleia, Cotiaeium, Midiaeium, Dorylæum, and Cadi" (Strabo, *Geography*, 12.8.12).

Cibyra
"The Cibyratic district is reckoned among the largest jurisdictions in Asia" (Strabo, *Geography*, 13.4.17).

Daidala
"After the part of the coast [of Asia] opposite to Rhodes, the boundary of which is Dædala, in sailing thence towards the east, we come to Lycia, which extends to Pamphylia" (Strabo, *Geography*, 14.3.1).

441

Bithynia and Pontus
"Bithynia is bounded on the east by the Paphlagonians, Mariandyni, and by some tribes of the Epicteti; on the north by the line of the sea-coast of the Euxine ... on the west by the Propontis; on the south by Mysia and Phrygia Epictetus" (Strabo, *Geography*, 12.4.1).

Mount Olympus
"At the foot of Olympus is Bithynia, and, contiguous to the mountain ..." (Strabo, *Geography*, 12.8.8).

Nicaea and Nicomedia
"We then come to Nicæa, formerly called Olbia, and situate at the bottom of the Ascanian Gulf ... At the bottom of the gulf lies Nicomedia, a famous city of Bithynia" (Pliny, *Natural History*, 5.43).

Bithynion and Juliopolis (Juliopolitæ)
"In the interior of Bithynia are the colony of Apamea, the Agrippenses, the Juliopolitæ, and Bithynion" (Pliny, *Natural History*, 5.43).

Heraclea (Heracleia)
"Heracleia is a city with a good harbour, and of importance in other respects... The city belongs to the province of Pontus, which was annexed to Bithynia" (Strabo, *Geography*, 12.3.6).

Amisus
"There remain to be described the parts of Pontus, situated between this country and the districts of Amisus, and Sinope, extending towards Cappadocia, the Galatians, and the Paphlagonians" (Strabo, *Geography*, 12.3.38).

Cappadocia
Difficult to map
"Cappadocia consists of many parts, and has experienced frequent changes" (Strabo, *Geography*, 12.1.1).

Chammanene
"Both Chammanene and Laviansene are provinces of Cappadocia" (Strabo, *Geography*, 12.2.10).

Garsaura (Gareathyra) and Koropassos (Coropassus)
"Here the Taurus approaches this country, separating Cappadocia and Lycaonia from Cilicia Tracheia. It is the boundary of the Lycaonians and Cappadocians, between Coropassus [Koropassos], a village of the Lycaonians, and Gareathyra [Garsaura], a small town of the Cappadocians" (Strabo, *Geography*, 12.6.1).

Halys River
"Next after Phrygia it comes to the river Halys, where there is both a defile which must be passed before the river can be crossed and a great fortress to guard it. After the passage into Cappadocia ..." (Herodotus, *Histories*, 5.52).

Amaseia (Amasia), Comana, Garsaura (Archelais), Tyana, Zela
"Cappadocia has in the interior Archelais [Garsaura], a colony founded by Claudius Cæsar, and past which the river Halys flows; also the towns of Comana, watered by the Sarus, Neocæsarea, by the Lycus, and Amasia, in the region of Gazacene, washed by the Iris... In its remaining districts there is ... Tyana ... Zela ..." (Pliny, *Natural History*, 6.3).

Cilicia
Mount Amanus
"On the coast there is the town of Myriandros, and Mount Amanus, upon which is the town of Bomitæ. This mountain separates Cilicia from Syria" (Pliny, *Natural History*, 5.18).

Cilcian Gates, Melas River, and Tarsus
"But let us now return to the coast of Syria, joining up to which is Cilicia. We here find ... the Gates of Mount Amanus ... the Gates of Cilicia ... the free city of Tarsus ... and the river Melas, the ancient boundary of Cilicia" (Pliny, *Natural History*, 5.22).

Galatia
Ancyra (Ankara), Pessinous (Pessinus), and Taouion (Tavium)
"On this occasion also it seems that we ought to speak of Galatia, which lies above Phrygia, and includes the greater part of the territory taken from that province, as also its former capital, Gordium... Its towns are, among the Tectosages, Ancyra; among the Trocmi, Tavium; and, among the Tolistobogi, Pessinus" (Pliny, *Natural History*, 5.42).

Pompeiopolis
"It is believed that the city [of Pompeiopolis] was annexed to the vassal princes of Paphlagonia, and in 6 BC, after the death of Deiotaros Philadelphos, the last king of Paphlagonia, was annexed to the Roman province of Galatia" (L. Summerer and A. von Kienlin (Nov 2010). "Pompeiopolis. The Metropolis of Paphlagonia." *L'Anatolie des peuples, des cités et des cultures*, p. 116).

Antioch, Iconium, Lystra, and Derbe; Pisidia and Lycaonia
The Apostle Paul evangelized these cities (Acts 14:20-21, 2 Tim 3:11) during his first missionary journey then later wrote the epistle of the Galatians to these churches. Antioch is in Pisidia (Acts 13:14); Lystra and Derbe are in Lycaonia (Acts 14:6); therefore Pisidia and Lycaonia are included in Galatia on this map.

Judea
Galilee (Galilaea)
"Judæa extends far and wide. That part of it which joins up to Syria is called Galilæa" (Pliny, *Natural History*, 5.15).

Mount Hermon is at the northern boundary of Israel.
"And the children of the half tribe of Manasseh dwelt in the land: they increased from Bashan unto Baal-hermon and Senir, and unto mount Hermon" (1 Chronicles 5:23).

Lycia and Pamphylia
Mount Solymos (Solyma or Climax) and Glaucus River
"Lycia ... bounded on the northwest by the little river Glaucus and the gulf of the same name, on the northeast by the mountain called Climax (the northern part of the same range as that called Solyma), and on the north its natural boundary was the Taurus [Mountains], but its limits in this direction were not strictly defined" (William Smith, *New Classical Dictionary*, p. 454).

Balboura (Balbura) and Telmessos (Telmessus)
"Next [in Lycia] comes the Promontory of Cragus, and beyond it a gulf, equal to the one that comes before it; upon it are Pinara, and Telmessus, the frontier town of Lycia... It includes also in the interior the district of Cabalia, the three cities of which are Œnianda, Balbura, and Bubon" (Pliny, *Natural History*, 5.28).

Telmessos (Telmessus) is at the western border with Asia
"On passing Telmessus we come to the Asiatic or Carpathian Sea, and the district which is properly called Asia" (Pliny, *Natural History*, 5.28).

Perga and Side
"The towns of Pamphylia are Side ..., Aspendum, situate on the side of a mountain, Pletenissum, and Perga" (Pliny, *Natural History*, 5.26).

Melas River is the eastern border of Pamphylia with Cilicia
"On the mainland there are the towns of Myanda, Anemurium, and Coracesium, and the river Melas, the ancient boundary of Cilicia [with Pamphylia]" (Pliny, *Natural History*, 5.22).

Syria
Ptolemais and Mount Carmel
"Now Phoenicia and Syria encompass about the Galilees, which are two, and called the Upper Galilee and the Lower. They are bounded toward the sun-setting, with the borders of the territory belonging to Ptolemais, and by [Mount] Carmel; which mountain had formerly belonged to the Galileans, but now belonged to the Tyrians" (Josephus, *Jewish War*, 3.3.1).

Achaia, Macedonia, and Thrace
Nestos (Nestus) River, Cambunii (Cambunian) Mountains, and Olympus Mountains
"The boundaries of the Ancient Macedonian monarch, before the time of Philip, the father of Alexander, were on the south Olympus and Cambunian Mountains, which separated it from Thessaly and Epirus, on the east the River Strymon, which separated it from Thrace, and on the north and west Illyria and Paeonia, from which it was divided by no well-defined limits. Macedonia was greatly enlarged by the conquests of Philip. He added to his kingdom ... a part of Thrace on the east as far as the River Nestus ... On the conquest of the country by the Romans ... Macedonia was formed into a Roman province and Thessaly and Illyria were incorporated with it; but, at the same time, the district east of the Nestus was again assigned to Thrace. The Roman province of Macedonia accordingly extended from the Aegaean to the Adriatic Seas, and was bounded on the south by the province of Achaia.... Macedonia may be described as a large plain, surrounded on three sides by lofty mountains.... On the southern frontier were the Cambunii Montes and Olympus. The chief rivers were in the direction of east to west, the Nestus ..." (William Smith, *New Classical Dictionary*, p. 464).

Nestos River and Pindus Mountains
"The traditional boundaries of the geographical region of Macedonia are the lower Nestos River and the Rhodope Mountains on the east ... and the Pindus Mountains ... on the south" ("Macedonia." *Encyclopedia Britannica Online*, accessed 21 Feb 2022).

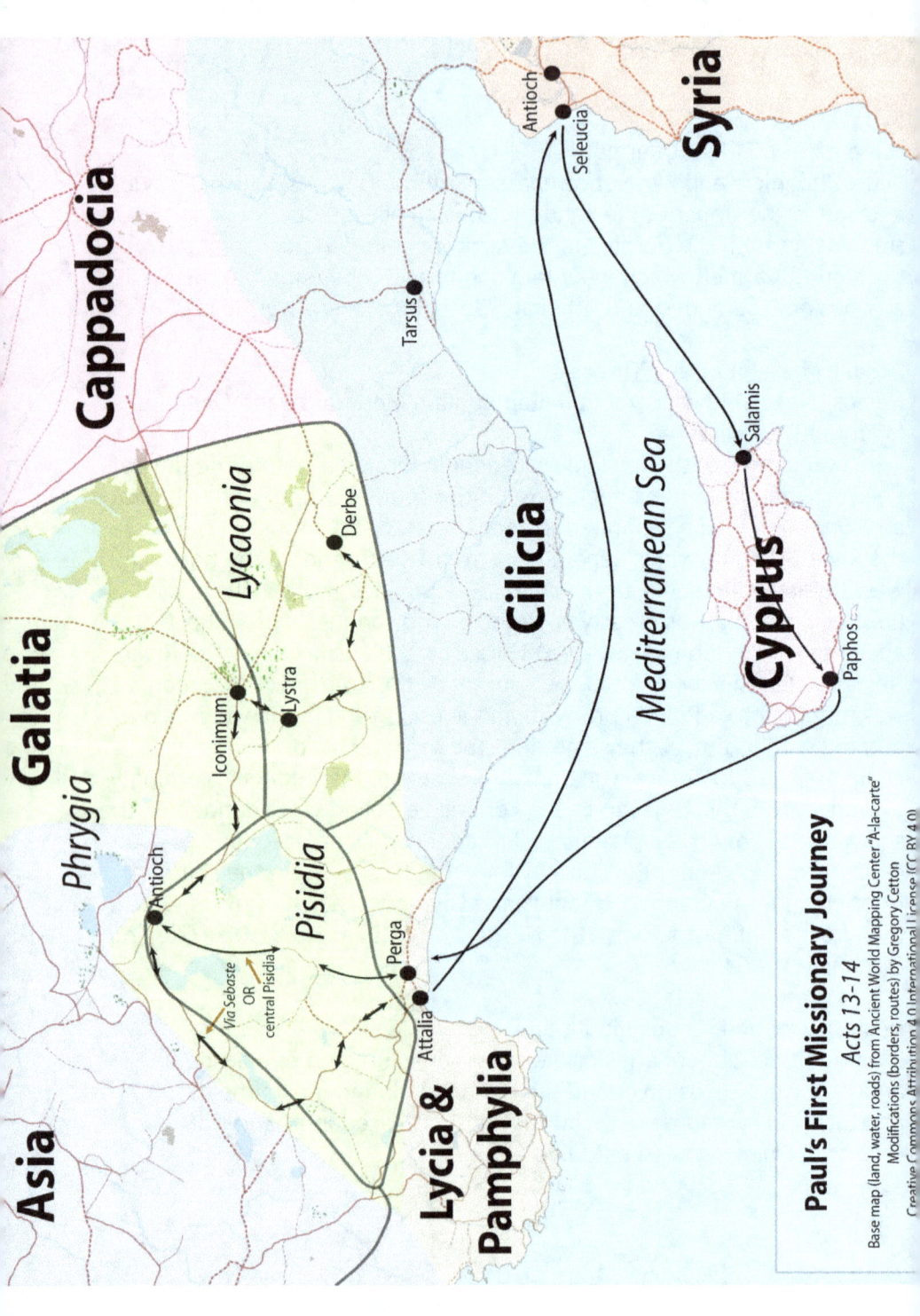

Asia

Cappadocia

Galatia

Phrygia

Lycaonia

Derbe

Lystra

Iconimum

Antioch

Pisidia

Via Sebaste
OR
central Pisidia

Perga

Attalia

Lycia &
Pamphylia

Tarsus

Cilicia

Syria

Antioch

Seleucia

Mediterranean Sea

Salamis

Cyprus

Paphos

Paul's First Missionary Journey
Acts 13-14

Base map (land, water, roads) from Ancient World Mapping Center "A-la-carte"
Modifications (borders, routes) by Gregory Getton
Creative Commons Attribution 4.0 International License (CC BY 4.0)

Paul's Second Missionary Journey

Acts 15-18

Base map (land, water, roads) from Ancient World Mapping Center "À-la-carte"
Modifications (borders, routes) by Gregory Cetton
Creative Commons Attribution 4.0 International License (CC BY 4.0)

Thrace

Bithynia & Pontus

Galatia

Cappadocia

Macedonia

Achaia

Mysia

Phrygia

Asia

Pisidia

Lycaonia

Lycia & Pamphylia

Cilicia

Cyprus

Syria

Crete

Mediterranean Sea

Tarsus

Antioch

Damascus

Tyre

Ptolemais

Caesarea

Jerusalem

Paphos

Derbe

Lystra

Iconium

Antioch

Perga

Patara

Rhodes

Coos

Samos

Miletus

Trogyllium

Ephesus

Chios

Mitylene

Assos

Troas

Samothrace

Neapolis

Philippi

Amphipolis

Apollonia

Thessalonica

Berea

Athens

Corinth

Cenchrea

Cyrene

Paul's Third Missionary Journey

Acts 18-21

Base map (land, water, roads) from Ancient World Mapping Center "A-la-carte"
Modifications (borders, routes) by Gregory Cetton
Creative Commons Attribution 4.0 International License (CC BY 4.0)

Paul's Voyage to Rome
Acts 27-28

Base map (land, water, roads) from Ancient World Mapping Center "À-la-carte"
Modifications (borders, routes) by Gregory Getton

Creative Commons Attribution 4.0 International License (CC BY 4.0)

The Simple Gospel

Christ died for our sins according to the scriptures; And that he was buried, and that he rose again the third day according to the scriptures
(1 Corinthians 15:3b-4)

For all have sinned, and come short of the glory of God (Romans 3:23)
"I am a sinner. I am not good like Jesus. I choose to do evil, and I choose to be evil."

For the wages of sin is death; but the gift of God is eternal life through Jesus Christ our Lord. (Romans 6:23)
"My sin deserves death. I have earned eternal separation from God. But Jesus Christ died for my sins and offers forgiveness as a free gift that I do not deserve."

That if thou shalt confess with thy mouth the Lord Jesus, and shalt believe in thine heart that God hath raised him from the dead, thou shalt be saved. For with the heart man believeth unto righteousness; and with the mouth confession is made unto salvation. (Romans 10:9-10)
"Lord Jesus, I know I am a sinner. I know I deserve to pay for my sins forever in hell. But I know that you died on the cross for me and rose from the dead. Please forgive my sins and give me the gift of eternal life."

For whosoever shall call upon the name of the Lord shall be saved.
(Romans 10:13)

452

About the Author

Dr. Gregory Cetton has loved the Bible since he began reading it as a child. He earned a degree in Biochemistry at Biola University and in Medicine at Loma Linda University. By day he works to keep his patients healthy, and by night he writes to encourage others to delight in the word of God. In his free time you can find him enjoying the mountains and deserts of Utah with his wife and three children.